JUSSI

Burton

BURTON
SNOWBOARDS

TREVOR ANDREW.DCP.ROMAIN DE MARCHI.KEIR DILLON.
DAVE DOWNING.SHANNON DUNN.TERJE HAAKONSEN.
VICTORIA JEALOUSE.ANNE MOLIN KONGSGAARD.
JUSSI OKSANEN.JOHAN OLOFSSON.ROSS POWERS.
GIGI RÜF.NICOLA THOST.SHAUN WHITE.NATASZA ZUREK.

ENTER BURTON.COM. KEYWORD: BUTTER.PHOTOGRAPHY: KEVIN ZACHER.
TO CHECK THE SEQUENCE. WHILE YOU'RE.ADDITIONAL PHOTOGRAPHY: JEFF CURTES.
THERE ORDER UP A FREE 03 GUIDEBOOK.NATE CHRISTENSON
NO COMPUTER? CALL US AT 00 800 287 866 13 (TOLL FREE).

FOR MORE JUSSI ACTION CHECK:
ROBOT FOOD'S *AFTERBANG*.

axel pauporté
jonas emery
wolle nyvelt
yannick amevet
tristan picot
flo mausser
thomas eberharter
jamie philip
jenny jones
risto matila
tuomo ojala
antti autti
heppu penti
marius otterstad
andreas borjegren
kevin jones
andrew crawford
tara dakides

Wolle Nyvelt
switch indy 720°

see Wolle in **Absinthe**films
new video
ViViD coming sept 2003

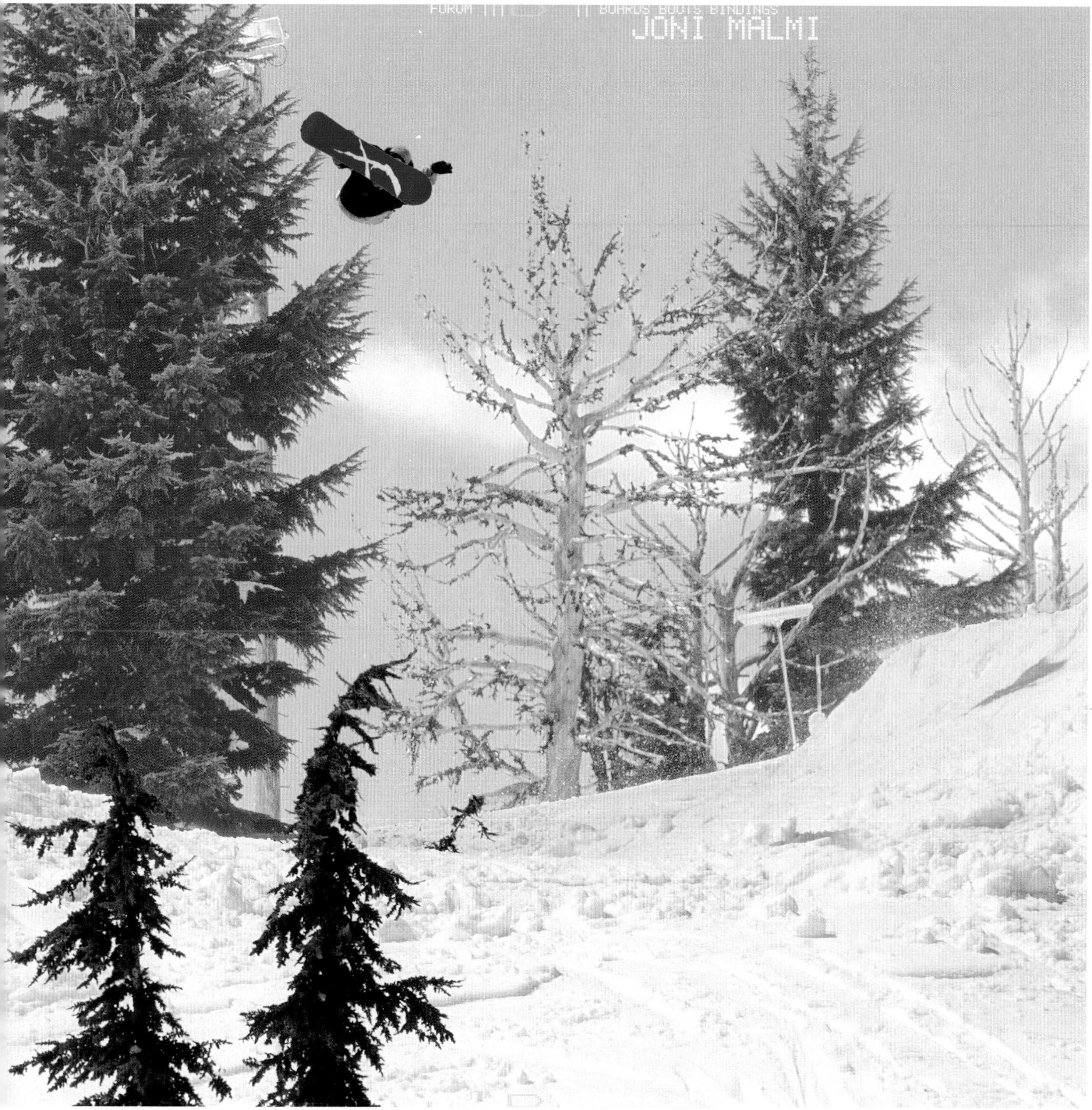
FORUM || || BOARDS BOOTS BINDINGS
JONI MALMI

jon cartwright alex schmaltz flo mausser gabe taylor marc-andré tarte per lØken heppu pentti

Editors_ Editor in chief: Alexander Rieser.
English editors: Jason Horton, Natalie Mayer.
French editor: Romu Clariond.
Italian editor: Ricky Felderer.
Art director: Algy Batten / slickcreative.com

Contributors_ Austria: Bernhard
Hechenberger, Rene Margreiter, Alexander
Rieser, Georg Schantl, Scharti. Germany:
Scharti. Switzerland: Philipo Berclaz, Franco
Furger, Fadri Jecklin, Florian Zimmermann.

France: Romuld Clariond, Guillaume Desmurs,
Marie-Laure Ducos, Youbi Ahmed. Finland:
Jaako Kantola. Norway: Jan Prokes. Sweden:
Niklas Bergh. Spain: Jorge Dominguez, Clive
Ripley. Scotland: Jason Horton

Photographers_ Philipo Berclaz, Pascal
Boulgakow, Pierre Canivenq, Jorge
Dominguez, Ricky Felderer, Bernhard
Hechenberger, Chris Holter, Stefan Hunziker,

Jaakko Kantala, Daniel Kudernatsch, Julien
Laurent, Espen Lystad, Peter Mathis, Scalp,
Georg Schantl, Vincent Skoglund, Christina
Stadler, Jeff Webb

Production_ Scanning: Alexander Wagner.
Production Manager: Alexander Rieser.

Publishers_ Clive Ripley, Garry Maidment.

Advertising and marketing_ Garry Maidment.

Distribution_ Clive Ripley

Contact_info@thesnowboardguideeurope.com

Published by_ Remedy ltd, Beaumaris
Regent house, LL58 8AB, UK
Tel: 0034 952141276

THE SNOWBOARD GUIDE EUROPE

ISBN NU 0-9543189-0-0

EDITORIAL

WELCOME TO THE LATEST INCARNATION OF THE SNOWBOARD GUIDE TO EUROPE. ABOUT SIX YEARS AGO, A GROUP OF DEDICATED SURFERS AND SNOWBOARDERS BASED IN LONDON PRODUCED A SERIES OF GUIDES UNDER THE NAME OF LOW PRESSURE. THESE GUIDES WERE THE FIRST OF THEIR KIND, GLOSSY BOOKS WRITTEN BY SURFERS FOR SURFERS, SNOWBOARDERS FOR SNOWBOARDERS, DIGGING DEEP FOR THE BEST SPOTS, WORLDWIDE. UNFORTUNATELY FOR THE REST OF US, PRODUCING THESE GUIDES LEFT THEM TOO LITTLE TIME TO ENJOY THEIR PASSION, AND THAT'S WHERE THEIR CHAPTER ENDS – HITTING THE ROAD AGAIN.

SIX YEARS LATER, AND THE SNOWBOARD GUIDE TO EUROPE RETURNS. THIS TIME ROUND WE HAVE WORKED WITH A NETWORK OF LOCAL RIDERS, JOURNALISTS, MAGAZINE EDITORS AND PHOTOGRAPHERS, SPREAD ACROSS THE FOUR CORNERS OF EUROPE, TO BRING YOU A GUIDE THAT PICKS UP WHERE LOW PRESSURE LEFT OFF, AND THEN SOME.

THIS IS NOT A RESORT GUIDE WRITTEN BY A SKI JOURNALIST IN AN OFFICE IN LONDON, IT'S A LOCAL'S GUIDE TO SNOWBOARDING IN EUROPE, WRITTEN BY THE REAL LOCALS. IT IS AIMED AT REAL SNOWBOARDERS, USUALLY TRAVELLING ON A REAL TIGHT BUDGET. WE'LL TELL YOU WHERE TO LOOK FOR THE BEST POWDER, THE CHEAPEST PLACES TO STAY, WHERE TO FIND THE BEST VALUE FOOD, AND WHICH BAR TO SPEND ALL THAT MONEY YOU SAVED ON THE WAY. WE DIDN'T TELL YOU ABOUT ALL THE BEST SECRET SPOTS IN EACH RESORT. YOU NEED TO EARN INFORMATION LIKE THAT, BY GOING THERE AND FINDING IT FOR YOURSELF. ALL WE DO IS POINT YOU IN THE RIGHT DIRECTION. THAT WAY, YOU MAY MEET MORE FRIENDLY LOCALS IN YOUR SEARCH FOR THE HIDDEN TREASURES OF EUROPE, AND WE WON'T HAVE TO FACE ANGRY LOCALS NEXT TIME WE GO BACK. AS WELL AS BEING AN INVALUABLE SOURCE OF INFORMATION, WE SINCERELY HOPE THAT THIS BOOK INSPIRES YOU TO HIT THE ROAD, AND DISCOVER FOR YOURSELF WHY EUROPE IS THE BEST PLACE IN THE WORLD FOR A SNOWBOARDER TO BE.

ntroduction
Austria
French Alps
French Pyrennes

Germany
Italy
Scandinavia
Scotland

Spain and Andorra
Switzerland
Artificial slopes
Summer camps
Backcountry camps
Heliboarding
Index

010 | 011

CONTENTS

»

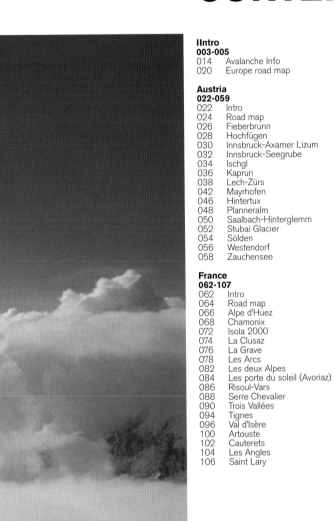

THIRTYTWO
ADVANCED
SNOWBOARD
FOOTWEAR

THE TM-TWO

SONIC WELDED INNER ANKLE H
BALLISTIC NYLON WATERPROOF
SONIC WELDED TPU RIDGES FO
RUBBER BACKSTAY WITH DIRECTIONAL G
WHY WOULDN'T YOU WANT THE TM-TWO?

REMOVABLE DUPONT HYTREL TONGUE STIFFENER

LEVEL 4

TRIPLE DENSITY ULTRALON

LEAVE A MESSAGE
WWW
THIRTYTWO
BIWEEKLY INTERVIEWS

THE LIGHTEST

LINER

BOOTS ON #1 #1 #1 #1 #1
PICK ONE
UP TO SEE
THE MARKET
{THE TEAM TWO SNOWBOARD BOOT BY THIRTYTWO}

NITROGEN FILLED
DAMPENING SYSTEM

THIRTYTWO

NAVY AND RED ALSO AVAILABLE

PLACE LOGO HERE

JOHN JACKSON
DIONNE DELESALLE
ROBERTA RODGER
RISTO SCOTT
CHAD OTTERSTROM
MARKKU KOSKI
TYLER LEPORE
WILLE YLI-LUOMA
JANNA MEYEN
KEVIN SANSALONE
NICOLAS DROZ
JONI MÄKINEN
MATT HAMMER

(1) THE TEAMS CHOICE

(2) THIS IS THE TM-TWO BOOT

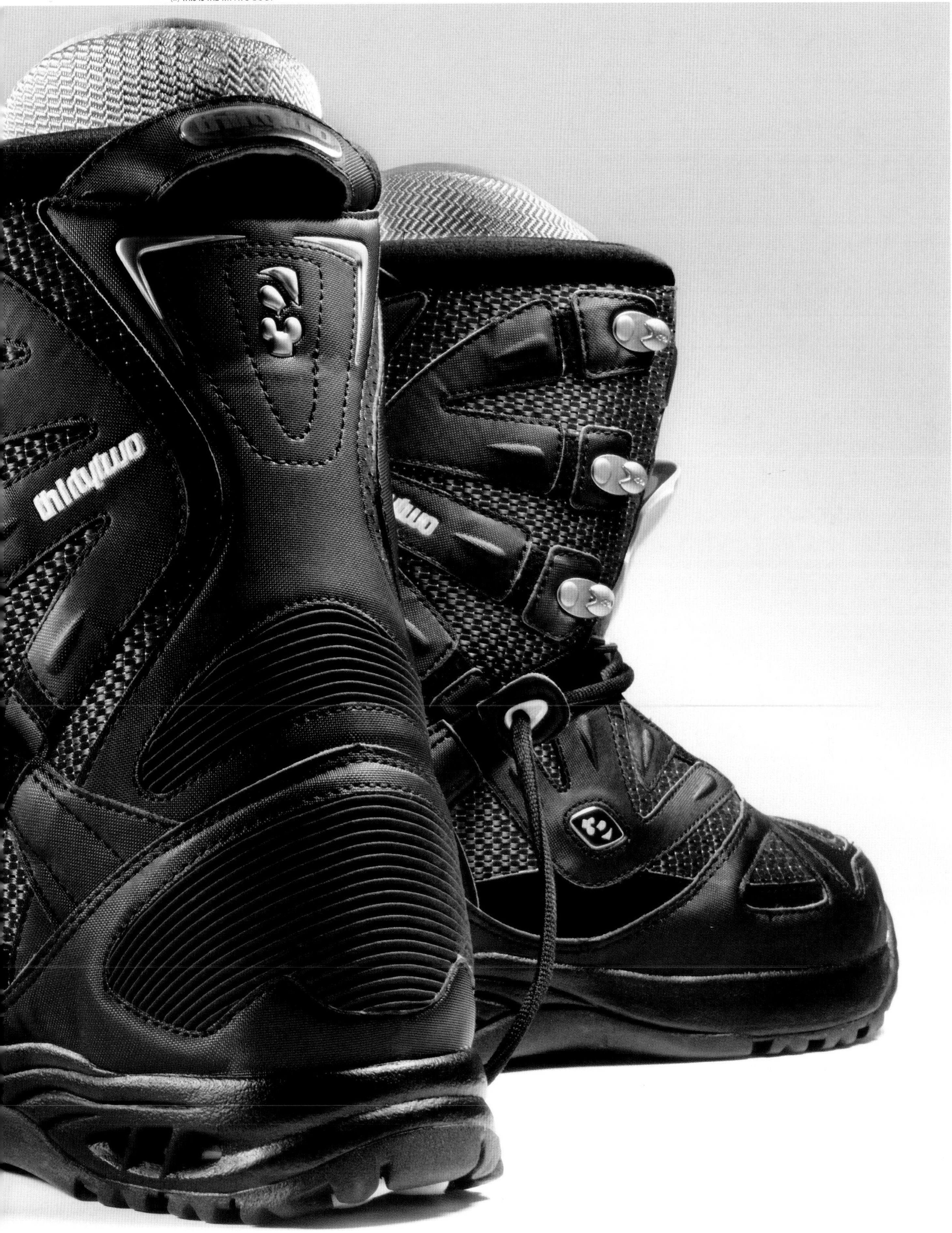

AVALANCHE

»

© Jeff Webb

EVERYONE KNOWS THAT AVALANCHES ARE DANGEROUS. YET, ON A FINE, SUNNY, POWDER DAY, VERY FEW PEOPLE SEEM WILLING TO BELIEVE THAT AN AVALANCHE COULD HAPPEN TO THEM. AND THIS INCLUDES THE ONES WHO INVEST IN AVALANCHE SAFETY EQUIPMENT. THE LATEST DEVELOPMENTS IN AVALANCHE GEAR DO NOT ONLY ADD TO THE DECEPTIVE FEELING OF BEING SAFE, BUT CAN EVEN LEAD SOME TO THINK THEY ARE EQUIPPED TO TAKE ON BIGGER RISKS – AND THIS CAN PROVE TO BE FATAL. AVALANCHE SAFETY EQUIPMENT DOESN'T IMPROVE YOUR CHANCES OF BEING CAUGHT IN AN AVALANCHE, JUST YOUR CHANCES OF BEING DUG OUT ALIVE! YOUR KNOWLEDGE AND LEARNED EXPERIENCE ARE YOUR BEST TOOLS IN HELPING TO REMAIN SAFE ON THE MOUNTAIN.

IT'S THIS SIMPLE: IF YOU WANT TO RIDE DEEP POWDER AND STAY ALIVE, YOU SHOULD TAKE AN AVALANCHE COURSE. AND, AT THE BEGINNING OF EACH WINTER, REVISE WHAT YOU'VE ALREADY LEARNED BEFORE HEADING OUT AGAIN.

The Do's and Don'ts of Freeriding_Points
_Never go off-piste without an avalanche transceiver, a probe and a shovel
_Always check weather and avalanche conditions
_Remain on-piste during 'HIGH' and 'EXTREME' avalanche danger periods
_Avoid riding steep slopes during 'CONSIDERABLE' avalanche danger periods
_Do not blindly follow tracks, especially if you do not know the area
_Never ride alone
_Different types of avalanches

Avalanche types_There are many types of avalanches, behaving in many different ways. The three main types are:

Slab Avalanche: The most common form of avalanche experienced by mountain users, and the most dangerous. This type of avalanche usually takes the form of an unstable layer of snow, which cracks away from the slope and can often be several metres deep. This type of avalanche is usually triggered by someone riding across an avalanche-prone slope. A slab avalanche can slide at speeds of up to 150 km/h. Around 75% of avalanche incidents involving skiers and snowboarders are of this type.

Dry, or Sluff Avalanche: Consists of loosely formed, dry snow in steep terrain, usually beginning at a precise point, or following a break in ice. Such avalanches can reach speeds of up to 400km/h, and can create an enormous amount of damage. The built up pressure and the vacuuming effect are so strong

© Christian Stadler

LOW
MODERATE
CONSIDERABLE
HIGH
EXTREME

© Christian Stadler

LOW
MODERATE
CONSIDERABLE
HIGH
EXTREME

»

014 | 015
AVALANCHE

EUROPEAN AVALANCHE DANGER SCALE

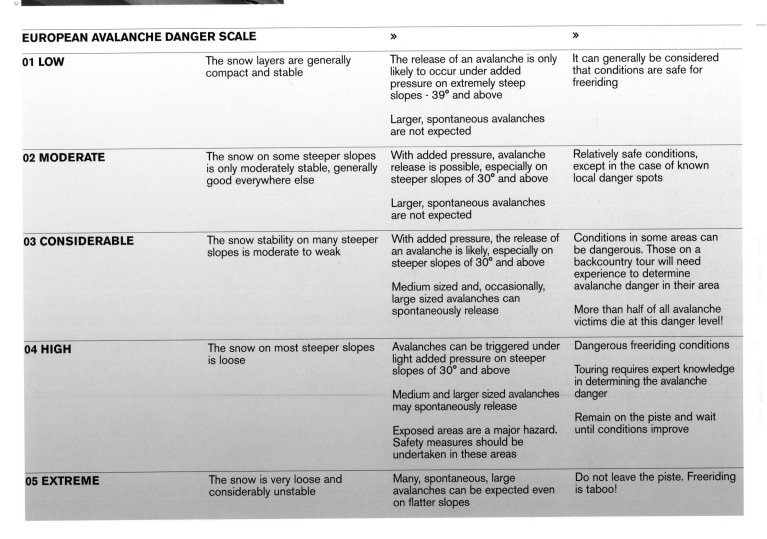

	»	»
01 LOW	The snow layers are generally compact and stable	The release of an avalanche is only likely to occur under added pressure on extremely steep slopes - 39° and above Larger, spontaneous avalanches are not expected	It can generally be considered that conditions are safe for freeriding
02 MODERATE	The snow on some steeper slopes is only moderately stable, generally good everywhere else	With added pressure, avalanche release is possible, especially on steeper slopes of 30° and above Larger, spontaneous avalanches are not expected	Relatively safe conditions, except in the case of known local danger spots
03 CONSIDERABLE	The snow stability on many steeper slopes is moderate to weak	With added pressure, the release of an avalanche is likely, especially on steeper slopes of 30° and above Medium sized and, occasionally, large sized avalanches can spontaneously release	Conditions in some areas can be dangerous. Those on a backcountry tour will need experience to determine avalanche danger in their area More than half of all avalanche victims die at this danger level!
04 HIGH	The snow on most steeper slopes is loose	Avalanches can be triggered under light added pressure on steeper slopes of 30° and above Medium and larger sized avalanches may spontaneously release Exposed areas are a major hazard. Safety measures should be undertaken in these areas	Dangerous freeriding conditions Touring requires expert knowledge in determining the avalanche danger Remain on the piste and wait until conditions improve
05 EXTREME	The snow is very loose and considerably unstable	Many, spontaneous, large avalanches can be expected even on flatter slopes	Do not leave the piste. Freeriding is taboo!

that it can totally demolish anything in and around its path. On a smaller scale, the main danger with sluff is that it can carry a person over a cliff or rock band.

Wet Avalanche: These are generally formed in spring or warmer conditions, when the snow heats up and becomes unstable. They generally start from a single point, spreading as they slide. Their progress is much slower than dry avalanches, but still dangerous. Once they stop, they set like concrete, and buried victims are left unable to move or breathe.

What will increase the avalanche danger?_The avalanche danger will generally increase with heavier snowfall, although other factors including temperature, time and wind also play a large role. Many people fall victim to an avalanche on the first 'good weather' day following heavy snowfall. Still, a common misconception is that waiting a few days until the snow has had enough time to settle, makes it safer – not necessarily.

Avalanches can be triggered by a variety of factors_heavy snowfall failing to bind to existing snowpack, people moving on the snowpack, and temperature shifts.

What role does temperature play in increasing the risk of avalanche danger?_The snow temperature is a deciding factor in determining how quickly, if at all, the snow will compact and bind together with the lower layers of snow. The colder it is, the less chance there is that the new snow will bind with the old snow, thereby increasing the risk of avalanche. This is why north facing slopes are often more dangerous than south facing slopes in the height of winter. South facing slopes are especially dangerous in the springtime, due to the increase in direct sunlight and air temperature, creating a heavier, wetter snow base that is more unstable.

What does wind have to do with avalanches?_Wind can have a major part to play in the formation of avalanche prone areas. Freshly falling snow is blown from the wind facing side of the slope and carried up and over the ridgeline, where it builds up, forming cornices and drifts, on the lee side of the hill. A breaking cornice can often be the cause for a larger avalanche, but perhaps more dangerous, are chutes and gullies which have been filled with snow, because these are harder to spot. Warning signs are slopes with waves or dunes. A good rule of thumb is to avoid such slopes, especially gullies and chutes that have been filled with snow. As well as building up the snow unevenly, wind changes the structure of individual snow crystals, often making them rounder and less binding with other snow crystals.

How do you know what the avalanche danger is?_The European Avalanche Danger Scale can be found at the valley lift station in every ski resort. Up to date information regarding the danger in that particular resort is also displayed on the notice boards. The ratings give a very general description of the entire

AVALANCHE

resort, which means certain slopes can be more or less prone to avalanching.

How big does an avalanche have to be before it can kill?_Even the smallest avalanche can be deadly. The weight of the snow depends on how wet or dry it is. 1 m2 of snow weighs on average 100 -300kg. In an avalanche, the snow gets compacted together and makes it almost impossible to move, let alone dig yourself out. There have been cases where people have suffocated beneath only a few centimetres of snow.

If you get pressed against a tree or rock, the pressure alone can be fatal. In such cases, helmets and back protection do increase the chance of survival.

How long can you survive underneath an avalanche?_In the worst case scenario, where the mouth and nasal passages of an avalanche victim are filled with snow and they are not rescued within the first 5- 10 minutes, chances of survival are extremely slim.

When the airways are free and there is little pressure on the victim's lungs, the chance of survival is somewhat better. On average, 50% of avalanche victims will die if not recovered within 30 minutes, and more than 75% within 45 minutes. This should be a good indication of the chance of survival for a victim that has to wait for outside help. In most survival cases, the victim was recovered by the people riding with them at the time.

How steep does a slope need to be before an avalanche releases?_Generally speaking, any slope you can ride down in powder is steep enough for an avalanche. Up to a certain point, the steeper the slope the greater the risk.

How do I recognise when I am in an avalanche danger zone?_A sign that you are in an avalanche danger zone is when the snowlayer begins to crack up, due only to the bodyweight of a rider. A hollow, cracking sound often accompanies this. It's often the case that an avalanche can release only seconds after the first alarm signs have been recognised, if not before. Attempt to leave the danger zone as quickly as possible. Stay

© Bernhard Hechenberger

aware of the snow conditions, specially during your hike. Keep your eyes and ears open to all alarm factors.

How much of a chance will I have to ride out an avalanche?_Very little. Never think that you will be able to ride away from an avalanche. Even if you have had this experience, it doesn't mean you'll be as lucky next time. Avoid slopes where you have to really think about the safety of you and your group. When you are riding, scan the terrain ahead and make mental notes of 'safe' points out of the fall-line to stop at, or head to in the event of a slide.

Riding in the forest, am I safe from avalanches?_Forests can protect you from larger avalanches, but a snow slab can release, even in a forest. Hollow areas are quite often formed, especially in pine forests, which are well suited to boarding - good characteristics for a danger zone. Avoid slopes with low trees and shrubs.

Are the off piste runs close to the piste, safe?_Avalanches can happen right next to the piste. Avalanche fences are generally

built on those off-piste slopes which threaten the safety of nearby pistes. This does not mean that slopes that are close to the piste without avalanche fences are safe. If you endanger others by riding an avalanche-prone slope near a piste, you may be liable for prosecution.

Are tracks a sign that a slope is safe?_A slope with tracks may still be dangerous. If a slope is not completely tracked out and seems suited to a powder run, the same steps need to taken as when you head on to a virgin run. The avalanche zone may only be a few metres away from other tracks.

Is it ever safe to ride off-piste alone?_Never ride alone in open terrain! When hiking and riding with two or more people, always keep a good distance apart. Riders should only descend a powder run one at a time, remembering to remain out of the danger zone while waiting for other riders to descend. The risk of avalanche remains, even after riders have completed the run, especially when two or three riders descend together.

What avalanche safety equipment can be found on

the market?_Whatever transceiver you decide upon, you will always need a shovel and avalanche probe in every backpack.

Electronic Avalanche Search Device (transceiver)
The Electronic Avalanche Search Device, is a battery run digital and/or analogue device which is carried on the body, which can send and receive a signal. It won't prevent you from being buried by an avalanche, but it can increase your chances of being rescued safely, if used properly. A transceiver takes a lot of practice to use well. Prices are generally between €150 and €300.
www.ortovox.com
www.barryvox.com
www.nic-impex.com
www.bcaccess.com

Avalanche-Ball: The Avalanche Ball is a ball which folds together and attaches to a back pack. A 6m long cord is then attached to the body itself. In the event of an avalanche, a rip cord releases the ball within a matter of seconds, allowing it to remain on the surface of the avalanche. In this way, it is relatively simple to locate a buried victim by following the cord down from the

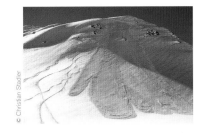

"NEVER GO OFF-PISTE WITHOUT AN AVALANCHE TRANSCEIVER, A PROBE AND A SHOVEL."

ball. The advantage of this system is that people without electronic searching devices can also aid in the search. The ball can then be easily folded together and used again. Price: approx. €200. www.avalanche-ball.com

Ava-Lung: A vest which works as an 'oxygen tank', increasing the survival chances of an avalanche victim. It works by placing a mouthpiece into your mouth as soon as you can, and the oxygen supplied enables you to remain beneath the snow layer longer. An electronic avalanche search device and/or an avalanche ball are still required. Price: between €175 and €230. www.avalung.com

ABS-Avalanche-Airbag: The only system that may actually protect you from being buried by an

avalanche. The ABS backpack has an Air Bag which, when released by the ripcord, inflates to a volume of 150l. This extra volume keeps the body above the surface of an avalanche. Price: Between €630 and €695. The high-pressure cartridges and release system need to be replaced following use. Price: €84. www.abs-lawinenairbag.de

Recco-System: The Recco System was a trend, for a while. A small signal sender (Recco Reflector) is built into the clothing of the rider. A specially made receiver is needed in the search for a victim, but is very difficult to use and generally only carried by the mountain rescue services. We do not recommend that you travel into open terrain, solely equipped with a Recco reflector (built into your

shoe or clothing). www.recco.com

Do mobile phones influence the signal of an electronic avalanche search device?_A mobile phone can be extremely useful when you are out on tour. But, the telephone should only be switched on when you need to make a call. It has been proven that the frequencies of a telephone can influence the incoming signals of an electronic search device.

What to do when you are caught in an avalanche?_By using a swim technique, you may have a chance to remain on the surface of a small avalanche. But, a snowboard works as an anchor and makes this almost impossible. If at all possible, unstrap your board.
_Before the avalanche comes to a standstill, go into a crouch position, try to bring the arms and hands in front of your face and create a space for your face and airways
_Save your energy, relax and try to breathe slowly
_Remain calm and wait for help

What can I do when a fellow rider is buried under an avalanche?_Try to keep the rider in sight for as long as possible and

then mark the point where they were was last seen. The longer the person remains under the avalanche, the less chance they have of surviving. Remain calm and begin the search at the point where the victim was last seen. If you have a mobile phone, call mountain rescue.
_Keep an eye open for any secondary avalanches
_Begin the search using an electronic avalanche search device and an avalanche probe. Search the area systematically marking your movements. Do not panic or run chaotically through the search area. Remain alert for cries of help or signs of life
_If you are alone and have not been able to find the person within the first 15 -20 minutes, go to the nearest lift station and return with help
_Once you have located the victim, dig the snow away as quickly as possible from the face to give them air
_Proceed with a first aid check. If the victim is unconscious lay them in the recovery position. If they are not breathing, proceed with mouth-to-mouth. If a pulse is not found, begin CPR.
_Protect the victim from the elements, e.g. cold and wind, by using a foil blanket or snowboard jacket.

AUSTRIA
GERMANY
SWITZERLAND

ITALY
FRANCE
SPAIN

SCOTLAND
NORWAY

SWEDEN
FINLAND

AVALANCHE INFORMATION

EUROPE

AUSTRIA »

Avalanche = Lawine
Info: www.lawine.at
Info: www.wetter.at
Avalanche Information
Kärnten +43 (0)463 1588
Oberösterreich + 43 (0)732 1588
Salzburg +43 (0)662 1588
Steiermark +43 (0)316 1588
Tirol +43 (0)512 1588
Vorarlberg +43 (0)5522 1588

GERMANY »

Avalanche = Lawine
Info: www.bayern.de/lfw/lwd/
Info: www.wetteronline.de/Bayern.htm
Avalanche Information
Bayern +49 (0)89/9214-1210

SWITZERLAND »

Avalanche = Avalanche, Lawine, Valange
Info: www.slf.ch
Info: www.meteoschweiz.ch
Avalanche Information
Switzerland +41 (0)848 800 187

ITALY »

Avalanche = Valange
Info: www.cai-svi.it
Info: www.meteoitalia.it/
Avalanche Information
Friuli-Venezia Giulia +39 0800 860 377
Liguria +39 010 53 20 49
Lombardia +39 014 78 370 77
Piemonte +39 0113 18 55 55
Südtirol +39 0471 27 11 77
Trentino +39 0461 23 89 39
Valle d'Aosta +39 0165 77 63 00
Veneto +39 0436 792 21

FRANCE »

Avalanche = Avalanche
Info: www.anena.org
Info: www.meteo.fr
Avalanche Information
Alpes Haute-Provence +33 (0)836 68 10 20 05
Alpes Maritimes +33 (0)836 68 10 20 06
Andorra +33 (0)836 68 10 20 99
Corse +33 (0)836 68 10 20 20
Hautes-Alpes +33 (0)836 68 10 20 05
Haute Garonne, Ariège +33 (0)836 68 10 20 31
Haute Savoie +33 (0)836 68 10 20 74
Isère +33 (0)836 68 10 20 38
Pyrénées Atlantiques/
Hautes Pyrénées +33 (0)836 68 10 20 65
Pyrénées Orientales +33 (0)836 68 10 20 66
Savoie +33 (0)836 68 10 20 73

© Georg Schardt **Rider** Flo Purtscher

SPAIN »

Avalanche = Avalancha
Info: www.ub.es/allaus/allaus.htm
Info: www.icc.es/allaus/maincas.html
Info: www.inm.es
Avalanche Information
Aragonesischen and
Navarresischen Pyrenäen +34 (0)906 365 380
Katalonischen
West-Pyreneän +34 (0)93 567 15 75
Katalonischen
Ost-Pyreneän +34 (0)93 567 15 75

SCOTLAND »

Avalanche = Avalanche
Info: www.sais.gov.uk
Weather info: www.meto.govt.uk

NORWAY »

Avalanche = Skred
Info: www.dnmi.no
Info: www.powderguide.no

SWEDEN »   »

Avalanche = Lavin
Info: www.smhi.se

FINLAND »

Avalanche = Lumivyöry
Info: www.fmi.fi

EUROPE ROAD MAP

Calais
N 43
A 26
Boulogne
N 1
Arras
D 925
Abbeville
Dieppe
D 925
N 28
D 901
Cherbourg
N 17
LE HARVE
N 15
N 31
A 13
ROUEN
N 1
N 13
N 13
A 13
CAEN
D 900
N 154
PARIS
N 175
N 138
BREST
N 12
Alençon
Chartres
A 10
N 165
N 154
A 10
RENNES
A 11
ORLÉANS
Quimper
LE MANS
N 157
N 10
N 20
N 24
A 81
N 137
N 23
Lorient
A 11
ANGERS
D 959
N 10
TOURS
BOURG
Vannes
N 165
N 23
N 147
N 76
A 71
NANTES
D 751
St. Nazaire
N 137
POITIERS
A 10
N 20
Niort
CLER
FER
N 141
LIMOGES
N 8
Saintes
Angoulême
N 215
N 10
Brive
N 89
N 20
BORDEAUX
Arcachon
N 250
N 20
Agen
A 62
Montauban
N 20
Albi
N 88
Bayonne
TOULOUSE
SANTANDER
BIARRITZ
A 64
N 117
N 113
DONOSTIA/
A 8
S. SEBASTIÁN
PAU
Tarbes
N 20
A 61
CARCAS
BILBO/
D 933
N 121
D 118
BILBOA
D 933
D 117
N 623
N
LOURDES
D 117
N 1
ÌRUÑEA/
Cauterets
GASTIEZ/
PAMPLONA
A 1
VITORIA
N 111
N 240
Logroño
A 15
Andorra
C 1
A 68
N 121
N 230
BURGOS
C
N 152
N 120
C
N 234
Soria
N 330
N 230
N 122
ZARAGOZA
N 240

AUSTRIA

022-059

AUSTRIA ROAD MAP

AUSTRIA »

Intro_Tanned ski instructors and cheesy Aprés Ski bars have been the symbol of Austrian winter tourism since the 60's. In some areas, this tradition still clings like sunglasses to a ski instructor's forehead. However, slowly but surely, many traditional ski resorts are waking up and investing in facilities for the snowboarding market. Although some Austrian mountains may seem small in comparison to France, Switzerland and Italy, the variety and quality of the riding is every bit as good. Many of the lower lying resorts have snowmaking facilities, almost always guaranteeing a valley run through to the end of the season. Arlberg is a paradise for freeriding, and can be considered to have some of the best terrain and conditions in Europe.

For those looking to ride through the summer, Austria has two camps, the SPC55 Camp on the Stubai glacier and the Base Camp in Sölden. Austria is a small country with a lot on offer.

INFORMATION »

Official Name_Republik Österreich
Capital_Vienna
Population_8.1 Million
Land mass_83.858km2
Language(s)_German
Currency_1 Euro = 100 Cent
Highest mountain_Großglockner 3.798m
International country code_0043
Police_133
Ambulance_144
Fire Brigade_122
Tourist Board_Tel: +43 (0)1-58 72 000
www.austria-tourism.at
Train Info_www.oebb.at
Tel: 05 1717
Weather Info_www.wetter.at
www.winterline.at

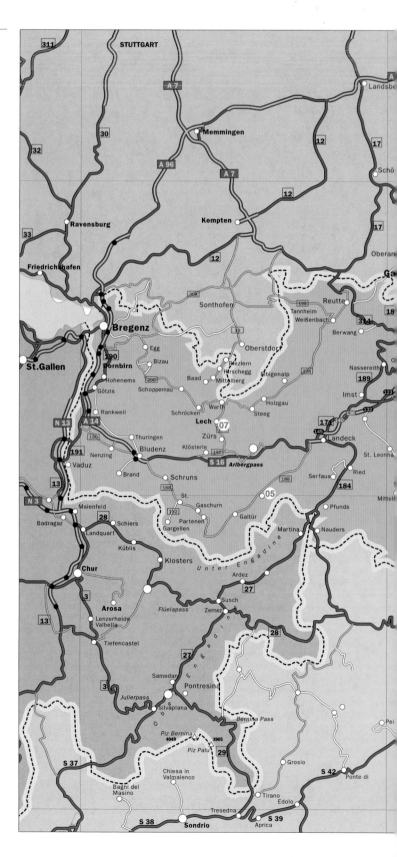

LOCATIONS »

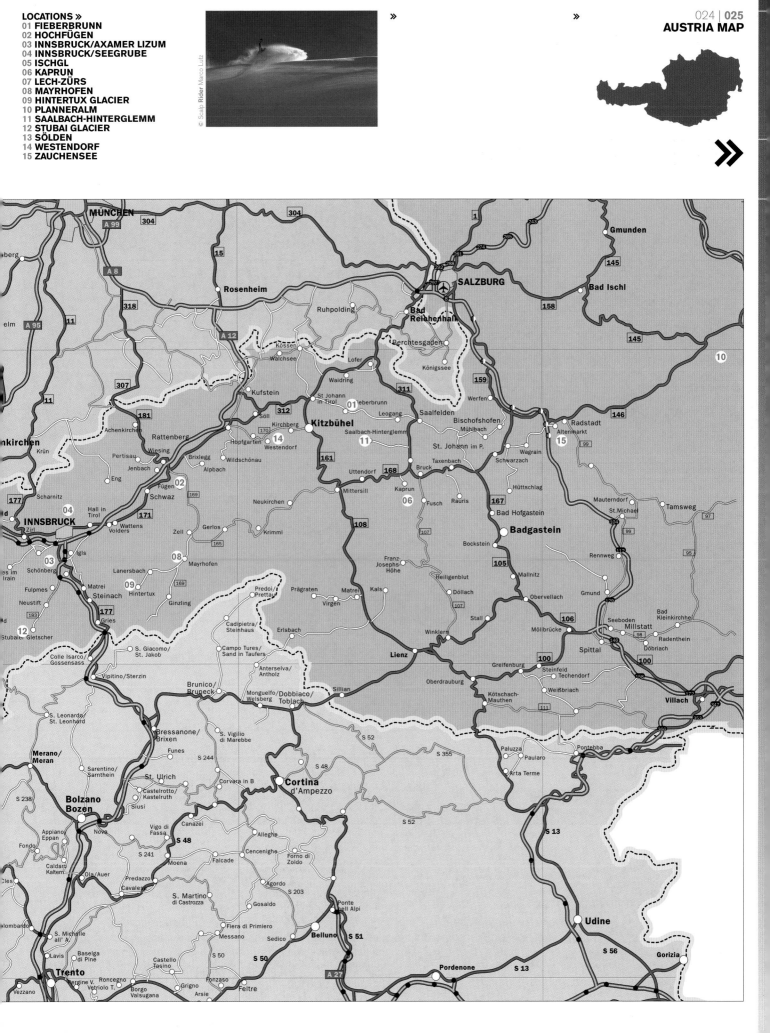

© Scalp Rider Marco Lutz

PROS & CONS »
+ When it snows, it really snows!
+ Floodlit halfpipe at the bottom of the resort.

– Some older style lifts.

"IN THE RIGHT SNOW CONDITIONS, YOU'LL FIND FIEBERBRUNN A GREAT PLACE FOR FREERIDING WITH A GOOD VARIETY OF TERRAIN. AND IT'S JUST A FEW METRES' HIKE ACROSS TO A LONG PLAYGROUND OF OFF PISTE LINES."

FIEBERBRUNN
AUSTRIA

»

FIEBERBRUNN »
www.schneedorado.at
tourist office tel: +43 (0)5354563330
location: Fieberbrunn
population:4000
altitude: 790 m

ON THE MOUNTAIN »
season: December - April
Lifts
vertical drop: 840–2020m
amount of lifts in total: 10
gondolas: 3
chairlifts: 3
T-bars: 4
Slopes
number of pistes: 35
snowmaking machines: 30
amount of easy runs: 10
amount of intermediate runs: 20
amount of advanced runs: 5
Facilities
night riding: yes
amount of halfpipes: 1
amount of funparks: 1
heliboarding: -
Events
www.lordsoftheboards.com
Lift-ticket prices in Euro
day: 28
week: 143
season: 330

SNOWBOARD TUITION »
Skischule Rosenegg
Tel: +43 (0)535452080
Skischule Widmann
Tel: +43 (0)535452297

SNOWBOARD SHOPS »
Sport Kogler
Tel: +43 (0)535452266

GETTING THERE »
By Car
Munich – Fieberbrunn: 135km
Munich - A8 towards Kufstein (Ger/Aut) -
then follow the signs to St. Johann
/Felbertauern - St. Johann - Fieberbrunn
Innsbruck - Fieberbrunn: 108km
Innsbruck - A12 towards Salzburg - take the
Wörgl Ost exit - follow the signs to St. Johann
/Felbertauern - St.Johann - Fieberbrunn
Salzburg - Fieberbrunn: 78km
Salzburg - B1 to Himmelreich (Aut/Ger) -
then follow the signs to Schneizlreuth -
Ger/Aut - Waidring - St. Johann - Fieberbrunn
By Train
Almost all express trains will stop at
St. Johann where you can then pick up a
regional train connection to Fieberbrunn.
By Air
Salzburg Airport: 78.5km
Innsbruck Airport: 110km
Munich Airport: 173km

© Stefan Hunziker **Rider** Urs Kröpfli

FIEBERRUNN »
Intro_ Fieberbrunn is a typical Tyrolean village on the border with the province of Salzburg. It's a well-known location for snowboarding and long time home to the 'Lord of the Boards' contest. As they say, 'Good things come in small packages' and Fieberbrunn is no exception. Despite the resort's relatively low elevation, because it's in the Kitzbühel Alps you can generally rely on good snow conditions. Freestylers can ride the floodlit halfpipe located by the *Streuböden* lift base station until 10.00 pm – a real bonus.

ON THE MOUNTAIN »
Snow reliability_ Fieberbrunn tends to get lucky with the snow. It normally snows half a metre more than it does in the neighbouring resorts of *St. Johann* or *Kitzbühel*. The addition of snow-making

facilities also guarantees the availability of good quality pistes.
Snow report
Tel: 00 43 (0) 5354 5630 4 - 22

Lift & Piste_ The valley lift station is located just a few minutes' drive from the town centre. To access the resort you can take the *Doischberg* chairlift or the *Streuböden* gondola. The lift system is not ideal, but the availability of long off piste runs makes the hassle worthwhile. Fieberbrunn has 3 gondolas, 3 chairlifts, 3 tow lifts, and 35km of piste, making it a relatively small area, but one where you can really let loose.

Freeriding_ In the right snow conditions, you'll find Fieberbrunn a great place for freeriding with a good variety of terrain. And it's just a few metres' hike across to a long

playground of off piste lines that run in parallel with all the obvious runs down into the valley. The better runs, though, are the classic lines of the *Pletzergraben* and the *Hörndlingergraben*. Beware! Even though the area doesn't look dangerous, there's still a risk of avalanches. If in doubt, ask.

Freestyling_ The legendary *Streuböden* halfpipe stays floodlit until 10.00pm. When you start to find the Funpark too small, you'll find plenty of ideal spots to build a big fat kicker. Plan on heading to Fieberbrunn around the time of the 'Lord of the Boards' contest, when you'll find the park and halfpipe in supreme condition. Fieberbrunn hosts many top-level pipe and corner contests, when you may be lucky enough to see such legendary riders as Terje Haakonsen and Stefan Gimpl in action.

"THE *STREUBÖDEN* HALFPIPE STAYS FLOODLIT UNTIL 10.00PM."

© Red Bull/Vitek Ludvik **Rider** Martin Cernik

© Peter Mathis **Rider** Reto Lamm

Carving_ Fieberbrunn is well suited to carvers, especially the *Doischberg* area, which includes a permanent race course for those who feel the need for speed. For such a small resort you'll find some great carving runs, even though you might find them a little tight at times.

Beginners_ Beginners are well catered for here in Fieberbrunn. *Weißbach, Hochkogel* T-bar or the valley run on *Streuböden* are all well suited to beginners. Fieberbrunn is also a friendly family resort.

Mountain Restaurants_ Not many choices here, so there's little worth mentioning. Your best bet is to eat at a restaurant down in the valley. On a sunny day, the view from the *Streuböden* restaurant terrace is good, but you'll have to compete with the hordes of punters who sunbathe there all day.

Nearby resorts_ St. Johann, St. Jakob/Pillersee, Waidringer Steinplatte and Kitbühel are all within half an hour's drive from Fieberbrunn.

IN THE TOWN »
Accommodation_ The price range for a standard room in Fieberbrunn starts from €15 - €20 per person. There are lots of pensions and hotels. But watch out! A room in town doesn't always mean that the town centre is within walking distance. Fieberbrunn sprawls over a fair distance and the walk home after a night in town can be torturous! Before you book a room ask how far it is to the actual town centre.

Fieberbrunn Tourist Office
Tel: 00 43 (0) 5356 304

info@fieberbrunn.at
www.fieberbrunn.com

Food_ Gasthofs are a dime a dozen. The *Alte Post, Neue Post, Pizzeria San Marco* and *La Pampa* can all be found close to the town centre. No one place is better than any other. There's also a supermarket in the village for visitors who are self-catering. The town of St. Johann, 11km away, has a McDonalds, some bigger supermarkets and a few nice restaurants.

Nightlife_ Like many of the smaller resorts, Fieberbrunn doesn't have a lot to offer in the way of nightlife, but there are a couple of good spots for a bevvy. *Cheers* is the new name of the old Londoner Pub and it's a good place for a beer. The locals can generally be found at the *Riverhouse* on the other side of the river, but later on in the evening people head for the *Tenne* dancebar. All three places are within a 3 minute walk of each other. If you're looking for a change, you can always opt for St. Johann or Kitbühel. A car would be handy, though, as taxis are expensive.

Other Activities_ Sledding, tandem paragliding and a visit to the après ski bars are all on offer. The Go-Cart track (open in the evening), can be found 20 minutes away in Saalfelden. Tandem flights can be booked at the Streuböden lift.

LOCAL TIP »
After a good snowfall when other resorts are closed, you can ride fine powder, pretty low risk, through the tree runs below the Streuböden lift.

PROS & CONS »

+ A good chance of decent snow thanks to its elevation and certain other factors.
+ Fügen is 5mins from the autobahn or motorway.
+ Many resorts accessible within a 20 mins drive.

– Takes 20 minutes to drive from the village of Fügen to the resort of Hochfügen.
– Small resort.
– Lots of tow lifts.

"SINCE THE NEW GONDOLA HAS BEEN BUILT, YOU HARDLY EVER NEED TO WAIT FOR A LIFT AT HOCHFÜGEN. THE RESORT HAS 12 LIFTS, 8 OF WHICH ARE TOW LIFTS. THE TRIP FROM FÜGEN TAKES AROUND 20 MINUTES"

HOCHFÜGEN
AUSTRIA

»

HOCHFÜGEN »
www.hochfuegenski.com
tourist office tel: +43 (0)528862319
location: Hochfügen
population: -
altitude; 630m
linked resorts: Spieljoch

ON THE MOUNTAIN »
season: December - April
Lifts
vertical drop: 1500-2400m
amount of lifts in total: 11
gondolas: 1
chair lifts: 3
drag lifts: 7
Slopes
amount of prepared slopes: 32
runs w. snowmaking machines: 6
amount of easy runs: 9
amount of intermediate runs: 17
amount of advanced runs: 6
Facilities
night riding: 2
amount of halfpipes: -
amount of funparks: -
heliboarding: -
Lift-ticket prices in Euro
1/2 day: 19.40
day: 27.70
week: 74.50
season: 240

SNOWBOARD TUITION »
Skischule Aktiv Fügen-Hochfügen
Tel: +43 (0)528863875
www.schischule-aktiv-fuegen.at
Skischule Total Telefon
Tel: +43 (0)528862233
www.skischule-total.at

GETTING THERE »
Car
Innsbruck - Fügen 50km
Innsbruck - A12 Inn Valley autobahn - towards Salzburg - Wiesing/Zillertal exit - Fügen
Munich - Fügen 141km
Munich - A8 towards Innsbruck - Kufstein - Wiesing/Zillertal exit - Fügen
Train
Train to Jenbach (between Innsbruck and Wörgl), then change to the Zillertal train.
Air
Innsbruck Airport 51km
Munich Airport 180km
There are also charter buses to Zillertal, but you'll need to ask what time they leave.

© Scalp Rider Andi Egger

HOCHFÜGEN »
Intro_Right at the entrance to the Ziller Valley you'll find the town of Fügen and it's from here that you can access the most beautiful resort in the whole valley, Hochfügen. The resort is only small, and a well kept secret for freeriders and kicker builders, and what's more, it generally gets more snow than the surrounding resorts. The small but fun resort of Spieljoch is also accessible from Fügen.

ON THE MOUNTAIN »
Snow reliability_When there's no snow at Hochfügen, you won't find snow anywhere else in the Ziller Valley either, except of course up on the Hintertuxer Glacier.

Notwithstanding that, you'll generally enjoy more snow in Hochfügen than anywhere else in the valley. The resort begins at 1400m and rises up to 2400m, thus ensuring a good snowbase. And when there isn't enough snow, the lift company will simply turn on the snow making machines.
The pistes are usually kept in good condition.
Log onto www.hochfuegenski.com for snow reports and live webcam pictures.

Lifts & Piste_Since the new gondola has been built, you hardly ever need to wait for a lift at Hochfügen. The resort has 12 lifts, 8 of which are tow lifts. The trip from Fügen takes around 20

minutes. The Spieljoch resort is accessible directly from Fügen. Spieljoch has 8 lifts, 4 of which are tow lifts. A 7km run will bring you back to Fügen. An excursion to Spieljoch is worth the effort.

Freeriding_For those who like hiking with all the gear, Hochfügen is the place to go. The terrain is ideal for long powder runs, or at least, it used to be. These days, you'll have to get to the lift early if you want to avoid your freshies being tracked out. Inexperienced freeriders should content themselves with the powder runs next to the piste before they think about taking off on a crazy hike. Don't underestimate the danger of avalanches here.

"FOR THOSE WHO LIKE HIKING WITH ALL THE GEAR, HOCHFÜGEN IS THE PLACE TO GO. THE TERRAIN IS IDEAL FOR LONG POWDER RUNS, OR AT LEAST, IT USED TO BE. THESE DAYS, YOU'LL HAVE TO GET TO THE LIFT EARLY"

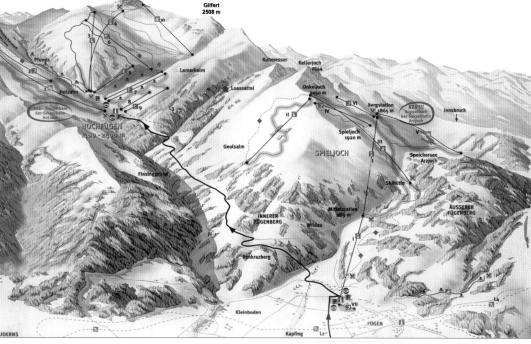

Freestyling_There's no park on the Hochfügen. The local freestylers build their own backcountry booters to join up with the dream powder runs. There are plenty of good spots and you'll be able to see them easily from the lift. There's a fairly average park on Spieljoch. Despite the shortcomings of the resort, you'll still see some great freestylers around Fügen.

Carving_Hochfügen has very few lifts and therefore very little piste. More for the chilled carver. The Holzalm lift is the exception, it's ideal.

Beginners_This resort is ideal for beginners. Two flatter tow lifts right next to the valley station create the perfect environment for learning, and there's nothing too challenging in terms of pistes.

Mountain Restaurants_The mountain restaurant next to the gondola is not fantastic, but the pizzeria on the first floor isn't bad. Or you could try the Almhof at the valley lift station (where there's also a very good snowboard school, by the way). The Après-Ski scene is probably at its best at the Kristallbar.

Nearby Resorts_Spieljoch -

access it via the gondola from Fügen, closer than Hochfügen. Kaltenbach involves a 10 minute drive

IN THE TOWN »
Accommodation_The cheapest room you'll find will cost between €15 and €20 per person. Even though there are lots of guest houses and hotels here, it's still best to book early. Also ask about the hotels in Hochfügen as they often have special package deals. Fügener Tourist Office
Tel: +43 (0) 52 88 62 262
email: tvb.fuegen@tirol.com
www.fuegen.cc or
www.hochfuegenski.com

Food_The Hotel Alpina serves a wide range of good food, as does the Hoppenda. Further recommendations include the Hotel Schiestl and the Piz Pub, yum…!

Nightlife_The Rosso, next to Hotel Alpina is chilled and plays good music. The local hangout Shapeso is also a relaxed place with great cocktails. The Piz Pub is a pizzeria and pub in one – right next to the Spieljoch lift. A visit to Rainer's Pub is good for one or two beers. A ski village classic is the Zillertaler Tenne just on the edge

"THIS RESORT IS IDEAL FOR BEGINNERS."

of the town, and its competition, the Badwandl. The two local discos have the same style, play the same type of music and are only a few kilometres apart. As usual, a great place to stop… when you're really drunk.

Shopping_We particularly recommend a shop in the neighbouring village of Uderns. It's called Snowboard Department Rainer, it's right on the main street, and you can't miss it. Just look out for the banners.

Other Activities_The Go-Kart track at Uderns is excellent fun, or you could try tandem paragliding with Stocky Air. www.zillertal.com/fly

LOCAL TIP »
Brändy - Hammer Team Rider from Fügen_"If you're looking for good snowboard info and lessons then stop in at Cosi im Almhof. It's the best snowboard school in the village."

INNSBRUCK AXAMER LIZUM
AUSTRIA

AXAMER LIZUM »
www.axamer-lizum.at
Tourist office tel: + 43 (0)523468178
location: Axams
population: 5000
altitude: 868m
linked resorts: Seegrube-Nordkette, Patscherkofel, Glungezer, Stubaier Gletscher

ON THE MOUNTAIN »
season: November - April
lifts
vertical drop: 1583 -2304m
amount of lifts in total: 10
gondolas: 1
chair lifts: 5
drag lifts:4
Slopes
amount of prepared slopes: 41 km
snowmaking machines: 20
easy runs: 4 km
intermediate runs: 27 km
advanced runs:10 km
Facilities
night riding: -
amount of halfpipes: 1
amount of funparks: 1
Heliboarding: -
Lift-ticket prices in Euro
1/2 day:23
day: 27
week: 132
season: 270

SNOWBOARD TUITION »
Olympic ·
Tel: +43 (0)523465400
www.schischule-olympic.com

SNOWBOARD SHOPS »
Sport 2000 Apperl
Tel: +43 (0)523468390

GETTING THERE »
Car
Munich - Innsbruck 160km
Munich A8 - A12 - in direction of Innsbruck
Geneva - Innsbruck 560km
Geneva - Bern - Zurich - St.Gallen - Au (Swiss/It) - Bludenz - Arlberg Tunnel (Toll) - Landeck - Innsbruck
Milan - Innsbruck 391km
Milan - Brescia - Garda - Brenner - Innsbruck
Innsbruck - Axamer Lizum 18km
Innsbruck - Innsbruck West - Götzens - Birgitz - Axams - Axamer Lizum
Train
When you get to the main train station at Innsbruck, take the Post bus to Axams.
Journey time 20 minutes, price: €2.18
Milan - Innsbruck approx. 5hrs 20min
Munich - Innsbruck approx. 2hrs 30min
Zürich - Innsbruck approx. 3hrs 50min
Air
Innsbruck Airport 18km
Taxi to Axams around €21.80

© Georg Schantl **Rider** Flo Örley, Flo Puntscher

AXAMER LIZUM »
Intro_The Winter Olympics village of Axams is 878 metres above sea level and is on the way to Khutai - Sellraintal, some 11kms from Innsbruck. Like its immediate neighbours, Axams is very much a typical Tyrolean village. Travel a further 8km and you come to Lizum, or Lizzn as the locals call it, and together these 2 villages form the resort of Axamer Lizum. With just 40km of piste, it's not exactly a major resort, but it does have plenty of freeriding and freestyle potential. The Innsbruck Super Ski Pass enables you to use this resort along with 6 others, including the Stubaier glacier and the Nordkette - Seegrube.

ON THE MOUNTAIN »
Snow reliability_The Lizum is a well-known snow trap given its elevation of between 1583 - 2340m. The snow conditions are good between Nov/Dec until the end of April. 20 snow making machines ensure a secure snow base. For general information check the website at www.axamer-lizum.at or call the Snow Phone on +43 (0) 5234 682 40 for the latest snow reports.

Lifts & Piste_No fears of long queues at the lifts here. The package holiday crowd don't usually end up in Lizum, and the relatively quiet nightlife means that the Après- Ski set don't bother with the place either. With 9 lifts to look out from, you'll soon see where the best places are. A hot tip: the Innsbrucker Gletscher Ski Pass includes the resorts of Seegrube-Nordkette, Glungezer, Patscherkofel, Schlick 2000 and the Stubaier glacier, and the free ski bus can take you to all of them. Of especial interest is the Seegrube - Nordkette resort, which can be accessed directly from Innsbruck by taking the Hungerberg lift. Great freeriding and a good funpark in one of Europe's steepest resorts - www.nordpark.com. Another alternative would be the Innsbruck Super Ski Pass which can also be used in Kitzbühel or Arlberg.

Freeriding_Freeride heaven. Standing right next to the valley lift stations, an experienced rider will immediately see the off piste opportunities the place has to offer. A short hike gives you access to some very heavy chutes and cliffs, which demand respect. The terrain fulfils every possible desire, from extreme lines to mellow powder runs. But you need to exercise great caution in Lizum, because after a new fall of snow the danger of an avalanche is never far away. Find out more about the latest avalanche situation from the locals or better still from the Avalanche Commission. From the summit station of the Lizum train at Hoadl (2340m), if there is no avalanche danger, you can ride down wide fields of powder, then through trees into the valley below.

The Snowboard School Axamer Lizum runs guided tours (Tel: +43 (0) 5234 88 68), as does the Alpine School Innsbruck (+43 (0) 512 54 60)

Freestyling_The coming season promises a better funpark thanks to the efforts of the pro shaping company Mellow Constructions run by Tommy 'Mellow' Marsh. Once this has been built, there'll be no concerns about the quality of the park. People don't come to Axams for the halfpipe at the foot of the women's downhill run, but it is regularly maintained. The terrain at Lizum offers heaps of windlips, cliffs and natural jumps which will satisfy any freestyler. Countless jumps can be hit when riding in parallel with the women's downhill run.

Carving_ Excellent conditions await you. TIP: Take the first gondola run in the morning and ride down the well-prepared women's downhill piste. The runs

four star hotel - the Lizumerhof - for those who want a little extra. Private rooms or holiday apartments are cheaper options and the neighbouring villages of Birgitz and Götzens also offer such accommodation. Due to the complete lack of nightlife in these villages, we would recommend you shack up in Innsbruck, for example at the Hotel Central - which has packages including overnight accommodation, transfer to and from the resort, lift passes and

Indian try Da Vento, near the Altstadt, opposite the post office in Adolf Bichler platz. For a quick feed you can visit the local kebab shops or, if you have to, McDonald's.

Nightlife_ Bini's is the recommendation from Axamer local Tommi U. For real nightlife, your best bet is to go to Innsbruck. There are lots of different bars at the Bögen - alongside the railway line - and all over Innsbruck, e.g. Jimmy's and for later in the

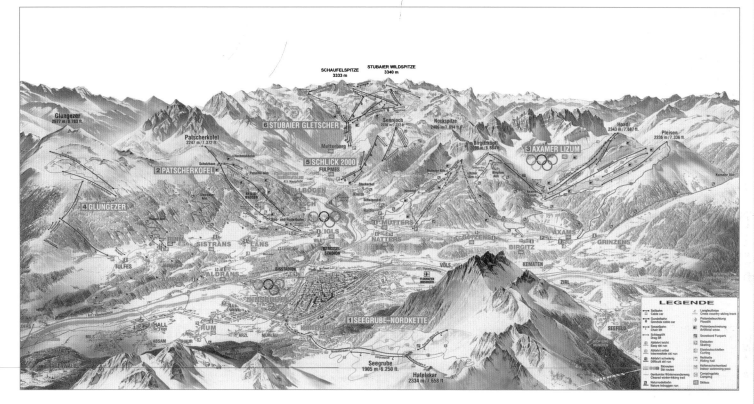

provide enough room for even hardcore carvers, especially early in the morning, before the crowds arrive.

Beginners_ For those who can turn their boards, you'll not have too many problems making it down the piste. For those of you still at the bottom of the learning curve, there are two practice lifts by the valley lift station. Info regarding courses or private lessons can be obtained from the Snowboard School Axamer Lizum Tel: +43 (0) 5234 88 68 (ask for Didi) or at the Snowboard School Olympic Tel: +43 (0) 5234 74 15

Mountain Restaurants_ From the self-service restaurant at Hoadl, you'll be treated to a breathtaking view of the surrounding mountains. However, the locals consider this to be an expensive tourist trap. They prefer the Dolennest, halfway down the women's downhill run, and it's certainly a great place for a midday chill. Next to the car park there's the Lizum Alm which serves traditional food at acceptable prices.

IN THE TOWN »
Accommodation_ Axams has one

meals - www.central.co.at. The free ski bus also takes you to the resort, which is about 9km from Innsbruck. For further information contact the Innsbruck Tourism Office - Tel:+43 (0) 512 81 78 or www.innsbruck-tourismus.com.

Food_ For those catering for themselves, there are two supermarkets in Axams, supplying all those important and not so important things you need for survival. Most of the hotels have their own restaurant serving traditional and international meals. For a cosy meal in front of an open fire, you can head to the Bürgerstuben or the Kögele. Italian specialities can be enjoyed at restaurant Madonna or in the pizzeria at the Freizeitzentrum Axams. Innsbruck, of course, has an unlimited choice of places to eat. Apart from the local and foreign dishes served at the Theresien Bräu, you can get well-poured beer. Cheaper midday meals are served alongside Tex-Mex food at the Krahvogel in Anichstraße. If you're fond of Asian food, try the Thai restaurant on the Sillgasse or for a reasonably-priced

evening, downstairs to Blue Chip. DJs play music from Hip-Hop to down tempo at the likes of the Innkeller or the Couch Club. A harder music scene can be found at Prometheus in the Altstadt. The early hours of the morning are still pumping at the Plateau in the Bögen district.

Other Activities_ The public swimming baths with its outdoor heated pool is great for relaxing and also has both a sauna and solarium facilities. For the hyperactive, there's a sledding night every Wednesday organised by the Tourist Office - sled ride, transfers and a stop over in one of the local huts, and all for €7. Otherwise head to Innsbruck to make the snowboard shops a little richer and the pubs a little more unsafe.

LOCAL TIP »
"The Lizum will fulfil your every heart's desire, from the great variety of off piste terrain, right down to its close proximity to Innsbruck. However, watch out for speed limits and radar controls on your way home. The money grabbing gendarmes are usually watching."

"NO FEARS OF LONG QUEUES AT THE LIFTS HERE. THE PACKAGE HOLIDAY CROWD DON'T USUALLY END UP IN LIZUM, AND THE RELATIVELY QUIET NIGHTLIFE MEANS THAT THE APRÈS-SKI SET DON'T BOTHER"

CHECKLIST»

+ Steep freeriding terrain
+ Good freestyle park
+ 15 minutes from Innsbruck

- Relatively small resort with very few lifts
- Crowded in the holiday periods and on weekends
- High avalanche danger, due to the steep terrain

"BEGINNERS MAY FIND IT A BIT TOO HECTIC. THE HUNGERBERGBAHN TRAIN TRANSFERS YOU FROM THE CITY TO THE NORDKETTEBAHN, JUST MINUTES AWAY FROM SEEGRUBE."

INNSBRUCK SEEGRUBE
AUSTRIA

SEEGRUBE»
www.nordpark.com
tourist office tel: +43 (0)51259850
location: Innsbruck
population: 113000
altitude: 789 m
linked resorts: Seegrube-Nordkette, Patscherkofel, Glungezer, Stubaier Gletscher

ON THE MOUNTAIN »
season: December - April
Lifts
vertical drop: 860-2260m
amount of lifts in total: 4
gondolas: 2
chair lifts: 2
Slopes
amount of prepared slopes: 14
runs w. snowmaking machines: -
amount of easy runs: 1
amount of intermediate runs: 8
amount of advanced runs: 5
Facilities
amount of halfpipes: -
amount of funparks: 1
Lift-ticket prices in Euro
1/2 day: 17
day: 22.50
week: 106
season: 200
Events
The Jam: www.thejam.tv

SNOWBOARD TUITION »
Ski- und Snowboardschule Innsbruck
Tel: +43 (0)6763056228
www.skischool-innsbruck.com

SNOWBOARD SHOPS »
Burton Store
Hallerer Straße 111
Tel: +43 (0)5122300
www.burton.com
Dollarshop Innsbruck
Viaduktbogen 16
Tel: +43 (0)512561150
www.dollarshop.at
Sport Spezial
Blasius Hueber Straße 14
Tel:+43 (0)12286707

RESORT NAME »
Car
Munich - Innsbruck 160km
Munich - A8 - (Ger/Aut) - Kufstein - Wörgl - Innsbruck
Zürich - Innsbruck 280km
Zürich - St.Gallen - Exit Au (Swiss/Aut) - Bludenz - Arlberg Tunnel - Landeck - Innsbruck
Milan - Innsbruck 391km
Milan - Brescia - towards Bolzano - Brenner Pass (It/Aut) - Innsbruck
Train
Main train station Innsbruck (Hauptbahnhof)
Munich - Innsbruck approx. 2 hours
Zürich - Innsbruck approx. 4 hours
Milan - Innsbruck approx. 5 hours 20 min
www.oebb.at
Air
Innsbruck Airport
www.flughafen-innsbruck.at

© Christian Stadler

SEEGRUBE »
Intro_Seegrube lies on the steep slopes of the Nordkette, high above the capital of the Austrian Tyrol, Innsbruck. Freestylers and freeriders alike, plus those just looking for a bit of sun on the south facing slopes, all head to Seegrube. It's quite a busy resort, so beginners may find it a bit too hectic to learn here.
The Hungerbergbahn train transfers you direct from the city to the Nordkettebahn, just minutes away from Seegrube.

ON THE MOUNTAIN »
Snow reliability_The resort begins at 900m and rises up to 2334m above sea level. Because the slopes face south, the snow melts quickly and riding down to the valley is seldom possible. And even when it is, it's usually too icy to be any fun. The Nordkette gets a lot of snow due to the 'damming' effect of the surrounding mountains. You could almost say it often gets too much snow, in terms of avalanche danger.

Lifts & Piste_Luckily for you, most tourists arrive here without skis or snowboards, coming simply to enjoy the sun and the scenery. Also, many Innsbruck residents avoid Seegrube because of its steep terrain and limited lift facilities. The Hungerberg train brings you from the city centre to the Nordkette lift in a matter of minutes, and from here there are two chairlifts to take you up to the top.

Freeriding_There are two real reasons to ride at Seegrube and the first one is its extreme freeride terrain. However, for those with limited experience of off piste riding, this is a dangerous place. The terrain is very steep and prone to avalanches. Be especially careful of heavy rocks falling, some of which occasionally even find their way through the trees.
   The SAAC organises avalanche awareness camps at different resorts every year. Dates and locations can be found at www.saac.at

Freestyling_The other reason for coming here is the Skyline Park.

Although there's not a lot here, what they do have is perfectly shaped. The 'chill zone' is equipped with deck chairs, hammocks and a great sound system. www.nordpark.com
   The highlight of the season is The Jam, a three-day freestyle event full of great riding, partying and music. The provisional dates for 2003 are 27.01.03 - 31.01.03, more at www.thejam.tv

Carving_Carvers shouldn't even bother bringing their boards, just their shorts and sunscreen.

Beginners_Beginners would be better off travelling to Axamer Lizum. However, there is a nice practice slope in Seegrube, and during good weather it is warmer here than Axamer Lizum. For lessons head for Rudi's Skischule, located in the resort.

Mountain Restaurants_Tyrolean specialities and traditional ski hut food are served in the self-service restaurant on Seegrube. The views and the sunny terrace draw a lot of tourists, and don't forget your

© Georg Schanti **Rider** Flow Daniaux

"THERE ARE TWO REAL REASONS TO RIDE AT SEEGRUBE AND THE FIRST ONE IS ITS EXTREME FREERIDE TERRAIN. HOWEVER, FOR THOSE WITH LIMITED EXPERIENCE OF OFF PISTE RIDING, THIS IS A DANGEROUS PLACE. THE TERRAIN IS VERY STEEP AND PRONE TO AVALANCHES. BE ESPECIALLY CAREFUL OF HEAVY ROCKS FALLING, SOME OF WHICH OCCASIONALLY EVEN FIND THEIR WAY THROUGH THE TREES."

"THE RESORT BEGINS AT 900M AND RISES UP TO 2334M ABOVE SEA LEVEL. BECAUSE THE SLOPES FACE SOUTH, THE SNOW MELTS QUICKLY AND RIDING DOWN TO THE VALLEY IS SELDOM POSSIBLE. AND EVEN WHEN IT IS, IT'S USUALLY TOO ICY TO BE ANY FUN."

sunscreen. Mountain huts such as the Bodensteiner Alm and the Arzler Alm are only accessible via off piste runs and aren't always open – ask the lifties first. After a day's boarding, it is practically obligatory to have a gluhwein (mulled wine) at Martin's Schirmbar at the base of the Nordkettebahn. Then head next door to Gasthof Klamm and try some fine Tyrolean food.

IN THE TOWN »
Accommodation_ The Restaurant-Hotel Seegrube is right in the middle of the resort - call them on +43 (0) 512 293 375.
   Your best bet, however, is Innsbruck, which has countless hotels and guesthouses. At around €10 per night, the cheapest option is the youth hostel, but you'll have to share a room with five other people - www.youth-hostel-innsbruck.at
The neighbouring villages are also

recommended, as they'll generally be cheaper and more scenic than Innsbruck . The Hotel Central often has some really cheap package deals - www.central.co.at.

Further information
InnsbruckTourist Office
Tel: +43 (0) 512 81 78
www.innsbruck-tourismus.com

Food_ Think about taking the night gondola to Seegrube and enjoying the cuisine of the mountains, on the mountain. Best to make a reservation though:
Tel: +43 (0) 512 293 375. Tyrolian cuisine is also on the menu at the Ottoburg, Gasthof Steden and the Theresienbräu. Das Chili's in the Bozner Platz is known for its Tex-Mex meals.

Vegetarian food
Phillipine, Tempelstraße 2
Tel: +43 (0) 512 58 91 57.
Compared to the limited menu found in most Austrian resorts, Innsbruck has it all – even sushi and curry!

Nightlife_ Martin's Schirmbar is

the first stop for a beer, but this is where the traditional cheesy Après Ski ends. Innsbruck is home to a number of good bars and clubs such as Jimmy's, Blue Chip, Innkeller, the Couch Club, and Plateau, to name but a few. Innsbruck is a university town and there's almost always something going on - except perhaps in summer, when the students disappear.

Other Activities_ There's always something to do in Innsbruck from swimming pools, saunas and fitness studios, through to night-time sledge runs. Theatres, concerts and museums are all here too. Metropol, Ciniplexx, Leokino and Cinematograph all show films in English.

LOCAL TIP »
Keep informed about the snow and avalanche conditions before heading off piste in Seegrube. Remember: it's dangerous to follow tracks into the off piste terrain.

Snow and weather reports
www.tirol.com/nordkette

PROS & CONS »
+ Snow reliability.
+ Modern, fast lifts.
+ Good fun park - easily accessible freeride terrain.

– Often overcrowded, especially in the holiday periods around Christmas and in February.
– Food and accommodation very expensive.
– Masses of drunken tourists.

ISCHGL
AUSTRIA

"SICK RUNS CAN BE STARTED FROM THE PALINKOPF, HEADING TOWARDS THE GAMPANBAHN END STATION. ONE NOVELTY IN ISCHGL IS THAT YOU CAN CROSS THE BORDER INTO SWITZERLAND."

ISCHGL »
www.ischgl.com
tourist office tel: + 43 (0)544452660
location: Ischgl
population: 1350
altitude: 1400m

ON THE MOUNTAIN »
Season: December to May
Lifts
vertical drop:1400-2872m
amount of lifts in total: 41
gondolas: 5
chair lifts: 17
drag lifts: 19
Slopes
amount of prepared slopes: 200 km
runs w. snowmaking machines: 25%
easy runs: 30 k
intermediate runs: 130 km
advanced runs: 40 km
Facilities
night riding: -
amount of halfpipes: 2
amount of funparks: 6
heliboarding: -
Lift-ticket prices in Euro
1/2 day: 29
day: 37.50
week: 184
season: 520

SNOWBOARD TUITION »
Ischgl Schischule
Tel: +43 (0)54445257
www.ischgl.info/schischule

SNOWBOARD SHOPS »
Sport Zangerl
Tel: +43 (0)5444518

GETTING THERE »
Car
Innsbruck - Ischgl: 100km
Innsbruck - Landeck - Ischgl
Munich - Ischgl: 195km
Munich - Garmisch - Landeck - Ischgl
Zurich - Ischgl: 210km
Zurich - Bludenz - St. Gallenkirchen (alternatively the Arlbergpass) - Ischgl
Train/Bus
Train connection to Landeck, then take the Post bus to Ischgl. The bus leaves every 1-2 hours from Landeck.
Air
Innsbruck Airport - Ischgl: 102km
Munich Airport - Ischgl: 233km
Zurich Airport - Ischgl: 218km

© Peter Mathis **Rider** Tommy Brunner

ISCHGL »
Intro_Ischgl was quick to see the potential of snowboarding and was a pioneer in the integration of boarding into ski resorts. In the past, the town was able to claim to have one of the best and the biggest fun parks in the Alps. Even though these days you can find many fun parks that are better, this resort is still known as one of the top spots for freestylers and freeriders. The nightlife is extreme and after a few beers you may well find yourself singing along to some of those stupid après ski songs. Ischgl means going hard... on the mountain and in the bars.

ON THE MOUNTAIN »
Snow reliability_Towards the end of the Paznauntal (Paznaun Valley), in the surrounding Silveretta mountains, is the little village of Ischgl at 1400m. The resort itself is more than 2000 metres above sea level, its highest peak being the Palinkopf at 2864m. Snow here is generally abundant and easily covers the winter season, which starts in December and continues until the end of April. More than 250

individual snow making machines ensure that even the most popular runs continue to be rideable, including the valley run.

Lifts_When it comes to lift facilities, Ischgl is one of, if not the, most modern resort in the European Alps. In the village alone there are no fewer than three different gondolas to carry you up to the Paratschgrat or the Idalp.

The speed and efficiency of the lifts generally means that there's very little hanging around. On the Idalp, the resort's centre and the meeting point for the ski & snowboard school, you may find that the lifts to the Idjoch are busier, but if that's the case, we'd suggest that you head down to the Höllbodenbahn and take a ride to Palinkopf instead. For those wanting to head to the funpark, you'll have no other choice than to wait patiently in line for a ride on the Idjoch or Flimjochbahn. And your reward? A ride on the world's first 8 seater chairlift with optional bubble for those colder days!

Freeriding_When it comes to freeriding, Ischgl has a ton on offer.

Less experienced riders should look for the powder runs alongside the piste. But even on these runs a note of caution is needed because the snow can hide treacherous rocks or 'sharks'. The backcountry is really only suitable for experienced freeriders or those accompanied by a mountain guide. But it's all here; tree runs, cliff drops, steep chutes and long powder runs. The Paratschgrat is a starting point for many a dream run and it includes loads of jumps. In good snow the recommendation is to take one of the runs down to the Paznauner Taja lift station. A stash of sick runs can be started from the Palinkopf, heading towards the Gampanbahn end station. One novelty in Ischgl is that you can cross the border into Switzerland and ride down to Samnaun. You may be asked for your passport, so don't forget to carry ID. Finally, and on a serious note of caution – always remember that the open and accessible terrain in Ischgl lulls many people into forgetting the dangers that constantly surround you on the mountains – ride safe!

"ISCHGL HAS ALWAYS PLAYED A LEADING ROLE WHEN IT COMES TO FUN PARKS AND HALF PIPES. SADLY, IT SEEMS THAT THEY'VE BEEN FALLING BEHIND OF LATE, WHICH MEAN THERE'S STILL A BIT OF CATCHING UP TO DO"

Freestyling_ Ischgl has always played a leading role when it comes to fun parks and half pipes. Sadly, it seems that they've been falling behind of late, which mean there's still a bit of catching up to do if they're to remain contenders. Having said that, though, you'll still find the fun park to be one of the biggest in the Alps. The Boarder's Paradise park is just below the Idjochbahn and freestylers will find a whole series of kickers, a Quarter, a Half-pipe and jib terrain to let loose on. Entry into the park is open to all, which is why there are so many kids on skis who not only damage the jumps but constantly get in the way. In Samnaun you'll find a half-pipe that's not usually used that much. To the left and right of the Visnitzbahn, you'll find lots of ideal places to build a kicker, and it won't take long to find natural jumps and cliffs too. In short, Ischgl has everything for everyone.

Carving_ Over 200km of groomed runs, many of which are wide and not too steep, draw a good proportion of Hard-booters and Ski-Carvers. The year 2000 saw Ischgl receive the international award for Best Ski Resort, due, amongst other reasons, to its modern lifts and outstanding quality in piste preparation. Those who really want to know can test their speed on the High Speed Run below the Vellilbahn.

Beginners_ To be honest, beginners can find less expensive and better resorts to learn in. Snowboard beginner lessons are generally held on the Idalp, an area only accessible via the gondola. At the height of the season, you'll find this area teeming with people and because the runs back down aren't suitable for beginners, getting back down the mountain will involve taking the gondola. As a beginner, it would be impossible to take full advantage of this amazing resort, so we recommend you start off in a more beginner-friendly resort and save Ischgl for when you're ready to do the place justice.

Mountain Restaurants_ The restaurants offer good food, but they ain't cheap. The restaurant on the Idalp is often full, yet it's also the one that's most accessible from the fun park. Those of you

hungry for a pizza should head to the restaurant Schwarzwand on the Hollenkar. The pizzas aren't any more expensive than the ones you get in the village, but they're big and taste as if they're made by Italians. Eating on the Samnaun side in Switzerland means you'll have to dig even deeper in your wallet. Sitting in the sun on the terrace of the Sattel restaurant, you can gaze across at great views of some hairy runs. But the breathtaking views are matched by breathtaking prices.

IN THE TOWN »
Accommodation_ The town of Ischgl is not very big so it's easy to access the gondolas, bars and restaurants on foot.
One of the cheaper hotels is the ***Hotel Charly, which in the low season will cost you €69.- including breakfast and an evening meal. Cheaper again are the Garnis, for example: the Helvetia, from €39.- (low season) up to €47.- (high season) inc. breakfast. Cheaper again and located near the Paratschgratbahn is the Gastheim Alma from €28.- (LS) up to €32.- (HS). If you've got wheels,

"THE RESTAURANTS OFFER GOOD FOOD, BUT THEY AIN'T CHEAP."

you can find even cheaper accommodation outside the town.

Food_ It's not hard to find good food in Ischgl, but those of you on a low budget will soon become regular customers at the local supermarkets. The local restaurants serve everything from traditional Austrian food, Swiss fondues, Italian cuisine to Tex-mex. At the Gasthof Goldener Adler you can feast on traditional Austrian cooking in a rustic atmosphere for a reasonable price. For those with a little less money we would recommend Pizzeria La Nona. But even in the pricier restaurants you'll usually find a good value daily special. It's worth taking a tour to check out the prices, and who knows, the money you save could buy you an extra beer.

Nightlife_ Ischgl's nightlife is renowned but it's not perhaps to

everybody's taste. Hordes of tourists storm the high season period turning this tiny town into a party island in the middle of the Alps. The first inhabitants must have had an idea about this town when they named it "Yscla", which when translated means 'island'. Those of you who want to party hard and are immune to dodgy après ski songs and drinking games, have come to the right place. Après Ski parties begin at Niki's Stadl, the Kitzloch or Kuhstall and continue on into the early hours of the morning at the Wunderbar, Posthörndl or the Höllboda.

Other Activities_ If you still have the energy after snowboarding and/or partying, why not head down to the swimming pool, have a massage or sweat it up in a steam bath. Other options include indoor tennis and squash courts. Further information from the Ischgl Tourist Centre.

> "FREERIDERS WILL FIND A GREAT PLAYGROUND IN THE LANGEWIED AREA. THE UPPER SECTION OF THE GLACIER OFFERS A SMALLER AREA OF CORNICES, QUARTERS AND CLIFFS WHERE YOU CAN LET LOOSE."

KAPRUN
KITZSTEINHORN_AUSTRIA

»

KAPRUN »
Tourist office tel: +43 (0)65478621
location: Kaprun
population: 2916
altitude: 800–3029m

ON THE MOUNTAIN »
season: Kitzsteinhorn all year
the rest December to April
Lifts
vertical drop: 800–3029m
amount of lifts in total: 28
gondolas: 6
chair lifts: 6
drag lifts: 1
Slopes
amount of prepared slopes: 55 km
runs w. snowmaking machines: 7 km
amount of easy runs: 12
amount of intermediate runs: 9
amount of advanced runs: -
Facilities
night riding: -
amount of halfpipes: -
amount of funparks 1
heliboarding: -
Lift-ticket prices in Euro
1/2 day: 16
day: 20,50
week:135

SNOWBOARD TUITION »
Skischule Oberschneider
Tel: +43 (0)65478232
www.ski-kaprun.com

SNOWBOARD SHOPS »
Subway Snowboard shop
Tel +43 (0)6547838835
Website www.subway-snowboardshop.at

GETTING THERE »
Car
Munich - Kaprun: 180km
Autobahn (motorway) towards Salzburg - take the Siegsdorf exit - Lofer - Saalfelden - Zell am See - Kaprun
Innsbruck - Kaprun: 150km
From the Inntalautobahn (Inn Valley motorway) take the Wörgl exit towards Felbertauern as far as Mittersill - Kaprun
Vienna - Kaprun: 400km
A1 motorway to Salzburg - Tauernautobahn as far as Bischofshofen - Bruck - Kaprun.
Train
Take the train to Zell am See, then by bus or taxi to Kaprun (approximately 8 km)
Air
Salzburg Airport - 99km
Innsbruck Airport - 154km
Munich Airport - 218km

© Red Bull/Richie Hopson **Rider** Chris Polascheck

KAPRUN »
Intro_Kaprun and the 3,203m Kitzsteinhorn was Austria's first developed ski resort. Mountain enthusiasts beat a comfortable path to the high alpine terrain of the Schmiedinger and Maurerkees Glaciers. Kaprun is located at the start of the Kapruner Valley. It's normally a quiet little place, but very soon turns into a wild party town in the high season.

ON THE MOUNTAIN »
Snow reliability_Good snow conditions can be expected to last right through until the end of April. Because the sun shines down on many of the pistes, though, during the spring and summer months the snow conditions aren't always ideal. The lower sections between the Alpincentre and Langwiedboden are equipped with snow making facilities. This allows the resort to keep running for as long as possible. In the summer season, the Kitzsteinhorn is reduced to 8 working lifts. Outside the secured piste the glacier often opens up, exposing many crevasses. Useful information regarding snow conditions, live cams etc can be found at www.kitzsteinhorn.at.

Lifts_At weekends and during the high season, get to town early! This means well before 9.00am if you want to get a parking space and avoid long queues.
The Gletscherjet 1, located at the bottom of the resort, is generally the fastest ride to the top. The Gletscherjet 2 is set to open sometime after October 2002. The new lift will provide a fast connection to the Alpincentre and will help relieve the pressure on the quad chairlift. From the Alpincentre you can ride the Gipfelbahn (a gondola for 60 people) up to the summit station at 3,029m. Considering the size of the resort, the public on the Kitzsteinhorn seem to spread themselves out well. The upper section of the resort is made up mostly of t-bars and poma lifts, so prepare yourselves for that nice burning sensation in your thighs!

Freeriding_Freeriders will find a great playground in the Langewied area. The upper section of the glacier offers a smaller area of cornices, quarters and cliffs where you can let loose. Every time you ride over a hill, you're faced with endless possibilities. One disadvantage, though, is that most of the off piste terrain is close to the lifts which means it's accessible to everyone. You'll need to be quick if you're after freshies. Your best source of information about guided tours is the Snowboard School at the Alpincentre.

Freestyling_Don't forget every rider's essential piece of equipment, your shovel. There are countless locations where you can build a kicker on this mountain. To get to the official funpark, just below the summit station on the glacier plateau, you'll need to ride up on the Gipfelbahn or the Kitzlifte t-bar. Eagerly awaiting you is a series of table and corner jumps, a well-built quarterpipe and a wave train. For those who find this funpark boring, there's only one place to go - Langwied! Freeride through a funpark, courtesy of Mother Nature. No one could have built it better!

Carving_A carver's paradise. The Kitzsteinhorn piste offers a splendid carving environment. The open and gradually sloping terrain of the Magnetköpfl is an ideal place to go and test your edges. Due to the abundance of not-so-challenging slopes, though, you'll find a lot of beginners here trying to keep their equipment under control.

Beginners_The Scmiedingerliften on the Magnetköpfl and the Maurer-Gletscherliften offer good training runs for those of you who are still learning. These areas are available to all and are well used by the snowboard school. Another perfect area for beginners can be

© Red Bull/Dieter Happ. **Rider** Grill Ulrich

"DON'T FORGET EVERY RIDER'S ESSENTIAL PIECE OF EQUIPMENT, YOUR SHOVEL. THERE ARE COUNTLESS LOCATIONS WHERE YOU CAN BUILD A KICKER ON THIS MOUNTAIN."

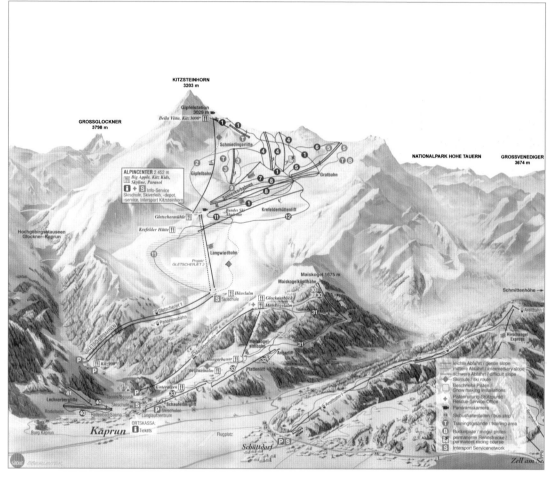

Zur Mühle with its surrounding camping areas is not too far from the town centre. Aside from their culinary delights, you'll also find an outdoor swimming pool, open all year round (it's 28°C in winter!).

Nightlife_ The Baumbar (literally means the Tree Bar and you'll see why) has live music and holds regular events, and is one of the classic spots in Kaprun. This is where to go for the Zum schnellen Bier (which literally means 'to a fast beer'!), enjoyed by just as many locals as tourists. Charly's Kneipe, Kitsch & Bitter and the Music Cafe Winkler are all next door to each other on Geschäftzeile. They sometimes feature live music too. These bars are decked out like saloons from a Lucky Luke comic, only smaller. Or there's the bowling at the Sportsbar, while the Musikpavillon and the outdoor bar in the Salzburger Platz, the town centre, is an ideal place for a cold beer after a day on the mountain.

Other Activities_ Swimming pool, sauna, massage, fitness centre, tennis, indoor squash courts, cinema.

"A CARVER'S PARADISE. THE KITZSTEIN-HORN PISTE OFFERS A SPLENDID CARVING ENVIRONMENT. THE OPEN AND GRADUALLY SLOPING TERRAIN OF THE MAGNETKÖPFL IS AN IDEAL PLACE."

found further down the mountain at Lechenberg. When you get slightly more advanced, you'll find the Maiskögel, with its nice runs down into town, ideal. At the end of your run you can jump straight onto the Maiskögelbahn and head back up. Information and links to prices and deals from the snowboard schools can be found at www.kitzsteinhorn.at.

Mountain Restaurants_ Since the 5 self-service restaurants are all run by the lift company, you don't exactly have a free choice when it comes to looking after your rumbling stomach. However, the restaurant Bella Vista definitely offers the best panoramic views. Then there are the Big Apple and Gletschermühle at the Alpincentre. You might also check out the Krefelderhütte, half way between the Alpincentre and Langwiedboden. Last but not least,

there's the Häuslalm near Langwiedboden featuring a large terrace facing the sun and the typical, deafening ski party music. The lift company's monopoly on the restaurants is clearly reflected in the restaurant prices, which don't necessarily reflect the quality of the food.

IN THE TOWN »
Accommodation_ Depending on your comfort needs, you can find a night's accommodation with breakfast in a 2, 3 or 4 star hotel. Prices range between approx. €30 and €70.

Kaprun has an unusually large number of holiday apartments available for rent, making this option one of the cheapest if you're travelling in a group. Naturally, you'll also find well-equipped and inexpensive guest houses throughout the town. Because Kaprun is not a very big

place, most of the accommodation is near the centre, which makes it easy to get around. Ski buses make it easy to get to the glacier lifts. Information and booking services, including a directory listing the apartments available can be found at www.kaprun.at.

Food_ You'll find everything your heart desires, in terms of groceries that is, at the large supermarket in the town centre. The tasty food at the Tex-Mex restaurant, the Zucchini, is highly recommended. The prices are a bit on the steep side, but the portions are generous and there's a great choice of vegetarian dishes. Most of the restaurants in the village are hotel restaurants offering a limited menu. On the road to the glacier, approximately 4.5km out of the town, you'll find the Künstleralm, which serves traditional dishes and home-reared meat. The Gasthof

PROS & CONS »
+ Good snow base guaranteed.
+ Outstanding freeride terrain.
+ Lift use restricted to 14,000 visitors per day.

- Expensive, both on the mountain and in the villages.
- Very little car parking available near the lifts.
- Flexenpass (the only road in or out) is often closed after a heavy snowfall.

> "THE WHOLE OF ARLBERG, AND ESPECIALLY LECH AND ZÜRS, IS WELL KNOWN FOR ITS DEEP POWDER RUNS. THE VARIETY OF UNTRACKED POWDER SLOPES, CHUTES, ROCK FACES AND OFF PISTE RUNS IS HUGE."

LECH-ZÜRS
AUSTRIA

»

LECH-ZÜRS »
www.lech-zuers.at
Tourist office tel: +43 (0)558321610
location: Lech
population: 920
altitude: 1450m

ON THE MOUNTAIN »
season: December to April
Lifts
vertical drop: 1304-2811m
amount of lifts in total: 32
gondolas: 4
chair lifts: 18
drag lifts:10
Slopes
amount of prepared slopes:110 km
snowmaking machines: 120
easy runs: 44 km
intermediate runs: 44 km
advanced runs: 22 km
Facilities
night riding: -
amount of halfpipes: 1
amount of funparks: 2 Funpark, BoarderX
heliboarding: yes
Lift-ticket prices in Euro
1/2 day: 28
day: 37.5
week: 196
season: 635

SNOWBOARD TUITION »
Skischule Lech
Tel: +43 (0)55832355
www.skischule-lech.com
Skischule Zürs
Tel: +43 (0)55832611
www.skischule-zuers.at

SNOWBOARD SHOPS »
Snowboard center stuff
Tel: +43 (0)55832328
Strolz
Tel: +43 (0)5583236128

GETTING THERE »
Car
Innsbruck - Lech: 120km
Innsbruck - Landeck - Arlbergpass - Flexenpass - Lech
Zürich - Lech: 185km
Zürich - Bludenz - Arlbergpass - Flexenpass - Lech
Munich - Lech: 212km
Munich - Garmisch - Landeck - Arlbergpass - Flexenpass - Lech
Milan - Lech: 336km
Milan - San Benidino (Swiss) - Mesocco - Sarganserland exit - Unterweitersdorf (Lichtenstein) - Bludenez - Langen a. A. Flexenpass - Lech
Train/Bus
To Langen am Arlberg by train, then by bus or taxi (approx. 20 minutes).
Air
Innsbruck Airport: 118km

© Scalp **Rider** Antonin L.

LECH-ZÜRS »
Intro_ Without doubt, the Arlberg is considered to be one of Europe's finest regions. The towering mountain range is first in line for every incoming low-pressure system. Riding up to your front door in knee deep powder is commonplace. The traditional feel of these two villages has been preserved to give an authentic Austrian experience, a policy that stems from the fact that many of the rich and famous enjoy their holidays in Lech-Zürs. This, unfortunately, has its effect on prices in the villages, but as long as you don't dine in posh restaurants or buy a round of

drinks in the Après Ski bar, you won't find it any more expensive than other well-known resorts such as Chamonix or St. Moritz.

ON THE MOUNTAIN »
Snow reliability_ Lying between a range of imposing mountains are the villages of Lech (1450m) and just 4 km away, Zürs, proudly situated at 1716m. The low-pressure systems sweeping onto the Arlberg from the north-west usually bring fantastic snow.
Even when the Tyrol or the rest of Voralberg are having a poor season, you'll often find there's enough snow to go round in Lech-Zürs. Before you set off, though,

you should always find out whether or not the Flexenpass is open.

Lift_ The nobility of this resort quickly ends once you arrive at the lifts. Some lifts have been converted into more modern quad and six-person chairlifts, but you still come across many relics from the 60s. Despite the age of some of the lifts, it's rare to find yourself having to queue for too long. The lift company has restricted the number of people who can use the lift to 14,000 per day. Still, if you're at the wrong lift at the wrong time, you'll have some waiting to do – but then that's true anywhere.
You can ride up on the

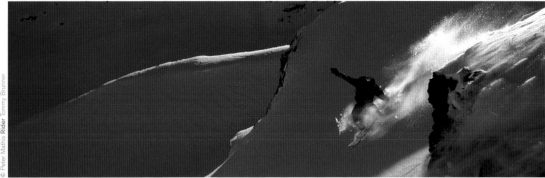

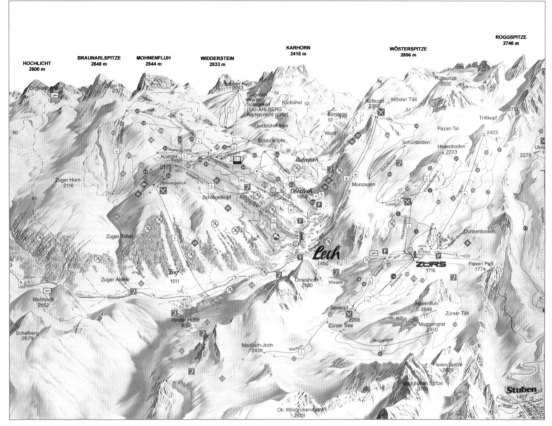

"HEADING OFF PISTE OR INTO THE BACKCOUNTRY, MAKE SURE YOU CHECK THE LATEST AVALANCHE REPORTS AND THAT YOU ALL HAVE BEACONS, AVALANCHE PROBES AND SHOVELS."

Rüffikopfbahn then board down to Zürser Seite. Unless you use the lifts on the opposite side in Zürs, you can only get back by bus. You can then travel up to Madljoch for an off-piste run down to Zug and Lech. An Arlberg ski pass will let you go riding at the neighboring resorts of St. Christoph, St. Anton and Stuben too, all of which are accessible by bus and car.

Freeriding The whole of Arlberg, and especially Lech and Zürs, is well known for its deep powder runs. The variety of untracked powder slopes, chutes, rock faces and off piste runs is huge. As always, we recommend that you

take a tour with a mountain guide, even though you can see a lot of the runs from the lift. Divide the cost between a few riders and hiring a guide becomes fairly affordable. For those of you heading off piste or into the backcountry, make sure you check the latest avalanche reports and that you all have beacons, avalanche probes and shovels. Although the resort is full of snobs and fur coats, you'll still have to beat the powder monkeys to the freshies.

Zürs After a fresh snowfall you'll find the Trittkopf has some great lines to ride. But be careful! There's

always a strong risk of an avalanche in this resort. Keep a close eye on the cornices that are just waiting to swallow up you and your friends. Inexperienced freeriders should stick to the off piste runs 4 and 5. Another classic run is off piste run 33, travelling down to Zug/Lech, with its starting point at Madljoch. If you want to ride to Lech, stay on as high a traverse as you can. Your calf muscles will burn but the reward is a great run with some nice natural bowls.

When you get to the top of the Muggengratbahn, you'll find a variety of runs which head back down to Zürs. One of these is

called the Zürser Täli. It's not difficult, but it provides some spectacular freeride terrain. On a good day you can shred through the powder right down to the car park.

Lech A fantastic ride can be had from the Kriegerhorn down the off piste run 49 to Zug. Towards the end of this run you'll find an area that's being re-forested. Ride through here and you will, quite rightly, risk your lift pass. Next to the Steinmähderbahn you won't find any trees, just big cornices and gullies full of snow. The final run down to Zug isn't really worth the bother, so a better bet is to finish

LECH-ZÜRS
AUSTRIA

© Peter Mathis

» at the bottom station of the Steinmähderbahn and take the next chair to the top. The top of the Zuger Hochlicht is the starting place for a lot of off piste runs and offers something for everyone.

Lech and Zürs are great starting points for incredible multi-day tours. Your best source of info is the ski schools. In Zürs, you can charter a helicopter and get dropped off at any one of the many summits in the area.

Freestyling_Lech/Zürs may be a freeride Mecca, but they haven't forgotten the freestylers either. There's a reasonably good funpark underneath the Schlegelkopfbahn. The terrain includes a halfpipe, regularly shaped by Pipe Dragon, a quarter,

a corner, a table-top and a few rails. And you'll find natural bowls, hits, rollers, and excellent spots to build kickers throughout the entire resort.

Carving_There are many runs that are wide and not too steep, making it ideally suited to the carvers amongst you. But if your only ambition is to remain on the piste and carve, you'd be better off at another resort.

Beginners_If you're looking to learn to snowboard in this area, then head to Lech. Behind the church you'll find a nice, easy piste to practice on until you're ready to head to Oberlech. Here you'll find other easier runs where you can test out your new-found skills.

Mountain Restaurants_Compared with many other large resorts, Lech/Zürs has few mountain restaurants and you'll be forced to choose between the expensive and the mega-expensive. The quality of the food is without a doubt excellent, matched only by the amazing panoramic views from the terrace. You'll soon forget how expensive everything is... until you get the bill! For those of you running a little short on cash, the only real option is to head to the supermarket in the village. For those of you packing more than your fair share of the green, dining at the Alter Goldener Berg restaurant in Oberlech allows you to shed your wealth in style with caviar and quails eggs.

IN THE TOWN »
Accommodation_Zürs Look at the huge collection of expensive hotels and the scarcity of cheap guest houses and you'll soon get an idea of who this town was built for. An amazing resort, but as soon as the lift closes down you won't find a lot of action, except in a few trendier bars where you can drink a glass of champagne and be entertained by mundane tales of the day's adventures on the mountain, darling.

Guesthouses (Pensions)
Haus Jahn Tel: 05583/2257
Haus Küng Tel: 05583/2556
Längenfelder Pension Garni
Tel: 05583/234-0
Haus Dr. Murr Tel: 05583/2280
Schweizerhaus Tel: 05583/2463

© Peter Mathis **Rider** Thommy Brunner

Lech Not much cheaper, but you do at least have more choice. The village is not actually bigger, but it stretches out over a greater distance. The further you get from the village centre and the lifts, the cheaper the accommodation.

Guest houses
Including breakfast, close to the lifts
Pension Brunelle: from 27 - 29€,
Tel: 05583/2976
Pension Loacker: from 33€
Tel: 05583/2967 and
Haus Armella: from 29 - 31€
Tel: 05883/2420.

Food_Despite its mere 920 inhabitants, you can dine at no fewer than 11 restaurants, the likes of which you will find in Gault Millau. Excellent food is not a problem, it's cheap eats that are hard to find. Those of you who are looking for a culinary holiday and who have a bulletproof credit card should try the following: Kultur Restaurant/Bar Fux (Euro-Asian style cooking), Post (traditional style cooking), Montana (French Cuisine, traditional), Hus. Nr. 8 (the old Walsterstube, local, traditional). Inexpensive, good quality food is served at the Cafe Ambrosius or the Restaurant Schneider. The pizzas in Pizzeria Charly are tasty and big and the price is reasonable. But if it's fast food you're after, don't come here. Once again the supermarket is the only place to fill your stomach on the cheap.

Nightlife_After a day on the mountain, everyone heads onto the main street with its cafes and après ski bars to see and be seen. After a glass of 'Glühwein' you can amuse yourself observing pseudo skiers in their furs, Gucci sunglasses and Prada leggings, marching proudly up and down the street. S'Pfefferkörndl is the preferred place for the younger crowd and ideal for meeting new people. Many hotels have bars and discos which are expensive, but generally busy. In Fux you can enjoy slurping down a cocktail and smoking a cigar while relaxing in the jazz bar. Things are a little more casual in the American Bar, where live concerts and DJ's create the atmosphere. You'll discover that the nightlife in Lech can be wild and untamed, with the added advantage of having fewer morons singing and stomping along to every après ski song.

"LECH/ZÜRS MAY BE A FREERIDE MECCA, BUT THEY HAVEN'T FORGOTTEN THE FREESTYLERS EITHER. THERE'S A REASONABLY GOOD FUNPARK UNDERNEATH THE SCHLEGELKOPFBAHN. THE TERRAIN INCLUDES A HALFPIPE, REGULARLY SHAPED BY PIPE DRAGON, A QUARTER, A CORNER, A TABLE-TOP AND A FEW RAILS. AND YOU'LL FIND NATURAL BOWLS, HITS, ROLLERS, AND EXCELLENT SPOTS TO BUILD KICKERS THROUGHOUT THE ENTIRE RESORT."

PROS & CONS »
+ Party Town.
+ Best funpark in the Ziller Valley.
+ Close to the Hintertux glacier.
+ Many different resorts are accessible in half an hour.

− The mountain is overcrowded at high season.
− Loud, cheesy, après ski atmosphere in town.
− A lot of traffic and traffic jams on the valley road.

> "FOR FREERIDING IN GOOD SNOW CONDITIONS YOU'LL FIND THE POWDER RUNS IN MAYRHOFEN ARE SOME OF THE FINEST AROUND."

MAYRHOFEN
ZILLERTAL_AUSTRIA

»

MAYRHOFEN »
www.mayrhofen.com
tourist office tel: +43 (0)528567600
location: Mayrhofen
population: 3679
altitude: 630m
linked resorts Hippach, Finkenberg, Tux

ON THE MOUNTAIN »
Season: early December to late April
Lifts
vertical drop: 630-3250m
amount of lifts in total: 45
gondolas: 7
chair lifts: 18
drag lifts: 20
Slopes
amount of prepared slopes: 143 km
snowmaking machines: 117
easy runs: 42 km
intermediate runs: 84 km
advanced runs: 17 km
Facilities
night riding: -
amount of halfpipes: 1
amount of funparks: 1
Heliboarding: -
Lift-ticket prices in Euro
1/2 day: 22
day: 31
week: 164
season: 360

SNOWBOARD TUITION »
Snowboardschule Mayrhofen TotaL
Tel: +43 (0)528563939
www.snowboard-mayrhofen.at

SNOWBOARD SHOPS »
Local Sport
Tel: +43 (0)528564444
www.chillertalerlocal.com

GETTING THERE »
Car
Innsbruck - Mayrhofen: 73km
Innsbruck - A12 - Exit Jenbach/Zillertal - Uderns - Zell - Mayrhofen
Munich - Mayrhofen: 164km
Munich - A8 direction Innsbruck - Kufstein - Exit - Jenbach/Zillertal - Uderns - Zell - Mayrhofen
Train
Train to Jenbach (located between Innsbruck and Wörgl), change for the small Zillertal train line. Getting to Mayrhofen takes a bit of time, but you can take in the sights as you travel through the Ziller valley.
Air
Innsbruck Airport 74km
Salzburg Airport 176km
Munich Airport 203km

MAYRHOFEN »
Intro_ Mayrhofen is the largest town in Zillertal (Ziller Valley) and also the liveliest town in the valley. Entering the Zillertal, you'll drive for about half an hour before arriving at Mayrhofen, two thirds of the way down the valley. Once in town, you won't need your car again until you leave. The main 'Penkenbahn' gondola starts from the middle of the village and the 'Ahornbahn' is within walking distance. A popular holiday destination for young people, with a thriving British scene, Mayrhofen could never be described as a sleepy village. This place goes off!

ON THE MOUNTAIN »
Snow reliability_ With snow making machines on every corner at Penken, a good piste is guaranteed. Ahorn is just as well equipped and creates optimal conditions, especially for beginners. In the event of poor snow conditions you can head to the fun park at Penken.

For snow conditions
Tel: +43 (0) 5285 676033 or www.ski-zillertal3000.com

Lifts/Piste_ Access to everything is easy in Mayrhofen! The Penken gondola travels up to the most interesting mountain, and leaves direct from the town centre. Penken is also accessible using the Horbergbahn situated 2km outside Mayrhofen, or, a further 4km away, the Finkenberger Almbahn. To avoid long waiting periods at the Penkenbahn during the high season, start early in the morning or head to the Horbergbahn. Situated within walking distance from the town centre is the Ahornbahn, which transports you to a smaller area more suitable for beginners.
Mayrhofen, Finkenberg and Tux have joined forces to create the largest resort in the Zillertal. It goes under the name *Ski-Zillertal 3000*.

Freeriding_ In good snow conditions you'll find the powder runs in Mayrhofen are some of the finest around. Penken has a lot of off piste on offer without long hikes up the mountain. The terrain here has everything that's needed for fun freeriding. The only thing that is really missing are the longer runs that you find in Arlberg. The only valley run towards Mayrhofen is the ski route over the Horberg, which mainly runs through the forest.
The extra lift on the Wanglspitz has opened up a new and exciting run, not without danger, that is only suitable for experienced freeriders. A dream run that almost swallowed me up. Respect the mountain!

"ONE THING YOU NEED TO KNOW, IN MAYRHOFEN YOU'LL FIND YOURSELF IN THE MIDDLE OF A CONSTANT APRÉS SKI SCENE. DO NOT EXPECT TO HEAR GOOD MUSIC ANYWHERE, UNLESS YOUR TASTES INCLUDE DJ ÖTZI AND THE LIKE."

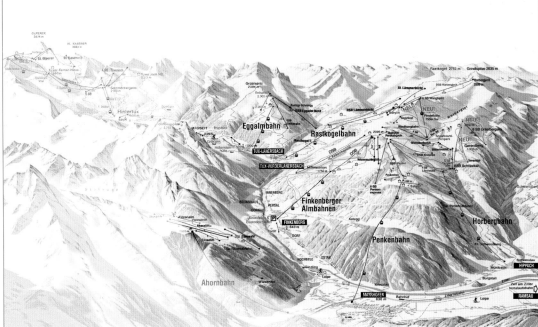

Freestyling_Very freestyler friendly at Penken. The fun park, which was built 2 years ago, is well developed by Tirolean standards. It includes a pipe, corner, kickers and rails. The pipe itself is often not much to speak of, but the kicker-combo is generally kept in a good state. Austrian pro riders such as Beckna, Wolle Nywelt, Steve Gruber, Andi Egger and Friedl Kolar can often be seen shredding through Penken and the park. Further developments for the park are planned for the coming season 2002/03. In good snow conditions, out in the backcountry, you can find loads of spots to build big fat kickers without having to shovel all day.

Carving_Generally speaking, Penken is an ideal carving mountain. The steeper runs and rolling off piste terrain would allow for big long turns except for the fact that in the high season, December to March, it's almost impossible to complete a turn because of the ridiculous number of people there. Carvers will probably have more fun riding on the Hintertux glacier.

Beginners_Mayrhofen is also ideally suited to beginners. Penken has some flatter and intermediate runs that are great for learning. You may find that Ahorn is a little less hectic. To start, take the gondola to the top. There you will find a few t-bars and a chairlift, situated on a plateau, ideally suited to those of you with a little more skill. The sensational views from the Ahorn across to the mountains opposite are another attraction in this area.

Mountain Restaurants_It won't matter if they're big or small, the restaurants are all the same. Busy, relatively cheap and cheerful. A personal tip is the Pyramide on the Schafskopf – a rustic hut with good food and an amazing view.

IN TOWN »
Accommodation_You'll find that the price of a room starts from €15 - €20 per person. There are plenty of hotels and guesthouses, and your best bet is to ask early at the tourist office, as Mayrhofen is often booked out completely.

Mayrhofen Tourism Board
00 43 (0) 52 85 6760
mayrhofen@zillertal.tirol.at
www.mayrhofen.com.

Food_Amongst the large range of restaurants, you'll find that prices will not vary too much. Here are some personal tips: The best pizzeria is Sidan located by the Horbergbahn. Good service and a price to match are available at Everest's, on the way to the Ahornbahn. Cafe Tirol has good food and a nice atmosphere and is located half way along the main road. The Chinese Restaurant located next to the Scotland Yard Pub is tasty though not known for its cleanliness. The traditional style Wirthaus zum Griena has an excellent Tirolean menu in a rustic setting. If you fancy something a little less 'traditional' you should head to Mo's for burgers and fries, or Mamma Mia! Pizzeria, both near the centre of town.

Nightlife_One thing you need to know, in Mayrhofen you'll find yourself in the middle of a constant apräs ski scene. Do not expect to hear good music anywhere, unless your tastes include DJ Ötzi and the like. Beginning in the afternoon and continuing until about nine in the evening, you'll see every apräs ski bar full to the brim. It doesn't matter if you're on the mountain or in the valley, you won't be able to miss the aprés ski bars and you'll definitely be able to hear them, even from the gondola.

In the evening, most riders head to the Scotland Yard Pub. A classic British pub, where the sound is a little easier to handle. A little different, but easy going, is Apropos. Don't be scared off by the transvestite photos! An easy place to get yourself drunk is the Arena or the Schlüsselalm, which will provide you with the typical sounds of Mayrhofen.

Other Activities_Sledding, Ski-doo riding, Tandem paragliding, etc are all available in winter through:

Action Club Zillertal
0043 (0)664 18 18 98,
www.action-club@zillertal.com

LOCAL TIP »
Rudi Kröll, Völkl Team Rider_"In winter you'll find a party every week among the locals and season workers - generally more happenin' than hanging out in the bars and discos. Get to know some locals, keep your ears open and pretty soon you'll find out where it's all going on."

At the end of the season, The resort of Heiligenblut called out of the blue telling us they were clearing the road up to Grossglockner, Austrias highest mountain. Not only that, if we wanted to bring some riders along, they'd gives us a couple of cats, a few snowmobiles and no less than 40 huskies to do what we wanted with. What an offer! The result was this; Marc Andre Tarte, sick Cab 5 to road gap.
We're sorry we couldn't fit in the huskies.

WWW.METHODMAG.COM

METHODMAG
VIDEOMAGAZINE
GUILTY AS CHARGED

"THE EXPOSED TERRAIN AND STRONG WINDS MEANS THERE'S ALWAYS A STRONG RISK OF AN AVALANCHE HERE. GREAT TERRAIN, PERFECT FOR EARLY AND LATE SEASON POWDER – BUT IT'S VERY DANGEROUS."

HINTERTUX GLACIER
AUSTRIA

HINTERTUX »
www.hintertuxgletscher.com
tourist office tel: +43 (0)52878506
location: Tux
population: 1922
altitude: 1300m
linked resorts Finkenberg, Mayrhofen, Hippach

ON THE MOUNTAIN »
season: all year
Lifts
vertical drop: 1500–3250m
amount of lifts in total: 24
gondolas: 6
chair lifts: 8
drag lifts: 10
Slopes
amount of prepared slopes: 89 km
snowmaking machines: 10
easy runs: 23 km
intermediate runs: 62 km
advanced runs: 4 km
Facilities
night riding: -
amount of halfpipes: 1
amount of funparks: 1
Heliboarding: -
Lift-ticket prices in Euro
1/2 day: 24
day: 34
week: 181
season: 465

SNOWBOARD TUITION »
Skischule Hintertux
Tel: +43 (0)528787363
www.skischule-hintertux.at
Ski & Snowboardschule Lanersbach
Tel: +43 (0)528787340
www.schischule.lanersbach.at

SNOWBOARD SHOPS »
Luggi`s Ski & Snowboardschule
Tel: +43 (0)528786808
www.luggis-schischule.at

GETTING THERE »
Car
Innsbruck - Hintertux 92km
Innsbruck - A12 – JenbachZillertal exit - Uderns - Zell - Mayrhofen - Hintertux
Munich - Hintertux 218km
Munich - A8 towards Innsbruck - Kufstein - Jenbach/Zillertal exit - Uderns - Zell - Mayrhofen - Hintertux
Air
Innsbruck Airport 93km
Munich Airport 222km

HINTERTUX GLACIER »
Intro_One of Austria's best glacial ski resorts is to be found at the end of the Ziller Valley, known locally as Zillertal. The 'Glacier Bus' gondola carries you up to 3250m. At this elevation, even if the weather leaves a lot to be desired, the snow conditions are generally very good. The communities of Tux and Lanersbach are close by and if you're looking for a wild night out, head down the valley to Mayrhofen. In fact, if you're holidaying anywhere in the Ziller Valley, you really should try to visit the glacier at least once - you won't be disappointed.

ON THE MOUNTAIN »
Snow reliability_The snow conditions on the Hintertux Glacier usually reflect the conditions in the rest of the Tyrol - if it's bad on the glacier, it's bad everywhere else too. But all things considered, it's no wonder that the Hintertux Glacier is Austria's best glacial resort - the pistes are always well groomed and the presence of snow-making facilities guarantees a run down to the middle station.

Lifts_Since the introduction of the new 'Gletscherbus' (glacier bus), waiting times in the morning are a thing of the past. And when the resort gets too crowded, the old gondola is also brought back into commission, so generally speaking you can be up on top and ready to rock by 9 or 10 o'clock. Once you're up on the glacier you'll have your pick of 22 lifts and 86 km of piste. It gets pretty busy in the early season though, so once you're up you'll find yourself in a few lift lines.

Nearby Resorts_Within 5 minutes of the glacier there are two other areas worth visiting, the Rastkogelbahn and the Eggalmbahn, but neither of them has a glacier. Further down the valley there are other great spots to explore such as Zell am Ziller, Gerlos, Hochfügen and of course Mayrhofen.

Freeriding_Freeriding on the glacier is not for the uninitiated. Every year, riders die in the glacial crevasses and many more are lucky not to. Only very experienced riders should be out here, and even then they should stay on the piste unless they've really done their

© Scalp Rider Philipp Kratter

homework, or better still are in the company of an experienced local. The exposed terrain and strong winds means there's always a strong risk of an avalanche here. Great terrain, perfect for early and late season powder – but it's very dangerous.

Mountain Sport School Tux (Bergsportschule Tux) - for high alpine touring and guiding.
Tel: + 43 (0) 5287 87372
info@bergsportschule-tux.at
www.bergsportschule-tux.at

Freestyling_Unfortunately the SPC Camps (see Stubai Glacier)

are no longer held on the Hintertux Glacier. But in spite of this, there's still the good chance of a funpark for the whole winter under the Olperer. The rideability of the park is variable - while it's often well shaped and prepared, at other times the wind just blows it to pieces. In other words, there's no absolute guarantee that there'll be a funpark, so best to check before you set off.

Carving_Carvers will find the Hintertux Glacier eminently suitable for the cutting edges of their race boards. Well-prepared,

© Scalp **Rider** Steve Gruber

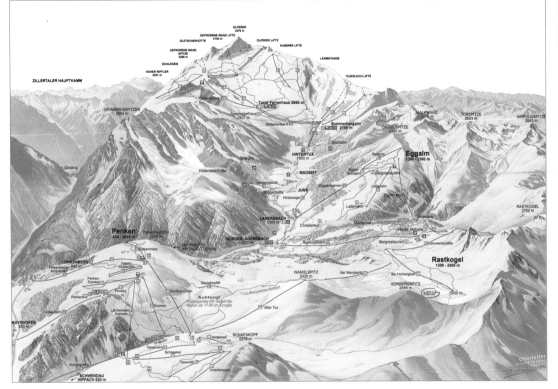

"AUSTRIA'S BEST GLACIER IS FOUND AT ZILLER VALLEY"

Nightlife_ Hey, this is Austria, so for Après Ski there's always plenty of opportunities to down large quantities of beer to the Techno beat of some dreadful Euro Pop. The closest real party town is Mayrhofen, about 20 minutes drive from Hintertux (see Mayrhofen). But there are a few other options a bit closer to home, i.e. within a 5 minute drive including Tux 1 in Tux, Pfiff in Vorderlanersbach, or Postkastle, Keller in Lanersbach.

Shopping_ Ski and Snowboard shops are as plentiful here as sand on the beach. Our favourite is 'Sport Mader' in Vorderlanersbach, just 5 minutes' drive from Hintertux. The local 'core' shop is called 'Insider' and you'll run across it on the way to the Rastkogelbahn in Vorderlanersbach.

Tel: +43 (0) 5287 86109
www.insider-sportshop.com
info@gmx.at

Other Activities_ Well recommended is a tandem paragliding flight from the glacier down into the valley. The adrenaline levels run high and the views are amazing.

Contact: Peter Bacher
Tel: +43 (0) 676 4308 023

Erlebnis Club Tuxertal
Tel: +43 (0) 5287 87287,
erlebnis@aon.at, www.natursport.at

Zillertaller Fugschule:
www.aktivcenter-tux.at for tandem flights, sledding evenings, snow shoe tours, inner tubing, etc.

LOCAL TIP »
Christian Schartner_"When you want to go boarding on the glacier, get up early, turn on the TV and check out the live panorama mountain cam to check the wind and the weather. If the wind speed exceeds 30km/hr, better head to a lower lying resort, even if the sun is shining."

long and wide runs create a haven for racers, except during the early season. October/November is a very busy time, so you might do better riding during the week rather than heading into a weekend.

Beginners_ Although the terrain is well suited to beginners, the rarefied air at 3000m generally means they get very tired very quickly. It's usually recommended, then, that beginners take their first few lessons further down the valley before heading up to the glacier to enjoy the views.

Mountain Restaurants_ The restaurants here are all as expensive as each other, no matter where you go. However, the Tuxerfernerhaus serves good value beer and is a good meeting place. There's also a picnic area if you've taken a packed lunch. Provided you book in advance, you can stay overnight at the more traditional Spanagel-Haus and sleep on a mattress.

IN THE TOWN »
Accommodation_ The cheapest rooms go for around €15 - €20 per person per night. To get the

best deals on the many guest houses and hotels here, make sure you book early.
The Tuxer Tourist Board is in the centre of Lanersbach.
Contact them on:
Tel: +43 (0) 5287 8506 or at info@tux.at www.tux.at

Food_ Not much difference in the prices at most restaurants, but here are a few suggestions: Pizzeria - Didi's Pub in Hintertux, Klein & Fine (including Tex Mex snacks) in Lanersbach, Grillkuchl in Lanersbach and Gasthoffe Forelle in Vorderlanersbach.

"THE PLANNERALM IS DEFINITELY NOTHING SPECIAL FOR FREERIDERS. YET HAVING SAID THAT, AND DESPITE THE FACT IT'S SO SMALL, THERE ARE A COUPLE OF DECENT FREERIDING SPOTS."

PLANNERALM
AUSTRIA

PLANNERALM »
Web address: www-planneralm.at
Tourist office tel: +43 (0)36832206
location: Donnersbach
population: 1134
altitude: 1600 m
linked resorts: Riesneralm/Donnersbachwald, Tauplitzalm, Loser/Altaussee

ON THE MOUNTAIN »
Season: December – end of April
Lifts
vertical drop: 1600-2000 m
amount of lifts in total: 6
gondolas: 0
chair lifts: 2
drag lifts: 4
Slopes
amount of prepared slopes in km: 16
runs w. snowmaking machines: 0
easy runs: 2 km
intermediate runs: 10 km
advanced runs: 4 km
Facilities
night riding: no
amount of halfpipes: no
amount of funparks: 1
heliboarding: no
Lift-ticket prices in Euro
1/2 day: 19.50
day: 24.50
season: 254

SNOWBOARD TUITION »
Skischule Reiter
Tel: +43 (0) 36838130
Website www.sportpension-reiter.at

SNOWBOARD SHOPS »
Sport Schöttl
Tel: +43 (0)36838107
Website www.sport2000.at

GETTING THERE »
Car
Salzburg - Planneralm 136km
Salzburg - A10 Eben exit - via Schladming - Trautenfels - Irdning - Planneralm
Bus/Train
Salzburg - Stainach station - Irdning approx. 2hrs 40min
Graz - Stainach station - Irdning approx. 2hrs
www.verbundlinie.at
Air
Salzburg Airport 142km
Graz Airport 164km

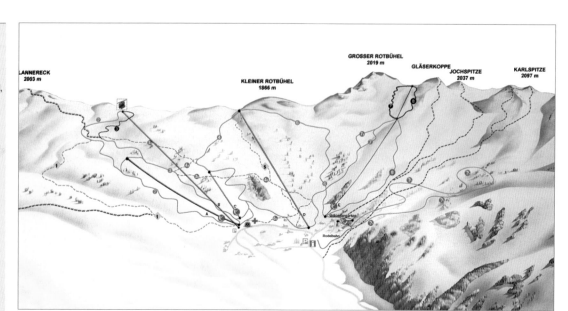

PLANNERALM »
Intro_The Planneralm is a laid back resort in the Steiermark – Styria region of Austria. Driving up the mountain to an altitude of 1600 m, you'll find a few houses and a small but beautiful resort. The best thing about Planneralm is that it isn't nearly as hectic as many larger ski areas. It's a great place for a relaxing snowboard holiday, but not ideal if you're a hardcore party animal. Freestylers will definitely have a bit of fun here, especially in the Snow Valley Park. But the core freeriders among you shouldn't get too excited about what awaits you here!

ON THE MOUNTAIN »
Snow reliability_The Planneralm has no snow making facilities, but generally speaking they still have a decent snow base. The village is situated 1600m above sea level and the resort is at 1850m. For those looking to build 'backcountry' kickers, the Planneralm has quite a few excellent spots. Snow Telephone: +43 (0) 36 83 81 28

Lifts_The Planneralm is a very small resort with just two quad chairlifts, three tow lifts and a baby lift. The lifts leave from the village, which is handy. Public holidays and weekends can be busy, but even so you won't have to queue for too long. Basically this is a mellow family resort, but this is what makes it good for backcountry freestylers.

"BEGINNER CARVERS ONLY. THE RUNS ARE FLAT AND SHORT, NOT IDEAL FOR ADVANCED CARVERS."

Freeriding_The Planneralm is definitely nothing special for freeriders. Yet having said that, and despite the fact it's so small, there are a couple of decent freeriding spots. The Schober Spitz (a face accessible via a short hike along the ridgeline) will definitely appeal to the freeriders amongst you. The run down to Donnersbach Wald is another good tip. The runs here are not extremely long, not very steep, and are really more suited to the less adventurous rider. If you're searching for Chamonix style freeriding, this ain't the place.

Freestyling_Will the Snow Valley Park be built or not? Check the website: www.planneralm.at/snowvalley

© Jan Zach **Rider** Bernd Mandlberger

which tells you all about the Snow Valley Park in the coming season. There's one for sure, though, the Planneralm is ideal for backcountry booters. You don't have to travel far from the resort so consequently there is no hiking. A few smaller rails can also be found in the village. The Planneralm was also involved in the Ästhetiker Tour 2002 – check out www.ästhetiker.com

Carving_Definitely for beginner carvers only. The runs are flat and short, not ideal for advanced carvers.

Beginners_If you are just learning to snowboard you'll not find a better place. The lower section of

> "THE PLANNERALM HAS NO SNOW MAKING FACILITIES, BUT GENERALLY SPEAKING THEY STILL HAVE A DECENT SNOW BASE. THE VILLAGE IS SITUATED 1600M ABOVE SEA LEVEL AND THE RESORT IS AT 1850M."

© Daniel Kudernatsch **Rider** Klaus Hofmeister

the resort is ideal for learners. You can find your feet in the safe knowledge that no one is going to run you down. Perfect!

Mountain Restaurants_ The self-service *Lackner* restaurant is next to the piste and is a popular meeting place for riders. We also recommend the *Dornbusch Hütte,* which is also right next to the piste. It doesn't matter which restaurant you decide to go to on the Planneralm - they all take five minutes to get to.

Nearby Resort_*Riesenalm* – lift card is available for both resorts - 40min. Other resorts covered by the lift pass are the *Tauplitz Alm,* Planneralm and Loser.

IN THE TOWN »
Accommodation_ The price for a room is around €20 per night per person. If you want to go self-catering, you should be able to find a room for around €10 per person.

The Planner Hütte has mattresses in the hut where you can sleep, and this is the cheapest option in town Tel: +43 (0) 36 83 81 36

For those looking for an apartment, try Sport Schöttl
Tel: +43 (0) 36 83 81 07

Planneralm Tourist Office
Tel: +43 (0) 36 83 22 06 or
Tel: +43 (0) 36 83 81 28
Internet - www.planneralm at click on '100% Family' for further offers

Food_ Planneralm - Gasthaus Reiter
Donnersbach - Gasthof Rütscher
Irdning - Gabriel: an old traditional village guesthouse.
   Unfortunately, there are no local secrets for large portions at cheap prices, but the above restaurants offer good quality meals and service for the right price.
   The closest supermarket is in Donnersbach.

Nightlife_ It's lucky that the Aprés-Ski scene has by-passed the Steiermark, where peace and quiet are the watchwords for a good time here. The Planneralm does have a few bars but if you go anywhere check out The Rock first. Donnersbach is a ghost town, a

better option is to drive further along to Irdning, where you can spend the evening in the Collosseum.

Other Activities_ Sledding and tandem paragliding. During a full moon, the Planneralm is ideally suited for a midnight powder run - but be careful, no one is going to dig you out of an avalanche at night.

LOCAL TIP »
TIP 1: After fresh snow, take an early morning hike up the Gläserkoppe.

TIP 2: Sport Scherz in Donnersbach let you use their snow skates free of charge!

© Scalp Rider Marco Lutz

"POWDER JUNKIES SHOULD MAKE THEIR WAY TO THE SUNNYSIDE AREA."

SAALBACH-HINTERGLEMM
AUSTRIA

SSAALBACH-HINTERGLEMM »
www.saalbach.com
tourist office tel: +43 (0)6541680068
www.saalbach.com
tourist office tel: +43 (0)6541680068
location: Saalbach
population: 3100
altitude: 1003
linked resorts: Leogang, Zell am See, Kaprun

ON THE MOUNTAIN »
Season: December to April
Lifts
vertical drop: 1003-2096
amount of lifts in total: 52
gondolas: 7
chair lifts: 15
drag lifts: 30
Slopes
amount of prepared slopes: 200 km
runs w. snowmaking machines: 80%
amount of easy runs: 90 km
amount of intermediate runs: 95 km
amount of advanced runs: 15 km
Facilities
night riding: yes
amount of halfpipes: 1
amount of funparks: 1
Heliboarding: -
Lift-ticket prices in Euro
1/2 day: 26,-
day: 33.5,-
week: 176.5,-
season: 395,-

SNOWBOARD TUITION »
Saalbach Snowboard Schule
Tel: +43 (0)654120047

SNOWBOARD SHOPS »
Tunnel
Tel: +43 (0)654120047

GETTING THERE »
Car
Munich - Saalbach: 180km
Munich - Autobahndreieck Inntal - Oberaudorf - Waidring - Gumping - Saalbach
Bozen - Saalbach: 277km
Bozen - Brenner - Innsbruck - Wörgl - Felbertauern/St.Johann - Lofer - Saalfelden - Saalbach
Vienna - Saalbach: 414km
Vienna - Linz - Salzburg Süd - Bischofshofen - Zell am Sell - Saalbach
Train
To Zell am See station then take a Post bus or a taxi for the 18km journey to Saalbach.
Air
Salzburg Airport: 84km
Innsbruck Airport: 167km
Munich Airport: 218km

SAALBACH/HINTERGLEMM »
Intro_ These two towns aren't your typical Pinzgauer villages, but there's a nice friendly atmosphere in the town centres now that traffic's been banned.

Thanks to the position and terrain of the Hohe Tauern in Saalbach-Hinterglemm, the mountain is pretty much guaranteed a relatively good snow base. Despite this, though, hard work has still been needed to survive the last couple of warmer winters. Most of the piste can now be supplied with artificial snow thanks to the recent addition of modern snow-making facilities at the resort. The towns, which have a combined population of 3,100, are dominated by hotels, restaurants and guesthouses (pensions) providing 16,000 beds for visitors.

ON THE MOUNTAIN »
Snow reliability_ The beginning of December usually brings heavy snowfalls, making for a good start to the winter season. This is the perfect time to shred it up without riding slalom through crowds of people. In January, we recommend you contact www.saalbach.com or phone +43/(0)6541/6800-40 to check on the latest snow conditions. February is often the month that provides the best snow conditions, but it's also, unfortunately, the busiest. But thanks to colder temperatures and the new snow making facilities it's now possible, even if only on the piste, to ride right through into the middle of April.

Lifts_ If you're not the type to be first at the lifts in the morning, you should probably forget taking the Bernkogel Sesselbahn (chairlift) in Saalbach. Try the Kohlmaisgipfelbahn instead, or at the other end of the resort look out for the Zwölfer-Nordbahn, which takes you up to the Zwölfer at 1,984 metres. From the Zwölfer, you can catapult yourself down the entire side of the mountain, staying in the shadows, before ending up in Vorderglemm. If everything goes to plan, the beginning of the 2002/2003 winter season should see a new gondola, including a middle station, on Shattberg. The resort is serviced by some 55 lifts, including 30 tow-lifts, but don't let this scare you off. Most of these are short connecting or practice lifts. In general, the chairlifts and gondolas are modern and fast moving.

Freeriding_ In off-piste areas, you'll constantly come across runs peppered with small cliffs and ledges. There are also some reforested areas. Even if you don't respect Nature, you should at least learn to recognise these closed-off areas out of love for your liftpass. The ski resort signposts the restricted areas to stop you slicing through baby trees.

First thing in the morning real powder junkies should make their way to the Zwölferkogel and the Hochalm sunnyside area. Awaiting you at Zwölfer is a sharp, steep and variable off-piste run. As you arrive at the bottom, head up the other side of the valley to the Hochalmbahn and Spieleck chairlift. From the open powder fields on the upper section of the Spieleckkogel, things head down through the steeper, wooded slopes and cliffs. The 1st Snowboardschool Saalbach offers guided tours into the unknown. Check it out at: www.board.at or Email:school@board.at

Freestyling_ The Hohe Penhab (Seekar) area is ideally suited for building a fat kicker in the snow. If you don't want to carry a snow-shovel, head to one of the resort's two, well prepared fun-parks. You'll find one at the base of Shattberg West in Hinterglemm, where you can ride under flood lights until 9.30pm. The other park/pipe, located on the Polten lift, is professionally shaped by Mellow Constructions (Tommy Marsh - www.mellow.at). You can reach this park (the better of the two) by travelling from

Vorderglemm using the Schönleiten lift. Another option is the halfpipe at the Forsthofalm.

Carving_A designated carving piste on the Bernkogel, and a slalom course on the Hochalm in Hinterglemm, make this area ideal for carvers.

Beginners_ Six ski and snowboard schools in Saalbach-Hinterglemm make this resort very learner-friendly. The shop, office and board-rental point at the 1st Snowboardschool is a great starting place, and they also offer freestyle and freeride courses. Both beginner areas are located close to the town centre and are easy to get to. This also means that the upper areas here are often overcrowded due to the lifts being used as a short cut between the Kohlmaiskopf and the Bernerkogel. In the lower areas, there's a practice lift you can use free of charge. Two-thirds of the resort's sunny side is mostly made up of blue runs around the Hochalm - Reiterkogel - Bernkogel areas.

Mountain Restaurants_ With 40 restaurants on the mountain, ranging from the big self-service restaurants to old-style huts, you'll be spoilt for choice. Reasonably priced restaurants include: Similalm, at the valley station of the Limberglift, Panoramaalm or Berger Hochalm between the Kohlmaiskopf and the Bründlkopf, and the Rosswaldhütte and Wieseralm in the Hochalm area.

"THE HOHE PENHAB (SEEKAR) AREA IS IDEALLY SUITED FOR BUILDING A FAT KICKER IN THE SNOW. IF YOU DON'T WANT TO CARRY A SNOW-SHOVEL, HEAD TO ONE OF THE RESORT'S TWO, WELL PREPARED FUN-PARKS. YOU'LL FIND ONE AT THE BASE OF SHATTBERG WEST IN HINTERGLEMM."

"THE BEGINNING OF DECEMBER USUALLY BRINGS HEAVY SNOWFALLS, MAKING FOR A GOOD START TO THE WINTER SEASON"

away at the *Castello*. The dance floor is pumping to house music in the *Classic Bar*. For an extra few Euros, you can even have your own private dancer in a side room. The well known *Arena Disco* also supplies Go-Go girls, but these keep a few more of their clothes on.

Tip: The village taxi companies standardise their prices through the winter. Alongside the regular taxis, you'll also find private taxi firms which are much more expensive - check with the locals what you should expect to pay for a taxi.

Other activities_For something different, splash out €7 and head up from Saalbach to Spielberghaus with the piste grooming machines. In addition to the great food, you'll almost always find a good party and later on you can get back to Saalbach down the floodlit sled run. In Hinterglemm you can relax in the indoor swimming pool or, just to finish you off after a day's boarding, you could always have a game of squash, or play ice hockey at the ice rink.

LOCAL TIP »
Stefan Gimpl, (F2-Rider)_"On a powder day, go to the Zwölferkogel and you'll find a super nice run underneath the lift. At the Westgrad Lift you have a nice small cliff to drop. If the snow isn't that good anymore, you still can go to the Leogang side where there's a nice funpark with kicker, corner and rails waiting for you."

IN THE TOWN »
Accommodation_Given all the *pensions* and hotels in Saalbach it's not hard to find suitable accommodation. Prices for bed and breakfast start at around €20.-, and go up to approximately €60.- per night for a four star hotel, including breakfast. It's also worth checking out the many special package deals on offer. The local ski bus runs between Saalbach and Hinterglemm and it's free to holders of a valid ski pass. Once you're in the town, it's only a short walk to the lifts.

Food_The number of eateries in the valley make it hard to decide where to get a great meal at the end of a long day. The portions are generous at the Pizzeria Wallner and the price is good too. For great Mexican food, head to PipaMex but expect to pay a bit more. Haider's Pizzeria serves big, outstanding pizzas as well as other Italian specialities at a reasonable price. Generally speaking, the restaurants in Saalbach/ Hinterglemm are expensive, so it pays to compare the prices and the specials boards.

Nightlife_Après ski parties generally go on into the early hours of the morning. But you need to watch out - the valley has very strict traffic regulations and these are stringently enforced, especially during organised party events. Try using taxis instead so you don't get to know the local police.
The Skibums (mainly Swedish and English) all meet at *Bobby's Pub,* which serves cheap snacks and the cheapest beer in the whole of Saalbach. The music varies from pop and hip hop to live bands. Live bands can also be heard not far

© Georg Schartl **Rider** Caroline Erhenstrasser, Christoph Egger

PROS & CONS »
+ Freeriding at Stubai, a joy for off-piste riders.
+ Good quality snow throughout the whole year.
+ 40km from the capital of the Tyrol, Innsbruck.

– Weekends and holiday periods are full on.
– Long transfer from the town to the resort

"POWDER, POWDER AND MORE POWDER - THE STUBAI GLACIER IS RENOWNED FOR ITS HEAVENLY SNOW CONDITIONS. BECAUSE OF THE GEOGRAPHICAL POSITION OF THE GLACIER"

STUBAI GLACIER
AUSTRIA

»

STUBAI GLACIER »
www.stubaiergletscherbahn.com
tourist office tel: +43 (0)52262228
location: Neustift
population: 4000
altitude:1000m

ON THE MOUNTAIN »
season
Winter: Nov-April
Summer: May-Sept
Lifts
vertical drop: 1700-3200m
amount of lifts in total:19
gondolas: 4
chair lifts: 6
drag lifts: 9
Slopes
amount of prepared slopes: 53
runs w. snowmaking machines: -
amount of easy runs: 20
amount of intermediate runs: 13
amount of advanced runs: 5
Facilities
night riding: -
amount of halfpipes 1
amount of funparks 1
heliboarding: -
Lift-ticket prices in Euro
1/2 day: 21.50
day: 32
week: 177.70
season: 430.60

SNOWBOARD TUITION »
Skischule-Neustift
Tel: +43 (0)52262540
www.schischule-neustift.com

GETTING THERE »
Car
Innsbruck - Neustift: 24km
Innsbruck - Autobahn towards Brenner -
Schönberg exit (toll) - Telfes - Fulpmes -
Neustift
Verona - Neustift: 270km
Verona - Brenner (toll) - Stubaital junction
(toll) - Telfes - Fulpmes - Neustift
If the toll charge of €3.50 is too expensive,
then drive the old Bundestrasse (main road)
to Neustift.
Innsbruck Süd exit - Brenner Bundestrasse
B182 towards Steinach/Matrei/Brenner -
turn off at Schönberg/Stubaital - Mieders -
Kampl - Neder - Neustift.
This route takes 20 minutes longer
Train
Innsbruck train station and then continue by
bus on the Stubaital line
Air
Innsbruck Airport - 25km
Continue by bus on the Stubaital line
Munich Airport - 228km

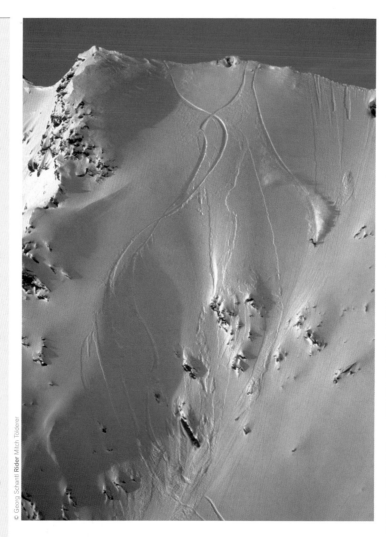
© Georg Schanti **Rider** Mitch Tölderer

STUBAI GLACIER »
Intro_At the end of the Stubai valley, you'll find Austria's largest and most popular glacial resort. Apart from the great freeride terrain, there's also a great environment for the freestylers among you. The Stubai glacier is not only a rocking place in winter, it's also the home of the SPC Summer Camps which were first set up in the Summer of 2002. Entertainment and accommodation can be found in the normally peaceful little town of Neustift, some 17km away from the glacier. But at the right time, when the tourists start to pour in, the town turns into a lively, happening place to be.

ON THE MOUNTAIN »
Snow reliability_Powder, powder and more powder - the Stubai glacier is renowned for its heavenly snow conditions. Because of the geographical position of the glacier, you can count on a change in the weather every few days. This generally means fresh snow throughout the winter months. Great powder can be found right until the end of May.

Lifts_During the main holiday periods and at weekends, you'll want to get to the valley lift station, the Muttersberg, before 9.00am, in the hope of avoiding long queues of traffic. It's not unusual to find getting on for 14,000 visitors all arriving on the glacier in the morning, all trying to get a ride in one of the two gondolas up to the resort. We'd recommend you take the Eisgratbahn which brings you

to just below the summit of the Schaufelspitze in about 20 minutes. Many of the 21 lifts are modern quad and six-person chairlifts. Generally speaking, you won't have to wait too long. The chaos of the morning might well be repeated in the afternoon unless you decide to wait it out at the Mutterbergalm après ski bar down below the valley station. Remember to designate a driver for the return journey so you make it through the regular police checkpoints on the Neustift road.

Freeriding_Just like any other glacier, in Stubai you're in high alpine terrain. The glacier provides endless possibilities for experienced freeriders, but however experienced you are, we don't recommend you just head off piste without talking to the local guides first. There are off piste dangers just waiting to swallow up tourists, including countless hidden glacial crevasses. Once a week, the ski and snowboard school on the Neustift-Stubai glacier offers a guided tour of the resort. (Information on request and individually-guided tours available.) The off piste valley run - approx. 10km - is a variable and challenging ride for fantastic powder turns. For those whose motto when they ride is 'no pain - no gain', don't miss taking a ride down the Wilde Grub'n. At this point it's worth commenting that riders must pay serious attention when threats of avalanches are reported and sign posts are put up to show that particular areas have been closed off. Ignore them and you risk your own life and the lives of others.

Freestyling_The fun park and the half pipe are located below the summit of the Schaufelspitze. Both are accessible from the t-bar at the upper lift station of the Eisgratbahn. Since early summer 2002, the Stubai Glacier has been the home of the SPC Summer Camps (formerly held in Hintertux/Mayrhofen). This has had a positive effect on the development of the new fun park. Freestylers who want to do more than just hang around in a pipe or park for the whole day have no problems here. The glacier offers lots of natural obstacles, including jumps, small cliffs and drops which,

"THE STUBAI GLACIER IS NOT ONLY A ROCKING PLACE IN WINTER, IT'S ALSO THE HOME OF THE SPC SUMMER CAMPS."

© Daniel Kudernatsch

if you have a good eye, can be spotted from the lifts.

Carving_ Carving De Luxe - on your own secured carving piste on the Daunferner, where you can carve to your heart's content without the danger of mowing down a group of beginners. A traffic light ensures a 15 second interval between riders thereby ensuring you'll have your own space. For those who really want to know, there are two specific courses where you can time your runs. In the upper, more gradually sloping section of the Eisjochferners you'll find the Arthur course and close by, on a steeper slope, there's the Königslauf, or King's Run.

Beginners_ Group and private lessons are available for beginners wanting to improve their

snowboarding skills. The resort has built its own practice lift and beginner piste for this purpose. Most runs on the mountain require a little more skill to descend, but you can find easier slopes. These include the Fernauferner Nr.10, a half run down the Zufahrt Fernau Nr. 4 to the middle station and the Daunferner Nr. 7 taking the quad chairlift Rotadl lift from Gamsgarten.

Mountain Restaurants_ The modern restaurants operated by the Stubai Glacier Lift Company (partly self-service) at Gamsgarten, Eisgrat and the Jochdole are 3,105m above sea level and give amazing panoramic views. The service at the Fernau Mauer bar is fast but the food isn't cheap. Generally speaking, the quality of the food is OK and the portions

are reasonable as long as you don't pitch your expectations too high. The Dresdnerhütte near the middle station is also recommended. The menu includes all the classics to be found in a ski hut including; Germknödel (sweet yeast dumplings), sausage and chips, pea soup, as well as good quality regional cuisine at an acceptable price.

IN THE TOWN »
Accommodation_ Two camping grounds, loads of private rooms and inexpensive guesthouses to rent provide an endless choice of places to stay. For those wanting more, 3 and 4 star hotels are also available. Prices range from about €36 to €47 including breakfast. You'll find even more hotels and guesthouses into the road into the resort and you'll need a car or bus to get you to the resort. Groups can be accommodated at the Dresdnerhütte, which is on the glacier itself. A great option if you're planning an early morning tour.

Food_A tasty snack bar right next to the main bus stop provides the perfect solution to a hungry appetite at the end of a day on the mountain. A supermarket is ideally situated between the ski school office and the camping ground, not far from the centre of town and there's another one opposite the Schönherr Haus.
Restaurant Platzl in the Dorfplatz (Village Square) serves up a good selection of pizza, pasta and traditional fodder.

Nightlife_ The umbrella bar at Mutterbergalm is a good place to take in those first drinks after a heavy day on the mountain - Après ski in its purest form! As for the town – start at the Dorfpub and then head across the road to Ribeisl where you can drink cocktails while listening to Ambient and Trip-Hop sounds. Harri's Bar beats out the Drum & Base and Hip Hop. For those wannabe hippies and transients amongst you, head into the Nachtkastl. The happenin' Rumpl disco should be able to see you through the night. For those of you who enjoy paying girls to dance on your lap, head down to the Hully Gully strip bar.

Other Activities_ Ice climbing at Gamsgarten - on a 10m ice tower, the whole year round. To relax - the public indoor swimming pool (with wicked slide), public sauna, or a wholesome massage. The nearest cinema is in Innsbruck, and this, combined with a tour of the pubs and bars, is a recommended undertaking.

LOCAL TIP »
Mike Pearse, guitarist-singer and song writer with the local heroes Fuckchiwawa as well as a snowboard instructor_"For a small morning tour - hike through the Glamer's Grube to Daunkopf (approx.40mins). You'll then be rewarded with a 20 minute powder run which slides into Wilde Grube descent. Those wanting to save the cash should take day provisions with them, or head down to the Dresdnerhütte".

PROS & CONS »

+ Glacial resort - great conditions right through the winter.
+ Very few tow lifts.
+ Good party town.
+ Perfectly prepared pistes.

– Crowded.
– The town is loud, especially in the evenings.

SÖLDEN
AUSTRIA

SÖLDEN »
www.ski-soelden.com
Tourist office tel: +43 (0)52545100
location: Sölden
population: 3827
altitude: 1377
linked resorts: Hochsölden

ON THE MOUNTAIN »
season: December to end of May
Lifts
vertical drop: 1377–3250m
amount of lifts in total: 34
gondolas: 5
chair lifts: 19
drag lifts: 10
Slopes
amount of prepared slopes: 141 km
runs w. snowmaking machines: 35
easy runs: 45 km
intermediate runs: 73 km
advanced runs: 23 km
Facilities
night riding: yes
amount of halfpipes: 2
amount of funparks: 1
Heliboarding: -
Lift-ticket prices in Euro
1/2 day: 26
day: 29
week: 176
season: 501

SNOWBOARD TUITION »
Skischule Sölden/Hochsölden
Tel: +43 (0)52542364
www.ski-soelden.com

SNOWBOARD SHOPS »
Sport Riml
Tel :+43 (0)52543873

GETTING THERE »
Car
Munich - Sölden 190km
Munich - A12 Inntal Autobahn - Kufstein / Innsbruck - towards Bregenz - Ötztal exit-Sölden
From Italy - Sölden
A13 Brenner Autobahn - to Innsbruck - towards Bregenz - Ötztal exit - Sölden
Zürich - Sölden 268km
Zürich - via St. Gallen - Au (Swiss/Au) - Lustenau - Arlberg (Toll) - Landeck - A12 Ötztal exit - Sölden
Train
Main Train Station Innsbruck - take the regional train to Ötztal then by bus or taxi to Sölden
Air
Innsbruck Airport 85km
Munich Airport 230km

"THE 'GOLDEN GATE TO THE GLACIER' AS THE GONDOLA IS KNOWN, TAKES YOU FROM SÖLDEN TO THE TIEFENBACH GLACIER. THIS ALLOWS YOU NOT ONLY TO CHECK OUT HOCH SÖLDEN BUT ALSO THE GLACIAL WORLD."

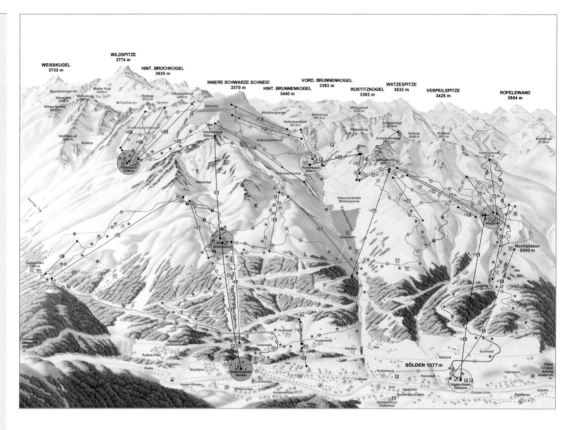

SÖLDEN »
Intro_ Some 65km south of Innsbruck, at the end of the Ötz valley, is the modern holiday town of Sölden. It's near some of Austria's highest resorts, including Obergurgl and Hochgurgl, and as the Tiefenbach and Rettenbach glaciers are close by a constantly good snow base is ensured.

The archaeological find of the ancient 'Ötzi' iceman has helped to promote the popularity of a region which has long been a hot spot for snowboarders from all over the world.

ON THE MOUNTAIN »
Snow reliability_ The Tiefenbach glacier is open almost the whole year round for skiing and boarding. You'll find the best conditions between October and April/May. The early season is often the best time to ride untracked powder, as the masses don't arrive until later. Further information can be obtained from www.soelden.at or www.glanzer.at. TIP: the local snowboarders are very quick at replying to enquiries regarding their home resort.

Lifts & Piste_ The modern lift facilities have the capacity to transport up to 60,000 visitors an hour, guaranteeing a great service and allowing you to access every corner of the resort without having to wait for long periods. It can get a little crowded during the holiday periods from 9 -10am. The 'Golden Gate to the Glacier' as the gondola is known, takes you from Sölden to the Tiefenbach glacier. This allows you not only to check out Hoch Sölden but also the glacial world. Sometimes you may have to wait for the weather to clear.

Freeriding_ High Alpine area - the best freeriding areas run down from the Gaislachkogel, it lies at just over 3000m. Outstanding off-piste riding that starts well above the treeline can also be had in Obergurgl/Hochgurgl. This part of the Ötz valley is fantastic for freeriding, but should really only be undertaken with a qualified local guide.

Freestyling_Sölden has as much to offer in winter as it does in summer. The Giggijoch funpark (kicker, fun box, rails, diamonds etc...) and the pipe, are both accessible using the Hainbacher or the Silberbrünnl quad chairlifts. In summer you'll also find a skate park (quarters, bank, boxes and rails) and skate pool in the glacier lift car park.

In addition to the various events organised here, you can also take part in the Base-Summer camps. For details of dates go to www.base.soelden.com

Carving_ The BASE Boarder park on the Giggijoch is also suitable for the carvers amongst you. A permanent racecourse and a speed-testing course have been built alongside the Easy-Cross course where hard booters can test their skills. The long, wide and well-prepared runs are also ideal for those travelling with a Super-G 180cm weapon.

Beginners_ The nearest, but small, beginner area, which is serviced by a chairlift and two tow lifts, is at Innerwald just above Sölden. The Sölden/Hoch Ski and Snowboard School will be happy to provide you with info about private and group

"THE BASE BOARDER PARK ON THE GIGGIJOCH IS ALSO SUITABLE FOR THE CARVERS AMONGST YOU. A PERMANENT RACECOURSE AND A SPEED-TESTING COURSE HAVE BEEN BUILT ALONGSIDE THE EASY-CROSS COURSE"

© Christian Stadler **Rider** Oli Holzmann

lessons. Call them on 00 43 (0) 5254 23640 (main office) For those who can travel down a blue run without a problem, head to the beginner area on the Giigijoch.

Mountain Restaurants_ With around 30 ski huts serving mainly the local Tyrolean food, and 6 self-service restaurants which between them cater for just about every taste, you can be assured of a good meal. Our recommendations include; the Gampe Alm, the Hühner Steige, or the Pizzeria 3000.

IN THE TOWN »
Accommodation_Sölden has accommodation to suit all budgets, from the finest five star hotels right through to cheap B&B places. If

you're travelling in a group, we recommend you book a holiday apartment. The Sölden campsite is open all year round and is only a two minute walk from the Gaislachkogel lift.

The main road runs right through the middle of the town, so it's often noisy and the noise of the traffic can often go on into the early hours of the morning, making it difficult to sleep.

Prices range from €30 per person/per night for a room or apartment in a well-equipped B&B, through to €230 per person/per night for a 100m 2 penthouse suite in the five star Hotel Central.

Food_ The cheapest option is to use one of the four supermarkets

in the town or, as an alternative, visit one of the fast food outlets - the Mounty Burger joint should satisfy your munchies. If you fancy some Italian, head to one of the pizzerias - e.g. Corso or Gusto. For traditional cuisine, try the Pfandl or Die Alm. Many of the hotels also have restaurants offering first class food. The best place for a romantic rendezvous is the Saitensprung or the Hotel Central.

Nightlife_ Take a walk along the main road where there are pubs and clubs every few feet. You'll also hear a wide range of music being played in Sölden's bars, but don't expect the prices to be cheap, especially during the high season. Tip: Don't waste your time in the

"THERE ARE PUBS AND CLUBS EVERY FEW FEET."

Après-Ski bars on the mountain, save your strength for the evening rampage.

Other Activities_Sölden has an indoor swimming pool with sauna and massage facilities and a fitness centre and cinema. There's also an indoor climbing centre, sledding and ice skating. If you've never been to Innsbruck, we'd recommend you put that right - it's a great place.

PROS & CONS »
+ Like the rest of the Wilder Kaiser Welt, Westendorf has a good snow record.
+ Relatively cheap resort.
+ The Funpark 'Boarder's Playground'.

− Westendorf is only connected with the Wilder Kaiser Ski Welt via the ski bus.
− Small resort, unchallenging terrain.

WESTENDORF
AUSTRIA

»

WESTENDORF »
www.westendorf.com
Tourist office tel: +43 (0)53346230
location: Westendorf
population: 3445
altitude: 800 m
linked resorts: Brixen, Hopfgarten/Itter/Kelchsau, Söll, Scheffau, Ellmau, Going

ON THE MOUNTAIN »
Season: December to early April
Lifts
Vertical drop: 800-1865m
amount of lifts in total: 13
gondolas: 2
chair lifts: 6
drag lifts: 5
Slopes
amount of prepared slopes: 40 km
runs w. snowmaking machines: 50%
amount of easy runs: 6
amount of intermediate runs: 10
amount of advanced runs: 1
Facilities
night riding: -
amount of halfpipes: 1
amount of funparks: 1
Heliboarding: -
Lift-ticket prices in Euro
1/2 day: 23
week: 148.50
season: 375

SNOWBOARD TUITION »
Skischule und Snowboardschule IDEAL
Tel: +43 (0)53342919
auner@alpenspektakel.at

SNOWBOARD SHOPS »
Rent & Sport
Tel: +43 (0)53346868
rentsport@westendorf.com

MAC Sport
Tel: +43 (0)53342900

GETTING THERE »
Car
Munich - Westendorf 127km
Munich - towards Innsbruck - Wörgl Ost exit - Brixental - Westendorf
Zurich - Westendorf 370km
Zurich - St Gallen - Lustenau - Arlberg - Innsbruck - Wörgl Ost exit - Brixental - Westendorf
Verona - Westendorf 343km
Verona - Brenner - Innsbruck - Wörgl Ost exit - Brixental - Westendorf
Train
A train departs for Westerndorf every 1-2 hours from Wörgl train station (approx. 65km from Innsbruck and 110km from Munich)
Air
Munich Airport 165km
Innsbruck Airport 82km

© Boardplay Westendorf **Rider** Rene 'Renilla' Margreiter

WESTENDORF »
Intro_Westendorf has lived in the shadow of its more famous neighbour, Kitzbühel for a long time. Fortunately, this small but scenic resort has not allowed this fact to dampen its spirits in the slightest. The great funpark has helped to make Westendorf a popular destination for snowboarders, and the high point of the season comes with the Shred Down Slopestyle Contest, a wicked freestyle event run by the local ruler Gogo. Westendorf now belongs to the Ski Welt Wilder Kaiser, and the 93 lifts combine to make this one of the largest resorts in Austria.

ON THE MOUNTAIN »
Snow reliability_Over the past four years, visitors to *Westendorf* have experienced the best snow conditions in the December and March periods. If the snow doesn't fall snowmaking machines are on hand to provide a decent cover. For further information, weather and snow reports call
Tel: +43 (0) 5334 200

Lifts_Westendorf is part of the *Ski Welt Wilder Kaiser* marketing group, but isn't actually connected to the larger area by any lifts. This isolation does have a positive side to it — the wild ski tourists don't seem to make it over here to the 13 lifts and 45km of prepared piste. If you're looking for a little variety, you can take the free ski bus and be in *Brixen i. T.* in around 10 minutes. The *Hochbrixen* gondola will then transport you into the larger resort.

Freeriding_There are 3 summits to choose from - *Choralpe*, Fleiding and the *Gampenkogel*, which provide freeriding without the long hikes. Your best bet would be the *Choralpe*, which opens up lines heading back down into Westendorf and the valley lift station. On fresh powder days, you'll find the locals riding at the *Fleiding* summit on the *111er* run. You'll need to get up early to get an untracked line here. At the end of the run is the legendary *111er* Bar, a great place to hang out, and a bus stop for the shuttle service back to the valley lift station, which leave at 20 minute intervals. Be careful though, the avalanche danger on this run can be high, so wear a transceiver. Just like anywhere else, respect the mountain and enjoy the ride…

Freestyling_Pro rider Reinhard 'Gogo' Gossner, on the best route to the Boarders Playground: "Head up the 6 person gondola towards *Choralpe*, and exit at the summit station at 1820m. Take the connecting path across to the *Fleidingberg* summit and access the tri chairlift. From the Fleidingspitze, you should be able to see the *Boarder's Playground*. The funpark has two brand new quad chairlifts for access. One returns to the *Fleidingspitze* and the other takes you to the *Gampenkogel* (1956m). There's no hiking in this park! The triple kicker combo and the rail line, which includes a rainbow, straight, kink and football goal, all follow each other in a line. The *Boarder's Playground* stretches over the entire length of the *Gampenkogel* quad chairlift. You can then chill out on the lift or in the 'chill out' area next to the container. A room is also available at the bottom of the chairlift for snowboarders to eat a picnic lunch."

Carving_At the *Talkaser* lift, there's a special carving piste with electronic timing just waiting for speed fiends. Whether beginner or expert, you can carve here until

"WESTENDORF HAS LIVED IN THE SHADOW OF ITS MORE FAMOUS NEIGHBOUR, KITZBÜHEL FOR A LONG TIME. FORTUNATELY, THIS SMALL BUT SCENIC RESORT HAS NOT ALLOWED THIS TO DAMPEN ITS SPIRITS. THE GREAT FUNPARK HAS HELPED TO MAKE IT A POPULAR DESTINATION FOR SNOWBOARDERS."

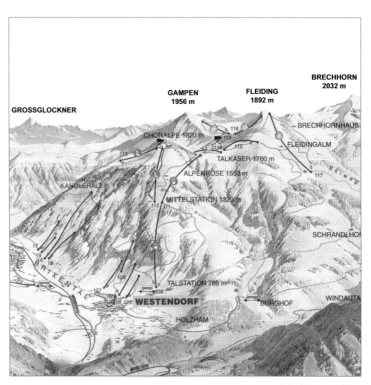

your edges glow. Once you've worked up a thirst, head down to the Après-Ski bar at the bottom of the *Talkaser* lift.

Beginners_Beginners will find ideal beginner terrain, all of it serviced by three lifts, within walking distance of the village. Intermediate beginners can head off to the *Talkaser* lift to practice their technique. If you're looking for professional lessons, check out the three different ski and snowboard schools, all based in the village.

Mountain Restaurants_The *Feriengasthaus Brechhorn*, opposite the funpark on the 119A piste, has a good atmosphere, overnight accommodation, a sauna and a nice Après-Ski bar. The *Fleidingeralm* is one of two restaurants on the Fleiding tri chairlift piste, both of which are very cosy and which serve good, traditional Tyrolean cooking. The *Alte Mittelstation* is also a classic mountain guesthouse on the valley run, and is a traditional rest stop on the way back down to the village.

IN THE TOWN »
Accommodation_There's accommodation to suit every budget here, whether it be a four-star spa hotel, an apartment, or a B&B. All the accommodation in *Westendorf* is within 5 - 10 minutes' walk from the valley lift station. For further info and

reservations call
Tel: +43 (0) 5334 6230

Food_*Westendorf* is well stocked with good restaurants and guesthouses, all within easy reach. Traditional Austrian cooking is available pretty much everywhere. Dishes worth trying include; *käsespätzle, germknödel* (yeast dumplings – yummy!) or *kaiserschmarren* (*Gasthof Schermer*). There's also Italian (*Pizzeria Toscana*) and French cuisine at *Chez Yves*. And, of course, there's the ubiquitous Spar supermarket.

Nightlife_*Westendorf* has a somewhat limited choice of bars and pubs. The centre of town is relatively small, making it easy to find a joint that's jumpin'. We can recommend *Wunderbar, Taverne Moskito Bar* and of course the *111-er Bar*.

Other Activities_*Westendorf* is well known for its good thermal currents, so it's a great place to go paragliding.

LOCAL TIP »
The Red Bull 'Jump and Freeze' contest is held every year in February. The name says it all. Contestants from all over Europe build their own flying machines and fly off the jump into an ice-cold pool of water. The event is held on the practice slope in the middle of *Westendorf*. A big crowd, a lot of fun, and a great party afterwards.

© Boardplay Westendorf **Rider** Reinhard 'Gogo' Gossner

"BEGINNERS WILL FIND IDEAL BEGINNER TERRAIN, ALL OF IT SERVICED BY THREE LIFTS, WITHIN WALKING DISTANCE OF THE VILLAGE. INTERMEDIATE BEGINNERS CAN HEAD OFF TO THE TALKASER LIFT TO PRACTICE THEIR TECHNIQUE."

PROS & CONS »

+ Good freeriding terrain.
+ Two impressive snowparks near by.
+ Close to several other resorts.

− Following a snowfall you'll need snow chains on the road into the resort from Altenmarkt!
− Almost always booked out in winter.

ZAUCHENSEE
AUSTRIA

ZAUCHENSEE »

www.zauchensee.cc
tourist office tel: +43 (0)64524000
location: Altenmarkt
population: 3300
altitude: 856m
linked resorts: Flachau, Wagrain, St. Johan, Eben, Filzmoos, Kleinarl

ON THE MOUNTAIN »

deason: December - April
Lifts
vertical drop: 1361-2188m
amount of lifts in total: 15
gondolas: 3
chair lifts: 6
drag lifts: 6
Slopes
amount of prepared slopes: 65 km
runs w. snowmaking machines: 23
easy runs: 23 km
intermediate runs: 15 km
advanced runs: 27 km
Facilities
night riding: -
amount of halfpipes: 1
amount of funparks: 1
heliboarding: -
Lift-ticket prices in Euro
1/2 day: 26
day: 32.5
week: 174
season: 355
Events
Ästhetiker Open
www.aesthetiker.com

SNOWBOARD TUITION »

Ski- und Snowboardschule Ruhdorfer
Tel: +43 (0)6643266170

SNOWBOARD SHOPS »

Tel: +43 (0)6643388840
Hauptstraße 9
Altenmarkt

GETTING THERE »

Car
Altenmarkt - Zauchensee 10km
Munich - Altenmarkt 198km
Munich - (Ger/Au) - Salzburg Stadt - A10 Tauern Autobahn - Eben im Pongau exit - Altenmarkt
Salzburg - Altenmarkt 66km
Salzburg Stadt - A10 Tauern Autobahn - Eben im Pongau exit - Altenmarkt
Train
Salzburg - Altenmarkt approx. 1 hour journey time (via Bischofshofen)
Munich - Altenmarkt approx. 3 hour journey time (via Bischofshofen)
www.oebb.at
Air
Salzburg Airport 68km
Munich Airport 237km
Bargain flights from London to Salzburg are often available. Check them out at www.ryanair.com

© Scalp **Rider** Mane Monsberger

ZAUCHENSEE »

Intro_ Zauchensee is part of the Salzburger Sportwelt Amadé, a conglomeration of ten winter resorts that between them encompass 25 villages and 270 lifts! The Sportwelt Amadé is highly regarded by the Austrian snowboard scene and is popular for two particular reasons. Firstly, for the quality of its freeriding terrain. Secondly because it's home to the annual Ästhetiker Jam. Last season the resort was redeveloped on a massive scale, including a new complex with bars, cafes, shops and a covered car park. Although this has resulted in the place now resembling a huge shopping mall, as soon as you're on the lift you quickly leave this all behind!

ON THE MOUNTAIN »

Snow reliability_ Zauchensee usually gets at least its fair share of snow, creating a good base throughout the season. The shape of the valley forces snow laden clouds to rise and then dump their load. Snow-making machines are also on hand should they be needed.
Snow reports
Tel: +43 (0) 6457 2800.

Lifts & Piste_ Zauchensee itself has 14 lifts, and from Roßkopf you can cross to the other side of the mountain where the resorts of Flachauwinkel and Kleinarl have a further 16. The connections to other resorts are easily accessible but it's worth keeping an eye on the snow conditions around Salzburg Land.

Freeriding_ Zauchensee is a fantastic freeriding spot. Alongside the lifts there are a number of steep powder runs, and experienced riders can drop in left of the Tauernkar lift and into a tree run that takes you right down into the valley − a vertical drop of 700 metres on pure powder if you hit it at the right time.
   Ride on the slightly antiquated Schwarzwand lift and you'll get a good view of what Zauchensee has to offer. On the right there's a very steep slope spread over ten smaller summits known as the Little AK. Caution: this is a high risk avalanche area. Just because there are tracks, that doesn't mean it's stable. When the new Panorama-Schrägaufzug opens next to the Schwarzwand summit lift station you'll also have access to the Gamskogel summit.

Freestyling_ You'll have your choice of two well-developed parks here. One is located in the 'freestyle zone' at Zauchensee, and the other in the neighbouring resort of Flachauwinkel. First take the Zauchenseebahn gondola, then ride down to the connecting lift to Flachauwinkel. Continue on the 6-seater chairlift and you'll arrive at Absolut Park. It might sound complicated but it's not, and will only take around half an hour. The park has a pipe, a kicker line, about 10 rails and obstacles, all lovingly tended by master shapers Max Rehrl and Sepp Harml, who keep the park in excellent condition.

Carving_ Carvers get their money's worth in Zauchensee. There's a wide selection of well-prepared pistes where you can really let loose. In the high season, though, the slopes are crowded with family groups so letting loose isn't an option.

Beginners_ Once you've got the basics, you'll find lots of blue and red runs, although Zauchensee isn't an ideal place to learn. In neighbouring Flachau the terrain is more beginner-friendly (and the nightlife is better too!).

"RIDE ON THE SLIGHTLY ANTIQUATED SCHWARZWAND LIFT AND YOU'LL GET A GOOD VIEW OF WHAT ZAUCHENSEE HAS TO OFFER. ON THE RIGHT THERE'S A SLOPE SPREAD OVER TEN SMALLER SUMMITS KNOWN AS THE LITTLE AK."

© Scalp Rider Friedl Kolar

"WE RECOMMEND THE GAMSKOGEL AND THE RAUCHKOPF, BOTH OF WHICH HAVE GREAT VIEWS AND GOOD FOOD. ON A CLEAR DAY YOU CAN EVEN SEE THE TOWNS OF TAUERN AND THE IMPRESSIVE DACHSTEIN MOUNTAINS IN THE FAR DISTANCE - AND WE MEAN FAR ... 200KM AWAY IN FACT."

Mountain Restaurants_There are plenty of ski huts in the resort, and to some extent you're spoiled for choice. We recommend the Gamskogel and the Rauchkopf, both of which have great views and good food. On a clear day you can even see the towns of Tauern and the impressive Dachstein mountains in the far distance - and we mean far... 200km away in fact.

IN THE TOWN »
Accommodation_Zauchensee is a hotel resort. Although the hotels are well located, they are probably not within the price range of most snowboarders. Cheaper options would be to stay in a pension or rent a holiday apartment in or around Altenmarkt which is about 10 km away. You should budget for at least €20 per night, and you'll need to book early. Altenmarkt/Zauchensee Tourist Office- Tel: +43 (0) 6452 5511 or +43 (0) 6452 5611 www.altenmarkt-zauchensee.at info@altenmarkt-zauchensee.at

Food_There are enough shops and restaurants in Altenmarkt to go round, but the later it gets, the quieter it becomes. The Mexican Restaurant, above the

Underground Snowboard shop is very good. The Pizzeria in the Arche Noah is also good, and the Metzgerei Schitter does a fine traditional 'Fleischkäse Semmel'. Self-caterers will be able to pick up supplies in Altenmarkt.

Nightlife_Altenmarkt isn't really a ski village, so it's not too lively in the evenings. Arche Noah turns into a pub at night while the Disco Internet is your typical village disco, only worth visiting after you've downed a few beers. The neighbouring town of Flachau has a lot more going on in the evenings.

Other Activities_Tandem paragliding flights, snow rafting, ice skating, and sledding are all here, and there's a big swimming pool 13 km away in Wagrain.

LOCAL TIP »
Rheinhard Schitter_"Get up early' is our tip. Those who follow this advice and go and ride next to the Schwarzwand lift on a good powder day will be treated to a great experience. Ema's Pub in Flachau has live music and a large screen showing snowboard videos, which should inspire your riding."

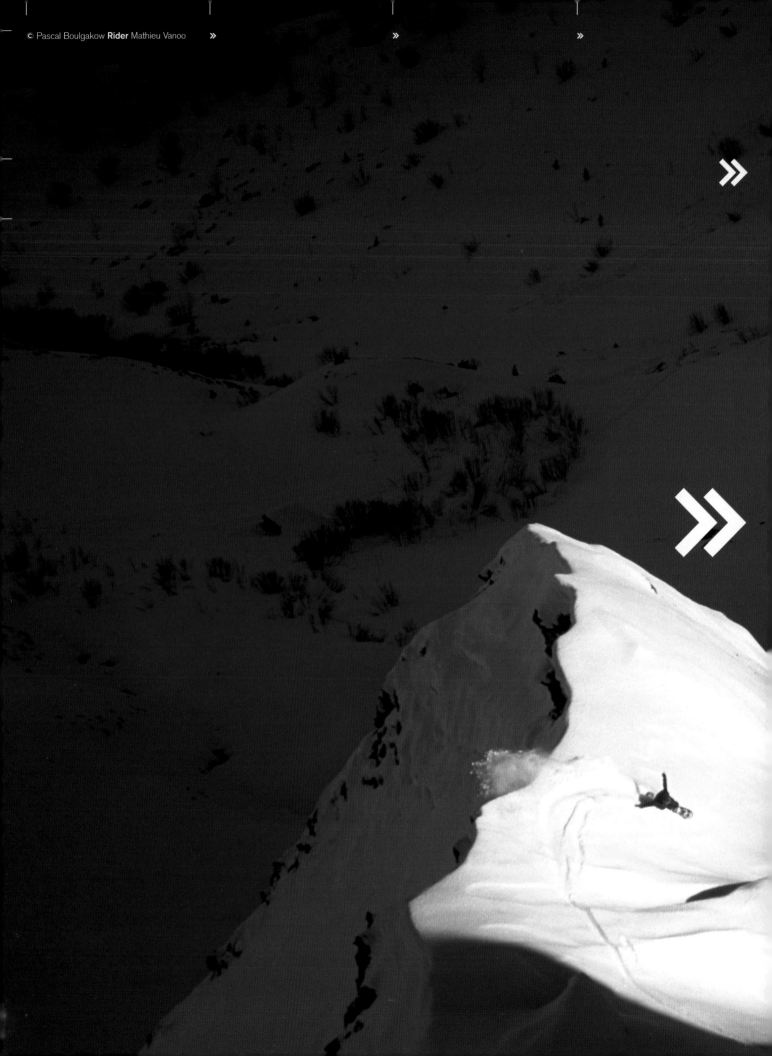

FRANCE
062-097

FRANCE MAP

FRANCE »

Intro_France is home to the largest range of winter resorts in Europe. The exact count of 319 is spread out over the Jura massif, the central massif, the Pyrenees and of course the Alps. The lift facilities here are often more modern than those elsewhere in the Alps, but the villages lack the charm of those you'd find in Austria, for example. Following the architectural excesses of the 60's and 70's which can be seen in Tignes and Les Arcs, they seem to have learnt from their mistakes and are now building with more regard to the natural alpine environment. The Pyrenees are a little behind with their lift facilities, but have some great riding spots, with a number of areas really making an effort to facilitate snowboarders. The prices here are also cheaper than those in the Alps.

Snowparks are improving, and resorts have come to realise that it is in their interest to improve their snowboarding facilities. France is a gigantic playground for freeriders, probably the best in the world. The Aprés Ski scene is varies from resort to resort, the better known spots including Chamonix, Three Valleys and Les Deux Alpes. But the reason France continues to be so popular is less to do with the drinking, and more to do with the fact that this country has the best terrain in Europe, if not the world.

INFORMATION »

Official Name_République Française
Capital_Paris
Population_58,89 Million
Land mass_543.965km2
Language(s)_French
Currency_1 Euro = 100 Cent
Highest mountain_Mont Blanc 4807m
International country code_0033
Police_17
Ambulance_15
Fire Brigade_18
Tourist Board_Maison de la France
Tel: +33 (0)836 68 31 12
www.franceguide.com
Train Info_www.sncf.com
Weather Info_www.meteo.fr

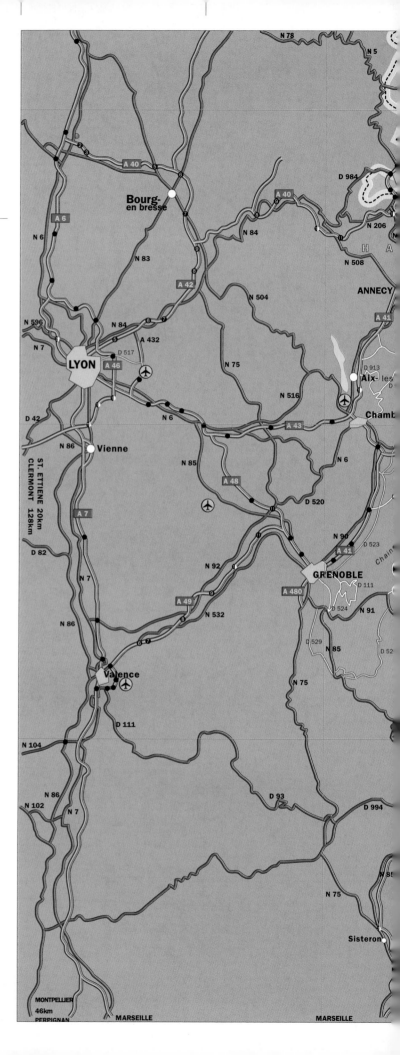

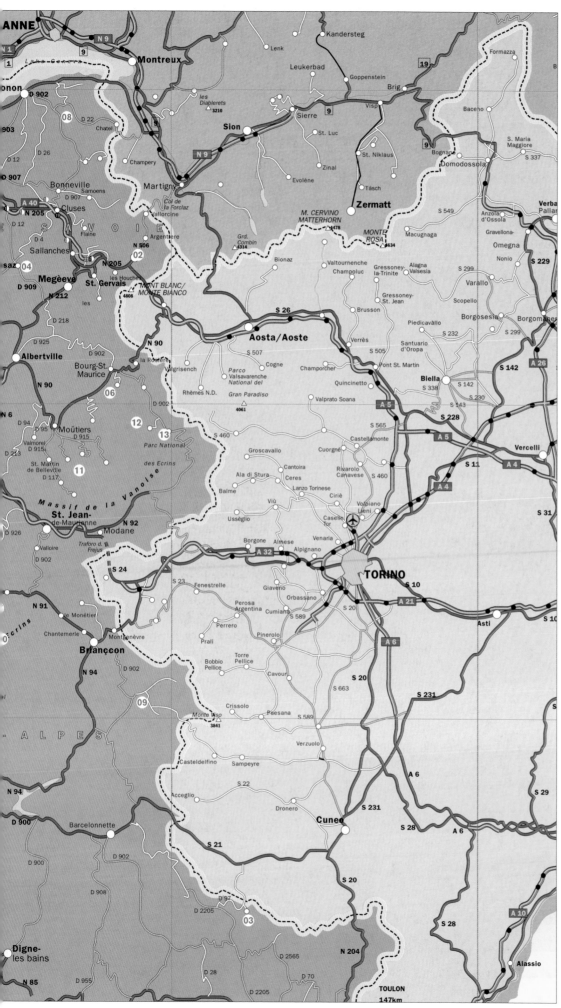

LOCATIONS »
FRANCE ALPS
01 **ALPE D'HUEZ**
02 **CHAMONIX**
03 **ISOLA 2000**
04 **LA CLUSAZ**
05 **LA GRAVE**
06 **LES ARCS**
07 **LES DEUX ALPES**
08 **LES PORTES DES SOLEIL**
09 **VARS/RISOUL**
10 **SERRE CHEVALIER**
11 **TROIS VALLÉES**
12 **ESPACE KILLY/TIGNES**
13 **ESPACE KILLY/VAL D'ISERE**

FRENCH PYRENNEES
SEE PAGE 192
14 **ARTOUSTE**
15 **CAUTERETS**
16 **LES ANGLES**
17 **SAINT LARY**

© Pascal Boulgakow

"ALPE D'HUEZ HAD ITS BEGINNINGS AROUND 1936. AT THAT TIME VERY FEW TOURISTS FOUND THEIR WAY INTO THE DAUPHINÉ ALPS."

ALPE D'HUEZ
FRENCH ALPS

ALPE D'HUEZ »
www.alpedhuez.com
tourist office tel: +33 (0)476114444
location Alpe d'Huez
population: 1700
altitude: 1860 m
linked resorts: Auris-en-Oisans, Vaujany, Oz-en-Oisans and Villard-Reculas

ON THE MOUNTAIN »
season: resort from December - April
Autumn altitude skiing from Oct- Nov
Lifts
vertical drop: 1860–3330m
amount of lifts in total: 115
cable cars: 5
gondolas: 10
chair lifts: 54
drag lifts: 46
Slopes
amount of prepared slopes: 236 km
snowmaking machines: 700
amount of easy runs: 37
amount of intermediate runs: 63
amount of advanced runs: 14
Facilities
night riding: yes
amount of halfpipes: 1
amount of funparks: 1
heliboarding: -
Lift-ticket prices in Euro
1/2 day: 25
week: 171
season: 801

SNOWBOARD TUITION »
French Ski School
Tel: +33 (0)476803169
www.esf-alpedhuez.com
International Ski School
Tel: +33 (0)476804277
www.alpedhuez.com

SNOWBOARD SHOPS »
Planate surf
Tel: + 33 (0)476806228
www.planetesurf.com

GETTING AROUND »
Auto
Grenoble - Alpe d'Huez 63km
Highway to Grenoble - then highway A480 - exit 8 Vizille-Les stations de l'Oisans - RN91 to Bourg d'Oisans - CD211 - Alpe d'Huez
Bus
Bus station Grenoble: daily buses to Alpe d'Huez, approx.1hr 30 min
Tel: +33 (0) 476 604 680 www.VFD.fr
Bus connections between Grenoble and major European cities
Tel: +33 (0) 476 461 977 www.intercars.fr
Train
Closest train station - Grenoble. TGV Paris/Grenoble approx. 3hrs 10 min
Info and reservations:
Tel: +33 (0) 836 353 535 www.sncf.com
Air
Lyon Saint-Exupéry Airport 150km
Tel: +33 (0) 472 227 221
Connecting bus also available - reservations necessary - Tel:+33 (0) 472 359 496
www.satobus-alps.com
Grenoble/St.Geoirs Airport 99km
Tel: +33 (0) 476 654 848
Connecting bus available:
Tel: +33 (0) 476 934 000
Geneva Airport 220km
Tel: +41 (0) 227 177 111
Connecting bus Geneva/Grenoble -
Tel: +33 (0) 438 021 333

ALPE D'HUEZ »
Intro_Alpe d'Huez had its beginnings around 1936. At that time very few tourists found their way into the *Dauphiné Alps*. Today, *Alpe d'Huez* is one of the best-known winter destinations in France, with a good choice of great runs. The road leading into the town is a legendary stage of the Tour de France. *Alpe d'Huez* is also the home of Salt Lake City Winter Olympic gold medallist, Isabella Blanc.

ON THE MOUNTAIN »
Lifts & Piste_*Alpe d'Huez* is a relatively large resort: 111 pistes (37 green, 32 blue, 28 red and 14 black) are serviced by 5 cable cars, 10 gondolas, 23 chairlifts, 46 tow lifts and 2 trains. The resort is spread over a number of areas, which are well connected by the Lift Company. Around 15 mountain restaurants are on hand to satisfy hunger on the piste and an army of 700 snowmaking machines is on constant standby.

Freeriding_*Alpe d'Huez* has been well provided for by Nature. Following a fresh snowfall, you can choose from endless freeride possibilities. Even a few days after snow has fallen, you can still find untracked powder. Check out the following runs – *Pyramide, Cheminées, Combe Charbonnière* or *Coulior du Cerisier*. It is also worth heading down to the other villages that are connected with *Alpe d'Huez* - Oz, *Vaujany* and *Villard Reculas* – the runs down are called *Parabole* and *Forêt*. These runs will also lead you through the pine forests - but watch out for the stock fences. Nice slopes!

Freestyling_Compared with the neighbouring resort of *Les Deux Alpes, Alpe d'Huez* hasn't always been that well equipped for the snowboarding scene, although this lack of motivation has been reversed in recent years. Last year saw the beginning of this transformation process, with the development of one of the best halfpipes in France. So good that the French Olympic team set up a new training base here and the FIS World Championships found a new location. The coming season, 2003, will see the development of a new snowpark including: tables - 4m to 15m, tabletops, rails (including a mailbox, fun box, rainbow and

kinked rail) - and a boardercross course. A Rossignol test centre will also enable you to test boards, as well as providing 'chill out' sounds and a grill kitchen. The snowpark will have its own tow lift.
As a freestyler, you won't have to just stay in the park. The backcountry here offers cornices and windlips with great potential.

IN THE TOWN »
Accommodation_*Alpe d'Huez* provides 32,000 beds for tourists during the winter, a massive

number for a village with a local population of just 1,700. Accommodation includes 15 hotels ranging from 1 to 4 star and scattered throughout the village. Prices start from around €23 at Vieux Logis and go up to around €217 in the 4-star Hotel *Chamois d'Or*. So there's something to suit everyone's budget. Seven real estate agents in the village will help those of you that don't have the time to look around for accommodation. Catered holiday apartments are on offer and are also classified from between 1 and 4 stars. There are also holiday houses and club hotels such as *Club Méd*. For further information or reservations call the Tourist Office on +33 (0) 476 114 444 or visit info@alpedhuez.com

Food & Nightlife_Those catering for themselves will have their pick of a number of grocery stores, bakeries and butchers. Around the town snack bars cater for the smaller appetite - *Gaston la Gauffre* is also

open later in the evening. For those wanting to try the local cuisine, head to *La Fromagerie,* where, as the name suggests, they serve speciality cheese dishes. Sporting is also popular, with a restaurant and bar area which converts into a disco later on in the evening. But before you go off dancing, head to the *Igloo*, the *Freeride Cafe* or the *Zoo*. The town also provides 4 games arcades where PS2-addicts can satisfy their cravings.

Other Activities_The region is

© Pascal Boulgakow

also the home of a legendary stage of the *Trophée Andros* - motor racing on ice - that begins at the start of the season. If you missed the actual event you still have the chance to try the ice track for yourself - Tel: +33 (0) 476 806 997. Helicopter flights to *Deux Alpes* are also available
Tel: +33 (0) 476 806 549. If you're looking to find a seat that stays on the ground or doesn't slip around the ice track, then head to one of the two cinemas, or go bowling, play billiards, bridge, squash, tennis, swimming, curling, carting, climbing, golf, snow scooters, paragliding or archery. Further information from the Tourist Office:
Tel: +33 (0) 476 114 444
info@alpedhuez.com
Website: www.alpedhuez.com

LOCAL TIP »
Richard Aurélien, Rossignol team rider and snowpark manager_"Alpe d'Huez is a small paradise for snowboarders.

"ALPE D'HUEZ HAS BEEN WELL PROVIDED FOR BY NATURE. YOU CAN CHOOSE FROM ENDLESS FREERIDE POSSIBILITIES. EVEN A FEW DAYS AFTER SNOW HAS FALLEN, YOU CAN STILL FIND UNTRACKED POWDER. CHECK OUT THE FOLLOWING RUNS – PYRAMIDE, CHEMINÉES, COMBE CHARBONNIÈRE OR COULIOR DU CERISIER."

Especially for freeriders who have the choice of easy off-piste runs right through to highly technical backcountry terrain. Summer camps are on the drawing board as well as the development of the pipe and park where the likes of Laurent Perraud and Julien Harricot can be seen riding."

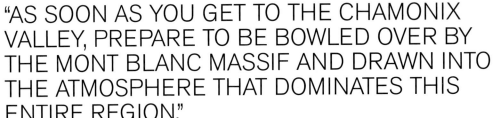
CHAMONIX
FRENCH ALPS

PROS & CONS »
+ The most unique freeriding terrain in Europe.
+ The best mountain guides in the world.
+ Wild nightlife.
+ Phenomenal panoramic views.

- Variable weather conditions.
- Ski areas are spread out and often unconnected.
- Expensive.
- Gets tracked out quickly.

CHAMONIX »
Web address: www.chamonix.com
Tourist office tel: +33 (0)450530024
Location: Chamonix
Population: 10,000
Altitude: 1035 m
linked resorts: Argentiere, Courmayeur

ON THE MOUNTAIN »
Season: December - begining of May
Lifts
vertical drop: 1035 – 3840 m
amount of lifts in total: 62
gondolas: 6
chair lifts: 16
drag lifts: 33
cablecar: 7
Slopes
amount of prepared slopes: 150 km
snowmaking machines: 47
amount of easy runs: 34
amount of intermediate runs: 27
amount of advanced runs:
Facilities
night riding: no
amount of halfpipes: -
amount of funparks: -
heliboarding: -
Lift-ticket prices in Euro
Day: 40
Week: 202.40
Season: 592

SNOWBOARD TUITION »
ESF Argentiere
Tel: +33 (0)450540012
ESF Chamonix
Tel: +33 (0)450532257
Evolution 2
Tel: +33 (0)450559022

SNOWBOARD SHOPS »
Zero G
Tel: +33 (0)450535844
Cham 7
Tel: +33(0)450559828
Sport Extreme
Tel: +33(0)450559850

GETTING THERE »
Car
Geneva - Chamonix: 81km
Geneva - Annemasse - Sallanches - St. Gervais - Chamonix
Zürich - Chamonix: 293km
Zürich - Bern - Fribourg - towards Vevey/Lausanne - Vevey exit - Martigny - Le Châtelard - Argentière - Chamonix
Milan - Chamonix: 243km
Milan - Santhià - Aosta - Courmayeur - It/Fr - Mont Blanc Tunnel - Chamonix
From southern France, drove via Chambéry and Annecy to Chamonix - Mont Blanc.
Train
Getting there by train takes ages. The closest mainline (TGV) station is Bellegarde. Access Chamonix Mont Blanc via Le Fayet.
Air
Geneva Airport
Tel: +41 (0) 227 177 111 - 1hr flight away
Shuttle bus to Chamonix - ATS
Tel: +33 (0) 450 536 397

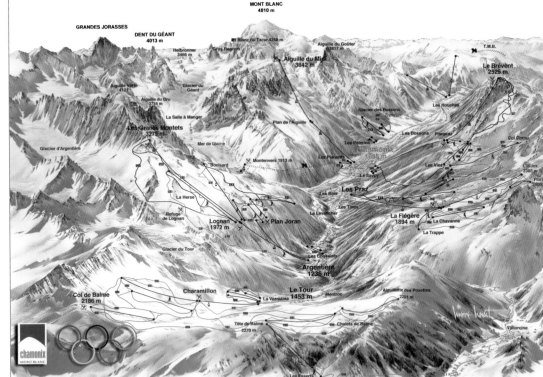

CHAMONIX »
Intro_This legendary town is widely regarded as the freeride capital of Europe. As soon as you get to the Chamonix valley, prepare to be bowled over by the Mont Blanc massif and drawn into the atmosphere that dominates this entire region. Steeped in Alpine history, Chamonix is a unique freeriding, climbing and touring area, and the home of the oldest Mountain Guides Association in the world. It's also where you'll encounter vast quantities of hardcore skiers and snowboarders all vying for first place in the lift queue.

ON THE MOUNTAIN »
Snow reliability_To describe Chamonix as a snow trap would be wrong. The piste on the Grand Montets can generally be assured of snow, but pistes such as the valley run often have very little snow because of their low elevation. There is very little snow making here. Of course, those slightly more familiar with the area will always find a bit of powder, but never without a hike. The season runs between December and the beginning of April, and on the Aiguille du Midi it lasts until May. For weather info call the Tourist Office: +33 (0) 450 530 024 info@chamonix.com www.chamonix.com

Lifts _You need to plan, as most areas are not linked to each other. Do your homework before you go riding. There are seven main areas - connected by various bus routes. Those accessible on foot from Chamonix include: Aiguille du Midi (Vallée Blanche) and Brévent (connecting lift to Flégère). Les Houches, Le Tour and Vallorcine are all accessible via the bus service. The valley station of the Grand Montets is located in Argentière, approximately 10km away from Chamonix. The best place to visit is Aiguille du Midi (summit station at 3842m) - a ride on the lift will cost around €28 and is not included in the Chamonix skipass. The summit areas of the Grand Montets and Brévent should be avoided during school holiday periods. There are a heap of good runs, and those worth mentioning are Cormu on Brévent, Index on Flégère, and the entire Grand Montets and Le Tour region. It doesn't matter where you plan to go in Chamonix, it's always best to get up early... or search for the quiet places.
Mountain Guides
Tel: +33 (0) 450 530 088

Freeriding_Chamonix's strength lies in its freeriding. You'll find some of the most extreme terrain in the world here and all just a short walk from the lifts.
150km of piste, 50 lifts and an outstanding terrain await you, from long wide powder fields to technical steep lines - it's all right on your doorstep. But remember - it doesn't matter where you go, this is high alpine terrain and any part of it outside the secured piste can be dangerous. Don't cut corners - hire a guide and you'll enjoy this amazing place much, much more.
For experienced snowboarders, the possibilities are immense. You could spend an entire week here

"YOU NEED TO PLAN, AS MOST AREAS ARE NOT LINKED TO EACH OTHER. DO YOUR HOMEWORK BEFORE YOU GO RIDING. THERE ARE SEVEN MAIN AREAS - CONNECTED BY VARIOUS BUS ROUTES."

© Jul **Rider** Laurent Gougain

and not ride a single red run or descend the same powder field twice. Some of the most interesting runs are on *Brévent*, for example *Les Pentes de l'Hôtel*, five minutes' walking distance from the summit cross at *Brévent*. At *Cornu*, you'll find some amazing lines. From the top of the tri-chairlift at Cornu, go down towards the connecting lift to *Flégère* - on the way you'lll discover some nice lines to either side of you, but be careful because heavy snow slabs tend to break off in this area. To return to *Brévent* from *Flégère*, you'll need to be at the lift before 4.30pm. On a fresh snow day, 5 minutes' walking distance from the summit of *Index*, you'll arrive on the ridge of the *Lachenal* for a great run which will take you down to the connection road. Without fresh snow, it can be a very hard mogul run.

A day trip to the *Vallée Blanche* is a must for every visitor to Chamonix. The ride on the gondola up to the summit of *Aiguille du Midi* is an amazing experience in itself, taking you up to 3842m. The »

© Peter Mathis

"CHAMONIX IS FIRST AND FOREMOST A FREERIDE RESORT, AND VERY LITTLE EFFORT HAS BEEN MADE IN THE WAY OF PIPES AND PARKS. THERE IS TALK OF A HALFPIPE AND SNOWPARK BEING DEVELOPED AT LE TOUR THIS COMING SEASON, 2003, BUT DON'T HOLD YOUR BREATH."

CHAMONIX
FRENCH ALPS

© Peter Mathis

» first section of the 20km run can be very challenging, whereas the *Vallée Blanche* itself is relatively flat. But it's still a great experience riding amongst the scenery of the biggest mountain in the European Alps. This run should only be undertaken with an experienced guide. Wear a climbing harness at all times and carry an avalanche beacon.

Queuing for the lift on a powder day at the *Grand Montets* is like being caught on the London Tube in the rush hour. However, once you get up there the area is very big, and if you get there early enough you'll always find a few runs which haven't yet been tracked out. A special recommendation is the *Pas de Chèvre*, a challenging run from the summit of Bochard, right via the *Mer de Glace* down to *Vallée*

Blanche. This is an incomparable ride, but here too you'll need a guide.

When the weather has closed in, or on a busy weekend, one option is to hit the backside of *Le Tour*, where you can ride right down into Switzerland. To get back though, you'll need to catch the train or have a car handy.

As the standard of riding in *Chamonix* is so high, following other people's tracks could prove fatal, so be warned.

Freestyling_ Chamonix is first and foremost a freeride resort, and very little effort has been made in the way of pipes and parks. There is talk of a halfpipe and snowpark being developed at *Le Tour* this coming season, 2003, but don't hold your breath. There's usually a poor excuse of a halfpipe at *Grand*

Montets (Lognan,) and that's about it. However, when there's fresh snow on the ground, there're plenty of great kicker spots, especially on the *Grand Montets* or *Flégère*.

Carving_ Carvers will be happy to hear that wide, steep, well-prepared pistes are just waiting to be torn up by sharp edges. Most carvers can be found riding at *Brévent, Flégère* and the *Grand Montets*.

Beginners_ Beginners should stick to the *Savoy* and *Planards* pistes, both of which are directly accessible from the town. Green and blue runs can be found lower down the *Brévent. Les Houches* is also good for beginners and intermediates. Generally speaking, *Chamonix* is very expensive for beginners.

Mountain Restaurants_ Like many French resorts, the mountain food here is mediocre and overpriced. The best options, though still not cheap, are the restaurants at the valley lift station of the gondola at *Brévent;* the summit station restaurant at *Flégère;* at Lognan on the *Grand Montets;* the valley lift station at *Le Tour;* and the summit of *Aiguille du Midi* - where at least the view is good. At the *Vallée Blanche*, the best rest stop is the *Requin Hut*. The most sensible solution is to eat a hearty breakfast and take a packed lunch with you.

IN THE TOWN »
Accommodation_ The cheapest accommodation to be had is in hostels: Le Vagabond or Le Bon Coin are two good places to stay in Chamonix, cheap and cheerful.

© Peter Mathis

© Jul **Rider** Douds Charlet

There are also some nice hostels in Montroc, just past Argentiére. Otherwise, take your pick of the 68 hotels in the town or book into a holiday apartment.
Reservations
Tel:+33 (0) 450 532 333
Email: reservation@chamonix.com.

Food_ There's no problem finding somewhere to eat, just finding somewhere to eat in your price range. There are a couple of supermarkets in the town centre, which is always helpful. Good sandwiches are made up very quickly at *Bélouga, Midnight Express* or *Poco Loco* - all lof them on the main street. The best pizzas in town are served up at Casa Valerio, but the biggest and cheapest are at *Pizza Hop* in *Chamonix sud*. There are numerous restaurants, but we

suggest *Le Munchie (Rue du Moulin), Jekyll (Chamonix sud),* and *Goophy* – near the train station. Traditional food is served at *Bergerie, Calèche* or *Les Drus*. In *Argentiére, L'Office* is a nice place for a good meal or a few drinks. On Saturdays there's a market in the town square where they sell local produce.

Night life_*Chamonix* is famous for its nightlife and it would be impossible to compile a complete list of places to go. After a hard day's riding you can head to the *Terrace, Micro-Brasserie, The Pub, Chambre 9,* the *Bar des Moulin* or *Cybar* - where you can also check your email. Later on, head to where the locals meet for some live acts at La Cantina. Wild Wallaby is a rowdy spot, while Goophy and Jekyll turn into bars at night.

L'Arbate has good live music. Choucas and Moonlight in south Chamonix are both great places for night owls. The Garage is the obligatory tacky tourist nightclub.

Other Activities_ Mountain biking, swimming, sauna, tennis, squash, ice skating, fitness, ice climbing, indoor climbing wall and a small skatepark are all available - centre.sportif@chamonix.com - bowling, panorama flights Tel: +33 (0) 450 541 382 - Sight-seeing tours - Mer de Glace, Aiguille du Midi... - Alpine Museum, casino, cinema. For further info contact the Tourist Office.

**LOCAL TIP »
Rossignol pro rider Nicolas Bache_**"This run is on the Brevent. It's very easy to access and it's really good fun, but the conditions

"THERE'S NO PROBLEM FINDING SOMEWHERE TO EAT"

need to be good because you're going to ride all the way down back to the town! Now, when you arrive at the top of the cable car, you'll see a restaurant on your right. Walk towards it and then behind the restaurant and carry on walking for a few minutes. You'll then come to the start of three couloirs. Pick any one, as they all join after a while into a bigger couloir with a 1500m vertical drop. It's such a good and easy run… snow allowing!"

ISOLA 2000

FRENCH ALPS

PROS & CONS »

+ High elevation.
+ Comfortable climate.
+ Sunny location.
+ Snowpark.

− Sometimes too much sun.
− Ugly concrete buildings.

ISOLA 2000 »
www.isola2000.com
Tourist office tel: +33 (0)493231515
location: Isola
population: 150
altitude: 2000m

ON THE MOUNTAIN »
season: December to April
Lifts
vertical drop: 2000-2610m
amount of lifts in total: 23
gondolas: 1
chair lifts: 10
drag lifts: 12
Slopes
amount of prepared slopes: 120 km
snowmaking machines: 165
amount of easy runs: 7
amount of intermediate runs: 35
amount of advanced runs: 5
Facilities
night riding: yes
amount of halfpipes: 1
amount of funparks: -
heliboarding: yes
Lift-ticket prices in Euro
1/2 day: 16
week: 118
season: 600

SNOWBOARD TUITION »
ESF
Tel: +33 90)493232800

SNOWBOARD SHOPS »
Ski centre
Tel: +33 (0)493231499
Ski set
Tel: +33 (0)493231277

GETTING THERE »
Car
Nice - Isola 2000 90km
Nice - N202 - Route de Grenoble - Isola - Isola 2000
Milan - Isola 2000 270km
Milan - Tortona - Asti - Alba -Madonna del'Olmo - Vindadio (It/Fr) - Isola 2000
Lyon - Isola 2000 359km
Lyon - Grenoble - Gap - Jausiers - Saint Maur - Isola - Isola 2000
Bus
Daily bus service from Nice to Isola 2000 (bus station, train station and airport). The ski bus leaves from Nice Bus Station. For ticket reservations Tel: +33 (0) 493 859 260
www.isola-2000.com
Train
Trains run daily to Nice from every major city in Europe. Info - Tel: +33 (0) 836 353 535
www.sncf.fr
Air
Nice - Côte d'Azur Airport 90km
Very cheap fares from Easyjet. Check it out at www.easyjet.com.
For airport info call: +33 (0) 493 213 030

ISOLA 2000 »

Intro_ Isola 2000 is located in the southernmost part of the Alps. The late 60s saw the development of the resort on the nearby snow covered mountain, approximately 17km away from Isola. Despite its unattractive architecture, typical of the period, the resort has all the comforts you could hope for. Its close proximity to Nice, just 90km away, makes this a great holiday destination, and on a sunny day you can see the Mediterranean sparkling in the distance.

ON THE MOUNTAIN »

Lifts & Piste_ Isola 2000 has 120km of connected piste right in the heart of pine forest. 50km of the pistes are sign posted - 7 green, 20 blue, 18 red and 5 black - and serviced by 24 lifts, including a gondola. The crowds rush to the resort early because this is when the lifts open. A fleet of 165 snowmaking machines ensure useable conditions when the natural snow refuses to fall. Six restaurants on the piste cater for the crowds.

Freeriding_ The resort is a large playground for freeriding and offers some good terrain. Its geographical formation makes for regular snowfalls throughout the entire season. You'll have a good view of the whole resort, making it quite easy to find the rideable lines, such as the chute at Mercière. This chute can be accessed by taking a short hike from the summit lift station of the Pelvos gondola. Those looking to ride the Tête Cabane or one of the Méné Couloirs should be aware that it is possible to ride way down past the bottom station as far as the road. How you get back to the resort is your problem! Due to the close proximity to Italy, you have access to helicopter transport, costing around €275.

Information
Tel: +33 (0) 493 587 724 or
Tel: +33 (0) 611 657

Freestyling_ The Isola snowpark has been classified as 'Good' by the ASF (Association Française de Snowboard). Official competitions are held here every year, and a pipe and boardercross course are available. As this guide was going to press, talks were still being held

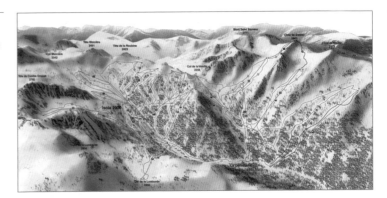

"THE RESORT IS A LARGE PLAYGROUND FOR FREERIDING AND OFFERS SOME GOOD TERRAIN. ITS GEOGRAPHICAL FORMATION MAKES FOR REGULAR SNOWFALLS THROUGHOUT THE ENTIRE SEASON."

regarding a new location for the park - so check with the resort what decision was made. The new location will also have a chalet and a sound system and someone will be employed full-time to manage the upkeep of the park.

For the latest information check with the Tourist Office
Tel: +33 (0) 493 231 515
www.isola2000.com

IN THE TOWN »

Accommodation_ Most of the hotels in this winter village are 3 or 4 star so obviously they won't be affordable to everyone. A 2 star hotel is located next to the piste and this has 36 rooms. Two apartment houses, Résid'hôtel and Les Adrets, both 3 star, offer small studios and apartments with up to 4 rooms. Between them they can sleep 1200 people. La Grange is a hut next to the summit lift station of the Grande Combe chairlift. But holiday apartments and private rooms are the most popular type of accommodation, and can be reserved (or bought!) through 4 different offices – 3 real estate

agents and one rental association.

Food & Nightlife_ Isola has two supermarkets, a number of bakeries, and specialty shops selling regional products (Tarine). Most people head to Le Crocodile, a small pub with a good atmosphere, for a drink or ten in the evening. Le Spot is also a popular bar, particularly in the afternoon. This bar is right next door to the Snowboard Shop ACS, where the friendly staff will be only too happy to sort out any problems with your equipment. The Cow Club and La Raclette are both restaurants serving local specialties and portions big enough to satisfy the hungriest appetite.

Other Activities_ Isola 2000 offers a wide range of activities including driving on ice, snow scooters (day and night), Cart X on ice, sledding, heli flights, solarium, sauna, spa, and ice skating.

Further Information from the Tourist Office
Tel: +33 (0) 493 231 515
info@isola2000.com

The Whazoo

emeric
Front

eye wear
www.quiksilver.com

PROS & CONS »
+ Good freeriding terrain.
+ Lively locals scene.
+ Protected north-facing valley.
+ Located midway between Chamonix and Annecy.

- Very little investment in the snowboarding scene.
- Very little sun.

"THE FUNPARK ON THE *AGUILLE* WAS BUILT IN 2001 RIGHT AT THE HEART OF THIS MASSIVE AREA. THE PARK INCLUDES A BIG KICKER, RAILS, HIPS, A QUARTER, AND A HALFPIPE - ALL SITUATED ON AN IDEAL 16° GRADIENT."

LA CLUSAZ
FRENCH ALPS

»

LA CLUSAZ »
Web address: www.laclusaz.com
Tourist office tel: +33 (0)450326500
location: La Clusaz
altitude: 1100
linked resorts: St Jean de Sixt,La Grand Bornard,Croix Fry Merdassier

ON THE MOUNTAIN »
season: mid December to Easter
Lifts
vertical drop: 1100 – 2600 m
amount of lifts in total: 55
gondolas: 3
chairlifts: 14
drag lifts: 35
cable cars: 3
Slopes
amount of prepared slopes in km: 132
snowmaking machines: 50
amount of easy runs: 26
amount of intermediate runs: 51
amount of advanced runs: 7
Facilities
night riding: yes
amount of halfpipes: 1
amount of funparks: 1
heliboarding: -
Lift-ticket prices in Euro
1/2 day: 20
day: 25
week: 143
season: 540

SNOWBOARD TUITION »
ESF
Tel +33 (0)450024083
PASSION GLISSECentre
Tel +33 (0)450025798

SNOWBOARD SHOPS »
Passion Glisse
Tel +33 (0)450025798

GETTING THERE »
Car
Lyon - La Clusaz: 170km
Lyon -A43 towards Chambery - A41 Annecy exit - La Clusaz
Geneva - La Clusaz: 50km
Geneva - A40 towards Bonneville - La Clusaz exit - Entremont - La Clusaz
Milan - La Clusaz: 32km
Milan - A4 towards Turin - then the A5 and follow the signs to Aosta - Mont Blanc Tunnel (It/Fr) - Sallanches - Bonneville - La Clusaz
Train
Annecy Station: 32km
Paris/Annecy takes 3 hours by TGV. Then by bus from Annecy/La Clusaz. Information: SNCF Tel: +33 (0) 836 353535
Air
Annecy/Haute-Savoie Airport: 36km
Daily flights from Paris Orly South and many other cities in France and Europe. Phone enquiries: +33 (0) 450 273006 or www.haute-savoie.cci.fr
Geneva Airport: 60km
Lyon/St. Expèry: 160km
Daily bus connections by Satobus
Tel:+33 (0) 472 359496
www.satobus-alps.com
For further info phone: +33 (0) 472 227221
www.lyon.aeroport.fr

LA CLUSAZ »
Intro_Two hours from Geneva, the mountain village of La Clusaz is set in impressive natural surroundings between Annecy and Chamonix. The main part of the resort lies on a north face which means the snow tends to retain its quality for longer, making for a good freeriding spot, despite the low altitude of the resort.

ON THE MOUNTAIN »
Piste and Lifts_With 400 hectares of pine-clad slopes, the village lies between five massifs. The resort has 56 lifts and 84 slopes that all in all stretch for more than 132km. During the past three seasons, 2 new lifts have been built to service the resort, including the Fernuy gondola (seats 16), and the quad chairlift on the *Aguille* (French for needle) which replaces the old t-bar. Fifty snow cannons are on hand to supply artificial snow in case Mother Nature fails to deliver. There's also a funpark on the *Aguille*.

Freeriding_The Freeride terrain is without a doubt the main attraction in this enormous resort. The best known area is the *Combe de Balme*, although *Bellachat* and the somewhat hidden hollow, *Étale*, are also popular freeriding areas. There are numerous secret spots which are easily accessible once you know where they are. Make friends with a few locals, and they'll be sure to show you some of these amazing runs. The *Étale* has lots of naturally formed kickers to ride, very seldom seen anywhere else in the world.

Aravis Challenge offer
Freeriding - Discovery tours
Half Day: €35 (8.45am - 1.00 pm)
Full Day: €52 (8.45am - 5.00pm)
Information: Tel +33 (0) 450 024193

Freestyling_The funpark on the *Aguille* was built in 2001 right at the heart of this massive area. The park includes a big kicker, rails, hips, a quarter, and a halfpipe - all situated on an ideal 16° gradient. The park will be further developed in 2003. Staff at the park are responsible for keeping it in peak condition, from shaping to looking after the chalet. The park has its own lift - the *Baby Lou* - reserved

C.Jul **Rider** Willy Forester

exclusively for the use of park riders. Snow making facilities will help maintain the quality of the park in times of snow no-show. This park is okay, but take a look for yourself on the funpark webcam at www.laclusaz.com.

IN TOWN »
Accommodation_La Clusaz has 22,800 beds located in 25 hotels - (7 three star, 13 two star, 1 one star, and 4 non-rated) - as well as countless chalets and holiday apartments. Accommodation can also be had at 2 apartment hotels, a club hotel, 2 sleep-over shelters,1 youth hostel, 7 houses renting out private rooms, 29 families offering a room to rent, 1 family guest house, 1 regular guest house and 1 luxury four star camping ground. The Reservations Office at La Clusaz Tour can find you good

accommodation at a good price. For example an apartment for four sharing costs around €539 per week. A privately rented apartment for six sharing costs around €474 per week. Half board accommodation in a 'two star' hotel is anywhere between €49 and €89 per night

Further info from La Clusaz Tour
Tel: +33 (0) 450 323833 or
infos@laclusaz.com
www.laclusaz-tour.com.

Food & Nightlife_You'll find no fewer than 166 shops in the area, including; supermarkets, bakeries, butchers, etc. Regional products are widely available, particularly the local cheese, which can be bought direct from the makers and is a recommended delicacy. For those looking for a good feed in a

© Pascal Boulgakow **Rider** Nicolas N'Guyen

MONT BLANC

MASSIV DE BALME 2600 m

MASSIF DE L'AIGUILLE 2400 m

MASSIVE DE L'ETALE 2400 m

MASSIF DE MANIGOD

relaxing atmosphere, head to the Restaurant *Arbè*. Most riders can be found hanging out at *Pub Salto* or at *Caves du Paccaly* during the evenings. There are a lot of discos to choose from, but none that really stand out. Your best bet is to go on a bar crawl to find which club is firing.

Other Activities_ Extra activities on offer include: snow-shoe tours, snow scooters, water fun park, sport and rehabilitation centre, ice rink, two paragliding schools, ice karting, winter 4x4 tours, winter hiking paths, sledding, nature trail, and the cinema.

More info from the Tourist Office Tel: +33 (0) 450 326500 or at infos@laclusaz.com.

LOCAL TIP »
Willy Forestier - Burton Team

Rider and a La Clusaz local_"La Clusaz is all about freeriding - the area's fantastic. When it comes to freestyle, though, not enough money's been invested in the funpark so they haven't really brought the park up to the standard we'd like."

Rudy Cohen - Salomon Team Rider and a La Clusaz local_"La Clusaz is an amazing playground. For the past three years I've been exploring this place and now I've settled here. I love the runs on *Balme* with its series of jumps, the freeride sessions at *Bellachat*, the life at the *Caves du Paccaly* and the good food at *Arbè*. The general rider standard is high, with riders such as Mathieu 'Vanoo', Willy Forestier, Nico N'guyen and Jonathon Collomb-Patton all remaining local to this area."

"THE FREERIDE TERRAIN IS WITHOUT A DOUBT THE MAIN ATTRACTION IN THIS ENORMOUS RESORT. THE BEST KNOWN AREA IS THE *COMBE DE BALME*, ALTHOUGH *BELLACHAT* AND THE SOMEWHAT HIDDEN HOLLOW, *ÉTALE*, ARE ALSO POPULAR FREERIDING AREAS."

PROS & CONS »

+ Extraordinary freeride terrain.
+ Unique position.
+ Extreme vibe.
+ Natural beauty.

- No place for beginners or intermediates.
- More or less shut off from civilisation.
- Non existent nightlife.

© Pascal Boulgakow Rider Jean Nerva

LA GRAVE
LA MEIJE_FRENCH ALPS

"THIS IS ONE MOUNTAIN WHERE SWALLOWTAIL BOARDS AND AVALANCHE TRANSCEIVERS OUT-NUMBER BAGGY PANTS AND OVERSIZED HEADPHONES"

LA GRAVE »
www.la-grave.com
tourist office tel: +33 (0)476799005
location: La Grave
population511
altitude: 1450m
linked resorts: Les deux Alpes

ON THE MOUNTAIN »
season: mid Dec. to the begining of May
Lifts
vertical drop: 1450 – 3550m
amount of lifts in total: 4
gondolas: -
cable car:2
chair lifts: -
drag lifts: 2
Slopes
amount of prepared slopes: 2
runs w. snowmaking machines: -
amount of easy runs: -
amount of intermediate runs: 3
amount of advanced runs: -
Facilities
night riding: -
amount of halfpipes: -
amount of funparks: -
heliboarding: -
Events
Derby de la Meije
Lift-ticket prices in Euro
day: 30
week: 149
season: 576

SNOWBOARD TUITION »
Alpes sport
Tel: +33 (0)476799740
Twinnel
Tel: +33 (0)476799221

GETTING THERE »
Car
Geneva - La Grave: 237km
Geneva - A41 towards
Annecy/Chambery/Grenoble - N91 via Le Bourge-d'oisans - La Grave
Bus
Connections with Grenoble and other European cities - Tel +33 (0) 476 461977 www.intercars.fr Daily bus service from the bus station at Grenoble to La Grave and return - Tel + 33 (0) 476 604680 www.VFD.fr
Train
Take the TGV that goes direct from Paris to Grenoble (3 hours)
Info - SNFC Tel +33 (0) 836 353535
Connecting bus info -
Tel +33 (0) 820 833833/
+33 (0) 476 805122; www.sncf.fr
Air
Geneva Airport - La Grave: 225km
Lyon Airport - La Grave: 171km
Grenoble Airport - La Grave: 124km

© Pascal Boulgakow

LA GRAVE »
Intro_La Grave - La Meije is a very special resort with a unique character. Located between *Serre Chevalier* and *Les Deux Alpes*, the town feels like a place lost in time. The vibe here is unlike any other mountain resort, perhaps a little like Chamonix, without the crowds. The tourism industry hasn't seemed to have made much of an impression here; and that's just the way the locals like it. La Grave should stay as it is; a town for mountain folk, soul riders and nature lovers.

ON THE MOUNTAIN »
Freeriding_La Meije - La Grave consists of almost purely unprepared terrain. On the unbroken 2,150 elevated metres -

that's about a 9km run - you'll discover the deepest of deep powder. The mountain landscape, with its elongated glaciers, deep hollows, steep chutes, towering forests and the *Meije, Râteau,* and *Girose* glaciers, is breathtakingly beautiful. There are two main runs and countless other possibilities: either you take the favoured run for riders over the *Meije,* or take the *Chancel* where the terrain doesn't drop away quite as steeply. The *Reine Meije* rises proudly to a height of 3,983m, accessed by the only lift, the Glacier gondola. In two stages, and in around 30 minutes, you'll reach the *Col des Ruillans* at 3,200m. The *Trifides* and *Dôme de la Lauze* T-bars will lift you to 3,550m, and the only two prepared

pistes, where you can then access *Les Deux Alpes*. Beware! At these altitudes it's the mountain that makes the decisions - if there's too much snow, wind or cloud, the mountain stays closed. Temperatures can drop rapidly and you need to be equipped to cope with such conditions. The famous *Derby de la Meije* is held annually at the beginning of April. This involves a timed descent with skiers, monoskiers and snowboarders charging down from 3,564m to 1,416m as fast as they can with a free choice of route. Last year 950 participants took up the challenge amid a friendly, carnival atmosphere and there was a great party afterwards.

Those of you heading to La

"LA MEIJE - LA GRAVE CONSISTS OF ALMOST PURELY UNPREPARED TERRAIN. ON THE UNBROKEN 2,150 ELEVATED METRES - THAT'S ABOUT A 9KM RUN - YOU'LL DISCOVER THE DEEPEST OF DEEP POWDER."

Grave for the first time should take a tour with a mountain guide or ride with a well-informed local.

Freestyling_This is one mountain where Swallowtail boards and avalanche transceivers out-number baggy pants and oversized headphones, thankfully. You'll not find anything built for a freestyler, neither park nor pipe, and kicker building is rare. But jibbers, don't fret! If you find yourself in La Grave and the weather is good, set your bindings back and hit the steeps. For those who have never been here, check out the video Exposed and find out just what La Grave is about.

IN TOWN »

Accommodation_The town has 2,500 beds, including; 1 apartment hotel, 16 hotels (1 and 2 star), 1 family guesthouse, 8 huts, 3 hostels (only mattresses to sleep on), and 155 holiday apartments (from a studio to a whole house). La Grave is not your typical overrun village and that's part of the appeal.

La Grave La Meije Tourist Office
Tel +33 (0) 476 799005
ot@lagrave-lameije.com
Reservations:
Tel +33 (0) 476 799772
meije.tours@wanadoo.fr

Food & Nightlife_The town is not very big and the choice of what you can eat is relatively restricted but you'll find all the necessities are covered: Grocery stores, bars, restaurants (Le Vieux Guide), bakery and speciality shops. La Grave is the total opposite to Deux Alpes when it comes to nightlife. Those looking for one will get very cold in the process.

Other Activities_Not a large choice available, especially when the lift is closed due to bad weather, but there are educational mountain or nature courses available.
Tel:+33 (0) 476 799529
cerfam.lagrave@wanadoo.fr
   The mountain guides will help you with all your other activities, especially snowboarding off piste. In La Grave you should have a guide with you at all times. Mountain Guides: Tel:+33 (0) 476 799012
meijenet@aol.com
And for those that still have the energy, there's the natural ice rink at Pas l'ne, where you'll also find a restaurant and bar.

"THE MOUNTAIN LANDSCAPE, WITH ITS ELONGATED GLACIERS, DEEP HOLLOWS, STEEP CHUTES, TOWERING FORESTS AND THE MEIJE, RÂTEAU, AND GIROSE GLACIERS, IS BREATHTAKINGLY BEAUTIFUL. THERE ARE TWO MAIN RUNS AND COUNTLESS OTHER POSSIBILITIES: EITHER YOU TAKE THE FAVOURED RUN FOR RIDERS OVER THE MEIJE, OR YOU TAKE THE CHANCEL WHERE THE TERRAIN DOESN'T DROP AWAY QUITE AS STEEPLY."

PROS & CONS »
+ Some of the best off-piste terrain in France.
+ Healthy snowboard scene.
  Lively nightlife.
+ Popular with British riders.

- Neglected park.
- Relatively expensive.
- Gets too crowded during school holidays.

"THE OFF PISTE CAN SEEM ENDLESS - BUT OFTEN GETS TRACKED OUT FAST. HOWEVER, THE PISTES FACE IN ALL DIRECTIONS, SO NO MATTER WHAT THE WEATHER IS DOING, YOU'LL ALWAYS FIND SOMETHING TO RIDE."

LES ARCS
FRENCH ALPS

LES ARCS »
Web address: www.lesarcs.com
Tourist office tel: +33 (0)479071257
location: Les Arcs
population: 4000
altitude: 1600 m
linked resorts: Peisey,Vallandry, Villaroger

ON THE MOUNTAIN »
Season: Mid December to begining of May
Lifts
vertical drop: 1600 –3226 m
amount of lifts in total: 62
gondolas: 5
chair lifts: 30
drag lifts: 28
Slopes
amount of prepared slopes in km: 200
runs w. snowmaking machines: 44
amount of easy runs: 10
amount of intermediate runs: 95
amount of advanced runs: 17
Facilities
night riding: yes
amount of halfpipes: 1
amount of funparks: 1
heliboarding: -
Lift-ticket prices in Euro
1/2 day: 24.5
day: 34.5
week: 190
season: 570
snowpark access: 22
Events
Quiksilver Slopestyle Pro
17. – 20. of March 2003

SNOWBOARD TUITION »
Pierre Blanche ESF Tel. +33 (0)479074309
Les Arcs 1800 ESF Tel. +33 (0)479074031
Les Arcs 2000 ESF Tel. +33 (0)479074752

SNOWBOARD SHOPS »
Les Arcs 2000 Extreme surf +33
(0)479077604
Les Arcs 1800 Surf center + 33
(0)479415509
Pierres blancs New school surf +33
(0)479075491
Pierres blancs Extremis surf +33
(0)479074780

GETTING THERE »
Car
Lyon – Les Arcs 212km
Lyon – A43 Chambéry - Albertville - Gilly-sur-
Isère - Les Arcs
Geneva – Les Arcs 216km
Geneva - Saint Julien en Genevois - Annecy -
Albertville - Gilly-sur-Isère - Les Arcs
Milan – Les Arcs 274km
Milan - Santhià - Ivrea - La Thuille (It/Fr) -
Séez – Les Arcs
Train/Bus
Take the train to Bourg St.Maurice and then
continue your journey by bus to Les Arcs.
Lyon – Bourg St Maurice: journey time
approx. 3hrs
Geneva - Bourg St. Maurice: journey time
approx. 4hrs
Air
Lyon Airport 199km
Geneva Airport 216km
Milan Malpensa Airport 252km

LES ARCS »
Intro_With its fantastic off-piste terrain, Les Arcs is arguably the spiritual home of European snowboarding. It was here that the legendary 80's snowboard movie 'Apocalypse Snow' was made, starring the outstanding Regis Rolland. He charged the Les Arcs steeps like no one else has ever done since – and all on a board with rubber straps for bindings! The three villages, *Arc 1600, Arc 1800* and *Arc 2000* don't win any prizes for their architecture, but they have the saving grace of being very close to the lifts. A further American-style ski village connecting to *La Plagne* is in the pipeline. Over the years, Les Arcs has been home to many a pro rider, including Axel Pauporté, Danny Wheeler, Jamie Baker, Phil Lalement, Youbi Ahmed and Franck Screm to name just a few. And not without good reason...!

ON THE MOUNTAIN »
Snow reliability_*Les Arcs* often experiences strong winds, making some areas potentially dangerous. As with anywhere else, conditions vary greatly throughout the season. The best snow usually falls in January, while in April you'll generally be blessed with sunny days. If the weather is too warm, you can always head into the shaded forests.

Freeriding_The off piste can seem endless - but often gets tracked out fast. However, the pistes face in all directions, so no matter what the weather is doing, if you know where to look, you'll always find something to ride.
  One classic is *Secteur 2000*, which has a run (located behind *Aiguille Rouge*) that has a 2000m vertical drop, but always check out the danger spots with the ski patrol before you go. A safer option would be to take the run on the Dou de *l'Homme* chairlift side. Another classic run is past the avalanche barriers to *Villaroger*, where you'll find a nice forest run with well spaced-out trees. *Forêt du Mont Blanc* is another good option, especially in bad weather. A 1km long tree run can be found below the *Lanchette* chairlift, as well as on the *Arcosses* side. Another exciting run goes from the summit of *Transarc*, heads right round the Aiguille Grive and past

© Scalp **Rider** Laurent Gougain

Peisey. But you need to know where the hidden rock faces are so the countless runs from the *Aguille* Rouge are only suitable for experienced riders, preferably in the company of a local who's familiar with the area.
  When loads of snow has fallen, you can ride from the summit of Arc 1600 right down to *Bourg St.Maurice*, where you'll end up

about 150m from the return lift. It's a really nice slope with cornices to jump off, wide clearings and long curving banks. You can't go wrong, just follow the line of the lift down.
  The terrain here is big, with loads of opportunities for epic runs. But be aware of the dangers when riding off piste and respect the closed off areas – your best and »

"THE BEST SNOW USUALLY FALLS IN JANUARY, WHILE IN APRIL YOU'LL GENERALLY BE BLESSED WITH SUNNY DAYS."

© Pascal Boulgakow

"WITH ITS FANTASTIC OFF-PISTE TERRAIN, LES ARCS IS ARGUABLY THE SPIRITUAL HOME OF EUROPEAN SNOWBOARDING. IT WAS HERE THAT THE LEGENDARY 80'S SNOWBOARD MOVIE 'APOCALYPSE SNOW' WAS MADE, STARRING THE OUTSTANDING REGIS ROLLAND. HE CHARGED THE LES ARCS STEEPS LIKE NO ONE ELSE HAS EVER DONE SINCE."

"LES ARCS HAS TWO PIPES, ONE AT 2000 AND THE OTHER IN THE SNOWPARK. BOTH ARE MEDIUM SIZED, AND NEITHER IS SHAPED REGULARLY. THERE IS ALSO A BOARDERCROSS COURSE."

LES ARCS
FRENCH ALPS

» safest bet would be to take a guide with you for a couple of days.

Freestyling_ With its varied, natural jumps, Col des Frettes is an ideal place for freestylers, and the same goes for the area around Clocheret. The park, however, has been very poor in the past for a resort of this size. Badly shaped, badly maintained, and poorly laid out. Still, things can only get better! Les Arcs has two pipes, one at 2000 and the other in the snowpark. Both are medium sized, and neither is shaped regularly. There is also a boardercross course.

Carving_ Most carvers are drawn to *Transarc*. The terrain is wide open and the pistes are generally well groomed.

Mountain Restaurants_ The mountain restaurant of Arpette has a corner snack bar serving tasty crêpes and waffles. The trip to Encolie in Nancroix is also worthwhile.

IN THE TOWN »
Accommodation_ As far as accommodation goes, *Les Arcs* itself is unappealing, partly because it's expensive, partly because of the ugly apartment blocks that predominate. For the independent traveller, the best prices and service can be found off the mountain in *Bourg St.Maurice*, where you can access the lifts within 10 minutes and save a heap of cash in the process. *La Colonne* is a good hotel/restaurant/bar.

Accommodation prices range from Apartments: from €244 to €680
Holiday apartments with kitchen: from €297 to €427
Hotels: 2 star in Les Arcs: from €317 to €370 per person
All inclusive: from €451 to €467
2 star in Bourg St.Maurice: from €33 to €40 per person

Food_ One of the best places is Bois de la *Lune* in *Montvenix*, their tureen is delicious. The *Bulldog* at *1800* Les Arcs is worth checking out, but the *Mountain Café* on *1800* is a little on the expensive side.

Nightlife_*Santa Line* is the place to go at *Arcs 1800*, where you can listen to good music and avoid the snobby scene. The *Mountain Café* opens until 2am, while *Le Gabotte*

© Jul Rider Mathieu Crepel

© Pascal Boulgakow

is the meeting place for the older generation.
    Starting at *Café Sol* in *Arcs 1600*, you need only follow the crowd later on and you'll find the local club (which constantly changes its name!).
    There are three clubs in *Arc 1800*. The locals head to *Sing Island*, especially on Wednesdays, where you'll often find a good party going on. The *Fairway* is also a good spot, especially during the *Quik* Cup. The *Apocalypse* is the tourist trap – the club itself is nice, but the music and the bouncers...

Other Activities_ Events: The *Freeride des Arcs*, organised by the *Evoie du gros* Team, and the *Quik Cup*, both held in March. Snowboard shops: *Shops Arc 1800, New School, Arc Aventures, Intersport, www.snow* and *Christina Sport* in *Arc 1600*. *Piste Noire* is the best workshop in the area. Bowling, Cinema, Squash, Arcade Hall.

LOCAL TIP »
Axel Pauporté (Billabong, A. Snowboards, Electric)_ Grand Col is a classical freeride run, but so beautiful! But before you go, ask the guides, or even better, take one with you, specially if you do the first track! Ask also for the way back, it can be painfull according to the conditions.
    At Arcs 2000, take Grand Col chairlift. At the top, walk on the left, in the direction of the pass and of the refuge (about 20 minutes walk). You're now at the top of a nice and warmfull piece of run. Take care, the beginning is more exposed. It can be dangerous to do the first track. You will end by a long left crossing towards Villaroge, quite flat, so take care of the conditions. Two chairlifts will bring you back to the bottom of Arcs 2000. While you're here, stop at the restaurant 'Beliou la Fumée', nice atmosphere and awsome Savoie food.

SNOWBOARD

magazine ✳ ✳ ✳ ✳

Document

Sno OWBOARD

putting the pow! back into powder

✳ ✳ ✳ ✳

The 2001/

British Chan

Terje in Shef

ISSUE #9 £3.10 CHEAP

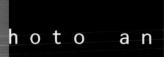

hoto an

PROS & CONS »
+ Lively village.
+ Strong snowboard scene.
+ Open both winter and summer.

– No tree runs.
– Pistes are often overcrowded.

"THE ANNUAL ORGANISATION DES MONDIAL DU SNOWBOARD EVENT, HAS BEEN GOING ON FOR TWELVE YEARS. THIS EVENT BRINGS THE FRENCH SNOWBOARD INDUSTRY TOGETHER"

LES DEUX ALPES

FRENCH ALPS

LES DEUX ALPES »
www.les2alpes.com
tourist office tel: +33 (0)476792200
location: Les 2 Alpes
population: 2051
altitude:1650 m
linked resorts: La Grave

ON THE MOUNTAIN »
season: end of Nov. to beginning of May
Lifts
Vertical drop: 1650-3650m
amount of lifts in total: 58
funicular railway 1
cable cars 4
gondolas: 2
chairlifts: 23
drag lifts: 28
Slopes
amount of prepared slopes: 200 km
runs w. snowmaking machines: 10
amount of easy runs: 18
amount of intermediate runs: 45
amount of advanced runs: 10
Facilities
night riding: yes
amount of funparks: 1
Lift-ticket prices in Euro
1/2 day: 25
day: 32
week: 153
season: 705

SNOWBOARD TUITION »
ESF
Tel: +33 (0)476792121
www.2alpes-esf.com
École de ski de St Christophe
Tel: 33 (0)476790421
www.ecole.ski.internationale@wanadoo.fr

SNOWBOARD SHOPS »
Atelier du snowboard
Tel: +33 (0)616832579
Kaemer shop
Tel: +33 (0)610565009
kaemer@vizzavi.net
Reservoir boards
Tel: +33 (0)476790234
resboards@aol.com
Sliders surf shop
Tel: +33 (0)476790915

GETTING THERE »
Car
Lyon - Les Deux Alpes 179km
Lyon - Grenoble - Exit Gap, Briançon -
Barrage du Chambon - Les Deux Alpes
Geneva - Les Deux Alpes 218km
Geneva - Saint Julien en Genevois -
Chambéry - Montmélian - Grenoble - Barrage
du Chambon - Les Deux Alpes
Milan - Les Deux Alpes 309km
Milan - Torino - Rivoli - Oulx (It/Fr) - Briançon
- Barrage du Chambon - Les Deux Alpes
Bus
Connect to Grenoble from other European
cities. Info - Tel: +33 (0) 476 461 977 or
www.intercars.fr Grenoble bus station - Les
Deux Alpes, daily connection, approx. 1 hour.
Info - Tel: +33 (0) 476 604 680 www.vfd.fr
Train
TGV direct Paris - Grenoble 3hours
Connection Grenoble - Les Deux Alpes by
bus. Info - Tel: +33 (0) 820 833 833
Air
Lyon St Exupéry Airport 166km
Connection to Les Deux Alpes with Sato
buses www.satobus-alps.com
Grenoble Airport 117km
Connect to Les Deux Alpes with the Monet
bus to the bus station, then the connecting
VDF Bus, which follows every flight arrival
from Paris. Info - Tel: +33 (0) 476 934 000
Monnet: +33 (0) 820 833 833

LES DEUX ALPES »
Intro_ Les Deux Alpes is situated in the Departement Isère, opposite Alpe d'Huez and around one hour's drive from Grenoble. An annual summer camp is held on the glacier, right next to the legendary freeride spot of La Grave.

ON THE MOUNTAIN »
Lifts & Piste_ In Les Deux Alpes, you can ride all year round – on the glacier in summer, which is accessed by the two-part Jandri Express. The resort is spread over 1200 hectares, 220km of piste and 58 lifts, including the Dôme Express, an underground railway cutting through the mountain.

Les Deux Alpes was one of the first French resorts to promote snowboarding. The annual Organisation des Mondial du Snowboard event, held in October, has been going on for twelve years. This event brings the French snowboard industry together to test boards, watch rider demos, and get drunk.

Freeriding_ This huge area opens up spots such as Fée, Chalance, Bellecombe, Selle, Vallons du Diable and the Posettes. The best lines can be found at Vallons de la Meije, where at 3600m, two glaciers almost merge. A free bus service brings you back to Les Deux Alpes, or you can walk back in 20 minutes. At the summit, you'll soon see that this is high alpine terrain, the mountain is rocky and exposed, and having a mountain guide or someone with local knowledge around would be a good idea. Reservoir Boards is a useful shop if you need your board fixing.

Freestyling_ The snowpark is situated on the Piste Toura at 2600m. It includes all the regular features: halfpipe, tables, and corners. Endless fun sessions go on here, as the DJ keeps things jumping, to the smell of a good BBQ. You'll also find a carving and boardercross course. The entire park is then rebuilt on the glacier, for the summer. At 3400m, you still have a halfpipe, tables, a big air and of course the DJ and BBQ.

Beginners_ Nursery slopes are to be found in the lower section of the resort. The local snowboard school has an internationally good reputation.

Primitive School
Tel: +33 (0) 476 790 932 or
+33 (0) 607 907 135
www.primitive-school-snowboard.com

IN THE TOWN »
Accommodation_ There is a wide selection of hotels and apartments. Hotels range from one to four stars, and their prices range between €32 and €50 per room. Apartments are obtained via letting agencies, and vary greatly in price depending on size, facilities and the time of year. You can stay in the village itself or in the neighbouring village of Venosc - a very 'alpine' village - around 8 minutes from Les Deux Alpes if

you take the six person gondola. Guests and locals receive a 20% discount on the Super Ski day pass.
Further info is available from the tourism office:
Tel: +33 (0) 476 792 200. Make reservations at the booking office - Tel: +33 (0) 476 792 438. Visit the website - www.les2alpes.com.

Food_ There are two supermarkets in the village. Countless sandwich bars sell snack food. Lovers of good Italian fodder should try the Spaghetteria. Local specialities are served at the Taverne. The Blue Salmon Farm is a good seafood restaurant.

© Jul Rider Dave Aubry

"NURSERY SLOPES ARE TO BE FOUND IN THE LOWER SECTION OF THE RESORT. THE LOCAL SNOWBOARD SCHOOL HAS AN INTERNATIONALLY GOOD REPUTATION."

© Pascal Boulgakow **Rider** Jean Valére

"THE SNOWPARK IS SITUATED ON THE PISTE TOURA AT 2600M. IT INCLUDES ALL THE REGULAR FEATURES: HALFPIPE, TABLES, AND CORNERS. ENDLESS FUN SESSIONS GO ON HERE, AS THE DJ KEEPS THINGS JUMPING, TO THE SMELL OF A GOOD BBQ."

Nightlife_ Bleuets is a cosy bar, although a bit on the small side. Le Bréselien and the Rodeo Saloon are both worth a visit, the saloon even has a mechanical bull to ride. If you're still in one piece, hit the clubs – Casa, l'Avalanche or Opéra. All three are 1-2km away, but a free shuttle is provided.

Other Activities_ After snowboarding, you can go bowling, dog sledding, ice skating, paragliding, or relax in a spa, sauna or pool, as well as cruise about on a snow scooter or practice driving on ice.
   In the summer, the glacier closes at 3pm. Your lift ticket also includes 10 trips on the summer toboggan run or the swimming pool, there is also mini golf, tennis, archery, go-karting, rafting, fishing and trampolining to choose from. A cinema, the Slalom, is also available. The summer snowboard scene has a reputation for being one of the best, and is as popular with the Brit's as it is with the French.

LOCAL TIP »
Yannick Amevet_"Les Deux Alpes is always a safe bet, you can ride all year round on the glacier and the snowpark gets better all the time. The off-piste terrain is amazing, especially the connection to La Grave. The village itself is not so attractive but the view over the Muzelle mountains at the end of the plateau is fantastic. The Aprés Ski scene is legendary, not to mention the nightlife."

"AT THE SUMMIT, YOU'LL SOON SEE THAT THIS IS HIGH ALPINE TERRAIN, THE MOUNTAIN IS ROCKY AND EXPOSED, AND HAVING A MOUNTAIN GUIDE OR SOMEONE WITH LOCAL KNOWLEDGE AROUND WOULD BE A GOOD IDEA. RESERVOIR BOARDS IS A USEFUL SHOP IF YOU NEED YOUR BOARD FIXING."

PROS & CONS »
+ Giant area.
+ Great funpark in Avoriaz.
+ Good freeriding.

− Apart from Avoriaz, the area is at a relatively low altitude.
− Often overcrowded.

LES PORTES DU SOLEIL
FRENCH ALPS

»

"TWELVE RESORTS ACROSS TWO COUNTRIES."

LES PORTES SOLEIL »
web address: www.lesportedusoleil.com
tourist office tel: +33 450740211
location: Avoriaz
population: 300
altitude: 1800m
linked resorts: Les Portes du soleil

ON THE MOUNTAIN »
Season: December -April
Lifts
vertical drop: 972-2466 m
amount of lifts in total: 211
gondolas: 14
chair lifts: 81
drag lifts: 116
Slopes
amount of prepared slopes in km: 650
runs w. snowmaking machines 400
easy runs: 170 km
intermediate runs: 380 km
advanced runs: 100 km
Facilities
night riding: yes
amount of halfpipes: 3
amount of funparks: 9
heliboarding: no
Lift-ticket prices in Euro
1/2 day: 26
day: 34
week: 184
season: 592

SNOWBOARD TUITION »
Emery
Tel: +33 (0)450741264
www.emeryproshop.com
ESF
Tel: +33 (0)450740565
www.esf-avoriaz.com
Ecole de glisse
Tel: +33 (0)450740218

SNOWBOARD SHOPS »
Emery
Tel: +33 (0)450741264
Website www.emeryproshop.com
Free Ride
Tel: +33 (0)450740036

GETTING THERE »
Car
Geneva - Avoriaz 70km
Geneva - via Annemasse - exit Thonon, Evian - Pont de Fillings - Taninges - Morzine - Avoriaz
Lyon - Avoriaz 215km
Lyon - A40 towards Geneva - via Annemasse - exit Thonon, Evian - Pont de Fillings - Taninges - Morzine - Avoriaz
Milan - Avoriaz 319km
Milan - Santhià - Lvrea - Morgex - Entrèves - Mont Blanc Tunnel - Saint Gervais les Bains - Cluses - Morzine - Avoriaz
Train
Thonon - Tel: +33 (0) 892 353 535
Cluses - Tel: +33 (0) 892 353 535
Grenoble (TGV) - Tel: +33 (0) 892 353 535
Because this resort is so big, your train route depends upon your final destination.
Further info can be obtained from www.portesdusoleil.com or www.sncf.com
Air
Geneva Airport to Avoriaz 70km
Lyon Airport to Avoriaz 209km

LES PORTES DU SOLEIL »
Intro_Portes du Soleil is situated right on the Swiss French border; a small part of the European Union inside Switzerland's closed border. Combined with the Swiss side, this is one of the largest resorts in Europe. Twelve resorts spread across two countries, 650km of piste, 208 lifts, 279 groomed runs and an area of 400km, at between 800m and 2466m altitude. Avoriaz, as well as being the highest resort in the area, has a snowpark that is widely regarded as the best in France.

ON THE MOUNTAIN »
Lifts & Piste_Despite the vastness of the area, navigation is a relatively simple affair – convenient buses and trains run between the villages. On arrival, you should study the piste map carefully to make the most of the resort. Don't forget your passport when travelling across to the Swiss side. Shuttle schedules and info is available from the local tourism offices:

Abondance
+33 (0) 450 730 290
Avoriaz
+33 (0) 450 740 211
Châtel
+33 (0) 450 732 244
La Chapelle d'Abondance
+33 (0) 450 735 141
Les Gets
+33 (0) 450 758 080
Montriond
+33 (0) 450 791 281
Morzine
+33 (0) 450 747 272
St Jean d'Aulpes/La Grande Terche +33 (0) 450 796 509
Association des Portes du Soleil +33 (0) 450 733 254
info@portesdusloeil.com

Freeriding_This whole area is a freeriders playground, a myriad of possibilities await you. Whether you're looking to slash some powder turns next to the piste, ride exhilarating tree runs, or a take a backcountry tour, this resort has it covered. The trees continue up to 1600m, and above that level, especially in Avoriaz, you'll find steep slopes with rocks to drop. Study your route carefully before taking a run – you can never be too careful. Les Portes du Soleil has runs known as Espaces Freeride which aren't groomed, but

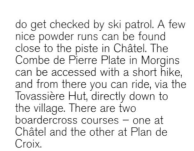

do get checked by ski patrol. A few nice powder runs can be found close to the piste in Châtel. The Combe de Pierre Plate in Morgins can be accessed with a short hike, and from there you can ride, via the Tovassière Hut, directly down to the village. There are two boardercross courses – one at Châtel and the other at Plan de Croix.

Freestyling_A few of the villages have good freestyle facilities. A 120m long halfpipe can be found in Super Châtel, along with a few kickers. The Les Gets snowpark in Mont Chéry has tables, a gap and a quarter, depending upon the amount of snow. The best park in Les Portes du Soleil, France even, is in Avoriaz, one of the original homes of European snowboarding. The pipe and snowpark are located at Arare in Avoriaz. The snowpark has various tables, rails, a good quarter, a good music system, deck chairs, and its own lift. Not surprising then, that this is home to some of France's best riders,

including Stéphane Lochon and Nico Droz. They say "Avoriaz was one of the first parks in France, and has continually developed through the input of local riders. In fact, the whole resort is a natural park, which has the added advantage of being connected to many other areas. In terms of riding, you'll always find something to do…"

And, if all you want to do is ride the park, you'll be pleased to know there's a cheaper pass that lets you do just that. Further info at www.snowparkavoriaz.com

Carving_The runs are not especially wide, which is surprising given the size of the resort. But, with over 279 runs, you'll find some room, somewhere.

Beginners_Beginners will find the Morzine area most suitable for learning. With over 3000 locals living here, it is the largest village in Les Portes du Soleil, and consequently has the most shops, and activities off the mountain.

"ON ARRIVAL, YOU SHOULD STUDY THE PISTE MAP CAREFULLY TO MAKE THE MOST OF THE RESORT. DON'T FORGET YOUR PASSPORT WHEN TRAVELLING ACROSS TO THE SWISS SIDE.."

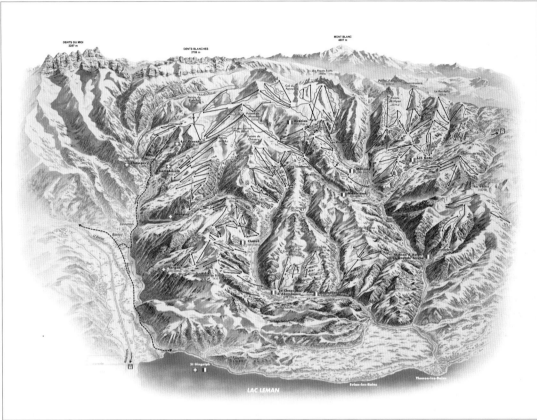

"WHETHER YOU'RE LOOKING TO SLASH SOME POWDER TURNS NEXT TO THE PISTE, RIDE EXHILARATING TREE RUNS, OR A TAKE A BACKCOUNTRY TOUR, THIS RESORT HAS IT COVERED. THE TREES CONTINUE UP TO 1600M, AND ABOVE THAT LEVEL, ESPECIALLY IN AVORIAZ, YOU'LL FIND STEEP SLOPES WITH ROCKS TO DROP."

IN THE TOWN »

Accommodation_ Avoriaz has been described as a Paris on snow, due to the large number of high-rise apartment blocks. If you opt for a hotel, you'll find plenty of choice - Les Dromonts and La Falise in Avoriaz, Fleur des Neiges Concorde, Les Airelles and Sportin in Morzine.

For further accommodation info, talk to the Association des Portes du Soleil
Tel: +33 (0) 450 733 254
Email: info@portesdusoleil.com

Food_ Self-caterers will find all they need in the various supermarkets. Try the regional cheese and sausage, available in specialist shops – just follow your nose.

In Avoriaz, Changabang is a good option for the smaller appetite. The decor is attractive, the food tasty. Les Intrets is a fondue restaurant that also serves raclette and stone grilled food at a reasonable price, as does Fontaines Blanche. The

Savoyard is a little more expensive, but the local specialities are delicious. L'Ètale is a similarly classy restaurant in Morzine.

Nightlife_ On the Châtel side, at Tunnel, the pumping music pours out onto the street. In Avoriaz, head to La Choucas – a two floored bar complete with stage to cavort on, open until 4am. For better or for worse, this is a popular spot with

the English crowd. Nightclubs such as Le Festival and Midnight Express are also an option, but we can't guarantee you'll have a good time…

Other Activities_800km of walking trails traverse the Portes du Soleil in the summer months, and some of them, including Sentier du Renard or Lac de Montriond are also

open in the winter.
The Indiana Parc in Morzine will take you back to your childhood -
Tel: +33 (0) 450 740 188
Hot air ballooning (approx. €185)
Tel: +33 (0) 450 759 400
Ice diving
Tel: +33 (0) 680 315 495
Ice climbing
Tel: +33 (0) 450 759 665
Snow kiting
Tel: +33 (0) 450 790 516

PROS & CONS »

+ Large resort.
+ Beautiful tree runs.
+ Good lift network.
+ Sunny slopes.

− Inconsistent snowfall.
− No real snowboard scene.
− Quiet nightlife.

VARS/RISOUL
FRENCH ALPS

»

VARS/RISOUL »
www.vars-ski.com
tourist office tel: +33 (0)92465131
location: Vars
population: 1000
altitude: 1650m
linked resorts: Vars Risoul– La Foret Blanche

ON THE MOUNTAIN »
season: beginning of Dec. to the end of April
Lifts
vertical drop:1650-2750m
amount of lifts in total: 56
gondolas: 1
chair lifts: 13
drag lifts: 42
Slopes
amount of prepared slopes:180 km
runs w. snowmaking machines: 45
amount of easy runs: 17
amount of intermediate runs: 77
amount of advanced runs: 10
Facilities
night riding: 12 pistes
amount of halfpipes: 2
amount of funparks: 2
heliboarding: yes
Lift-ticket prices in Euro
day: 25
week: 112
season: 515

SNOWBOARD TUITION »
Ecole du ski francais
tel: +33 (0)492465324
www.ski-ecole.com/vars

SNOWBOARD SHOPS »
Bivvi
tel: +33 (0)492466860
Les Cherpintirie
tel: +33 (0)492465210

GETTING THERE »
Car
Marseille - Vars 246km
Marseille - Aix en Provence - Sisteron - La Saulce - La Bâtie Neuve - Guillestre - Vars
Grenoble - Vars 163km
Grenoble - Le Pont de Claix - Vizille - Briançon - Guillestre - Vars
Torino - Vars 155km
Torino - Rivoli - Oulx (Fr/It) - Briançon - Guillestre - Vars
Bus
Aix en Provence bus station
Tel: +33 (0) 442 271 791
Grenoble - Tel: +33 (0) 476 879 031
Marseille - Tel: +33 (0) 491 081 640
Nice - Tel: +33 (0) 493 856 181
Train
Mont Dauphin train station, direct train from Paris and Marseille
Info - Tel: +33 (0) 836 353 535
TGV connection from Paris, Valencia, Aix, Grenoble
Info - Tel: +33 (0) 836 353 535
Oulx (Italy): TGV direct Oulx/Paris
Tel: +39 (0) 122 831 097
Air
Marseille Airport 242km
Free shuttle to Risoul every Saturday
Grenoble Airport 203km
Torino Airport 15km
Cuneo/Levaldigli Airport 96km

VARS-RISOUL »
Intro_Vars and Risoul combine to create one of the biggest winter sport regions in the Southern Alps - Forêt Blanche. This area, in Departement Hautes Alpes, the southern part of the French Alps, is well known for the highland forests which continue right up to 2500m. Get lucky with the snow, and you'll be spoiled for choice – dream tree runs and wide-open powder fields.

ON THE MOUNTAIN »
Lifts_The resort of Forêt Blanche has a lot on offer. It is a big area - 57 lifts service 180km of groomed slopes. The resort gets a lot of sun, so the snow making facilities are often much needed.

Freeriding_The area offers all different types of terrain, from forest through to deep powder fields, cliffs and chutes. Steep gnarly lines can be seen on one side of Vars, while the other side is covered in trees. Over 100 chutes await advanced freeriders; at least 20 of which are accessible from the lifts. The others are only accessible by hiking, but are definitely worth making the effort. Risoul has many forests, helping keep the snow on the ground for longer. Powder fields and cornices are also accessible. It doesn't really matter what sort of terrain you're looking for, you'll find it in Forêt Blanche.

Freestyling_The village of Risoul has tried hard to please snowboarders. Up until now, the best development has been the snowpark Surfland, which was opened in 1996. The park contains a floodlit 100m halfpipe, which is 25m wide and 3m high, a boardercross course and every type of table, kicker, gap as well as a few obstacles to ride around. A big advantage is that you can walk to the park, so you don't even need a lift ticket.
A contest, called Mix and Fly, is held every Thursday of the season. It's a mix of snowboarding and music, with international DJ's.
Another park, known as Gameboard, has been developed in Vars. The park is half in the trees and half on the piste. It consists of a halfpipe, a boardercross course, a big air, and a great sound system. The Mix and Fly sessions are held here once a week,

© Scalp Rider Wilk Forestier

throughout the season. A few well-treasured natural spots can also be found alongside the parks. Homme de Pierre in Risoul also has a few fun rails and cornices.

Carving_Vars and Risoul have several relatively wide runs, suitable for carving.

Mountain Restaurants_There are plenty around, but they are so expensive that we recommend you take your own lunch or travel down into the valley, where you don't have to blow the whole days budget in one swoop.

IN THE TOWN »
Accommodation_During high season, a room with full board can set you back as much as €123 per night. If you are on a real budget you can find rooms for as little as €30, depending on the time of year and the room. Holiday apartments can be organised through agents in Vars and Risoul; prices vary depending upon the style of apartment. Information regarding hotels, holiday apartments, hostels and guesthouses can be obtained from the respective tourism offices.

Vars - Tel: +33 (0) 492 465 131
Risoul - Tel: +33 (0) 492 460 260

"OVER 100 CHUTES AWAIT ADVANCED FREERIDERS; AT LEAST 20 OF WHICH ARE ACCESSIBLE FROM THE LIFTS. THE OTHERS ARE ONLY ACCESSIBLE BY HIKING, BUT ARE DEFINITELY WORTH MAKING THE EFFORT."

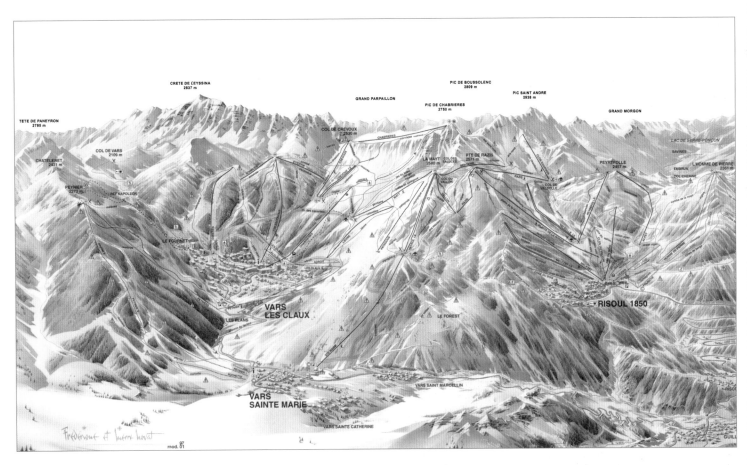

"A CONTEST, CALLED MIX AND FLY, IS HELD EVERY THURSDAY OF THE SEASON. IT'S A MIX OF SNOWBOARDING AND MUSIC, WITH INTERNATIONAL DJ'S. ANOTHER PARK, KNOWN AS GAMEBOARD, HAS BEEN DEVELOPED IN VARS. THE PARK IS HALF IN THE TREES AND HALF ON THE PISTE. IT CONSISTS OF A HALFPIPE, A BOARDERCROSS COURSE, BIG AIR, AND A GREAT SOUND SYSTEM. THE MIX AND FLY SESSIONS ARE HELD HERE ONCE A WEEK."

Food_There are more than 60 restaurants in the area. Regional specialities are served in every guesthouse and every hut. The good portions and good value of a burger and chips at Snack Attack is worth mentioning. La Delle en Pente is another. The Phil Burger is good when you're in a rush, the Barjo mountain restaurant in Vars has a large terrace in the sun with deck chairs – the ideal chill spot. There are also events on the mountain in the evenings, where you head up on a piste basher. Self-caterers will find a couple of grocery stores in Vars and Risoul, as well as a supermarket on the connecting road between the two villages.

Nightlife_Riders generally head to the Rider's Bar in Vars. The Grotte du Yéti is a good place to meet new people. The Morgan Club or the KGB is where people tend to head late evening. The Lem and the Point Show in Risoul are open until the early hours.

Other Activities_Forêt Blanche offers a number of alternative mountain activities, including over-nighting in an igloo, snowshoe tours, dog sledding and snow-mobiling. Classic alternatives such as a cinema or ice-skating are also available, as well a museum. In addition to this, Vars is one of the international mountains to hold speed skiing events.

"DESPITE THE SIZE OF THE RESORT, IT'S STILL RELATIVELY EASY TO TRAVEL FROM ONE POINT TO ANOTHER. ALL YOU NEED TO DO IS TAKE ONE OF THE 111 RUNS, ONE OF THE 77 LIFTS"

SERRE CHEVALIER
FRENCH ALPS

SERRE CHEVALIER »
www.serre-chevalier.com
tourist office tel: +33 (0)492249898
location:Serre Chevalier
population: 3500
altitude: 1200m

ON THE MOUNTAIN »
season: early December to late April
Lifts
vertical drop: 1200-2830m
amount of lifts in total: 77
gondolas: 9
chair lifts:19
drag lifts: 49
Slopes
amount of prepared slopes: 250 km
runs w. snowmaking machines: 38 km
amount of easy runs: 56
amount of intermediate runs: 32
amount of advanced runs: 13
Facilities
night riding: 15
amount of halfpipes: 1
amount of funparks: 8
heliboarding: -
Lift-ticket prices in Euro
1/2 day: 22
week: 153
season: 618
Events
World Snowboarding Championship 7th-9th March

SNOWBOARD TUITION »
Generation snow
Tel: +33 (0)492242151
www.generation-snow.com

SNOWBOARD SHOPS »
Generation Snow - surf shop
Tel: +33 (0)492242151
Krakatoa snowboard
Tel: +33 (0)492242647
Elixir
Tel: +33 (0)492244970
Elixirboardshop@aol.com

GETTING THERE »
Car
Geneva - Briançon: 267km
Geneva - Annecy - Grenoble - Gap/Briançon exit- via La Grave - Briançon
Milan - Briançon: 256km
Milan (Mailand) - Turin - Exit: Svincolo Settimo Towards Tangenziale - Montgenerve - (It./Fr.) - Briançon
Marseille - Briançon: 263km
Marseille - Towards Aix en provence - Tallard - Chorges - Savines Le lac - La Roche de rame - Briançon
Bus
Daily bus connections from Marseille, Nice +33 (0) 492 211200, and Grenoble +33 (0) 820 833833
Train
Direct Night Train Paris Austerlitz/Briançon
Grenoble - 108km: Bus-TGV - Connection from Grenoble
Oulx/Italy - 30km: TGV - Direct connection
Oulx/Paris Tel +39 (0) 122 83 1097
Air
Turin Caselle Airport 110km
www.airport.turin.it
Lyon Saint Exup_ry Airport 160km
Tel: +33 (0) 472 227221
Take the connecting Sato Bus,
Tel: +33 (0) 472 359496
Marseille Provence Airport 250km
Tel: +33 (0) 442 141414

© Scalp **Rider** Maggo Strehle

SERRE CHEVALIER »
Intro_Serre Chevalier is made up of four resorts.- Briançon (Serre Chevalier 1200), Chantemerle (Serre Chevalier 1350), Villeneuve (Serre Chevalier 1400) and Monétier-les-bains (Serre Chevalier 1500). The centres are situated within a few kilometres of each other and have been combined to create the winter sport resort of Grand Serre Che. With 300 days of sun per year, this is definitely one of the sunniest parts of the Alps. The architect, Vauban, renowned for his fortifications, played a major role in the building of the old part of town. Located a little further away are the livelier towns of Chantemerle and Villeneuve, right in the heart core of Serre Chevalier.

ON THE MOUNTAIN »
Snow reliability_Despite the size of the resort, it's still relatively easy to travel from one point to another. All you need to do is take one of the 111 runs, one of the 77 lifts or check with the timetable and be in the right place at the right time for

the connecting ski bus. The bus from Briançon runs every 20 minutes from 7.50 am until 5:30pm, also at 20 minute intervals from Monétier from 8:30am until 5:50pm. Twenty five percent of the resort is equipped with snow making facilities in case Mother Nature doesn't play her part. And, when a day is not long enough for snowboarding, during peak periods you can carry on into the night on the floodlit piste.

Tourist offices
Briançon
+33 (0)492 210850
office-tourisme-briancon@wanadoo.fr
Villeneuve +33 (0) 492 249898
contact@ot-serrechevalier.fr.

Freeriding_Serre Che is definitely one of the best freeriding areas in the Southern Alps, when the weather comes up trumps. Just a short hike opens up endless riding possibilities. The tree line rises to 2500m above sea level, opening up some brilliant tree runs where the snow remains fresher, longer. The classic backcountry freeriding

areas are to be found above the tree line. Monétier's season is generally the longest due to the better snow conditions. Should your board need repairing, head to 'Outland', a competent, well equipped shop.

Tel: +33 (0) 492 242883

Freestyling_The jib and jump fraternity will find funpark elements spread over the three towns. Big jumps and a variety of rails can be found at Briançon. Chantemerle contains a Boardercross course and Snowskate park. The best feature is definitely the massive half pipe, which can be found on the lower section of the piste in Villeneuve. The size of the pipe is perfect and on regular nights the floodlights stay on until 10.00pm. A park in the upper part of the resort was planned for 2001/02 and should be operating by next season. You may cross paths with the very friendly local stars, Guillaume Chastagnol, Sam Zartarian and British ex-pat Bud Gallimore.

"SERRE CHE IS DEFINITELY ONE OF THE BEST FREERIDING AREAS IN THE SOUTHERN ALPS, WHEN THE WEATHER COMES UP TRUMPS. JUST A SHORT HIKE OPENS UP ENDLESS RIDING POSSIBILITIES."

Mountain Restaurants_ The 250 km of piste are serviced by 77 lifts. Within the 111 designated runs, you'll find 13 black runs, 54 red runs, 23 blue and 21 green runs. When you need a break, you'll have no problem spotting the 13 restaurants next to the piste. They are not exactly cheap, but the toilets are handy..

IN THE TOWN »
Accommodation_ The hotels and apartments in Serre Che cater for everyone. Call the Serre Chevalier reservations centre:
+33 (0) 492 249880
resa@ot-serrechevalier.fr or
Briançon +33 (0) 492 210101

Restaurants & Nightlife_A number of supermarkets in Villeneuve and Briançon cater for those of you who wish to remain independent. If you can't be bothered cooking for yourself, you'll find a wide range of eating spots, from the fast food restaurants in Briançon, right down to the small, cosy eating places such as the Point Chaud, where

"THE JIB AND JUMP FRATERNITY WILL FIND FUNPARK ELEMENTS SPREAD OVER THE THREE TOWNS. BIG JUMPS AND A VARIETY OF RAILS CAN BE FOUND AT BRIANÇON. CHANTEMERLE CONTAINS A BOARDERCROSS COURSE AND SNOWSKATE PARK. THE BEST IS DEFINITELY THE MASSIVE HALF PIPE, WHICH CAN BE FOUND ON THE LOWER SECTION OF THE PISTE"

you'll eat great pizza. For a romantic meal for two, head down to the Loup Blanc in Chantemerle. La Marotte in Villeneuve is also good. Lovers of Italian cuisine should try Gusta Pasta in Briançon. The night owls meet up in Chantemerle and Villeneuve, in the Underground which includes a very international crowd; The Y(ti and the X-treme Bar in Chantemerle; the Grotte du Yeti (also international, you can even order your beers in English.) and the

Frog in Villeneuve are all popular. Once you've warmed up, you can then head on to the Bam-Bam, Bata or the Dune.

Other Activities_ If your idea of après ski goes beyond lifting a pint glass, you'll find plenty more on offer in Serre Che. Snow shoe tours, an ice race track, horse riding, ski-touring, ice skating on natural and artificial ice rinks, swimming, spa treatments, thalasso, tennis, snowmobiles, sky

diving, as well as five cinemas.

More infomation
Tel: +33 (0) 492249898
Email: contact@ot-serrechevalier.fr
or website, www.serrechevalier.com.

LOCAL TIP »
Sam Zartarian, local Pro_"The best areas to freeride are situated up high in the resort. Particularly in Monétier, you'll find some beautiful slopes. Those who like the tree runs should head to Chantemerle."

PROS & CONS »
+ High altitude.
+ Tree runs.
+ Huge area to explore.
+ Good infrastructure.

– Expensive.
– Gets crowded.

"THIS GIANT AREA INCLUDES THE WELL-KNOWN RESORTS OF MÉRIBEL, VAL THORENS, AND COURCHEVEL, ALONG WITH THE SMALLER LES MENUIRES, SAINT MARTIN AND BRIDES LES BAINS."

TROIS VALLÉES

COURCHEVAL, MERIBEL, VAL THORENS, LES MENUIRES_**FRENCH ALPS**

TROIS VALLÉES »

Web address: www.lestroisvallees.com
Tourist office tel:
Les Menuires +33 (0)479007300
Courchevel +33 (0)479080029
Méribel +33 (0)479086001
Val thorens +33 (0)479000808
Location: Meribel
Population: 12,000
Altitude: 1300
linked resorts: Méribel, Courchevel, Val Thorens, Saint Martin de Belleville, La Tania.

ON THE MOUNTAIN »

Season: December –April
Lifts
Vertical drop: 1300-3200m
amount of lifts in total: 196
gondolas: 41
chair lifts: 68
drag lifts: 87
Slopes
amount of prepared slopes in km: 600
runs w. snowmaking machines: 485
amount of easy runs: 101
amount of intermediate runs: 146
amount of advanced runs: 28
Facilities
night riding: yes
amount of halfpipes: 1
amount of funparks: 9
Heliboarding: no
Lift-ticket prices in Euro
1/2 day: 29
day: 39
week: 193
season: 850

SNOWBOARD TUITION »

Les Menuires ESF Tel +33 (0)479006143
Courchevel 1850 ESF
Tel +33 (0)479080772
Méribel ESF Tel +33 (0)479086031
Val thorens ESF Tel +33 (0)479000286

SNOWBOARD SHOPS »

Courchevel 1650 Sport Gliss
Tel +33 (0)479010943
Courchevel 1850 Snowcoco Surf
Tel +33 (0)479083761
Les Menuires Adrenaline sports
Tel +33 (0)479006249
Méribel Board Brains
Tel +33 (0)479085296
Méribel Exodus Surf
Tel +33 (0)479085372
Val Thorens Gliss & co
Tel +33 (0)479000404
Val Thorens Les balcons surf-ski
Tel +33 (0)479009080

GETTING THERE »

Car
Geneva - Val Thorens 151km
Geneva - (Swiss/Fr) - Annecy - Ugine - Albertville - Moûtiers - Val Thorens
Lyon - Val Thorens 209km
Lyon - A43 Chambéry - Montmélian - Gilly sur Isère - Moûtiers - Val Thorens
Bus
Connections every day to and from Moûtiers
Info - Cars de Belleville: +33 (0) 479 007 300
On-line reservations at www.altibus.com
Train
The closest train station is Moûtiers
Eurostar – 'London/Moûtiers' return every Saturday - Info SNCF +33 (0) 836 353 535
Air
Geneva Airport 152km
Chambéry/Aix Airport 120km, transfer with the ski bus to your village
Tel +33 (0) 479 352 174
Lyon/Saint Exupéry Airport 195km
Tel +33 (0) 472 359 496

TROIS VALLÉES »

Intro_ The Three Valleys (Les Trois Vallées) is one of the largest ski areas in the world, with over 600km of piste and 200 lifts. This giant area includes the well-known resorts of Méribel, Val Thorens, and Courchevel, along with the smaller Les Menuires, Saint Martin and Brides Les Bains. Each of the three main villages have their own valley, and each is a major resort in its own right.

Méribel sits in the centre valley. Architecturally, it has greater charm than its neighbours, and has a great party scene. It is especially popular with the British, who have re-christened it 'Merry-Hell' Courcheval, in the west valley, is made up of several smaller villages at different heights, and has some of the best terrain in the whole of France. It's also popular with the rich and famous, so expect prices to match.

At 2300m, Val Thorens is the highest resort in Europe. An excellent lift system and guaranteed snow base make this a popular resort, and package holidaymakers come here in their thousands. However, if you like your tree runs, you'd be better off staying elsewhere. In the same valley as Val Thorens, further down at 1815m, is the fourth largest resort, Les Menuires.

ON THE MOUNTAIN »

Lifts & Piste_ The Trois Vallées area is immense. Courchevel has 102 pistes, 67 lifts and 8 mountain restaurants. One highlight is the snowpark, another is the variety of backcountry terrain, which includes forests, open powder fields, rocks and chutes. 20% of the area has snow making, and by 2004 it should be up to 35%.

The Belleville Valley, which includes Saint Martin and Menuires, provides 300km of piste and endless backcountry runs, many of which remain untracked. Tree runs can be found in the lower sections of the mountain, along with a snowpark.

Val Thorens is located at an altitude of 2300m, at the foot of a glacier. 140km of pistes divide into 66 runs and one snowpark. A six day ski pass for Trois Vallées includes a day in one of the following resorts: Espace Killy (Tignes-Val d'Isère), Espace La Plagne, Les Arcs, Peisey

© Scalp **Rider** Youbi

Vallandry, Pralognan La Vanoise, Les Saisies.

Freeriding_ This is one of the biggest areas in the world, set in one of the best mountain ranges in the world – enough said.

Accessed from Les Menuires, the Pointe de la Masse in the Vallée de Belleville is a departure point for some great off piste runs down to Saint Martin - a vertical drop of around 1400m. Many more lines run down from Cime de Caron to Val Thorens – but be careful, this

area is rocky. Yet more good stuff can be found when riding from Vallons du Lou down to the lake bearing the same name.

On the westernmost point of the area, in Courchevel, a good route runs from Roc Merlet down into the Avals. A short walk will take you back to Courchevel 1650. If it's tree runs you're after, you'll need to lose some altitude. Many of the best tree runs can be found between Courchevel 1650 and La Tania, as well as in the Méribel area.

"THERE ARE NUMEROUS SNOWPARKS IN THE TROIS VALLÉES, PRACTICALLY ONE IN EVERY AREA."

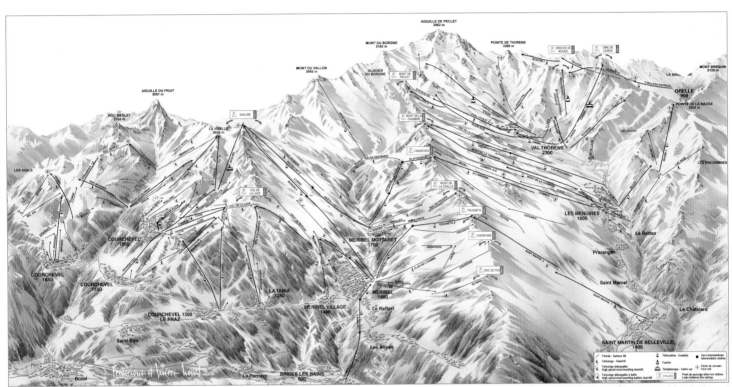

Freestyling_There are numerous snowparks in the Trois Vallées, practically one in every area. The park at Courchevel has a wide range of kickers and a large halfpipe. Méribel has two parks. One at Méribel Mottaret (2400m) – north facing, with two halfpipes, two quarters, three tables and a 650m long boardercross course. It has a chalet for riders to chill in, and two lifts service the park. The other snowpark is situated at Méribel in the Arpasson (1800m) area – consisting of a competition sized halfpipe (145m long, 20° pitch), a smaller pipe, and a 1000m long boardercross course. The snowpark at Val Thorens is situated in the Deux Lacs area. Two full time employees maintain the park, which has 10 hits, including tables, quarters and handrails, as well as a 110m long halfpipe and a kilometre long boardercross course.

IN THE TOWN »
Accommodation_The amount of accommodation on offer in Trois Vallées is huge, so we won't be able to include everything. A few pointers: Courchevel has a lot of hotels, 41 in total with 12 four star

hotels – a world record. The prices are high, with the cheapest room in high season costing around €64 per night. There are, of course, holiday apartments and guesthouses too, and you may be able to pick up a good deal. Of the four villages that make up Courchevel, Le Praz 1300 is probably the nicest and cheapest.

Méribel has the prettiest chalet style accommodation, far more charming than the 70's style blocks of Val Thorens, for instance. Méribel 's neighbouring village Mottaret is both cheaper and closer to the slopes.

Although ugly, Val Thorens is practical, being very handy for the slopes and offering plenty of decent value self-catering accommodation. Les Menuires is even more ugly, and even more cheap.

Further information can be obtained from each respective village's tourist office.

Courchevel
+33 (0) 479 080 029
www.courchevel.com
La Tania
+33 (0) 479 084 040
www.latania.com
Les Menuires
+33 (0) 479 007 300

© Val Thoren Tourist office

»

"THIS IS WHERE SOME OF FRANCE'S SOCIAL ELITE COME TO PLAY, BUT THAT DOESN'T MEAN YOU CAN'T PLAY HERE TOO. GENERALLY, THE HIGHER THE VILLAGE, THE HIGHER THE SOCIAL LADDER, AND THE HIGHER THE PRICES."

TROIS VALLÉES

COURCHEVEL, MERIBEL, VAL THORENS, LES MENUIRES_**FRENCH ALPS**

© Pascal Bougakow **Rider** Laurent Besse

» www.lesmenuieres.com
Méribel
+33 (0) 479 086 001
www.meribel.com
Saint Martin de Belleville
+33 (0) 479 089 309
www.st-martin-belleville.com
Val Thorens
+33 (0) 479 000 808
www.valthorens.com

Food_ Shopping in the villages can be done at the local grocery stores such as Forum in Courchevel, but also at the local butchers, bakeries, crêpes and pastry shops.

Dinner for two in Courchevel 1850, can be enjoyed in La Saulire, with good quality and service, but it may not fit into everyone's budget. In the area between 1650 and 1550, you'll find the prices a little cheaper. We recommend La Montagne, Le Caveau and La Cortona.

There are not quite as many restaurants in Méribel, but enough. Taverne do good pizza. For those who like Mexican food, drop in to the originally named El Poncho. This is also the right place to sample the regional delicacy Tartiflette, in any number of places. Most of the 50 or so restaurants in Val Thorens serve typically French fare: lots of fondue, a traditional favorite, and raclette – grilled cheese with potatoes and meat. And then, of course, there's the ubiquitous pizzerias.

Nightlife_ Courchevel:
This is where some of France's social elite come to play, but that doesn't mean you can't play here too. Generally, the higher the village, the higher the social ladder, and the higher the prices, culminating in champagne and canapés at 1850. Le Praz is the best combination of lively and economical.

Méribel:
This is the place where drinking is considered as important as snowboarding, where the clients rub shoulders and other body parts with the chalet girls, and the first language is English. A good night out should start in Scott's Bar and end in Dicks T-Bar, preferably with a few 'Grolle's' - a mix of liqueurs, Savoie brandy, coffee, and lemon - in between.

Val Thorens:
Has a very lively pub and club scene. French style wine bars, loud techno bars and English style pubs are all here. Spots worth a look include El Gringo, the Frog and Roast Beef, and the nightclub Malaysia.

Les Menuires:
Although not as kicking as nearby Val Thorens, there's still a few good spots to let your hair down, like the La Grotte du Yeti.

Other Activities_ There is a hell of a lot on going on in Les Trois Vallées.

With its own airstrip, Courchevel gives you the chance to take to the skies with flying lessons, helicopter flights or paragliding. It also has karting, snow shoe tours, climbing, sledding, snowmobiling, ice skating, fitness centre, squash, a cat rides, a cinema and other cultural events. At Val Thorens you can go sledding on Europe's highest sled run, enjoy a spa, sauna or Turkish bath, swim, play tennis, volleyball, football, roller hockey, squash, badminton, or table tennis. There's also a climbing wall, gym, basketball court and cinema. Les Menuires has swimming pools, ice-skating, snowshoe tours, sauna, gym, tire slides, freeride camps, snow scooters and paragliding. Méribel has much the same, as well as ice-karting.

Street clothing for girls who ride

Natasza Zurek   Minna Hesso   Keiko Yanagisawa   Christel Thoresen

Keiko Yanagisawa

NIKITA
www.nikitaclothing.com

PROS & CONS »

+ The size of the Espace Killy (a lifetime is too short to explore it all).
+ A thriving snowboard scene and a perfect snowpark.
+ High quality pistes.
–
– Expensive and posh.
– Busy, (avoid French school holidays!).
– Ugly buildings

ESPACE KILLY TIGNES

FRENCH ALPS

TIGNES »
www.tignes.net
tourist office tel: +33 (0)479400440
location: Tignes
population: 2200
altitude: 2000m
linked resorts: Val d'Isère (Espace Killy)

ON THE MOUNTAIN »
Season: November to May
Lifts
vertical drop: 1550-3460m
amount of lifts in total: 49
funniclar: 1
cablecars: 1
gondolas: 4
chair lifts: 24
drag lifts: 19
Slopes
amount of prepared slopes:150 km
runs w. snowmaking machines: 20 km
amount of easy runs: 41
amount of intermediate runs: 16
amount of advanced runs: 8
Facilities
night riding: yes
amount of halfpipes: 1
amount of funparks: 1
heliboarding: yes, but they take you to Italy
Lift-ticket prices in Euro
1/2 day: 26
day: 36.50
week: 173
season: 850
special fares Snow Space area for snowboarders: 19.5 for half day and 27.5 for one day.

SNOWBOARD TUITION »
Evolution 2
Tel: +33 (0)479400904
www.evolution2.com
The Snocool
Tel +33 (0)615345463
www.snocool.com
Snowboard Company
Tel: +33 (0)479062088
www.333school.com

SNOWBOARD SHOPS »
Bazoom (Didier)
Tel:+33 (0)479065603
Snow Barrel (Dédé)
Tel: +33 (0)479400047
Surf Feeling
Tel: + 33 (0)479065363

GETTING THERE »
Car
Paris – Tignes: 700km
Turin – Tignes: 203km
Geneva – Tignes: 180km
Take the motorway to Moûtiers and then the national road. Access is easy but avoid driving on Saturdays if you can!
Bus
Buses run from all major cities in Europe. From Bourg St Maurice to Tignes, there are daily connections via Autocars Martin (+33 4 79 07 04 49).
Train
Bourg St Maurice Train Station (Tel: + 33 8 36 35 35 35) and then by bus or car. In the winter, the daily Eurostar (www.eurostar.com) and Thalys (www.thalys.com) connections.
Air
Geneva airport: 165km
(Tel: + 41 22 717 71 11, www.gva.ch),
Lyon Saint Exupéry: 240km
(Tel: + 33 4 72 22 72 21) or
Chambery: 130km
(Tel: + 33 4 79 54 49 54).

TIGNES »
Intro_You can't go wrong here: you've got a summer glacier, beautiful high altitude freeriding, and a top of the range freestyle play area with one of the best snowparks in Europe. Tignes is a major ski resort in the French Alps and has played an important role in the history of snowboarding. From the light powder on the glacier down to the soft spring snow in Vallon de la Sache, the variety of runs and snow quality is almost endless. Four areas (Palafour, Balme, Glacier and Tovière) are connected in a star shape. You can go directly from Palafour to Balme and from the Glacier to Tovière, but you'll have to ski down to the resort itself to change from Balme to glacier or Tovière (which is a bit of pain on busy days...). The connection with Val d'Isère is on Tovière with four lifts.

ON THE MOUNTAIN »
Snow reliability_The best snow comes from the North (it's cold) or the Northeast. If it comes from the South / Southeast, it's a bit heavier and warmer. Pisteurs (snow patrol) can be found at the top of each area (the ones in Tovières are particularly freerider-friendly) and they are always happy to give you information about the snow conditions.

Lifts_On your way back from Val d'Isère, take the Borsat Express to avoid the crowds. There aren't many connection points between the two ski areas (just four) so avoid the critical time which is in the afternoon around 4pm (4.30 pm after February) when the whole world seems to be standing in front of you. If you are going from Tignes to Val d'Isère, take the Aeroski. To get to the Palafour area (where the snowpark is), be smart and take the Chaudannes chairlift in Lavachet, which is much quieter. Same story if you're planning to go to Tovières - take Paquis chairlift to avoid traffic jams.

Freeriding_Start by hiring a guide to ride the classic "North Face Trilogy" (for experienced riders only). Otherwise go to the top of the Funiculaire and further down on the left to the couloirs p1, p2 and p3 (experienced riders). The couloirs du Télégraphe are well trodden by ski instructors, they

don't hide any traps and are relatively safe.
From the top of Aiguille Percée, go straight up, walk for a while and drop down in the couloirs (steep at the beginning, so if you want to avoid it ski down the piste and connect further down under these couloirs). They lead to Les Vallons de la Sache, one of the best rides there is round here, down to Brévière area, overlooking Lake Chevril (created by a dam that destroyed the old Tignes village in the Sixties) and dotted with secret marvels all the way down. With good snow, the Grande Balme area is great too.

Freestyling_The snowpark on the glacier hosts one of the best Summer Camps in Europe and maybe you'll meet some of your favourite pros there. In the winter, Palafour's snowpark is one of a kind. Totoche looks after it with two half pipes (choice of small and large) and has established Tignes as a top European spot. The area around the snowpark is a perfect freestyle playground. Les Campanules is also a good spot, under Tuffes chairlift with lots of crazy windlips... only drawback, the lift is slow.

© Pascal Boulgakow Rider Seb Vassoney

© Pascal Boulgakow **Rider** Xavier B.

© Pascal Boulgakow **Rider** Pacome Allouis

disco in Tignes, or Caves du Lac (if you like British girls). The other pubs are considered boring according to the locals.

Other Activities_Skatepark (summertime only), cinema and a few good video game arcades. You can also go to the swimming pool or play squash at the sport centre (an interesting breathing experiment at 2000m above sea level!)

LOCAL TIP »
A warning: don't ride slopes called 'Mickey's Ears' just above the Lavachet (even if you see tracks): it looks like the easy way down to your flat in Lavachet but it is a giant mouse trap even for good skiers. The snow is very unstable here and you have no chance to gain speed and escape because it's flat at the bottom.

"THE PLANT USED TO MAKE GÉNÉPI IS PICKED IN THE MOUNTAIN AND EVERY LOCAL HAS HIS OWN SECRET SOURCES. GÉNÉPI IS A SWEET LIQUEUR MADE BY MIXING 40 SPRIGS OF GÉNÉPI, 40 LUMPS OF WHITE SUGAR AND 1 LITRE OF PURE ALCOHOL."

Carving_Go to Lanches, in Brévières area, and Palafour: the pistes are pure velvet.

Beginners_Plenty of beginners pistes from the centre of the resort Lac, easily located.

Mountain Restaurants_Take our advice; don't eat in a mountain restaurant, the food is usually bland and expensive (a Coke can be as much as 3.5 euros). Take yourself a picnic. A good local cheese (Reblochon, Beaufort or Tomme), cured sausage, some fresh bread and sit on a warm rock to enjoy the

view. It's ten times better (and cheaper). If you are really hungry or your mum forgot your packed lunch, try L'Alpage or Panoramic (with deck chairs… ahhh!). Remember the golden rule in France: the pistes are empty between 12.30pm and 2pm. Eat before, after or on the chairlift.

IN THE TOWN »
Accommodation_Le Diva and La Montana are expensive but have all le chic you need. Slightly more down market is La Tourmaline in Tignes Les Boisses village (5km but connected during the day and

until late at night by a bus service). For those who have wheels, there are a number of cheaper gites on the road from Bourg St Maurice, such as La Masure (on the way to Saint-Foys, 20 minutes from Tignes). They are more typical, cheaper places to stay and it really feels like you are in the mountains. You can easily book your accommodation by calling the Centrale de Réservation on 04 79 40 03 03 or online at www.tignes.net.

Food_For a quick lunch lounging in the sun: Le Croque Burger at the lake, l'Aspen and Evolution 2 Coffee Shop.
  For dinner: Le Stelvio (and its sidekick Boubak) for its meat cooked on hot stones and the local tipple Génépi. The plant used to make Génépi is hand picked in the mountain and every local has his own secret sources. Génépi is a sweet liqueur made by mixing 40 sprigs of Génépi, 40 lumps of white sugar and 1 litre of pure alcohol. Wait 40 days and drink! For more evening romance and live music, go to Le Caveau. Tartiflette, fondue and raclette are the traditional dishes to try. They are all based on melted cheese (beware of the overload!) with hot potatoes and cured meats.

Nightlife_Start your evening at Café de la Poste (drink and dance) or in Embuscade (pub), a local's lair. After that you don't really have much choice, so move on to the Blue Girl, one of the most active

© Scalp **Rider** David Pitschi

> "VAL D'ISÈRE HAS BREATHTAKING OFF-PISTE IN THE VANOISE NATIONAL PARK, AS WELL AS THE WHOLE OF ESPACE KILLY."

ESPACE KILLY VAL D'ISERE
FRENCH ALPS

»

VAL D'ISÉRE »
www.valdisere.com
Tourist office tel: + 33 (0)479060660
Location: Val d'Isère
Population: 1750
Altitude: 1850m
linked resorts: Tignes (Espace Killy)

ON THE MOUNTAIN »
season: end of Nov. to beginning of May
Lifts
vertical drop: 1785-3460m
amount of lifts in total: 50
furnicular: 1
cable cars: 3
gondolas: 2
chair lifts: 22
drag lifts: 22
Slopes
amount of prepared slopes: 150km
snowmaking machines: 250
amount of easy runs: 22
amount of intermediate runs: 93
amount of advanced runs: 15
Facilities
amount of halfpipes: 1
amount of funparks: 1
heliboarding: yes, but they take you to Italy
Lift-ticket prices in Euro
1/2 day: 26
day: 36.50
week: 172.50
season: 850

SNOWBOARD TUITION »
Snow Fun
Tel: +33 (0)479061679
www.snowfun.fr
Name:Altimanya
Tel: +33 (0)479062538
Evolution 2
Tel: +33 (0)479411672
www.evolution2.com

SNOWBOARD SHOPS »
Quiksilver
Tel: +33 (0)479419022
Killy Sports
Tel: +33 (0)479060553
Gérard Mathis Sports
Tel: +33 (0)479060993

GETTING THERE »
Car
Paris – Val d'Isere: 703km
Geneva – Val d'Isere: 186km
Turin – Val d'Isere: 132km
Follow the A43 motorway to Moûtiers and then switch onto national roads.
Bus
From all major cities in Europe.
You can also take a bus from the airports in Geneva. (Martin, Tel: + 33 4 79 06 00 42) or Lyon (Satobus Alpes, Tel: + 33 4 37 255 255)
Daily connections from Bourg St Maurice to Tignes via Autocars. Martin: +33 4 79 07 04 49
Train
to Bourg St Maurice train station
(Tel: + 33 8 36 35 35 35) and then bus or car (in winter, there's a direct train from London Victoria - Bourg)
Taxi numbers: AA Taxi
(Tel: + 33 6 09 51 90 99)
Bozzetto
(Tel: + 33 4 79 06 01 70)
Taxi Papillon
(Tel: + 33 6 08 99 93 96)
You can also rent cars at Europcar
(Tel: + 33 4 79 04 04 20)
Air
Geneva Airport
(Tel : +41 22 717 71 11 www.gva.ch)
Lyon Saint Exupéry Airport
(Tel: + 33 4 72 22 72 21)
Chambery Airport (Tel: + 33 4 79 54 49 54)

VAL D'ISERE »
Intro_Val d'Isère has breathtaking off-piste in the Vanoise National Park, as well as the whole of Espace Killy. The area is a freerider's heaven because of its combination of hugely varied terrain and hidden valleys. Val d'Isère is top class resort with a great atmosphere and a very well equipped ski area. La Daille is steep and busy, Bellevarde is the dramatic Olympic piste, Solaise and Fornet are more relaxed, and the glacier is always a treat. The five areas are connected and you don't have to ski down to Val d'Isère to change location. As the snow conditions can vary greatly (3cm of fresh snow in La Daille and 30cm in Le Fornet on the same day isn't unusual), keep your ears to the ground for the best conditions day by day.

ON THE MOUNTAIN »
Snow reliability_Five areas, with the potential for three different climates, make the snow capable of perfection whatever the season. The snow melts first on Bellevarde, then 10 days later on Solaise, then 15 days later on Fornet. On the same day you can ride in powder on Fornet and spring snow on Bellevarde. Consider hiring a guide to take you to the good spots. As the ski area borders the Vanoise National Park, you'll have a good chance to see wild animals such as mountain goats.

Lifts & Piste_Avoid rush hour at the Funival in La Daille. Take your car (or the free bus) and start your day in Le Fornet. Generally the lifts are really quick and there is little waiting. The Val d'Isère lift company has signed an agreement with the City Council to spend 76 million euros over the next 12 years, the equivalent of 2 modern chairlifts a year. The Fornet area is only connected to Solaise by a little tunnel and a black run. It takes quite a while to get from La Daille to Fornet, so check where the best snow is, and go directly to the spot. Tignes is connected to Val d'Isère (near the snowpark) with three lifts.

Freeriding_Endless freeriding in empty valleys is what you find most in Val d'Isère. Start on the glacier de Pissaillas or le Grand Vallon (in Vanoise National Park, the run ends up in the old village of Bonneval), towards Cugnaï or le Pays désert. Le tour du Charvet is a famous run but Fornet Wood is a dangerous lair in foggy weather with its 400 metre vertical drop. If you want to walk a bit, ask your guide to take you to Col de Pers, Pointe de Lores or Col de l'Iseran, all magnificent rides in a landscape that straddles three countries (Italy, France and Switzerland).

Freestyling_From the top of the sign to the hamlet of Fornet there are a variety of runs, mini valleys, wind lips and plenty of places to build your own kickers. On the Mathis piste, the turns in the woods have to be sharp, so you can let yourself glide with gravity and find your own natural jumps. Santons is a down-tempo riding area. The snowpark is not as good as the one in Tignes, so if you're a hardcore-snowpark-freestyler, don't stay in Val.

Carving_Start on the famous Olympic downhill run Bellevarde, the O.K (short for Oreiller-Killy) and Arcelle.

Beginners_There are 7 free lifts for beginners, 5 in the centre and 2 in La Daille. One nice peculiarity in Val d'Isère is that most of the easiest runs are found high at altitude between Bellevarde and Col de Fresse (take the Bellevarde gondola). Beginners have the rare chance to ski all day at 2500m with the Mont-Blanc and Grande Casse in view instead of being stuck at the bottom of the valley.

Mountain Restaurants_As usual, and especially in France, the food is over-priced, but you can find decent eats (meat and chips, Tartiflette and salad) for a reasonable price at the top of Solaise, in Le Signal, Col de l'Iseran or La Folie Douce on Bellevarde.

IN THE TOWN »
Accommodation_Outside Val and on the way to Fornet you'll find La Grangerie (a good spot), Le Sakura (apartments with mini-kitchens). Ask the Tourist Office for details of the apartments that come with hotel service, some are

"THE VAL D'ISÈRE LIFT COMPANY HAS SIGNED AN AGREEMENT WITH THE CITY COUNCIL TO SPEND 76 MILLION EUROS OVER THE NEXT 12 YEARS, THE EQUIVALENT OF 2 MODERN CHAIRLIFTS A YEAR."

© Scalp **Rider** Axel Pauporté

really reasonable, and they sleep either 4 or 6 people. Book with Val Hôtel (+33 479 06 18 90) or Val Location (+33 76 06 06 60) as they often have special deals (for example buy a 7 day hotel stay, get a free 6 days ski pass).

Food_La Taverne d'Alsace does excellent choucroute (Alsacian traditional dish with marinated cabbage). Nice restaurants can be found in Hôtel Le Tsantelina, L'Igloo (try the afternoon fondue) and La Pela. Avoid the restaurant in the Quiksilver shop unless you love half-cooked hamburgers! Tartiflette, fondue and raclette are the local specialities and they're delicious.

Nightlife_In a big ski resort like Val d'Isère, you often end up in the same places. Locals explain that there are countless little pubs but

the two best places to spend the night are Le Coq d'Or (opposite Hotel Kandahar), an excellent pub/disco and Dicks T Bar where you'll find a good funky atmosphere to burn all that extra energy left over after riding. Facing Le Coq d'Or, there's a yummy bakery that stays open until early in the morning - that will help cure a case of the munchies.

Other Activities_Cross country skiing, ice climbing or ice driving. The swimming pool is free with a seven-day minimum ski pass. Don't miss the Baroque church.

LOCAL TIP »
Try to get you and your mates photographed riding next to a cargneule, a typical mushroom-like rock formation in the area. It looks weird and you can pretend you've been skiing in a giant volcano.

"ENDLESS FREERIDING IN EMPTY VALLEYS IS WHAT YOU FIND MOST IN VAL D'ISÈRE. START ON THE GLACIER DE PISSAILLAS OR LE GRAND VALLON (IN VANOISE NATIONAL PARK, THE RUN ENDS UP IN THE OLD VILLAGE OF BONNEVAL), TOWARDS CUGNAÏ OR LE PAYS DÉSERT."

TICKET

INDEPENDENT

JUNIOR WORLD CHAMPIONSHIPS
FIRST TICKET TO RIDE WON BY ELIJAH TETER

10th NOKIA AIR & STYLE CONTEST
13 - 15 DECEMBER 2002, SEEFELD, AUSTRIA

X-TRAIL JAM
14-15 DECEMBER 2002, TOKYO, JAPAN

O'NEILL SB-JAM
29 DECEMBER 2002, DAVOS, SWITZERLAND

BURTON EUROPEAN OPEN
18-25 JANUARY 2003, LIVIGNO, ITALY

NESCAFÉ CHAMPIONSHIPS, LEYSIN
5-9 FEBRUARY 2003, LEYSIN SWITZERLAND

VANS TRIPLE CROWN OF SNOWBOARDING STOP 3
6-9 MARCH 2003, BEAR MOUNTAIN, CALIFORNIA, USA

BURTON US OPEN
10-16 MARCH 2003, STRATTON, VERMONT, USA

QUIKSILVER SLOPESTYLE PRO
17-20 MARCH 2003, LES ARCS, FRANCE

THE BATTLE
19-23 MARCH 2003, FALUN, SWEDEN

THE ARCTIC CHALLENGE
7-13 APRIL 2003, STAMSUND, LOFOTEN, NORWAY

FOR CONTACT INFO CHECK TTR ON: METHODMAG.COM

TO RIDE

SNOWBOARDING

THE SPIRIT OF SNOWBOARDING. S. 30 cm. JOHAN FORMGREN. SHAPER: THE BATTLE. FALUN, SWEDEN. PHOTO: ANDERS NEUMAN. DESIGN: DROIDY

TICKET TO RIDE

PROS & CONS »
+ Good spirit amongst snowboarders.
+ Sunny position.
+ Cheap lift tickets.

− Small resort.
− No nightlife.
− No shops.

ARTOUSTE
FRENCH PYRENÉES

ARTOUSTE »
artouste.tourisme@wanadoo.fr
Tourist office tel:: +33 (0)559053400
Location: Artouste
Population: 50
Altitude: 1400

ON THE MOUNTAIN »
Season: end of November to end of March
Lifts
Vertical drop: 1400 - 2400 m
amount of lifts in total: 10
gondolas: 1
chair lifts: 3
drag lifts: 6
Slopes
amount of prepared slopes in km: 21
runs w. snowmaking machines: 2
amount of easy runs: 2
amount of intermediate runs: 10
amount of advanced runs: 1
Facilities
night riding: no
amount of halfpipes: 1
amount of funparks: 1
Heliboarding: no
Lift-ticket prices in Euro
1/2 day: 13
week: 76
season: 198

SNOWBOARD TUITION »
Ecole du Ski Français d'Artouste Fabreges
Tel: +33 (0)559054197

SNOWBOARD SHOPS »
Ossau 2000
Tel: +33 (0)559054294

GETTING THERE »
Car
Toulouse - Laruns: 232km
Toulouse - Highway A64 - Pau or Soumoulou exit - Laruns
Bayonne - Laruns: 144km
Bayonne - Highway A64 - Artix - Pau - Laruns
Bordeaux - Laruns: 240km
From Bordeaux take the A10/N10/A64 - through Langon - Pau - Laruns
Pau - Laruns
From highway exit - towards Saragosse ending at Gan - N134/D934 - towards Laruns, Espagne, Col du Pourtalet.
Train
Trains run from Pau train station to Laruns - 37km Tel: +33 (0) 836 35 3535
Air
Pau Pyrénées Airport or
Tarbes Ossun Lourdes Airport 7km
Shuttle buses: Tel +33 (0) 559 02 4545

ARTOUSTE »
Intro_Artouste is a small resort with a lot of spirit. At 2100m it offers stunning views far into the distance. Snowboarders are welcome here, and there's a wealth of opportunities for freeriders and freestylers alike, indeed Artouste is the best equipped resort for freestylers in the whole of the Atlantic Pyrenees. The vibe is good, but quiet, in this typical mountain village. There are two small bars where you can go out for a beer or two, but that's about all.

ON THE MOUNTAIN »
Snow reliability_Artouste is in the Atlantic Pyrenees, and as the name of the mountain range suggests, it's near the ocean, which makes for variable weather. The big advantage of its position is that it is right in front of *Le Pic du Midi d'Ossau*. This natural barrier helps to stall the low pressure systems arriving from Spain and the northwest regions.
The disadvantage is that rain from the south is often drawn up here. So except during colder snaps, you'll generally experience softer snow conditions − not such a bad thing for freestylers.

Lifts_The gondola takes visitors up to Artouste, while on the mountain itself, 9 lifts service the rest of the resort. It's best to avoid holiday periods.

Freeriding_Although not exactly a freeride Mecca, *Artouste* is definitely a great playground, with lots of rolling terrain with hanging breaks, chutes and open powder fields offering a lot of fun. When that's not enough, you can always head to Gourette and the rolling terrain of *Pène Méne, Z or Lac d'Anglace*. Don't forget to ask about the snow conditions first, though, as it can often be surprisingly bad around here.

Freestyling_The main attraction of this resort is its facilities for the freestyler. Both the Pedrix piste at Col de l'Ours and the section at the start of the black Isards run are well set up for freestylers. You'll find a snowpark, halfpipe and boardercross course providing hours of entertainment. The park is filled with jumps and obstacles for every level of riding: quarterpipe, gap, funbox, slider, a pipe that's

"ALTHOUGH NOT EXACTLY A FREERIDE MECCA, ARTOUSTE IS DEFINITELY A GREAT PLAYGROUND, WITH LOTS OF ROLLING TERRAIN WITH HANGING BREAKS, CHUTES AND OPEN POWDER FIELDS OFFERING A LOT OF FUN. WHEN THAT'S NOT ENOUGH, YOU CAN ALWAYS HEAD TO GOURETTE AND THE ROLLING TERRAIN OF PÈNE MÉNE, Z OR LAC D'ANGLACE."

100m long, 10m wide and 1.5m high; plus a boardercross course which is 400m long, and steep. The local star, Gwen Martin, used to train here. Prepare to be impressed by the standard of riders in the park when the conditions are good. They mainly come over from Spain.

Carving_The only time carving is fun is when the kids are back in school, otherwise they're all over the place. The other problem is that if you can manage a fast-ish ride you'll be at the bottom before you can blink. Speed freaks are better served at *Gourette*. Artouste is more for freestylers.

Beginners_Except for the short towlift at *Ossau*, there's not much else around.

Mountain Restaurants_The *Panoramic*, with its cafeteria, bar and terrace offers an amazing view over the *Ossau* valley.

IN THE TOWN »
Accommodation_Artouste only has holiday apartments - for any other type of accommodation you'll need to go to Gabas or Laruns.
Gabas
Le Biscau(**) or Le Vignau (**)
Laruns
Hotel de France Lorry and Ossau:

(all 2**), Ferienheim l'Embaradère. Further information from the Maison de Fabrége Tourist Office - 64440 Artouste Tel: +33 (0) 559 0534 artouste.tourisme@wanadoo.fr

Food_There are a few bars and restaurants, with good sun terraces, right next to the piste. For a nice evening meal, head to the villages of *Laruns* or *Garas*. There's a grocery store in *Artouste* but for everything else, you'll need to go to Laruns

Nightlife_Virtually non-existent. The closest nightlife is in *Gourette*, where you can party until the early hours of the morning.

Other Activities_All 20km away in *Laruns:* cinema, sports centre with tennis courts, climbing wall, indoor pool, skate park. The second option is *Eaux Chaudes* (14km) with its health spa and hot springs.

LOCAL TIP »
Of all the resorts in the Atlantic Pyrenees, Artouste has invested the most time and money into developing a snowboard freestyle realm. Even the locals will tell you that unless it's a powder day, everything happens in the snowpark. The neighbouring resort of Gourette is much the same in this respect.

PROS & CONS »
+ A lot of variation in freeriding terrain.
+ Beautiful, typical mountain village.
+ Many other activities available.

− Small resort.
− No snowpark.
− Older lifts with limited capacity.
− Almost non-existent nightlife.

"THE CONDITIONS HERE ARE PROBABLY THE BEST TO BE FOUND ANYWHERE IN THE PYRENEES. DO NOT RELY ON THE SNOW MAKING MACHINES HERE, THERE ARE ONLY TWO OF THEM."

CAUTERETS
FRENCH PYRENÉES

CAUTERETS »
www.cauterets.com
tourist office tel: +33 (0)562925027
location: Cauterets
population:1300
altitude: 980m

ON THE MOUNTAIN »
season: end of November to begining of May
Lifts
vertical drop: 1850 - 2500 m
amount of lifts in total: 16
gondolas: 1
chair lifts: 5
T-bars: 9
cable car: 1
Slopes
amount of prepared slopes: 36 km
runs w. snowmaking machines: 2
amount of easy runs: 5
amount of intermediate runs: 15
amount of advanced runs: 2
Facilities
night riding: -
amount of halfpipes: -
amount of funparks: -
Heliboarding: -
Lift-ticket prices in Euro
1/2 day: 15
week: 121
season: 274
SNOWBOARD TUITION »
Ecole du Ski Français
Tel: +33 (0)562925816
Ecole de Ski Snow-fun
Tel:+33 (0)562925983

SNOWBOARD SHOPS »
No Limit's
Tel: +33 (0)562926248

GETTING THERE »
Car
Toulouse - Cauterets 206km
Toulouse - A64 - Tarbes - Pierrefitte-Nestalas - Cauterets
Bordeaux - Cauterets 266km
Bordeaux - Langon - Aire sur l'Adour - Tarbes - Argelés-Gazost - Cauterets
Bayonne - Cauterets 176km
Bayonne - Soumoulou - Lourdes - Argelés-Gazost - Cauterets
Train
The nearest train station is Lourdes, 30km away, which has a connecting bus service to Cauterets.
Air
Lourdes/Tarbes/Pyrénées Airport 40km
Pau Airport 70km
Toulouse-Blagnac Airport 210km

CAUTERETS »
Intro_ The snow comes in from the northwest at Cauterets. In the past, this factor made Cauterets a fairly popular winter destination as the season generally started before and ended after most of the other resorts in the Pyrenees. These days it's lagging a bit behind the times compared with other resorts, and needs to be modernised and redevelop its lift facilities.

Another problem with the village of Cauterets is that it is not directly next door to the pistes, which makes getting there slightly inconvenient as the access lifts to the resort are often overcrowded. The resort also does very little to accommodate snowboarders. But don't let all this put you off - it's still one of the more interesting places to visit in the Pyrenees!

ON THE MOUNTAIN »
Snow reliability_ The conditions here are probably the best to be found anywhere in the Pyrenees. Do not rely on the snow making machines here, there are only two of them. Further info from the tourist office
(Tel: +33 (0) 562 925 027) or from the webcam at www.cauterets.com

Lifts_ Two different lifts transport you to the resort. One is the cable car that leaves from the village and takes 12 minutes; the other is the gondola from *Cambasque,* which is roughly a 10 minute drive from the village. Both lifts are old, and when the resort starts to fill up you may find yourself standing in a queue for up to two hours. Unfortunately there is no other way up the mountain, unless you happen to have a chopper on standby. Once in the resort, things are a bit better, especially at the *Grand Barbat* chairlift.

Freeriding_ The *Grand Barbat* chairlift brings you up to the *Grand Barbat* ridge where you can take your pick of the 10 good, safe runs that all start from here. Travelling left along the path from the summit station of the *Brêche* chairlift, you'll arrive at a nice, steep slope that's wide and fat, and full of snow. There are also a few good lines under this same lift. When you head right along the path, stop at the hairpin turn and then drop over into a great snowfield. The run

© Scalp **Rider** Nicolas Watier

goes directly to the *Touyarolle* chairlift. Above, just after the beginning of the piste, you can go left. But be careful, the slope is not always stable! Ride parallel to the piste and be careful not to wander too far away, otherwise you'll have trouble getting back up. There are also a few rock ledges, where you'll need to take care. More experienced riders can look for the secret spot at *Cauterets,* Ilhéou, definitely the place to ride.

Freestyling_ The story going around at the beginning of last winter was that a new snowpark would be built with a hip, rainbow, mailbox and jukebox. But we guess

it wasn't so important to the resort, because nothing appeared. Nicolas Watier, winner of the French Cup Big Air 2000 and A Snowboard, Dragon and Gotcha Pro rider has been organising the *HO5 Freestyle at Cauterets* for the past two years. It shows the typical hospitality of the local Pyreneans.

Carving_ As you look down from the summit station terrace of the cable car, you can see that all the carving pistes are on the right hand side of the resort.

Beginners_ The *Lys* area is a dangerous undertaking in the high season, and beginners should

© Pierre Caniveng

"A SKATEPARK WAS BUILT IN THE 2001/02 SEASON WITH A FUNBOX, WALL, SPINE, PYRAMID, DIAGONAL RAMP, QUARTER, CURB AND A HANDRAIL."

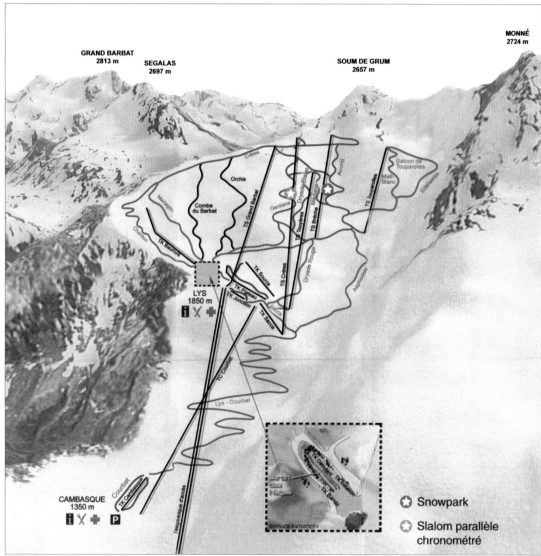

GRAND BARBAT
2813 m

SEGALAS
2697 m

SOUM DE GRUM
2657 m

MONNÉ
2724 m

LYS
1850 m

CAMBASQUE
1350 m

⭐ Snowpark

⭐ Slalom parallèle chronométré

(Tel: +33 (0) 562 925 297) is 2km away from the village, and it's a treasure.

For those catering for themselves, there are two supermarkets in the village.

Nightlife_Aside from Royalty - a bar which sometimes organises gigs - there is not much to do in the evening. There are a few other bars, but at 2.00am everyone goes home to bed. There hasn't been a disco here for about six years!

Other Activities_A skatepark was built in the 2001/02 season with a funbox, wall and 1.5m spine, a 3 sided pyramid, a diagonal ramp, a quarter, curb and a handrail. You might even get to meet Juju Maguy who lives here now. Unfortunately the park is situated on the shady side of the Gave river and is only usable in summer. You can also go and splash around in the natural thermal pools, or go skating at the ice rink. The place has two cinemas (420 seats and 190 seats) and a casino.

"TWO DIFFERENT LIFTS TRANSPORT YOU TO THE RESORT. ONE IS THE CABLE CAR THAT LEAVES FROM THE VILLAGE AND TAKES 12 MINUTES; THE OTHER IS THE GONDOLA FROM CAMBASQUE."

avoid it. Two tow lifts and two pistes can be found in the *Parc National des Pyrénées*, a beautiful spot which is ideally suited to beginner riders.

Mountain Restaurants_*Le Carrousel*: directly next to the piste, the only problem being that it's tough to get in!

Le Courbet: next to the bottom lift station of the Courbet gondola in Cambasque, is a little nicer.

IN THE TOWN »
Accommodation_*Cauterets* can accommodate 20,000 visitors and the accommodation ranges from 3 star hotels through to the family

orientated guesthouses and hostels.

If you can afford it, try the 3 star *Hôtel Résidence Aladin* (Tel: +33 (0) 562 926 000) in the middle of the village with spa baths, indoor and outdoor swimming pools, sauna, fitness room… everything your body needs.
The 2 star *Hôtel le Lion d'Or* (Tel:+33 (0) 562 925 287), again in the middle of town, is worth a visit.
La Pension Dulau (Tel: +33 (0) 562 925 105) is a nice family guesthouse run by the parents of Nicolas Watier.
All accommodation is within close

proximity of the village lift.
For reservations call
Tel: +33 (0) 562 925 027 or
Fax: +33 (0) 562 926 301

Food_For an acceptable price, you can eat at *Royalty* (Tel: +33 (0) 562 925 224) where you will also get to meet the local crew. Kebabs for the smaller appetite.
Boîte à Pizzas is also recommended (Tel: +33 (0) 562 926 363)
Chez Giovanni (Tel: +33 (0) 562 925 780) is a little more expensive, but they do wonderful pizza and pasta!
Ferme Basque

PROS & CONS »

+ A traditional Pyrenean village.
+ Lively town.
+ Very rider friendly.

– Ugly modern architecture.
– Unchallenging terrain.
– No decent snowboard shop.

"WITH ITS BEAUTIFUL VIEWS OVER THE LAKES AND FORESTS OF CAPCIR, LES ANGLES IS WIDELY REGARDED AS THE LEADING RESORT IN THE WESTERN PYRENEES."

LES ANGLES
FRENCH PYRENÉES

LES ANGLES »
www.les-angles.com
tourist office tel: +33 (0)468043276
location: Les Angles
population: 600
altitude: 1600m

ON THE MOUNTAIN »
season: November to mid April
Lifts
vertical drop: 1600–2400m
amount of lifts in total: 21
gondolas: -
chair lifts: 2
drag lifts: 18
cable car: 1
Slopes
amount of prepared slopes: 40 km
snowmaking machines: 202
amount of easy runs: 8
amount of intermediate runs: 23
amount of advanced runs: 2
Facilities
night riding: 1 piste
amount of halfpipes: 1
amount of funparks: 1
heliboarding: -
Lift-ticket prices in Euro
1/2 day: 19
week: 132
season: 240

SNOWBOARD TUITION »
Ecole du Ski Français
Tel: +33 (0)468044782

SNOWBOARD SHOPS »
No Limit's
Tel: +33 (0)562926248

GETTING THERE »
Car
Perpignan - Les Angles 91km
Perpignan - N116 - D118 - La Llagonne - Matemale - Les Angles
Barcelona - Les Angles 181km
Barcelona - Via Augusta - Rubi Norte - Puigcérda (Sp/Fr) - Les Angles
Toulouse - Les Angles 186km
Toulouse - A 620 towards Barcelona - towards Villesiscle - Lauraguel - D118 Couiza - Axat - Les Angles
Train
Mont Louis train station - Tel: +33 (0) 468 042 327
Air
Perpignan Airport 90km
Toulouse Airport 198km
Barcelona Airport 196km

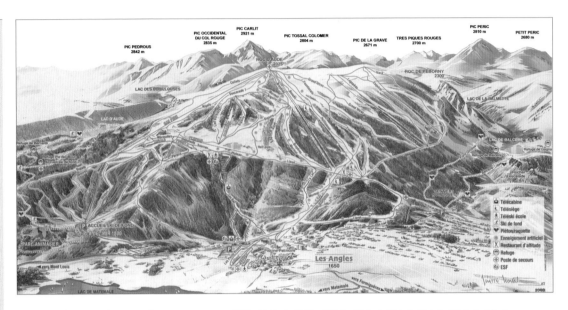

"LES ANGLES BUILT THE FIRST SNOWPARK IN THE PYRENEES BACK IN THE EARLY '90S. SINCE THEN, THE DESIGN HAS BEEN REGULARLY UPDATED AND THE PARK IS STILL THE BEST IN THE REGION. THERE'S A FANTASTIC PIPE IN THE MIDDLE OF THE FOREST, A DOZEN DIFFERENT HITS INCLUDING TABLES, A QUARTER, A HIP, AND THREE WELL PLACED RAILS."

LES ANGLES »
Intro_ Les Angles, at an elevation of 1650m above sea level, is just a short drive from Andorra and less than 100km from the Mediterranean. With its beautiful views over the lakes and forests of Capcir, Les Angles is widely regarded as the leading resort in the western Pyrenees, especially amongst snowboarders who come from far and wide to enjoy the excellent snowpark.

ON THE MOUNTAIN »
Snow reliability_ Compared with other villages in the centre of the Pyrenees, Les Angles generally receives less snow. This is due to its location on the Mediterranean side of the mountain range, but having said that, the snow that does fall remains well protected because the resort faces north-east and the shade from the many trees on the slopes keep the snow from melting. There are just over two hundred snow-making machines help keep the pistes white.

Freeriding_ Chamonix this ain't! The mountains at Les Angles are basically just big hills but the place is ideal for those into riding 30° backcountry, rather than 55° couloirs. And in any case, on a good powder day, the tree runs that head down into the village should satisfy even the best riders out there. Les Angles also has its fair share of secret spots. Ask for directions to Lake Balcere, Col Rouge or Versant Pla del Mir. After a short hike, you'll find enough rocks and steep chutes to guarantee a good time.

Freestyling_ Les Angles built the first snowpark in the Pyrenees back in the early '90s. Since then, the design has been regularly updated and the park is still the best in the region. There's a fantastic pipe in the middle of the forest, a dozen different hits including tables, a quarter, a hip, and three well placed rails. Two shapers pride themselves on keeping the hits perfect. Meanwhile, a hut pumps out the sounds of Wu-Tang, Sizzla, Fela, Prodigy and Offspring, adding to the general good vibe.

Throughout the season you'll find stress-free contests organized in which anyone can join in. The snowpark slogan for this year is 'SITAPAPEUR' which literally means 'if you're not scared…

Carving_ The pistes are well groomed with a gradual gradient,

© Pierre Canivenq

and most are suitable for carving. Some are a little tight, and on a busy day it may be difficult to find your own space.

Beginners_Beginners will love the terrain here for learning their first turns.

Mountain Restaurants_In Les Angles you can eat with your board still attached to your feet at 2000m, or ride down into the valley… The two valley restaurants, Pélerins and Jassettes, are ideal places for a friendly lunchtime break.

Another speciality at Les Angles is the Salle hors sac. Situated at the summit station of the 16-seater gondola, this restaurant offers seating for 160. Alongside the tables and chairs there's a charcoal grill and the aroma of local 'coustellous' or ribs will get your taste buds going.

IN THE TOWN »
Accommodation_A range of simple 2 star hotels, youth hostels and holiday homes can between them provide beds for 18,000 visitors to Les Angles. The three best two star Hotels are Le Coq d'Or, Le Bel Angle and Lllaret. The apartments at Panoramic are also worth checking out.
All accommodation in Les Angles is handy for the lifts.
For info call +33 (0) 468 043 276 or visit www.les-angles.com

Food_After coming down from the mountain, get stuck into an appetiser of tapas on one of the sunny terraces at the Bodéguita which has good music and is a regular meeting place for the locals. There are lots of restaurants here, but we recommend Les Arcades, Crêperie la Marmotte or Casa de l'Ours. Surf Burger will also fill a gap quite nicely.

Nightlife_Opposite Bodéguita is Tartane, very handy if you're not feeling very steady on your feet. The tacky lights projecting into the night sky will draw you in like a moth to a candle. If you like dancing the night away to house beats, you've come to the right place.

Other Activities_Bowling, ice rink, pool, fitness studio, sauna, trampolines, and a few skate spots.

© Pierre Canivenq **Rider** Jamet Huca

"THE MOUNTAINS AT LES ANGLES ARE BASICALLY JUST BIG HILLS BUT THE PLACE IS IDEAL FOR THOSE INTO RIDING 30° BACKCOUNTRY, RATHER THAN 55° COULOIRS. ON A GOOD POWDER DAY, THE TREE RUNS THAT HEAD DOWN INTO THE VILLAGE SATISFY EVEN THE BEST RIDERS."

PROS & CONS »
+ Great Après-ski scene with a southern flair.
+ A lot of variation in the terrain.
+ Strong local scene.
+ A good snowpark.

- The lift isn't right next to the village.
- Watch out for rugby players when you're out partying!

"IDEALLY SITUATED IN THE BEAUTIFUL AURE VALLEY, JUST 20KM AWAY FROM THE SPANISH BORDER."

SAINT-LARY
FRENCH PYRENEES

SAINT LARY »
www.saintlary.com
tourist office tel: +33 (0)562395081
location: Saint Lary Soulan
population: 1042
altitude: 830m

ON THE MOUNTAIN »
season: early December to mid April
Lifts
vertical drop 1700-2450 m
amount of lifts in total 32
gondolas: 1
chair lifts: 10
drag lifts: 20
cable car: 1
Slopes
amount of prepared slopes: 100
snowmaking machines: 90
amount of easy runs: 11
amount of intermediate runs: 30
amount of advanced runs: 7
Facilities
night riding: -
amount of halfpipes: 1
amount of funparks: 2
heliboarding: -
Lift-ticket prices in Euro
1/2 day: 19
week: 139
season: 365

SNOWBOARD TUITION »
Ecole du Ski Français
Tel: +33 (0)562984401
Ecole de Ski Internationale
Tel: +33 (0)562984580

SNOWBOARD SHOPS »
Snow Problemo
Tel: +33 (0)562400382

GETTING THERE »
Car
Toulouse - Saint Lary: 157km
Toulouse - towards Bayonne, Pau, Tarbes - via Lannemezan - Saint Lary
Barcelona - Saint Lary: 347km
Barcelona - take the NII via Igualada - Cervera - Lérida - Barbastro - Túnel de Bielsa (Sp/Fr) - Saint Lary
Bayonne - Saint Lary: 214km
Bayonne- Bretelle A64 - Lannemezan - Saint Lary. Take the A64 from Bayonne - Bretelle - Lannemezan - Saint Lary
Train/Bus
By the Atlantique Paris - Tarbes high speed link (TVG), then by the connecting bus to Saint Lary
Air
Tarbes Ossun Lourdes Airport 80km
Pau Uzein Airport 100km
Toulouse Balgnac Airport 150km

© Pierre Canivenq **Rider** Christoper Cecchinato

SAINT-LARY »
Intro_Saint-Lary is a scenic mountain village and a popular destination with winter sports enthusiasts. It offers a wide range of different activities and is ideally situated in the beautiful Aure valley, just 20km away from the Spanish border. The resort itself has many technical spots, and, thanks to input from the locals, the town now also caters for the snowboard scene.

ON THE MOUNTAIN »
Snow reliability_This resort should be outside the influence of any low-pressure system blowing in from the sea.. This generally means decent snowfall during the winter season. The only problem is that the warm temperatures here cause the snow to turn wet which makes sitting on it a rather damp experience. The best conditions are usually in March.

Tourist Office
Tel: +33 (0) 562 395 081
www.saintlary.com - the site shows footage from two web cams installed directly on the piste.

Lifts_The (relatively long) gondola, which leaves from the outskirts of the village, carries people up to *Plat d'Adet* as well as to the accommodation, bars and shop on the mountain. Unfortunately, at this elevation, you'll not find optimum conditions for off piste riding. But you can make the 10 minute drive up to *Espiaube* above the *Plat d'Adet*. A gondola starts from here that will take you directly to the snowpark and the freeride terrain of *Saint Lary*. Holiday periods should be avoided as it usually gets very crowded.

Freeriding_Try to remain at Terranère and the surrounding areas, or other boarder spots such as *Vallon de l'Oulle* (in the Pyrenean National Park) or at *Combe d'Aulon*. For experienced riders, it's worth booking a guide for a day to explore the hidden treasures of *Saint Lary*. You won't really want to spend time at *Plat d'Adet*, as the snow is not especially good. We'd recommend *Espiaube*, then a ride with the gondola to the snowpark and from

here into the best freeriding parts of the resort.

Freestyling_The snowpark and boardercross course are up on the summit of *Espiaube*. The halfpipe is located a little lower down and on the opposite slope to protect it from direct sunlight. *Saint Lary* has a great park and the various events draw a good standard of rider. The boardercross World Champion, Xavier Delerue says, "I was born and raised in Saint Lary, for me it is a source of inspiration and almost like a mother."

Carving_Carvers go out to play in *Espiaube*. Take special note of the region around Terra Nère.

Beginners_The snowboard school at *Saint Lary* offers first class snowboarding lessons. The beginner terrain up on the ridge of Les Saboures is ideally suited to learning, the piste being housed in a small bowl and with just a slight gradient.

Mountain Restaurants_We recommend the *Chalet Lou Rider* in *Espiaube*: the meeting place for

© Pierre Cariverq

"SAINT LARY HAS A GREAT PARK AND THE VARIOUS EVENTS DRAW A GOOD STANDARD OF RIDER."

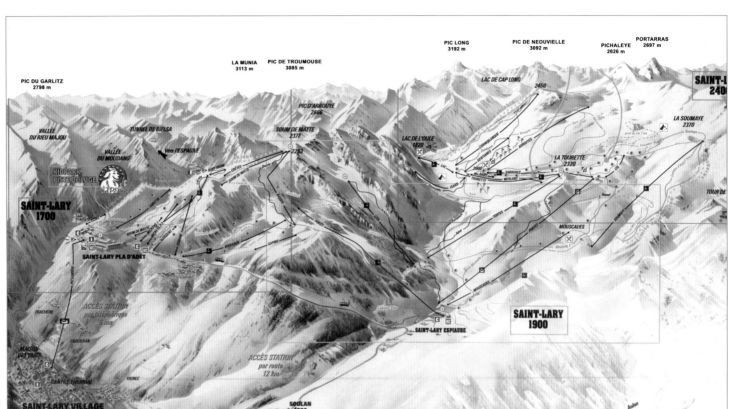

locals from the *Brown Bears*. Comfortable and friendly, with good food and a sunny terrace. The *Chalet de l'Oule* is next to the lake at 1800m. *Les Trois Guides - Saint Lary* 1900m - is also worth a visit.

IN THE TOWN »
Accommodation_*Chalet Lou Rider* in *Espiaube* is a fantastic place, immediately next to the lift in Espiaube. Cheapish and cosy, good food, and the parties and concerts in the evening will keep boredom at bay.

Chalet Lou Rider
Tel: +33 (0) 562 984 393
Fax: +33 (0) 562 984 102
Email: jml@lourider.com

La Refuge is also nice
Tel: +33 (0) 562 394 681
Fax: +33 (0) 562 400 328
Email: ahoc.carole@wanadoo.fr

Most of the accommodation is in the middle of the village or next to the valley lift stations serving the three resort areas. Reservations Tel: +33 (0) 562 394 092
Email: info@saintlary-resrvation.com

"TRY TO REMAIN AT TERRANÈRE AND THE SURROUNDING AREAS, OR OTHER BOARDER SPOTS SUCH AS VALLON DE L'OULLE OR AT COMBE D'AULON. FOR EXPERIENCED RIDERS, IT'S WORTH BOOKING A GUIDE."

Food_We recommend a visit to *La Grange* or *Pic Assiette,* both on the outskirts of the village. There are three options in the town centre; *La Sandwicherie* - under the trees, and where all the riders go - Spanish Tapas at *Gros Minet,* or the swanky *Les Chandelles* restaurant. The town also has a couple of supermarkets and a few shops.

Nightlife_Most of the activity is happening in the old part of the village. Start the night at the *Latino Bar,* which is under *Les Chandelles,* or at *Izard* or at *Desman KF.* For those whose stamina can take it, you'll probably

end up at Luna - where the music is sometimes great and sometimes unbearable, but it won't really matter anyway because most times you'll still have a fun evening and in any case you probably won't remember it in the morning.

Other Activities_To relax after a strenuous day, head to the landscaped swimming area at the Centre de Remise en Forme (fitness centre). It can also be fun to ride on Skidoos after the piste closes at 5pm, but only with a guide. Tel: +33 (0) 559 846 180 or +33 (0) 612 034 978.
For pure adventure try a ride behind the dog sleds at Vallon du

Portet - an amazing feeling. Set up your own bivouac or spend the night in a tent playing North Pole explorer, building igloos with overnight accommodation in an 'Eskimo hotel'.
Tel: +33 (0) 556 617 880 or +33 (0) 687 141 217

LOCAL TIP »
Chalet Lou Rider at Espiaube, is the best place to crash on the mountain. You can talk to Jean Mi about everything, and if your'e lucky, you'll even have him showing you the best riding spots or explaining the dangers of the area and later on dragging you through the bars in the village.

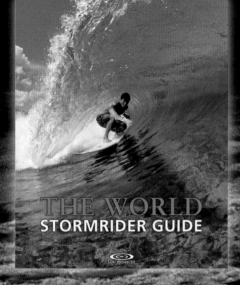

THE WORLD
STORMRIDER GUIDE

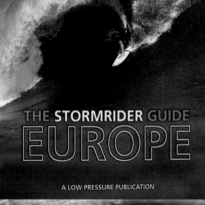

THE STORMRIDER GUIDE
EUROPE

A LOW PRESSURE PUBLICATION

If you don't go,

THE STORMRIDER GUIDE
NORTH AMERICA

you don't know

GERMANY
110-121

GARMISCH-PARTENKIRCHEN
DAMMKAR-MITTENWALD

OBERSTDORF
SUDELFELD

SPITZINGSEE-SCHLIERSEE

110 | 111
GERMANY
MAP

GERMANY MAP

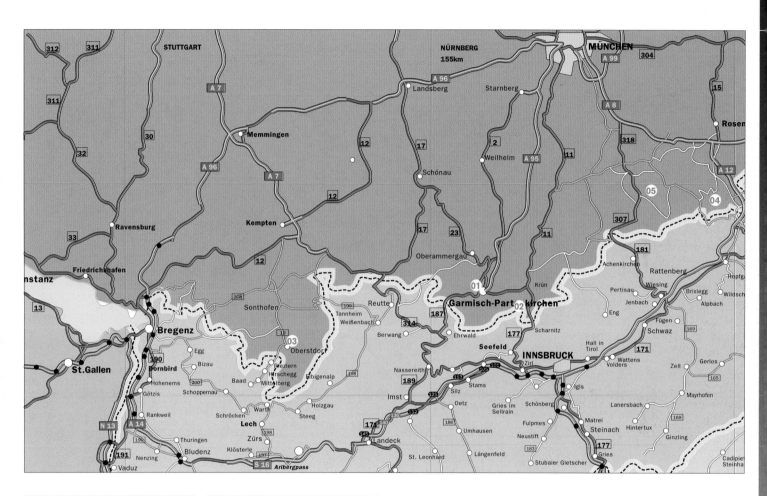

GERMANY »

Intro_The Alps only just creep across the southern border into Germany. Although the mountains here don't really compare to the neighbouring countries of Austria and Switzerland, there are a few fun areas to ride. The main place for snowboarders to check out is definitely Garmisch-Partenkirchen, where during the summer months, you'll find the yearly Gap 1328 Camp on the Zugspitze, Germany's highest mountain and only glacier. This part of the Alps doesn't really have big resorts; instead you'll stumble upon little treasures, like Dammkar - one mountain, one gondola, pure freeriding, and no groomed piste. Some of Germany's resorts, including Garmisch-Partenkirchen, lie within a one-hour drive from the Bavarian capital, Munich. This creates a perfect opportunity for city dwellers, and travellers, to stop over for a couple of days in the mountains.

INFORMATION »

Official Name_Bundesrepublik Deutschland
Capital_Berlin
Population_82,163 Million
Land mass_357,022 km2
Language(s)_German
Currency_1 Euro = 100 Cent
Highest mountain_Zugspitze 2963 m
International country code_0049
Police_110
Ambulance_110
Fire Brigade_112
Tourist Board_Germany Tourism
Tel: +49 (0)231 1816-186
www.germany-tourism.de
Train Info_Tel: (0800) 1 50 70 90
www.bahn.de
Weather Info_www.wetter.de

LOCATIONS »

01 GARMISCH-PARTENKIRCHEN
02 DAMMKAR-MITTENWALD
03 OBERSTDORF
04 SUDELFELD
05 SPITZINGSEE-SCHLIERSEE

"VERY FEW TOURISTS FIND THEIR WAY ACROSS TO WANK, WHICH IS GREAT"

PROS & CONS »
+ A well shaped park and superpipe on the Zugspitzplatt.
+ Glacial resort - the Zugspitze.
+ Annual GAP1328 summer camp / park.

− Overcrowded at weekends / holiday periods.
− Not cheap.
− Not many happenin' bars (unless you get them going yourself!).

GARMISCH
PARTENKIRCHEN_**GERMANY**

»

GARMISCH »
www.garmisch-partenkirchen.de
tourist Information tel: +49 (0)8821180700
location: Garmisch-Partenkirchen
population: 27.000
altitude: 720m
linked resorts: Zugspitze, Classic tour
(Alpspitze, Hausberg, Kreuzeck, Wank, Eckbauer)

ON THE MOUNTAIN »
season: beginning of November until beginning of May
Lifts
vertical drop:1334–2830m
amount of lifts in total: 38
gondolas: 8
chair lifts: 5
drag lifts: 24
rack rail: 1
Slopes
amount of prepared slopes: 72 km
runs w. snowmaking machines: 13
easy runs: 10.5 km
intermediate runs: 51.1 km
advanced runs: 10.4 km
Facilities
night riding: -
amount of halfpipes: 1
amount of funparks: 1
Heliboarding: -
Lift-ticket prices in Euro
1/2 day: 20
day: 34
week: 147
season: 529
special fares: 27 (Classic- AREA) 34 (Zugspitz-AREA)

SNOWBOARD TUITION »
Skischule Garmisch-Partenkirchen
Tel +49 (0)88214931
www.skischule-gap.de
Skischule Sport-Total
Tel: +49 (0)88211425
www.agentursporttotal.de

SNOWBOARD SHOPS »
Edge to Edge
Tel: +49 (0)882159501
www.snowboard-schule.de
Snowboard and Ski-Center Zugspitze
Tel: +49 (0)882174505
www.skiverleih-zugspitze.de

GETTING THERE »
Car
Munich – Garmisch-Partenkirchen: 88km
Munich – A95 GAP – Oberau – Garmisch-Partenkirchen
Innsbruck – Garmisch-Partenkirchen: 60km
Innsbruck – Zirl – Seefeld – Mittenwald – Garmisch-Partenkirchen
Train
Munich – Garmisch-Partenkirchen 1h 20min
Innsbruck – Mittenwald – Garmisch-Partenkirchen
Air
Munich Airport 126km
Innsbruck Airport 61km

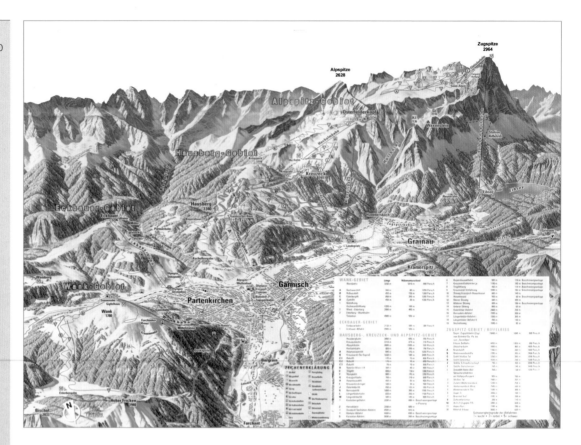

GARMISCH »
Intro_Garmisch–Partenkirchen is the top spot for snowboarding in the German Alps. You'll find everything you could want here, from a superpipe, a World Cup downhill run, powder runs to the Gap 1328 summer camp up on the Zugspitze, Germany's only glacial resort. The town of Garmisch-Partenkirchen, originally two towns which have gradually blended into one, is a typical Bavarian village in the scenic Alps between Innsbruck and Munich. Snowboard pros and amateurs from all over Europe meet up here (for the riding and the partying!) in May and June each year for the Gap 1328 summer camp.

ON THE MOUNTAIN »
Snow reliability_At 2964m, Germany's highest mountain, the Zugspitze, makes this a glacial region. The winter season begins in October and continues through 'til May. It's not necessarily the most challenging resort, but it is the only glacier in Germany. The 'Classic Ski Resort' is divided into the Osterfeldkopf at 2050m, the Kreuzeck at 1651m, and the Hausberg at 1340m, all of which are now connected and all of which now have snowmaking facilities. The unfortunately named Wank, at 1780m, is also part of the resort, but it's not connected by lift to the other three and it has no snow making facilities.

Snow reports
Tel: +49 (0)8821 797979
Fax: +49 (0)8821 7970
www.zugspitze.de - the official local Internet site with weather info and on-site camera. Email info on local weather and snow conditions can be received from: wetter@zugspitze.de

Lifts & Piste_In the Zugspitze resort it's not uncommon to have to queue. We'd recommend that you get to the resort early or take the Zahnradbahn.
There's one special run - the Riffelriss - for those of you with iron legs. Take the funicular railway up to the top and then ride down to the Eibsee, starting either through the window in the tunnel (although this is not usually open), or from the tunnel exit.
Osterfelder, Kreuzeck and Hausberg are all accessible from the gondola. The Bernadein run is our recommendation in the Osterfelder area. Very few tourists find their way across to Wank, which is great, especially after a fresh snowfall. You'll find several lifts, including two tow lifts, on the backside of the mountain.

Freeriding_Zugspitze to the right of the Sonnenkar lift there's an open powder run with countless cornices. Just ask one of the locals to point you towards the Wechtenabfahrt. The Neue Welt is a steep, off piste run for experienced riders. Due east from the Neue Welt there's another off piste run which leads down into Eherwald in Austria. This run requires gear for abseiling, and you'll need to have a guide with you.

Osterfelder this place, at the foot of the Alpspitze, is a fantastic area for freeriding. You'll find that even

© Christian Stadler

© Christian Stadler **Riders** Mini Karpf

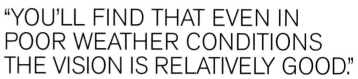

"YOU'LL FIND THAT EVEN IN POOR WEATHER CONDITIONS THE VISION IS RELATIVELY GOOD."

Osterfelder our tip is the *Hochalm.*

Kreuzeck lots of umbrella bars - they serve a great *Kaiserschmarn* (sweet omelette) at the *Kreuzalm-Hütte*

Hausberg lots of umbrella Après-Ski bars all over the place here. Both the *Bayernhaus* and the *Garmischer Haus* up on the summit station are good value. Cheap midday menus are available at the traditional *Sportgaststätte Hausberg,* directly located at the end of the runs.

Wank try the *Esterbergalm* in the summit station the *Sonnenalm,* a cosy restaurant with great views of Garmisch and the Wetterstein Massif.

IN THE TOWN »
Accommodation_The cheapest overnight accommodation is at the youth hostel in *Burgrain*

Burgrain
Tel: +49 (0) 882 129 80
or at one of the countless bed and breakfast places.

Garmisch Tourist Information Office
Tel: +49 (0) 882 1180-700 or
Tel: +49 (0) 882 118 022

Kurverwaltung Grainau
Tel: +49 (0) 882 198 1850
This can help and can let you have a list of places to stay.

Winter camping ground
Located between GAP and Grainau
Tel: +49 (0) 882 131 80.
The small town of Grainau is between Garmisch and the Zugspitz lift, and basically has no nightlife and no restaurants to speak of.

Food_You'll find a supermarket on every corner. Restaurants include the *Rassen Gasthof* and the *Frauendorfer* are on *Ludwigstraße,* and are great places to visit for those interested in trying traditional Bavarian cuisine. If you prefer Italian cuisine, though, we recommend *Renzo* in the

Rathausplatz (Town Hall Square). *Sausalito,* just across from the Partenkirchen Train Station caters for fans of *Mexican* fodder. The *Marienplatz* is the junk food centre, with a *McDonalds* and a *Pizza Hut.* And for something a bit different, check out the *African Lounge,* an exotic location serving African cuisine, and an ideal spot for a special night out.

Nightlife_There are lots of bars and discos in Garmisch, but none that really heat up, unless you heat them up yourself! *Peach's* and the *Musik Café* are both in the Marienplatz and are probably the first places you'd want to try. A party at the *Evergreen* next to the swimming pool can turn into a real fun night if you get the right dosage of booze, and parties are a regular thing during the Gap1328 Summer Camps. *The GAP1328 Sport Bar* (www.froski.com/sportsbar) is a popular hangout with the Gap1328 crew, locals and pro riders.

Other Activities_Two swimming pools, the *Zugspitzbad* in *Grainau* and the larger *Alpspitzbad* in Garmisch (which has a great range of diving boards), plus bowling, ice skating, paragliding, etc. And oh yes, there are also some beautiful lakes to swim in during the warm summer months. The *Hochland* cinema in Partenkirchen and the Cinema Centre Garmisch both have daily screenings of films in their original language (including English!)

LOCAL TIP »
Garmisch is very close to the Austrian border, and even though there are officially no border controls between the two countries, you'll still get stopped on a regular basis. The Bavarian border police have a particular appetite for snowboarders. You might also get to meet the regular police during organised events and parties, as they do their best to make sure Bavarian beer remains the number one drug in the region.

---

in poor weather conditions the vision is relatively good because the trees and shrubs provide some contrast. There's also a wide variety of runs directly below both the *Hochalm* lift and the *Bernadein* lift. If you're looking for a good tree run, try the *Hausberg* next to the *Kreuzjoch* lift.

The *Wank* is a good alternative on the weekends and during the main holiday periods when it can quickly get overcrowded elsewhere.

Freestyling_The freestyle arena is at the *Zugspitzplatt,* and includes a superpipe and funpark, both kept in excellent condition. Pro snowboarders such as Jan Michaelis and Xavier Hoffman can often be seen training here. Even more freestyle action can be viewed at the GAP1328 Summer Camps, which are held from the beginning of May until mid June. The park includes a superpipe, a normal pipe, straight jumps, corners and rails. For more info log onto www.gap1328.de

Carving_Carvers can have a lot of fun riding on the *Zugspitze* at *Wetterwandeck* or on the *Olympia* and *Kandaharr* valley runs at *Kreuzeck-/Hausberggebiet.* The slopes are always well prepared, but our tip would be the *Kandaharr* run, which is probably the cream of the crop.

Beginners_There are beginner-friendly slopes at *Hausberg* and on the *Zugspitzplatt.* The pistes are flat and entirely suitable for learning.

For info
www.sprenzel-Sport.de
Tel: +49 (0) 882 114 96 or
Tel: +49 (0) 882 152 033
www.snowboard-schule.de
Tel: +49 (0) 882 176 490
www.ski-and-more3.com
Tel: +49 (0) 882 158 300 or
Tel: +49 (0) 882 146 00

Mountain Restaurants_Zugspitze One self-service restaurant, the *Sonnalpin,* as well as two other restaurants with sunny terraces situated on the summit.

PROS & CONS »
+ 1300m vertical drop and 7km of long, off-piste runs.
+ Purely freeride terrain!
+ Avalanche Commission keeps regular checks but remember it's still an off piste alpine terrain.

– A long flat trail at the bottom which you have to cross to get to the lift.
– Without fresh snow, Dammkar becomes the longest mogul run ever.

DAMMKAR
GERMANY

"ONE GONDOLA, ONE LONG RUN BACK DOWN! THE KARWENDELBAHN GONDOLA WILL TRANSPORT YOU FROM MITTENWALD TO THE TOP STATION AT 2244M, WHICH IS JUST BELOW THE WEST SUMMIT OF THE KARWENDELSPITZE."

»

DAMMKAR »
www.dammkar.de, www.mittenwald-info.de
tourist office tel: +49 (0)882333981
location: Mittenwald
population: 8500
altitude: 920m

ON THE MOUNTAIN »
season: December - March
Lifts
Vertical drop: 920 - 2244m
amount of lifts in total:1
gondolas: 1
chair lifts: -
T-bars: -
Slopes
amount of prepared slopes: -
runs w. snowmaking machines: -
amount of easy runs: -
amount of intermediate runs: -
amount of advanced runs: 1
Facilities
night riding: -
amount of halfpipes: -
amount of funparks: -
Heliboarding: -
Lift-ticket prices in Euro
1/2 day: 18
day: 24
season: 220

SNOWBOARD TUITION »
Erste Skischule Mittenwald
Tel: +49 (0)88233582
www.skischule-mittenwald.de
Vereinigte Skischule
Tel: +49 (0)88238080
www.skischulevereinigte.de

GETTING THERE »
Car
Munich – Mittenwald: 104km
Munich – A95 towards Garmisch-Partenkirchen – Mittenwald
Innsbruck - Mittenwald: 39km
Innsbruck – Zirl – Seefeld - Mittenwald
Train
Munich – Garmisch - Mittenwald (approx. 2 hours)
Innsbruck – Mittenwald (approx. 1 hour)
Air
Innsbruck Airport: 143km
Munich Airport: 38km

© Christian Stadler **Rider** Vinzent Lups

DAMMKAR »
Intro_Could Dammkar be Germany's answer to La Grave? After the 97/98 winter season, the resort management decided it no longer had the money to keep the piste at Dammkar regularly groomed. This decision led to the creation of the first all-freeriding resort in the German Alps, much to the joy of the local freeriders. This resort now consists of one mountain, one gondola and 7km of pure off-piste runs.

ON THE MOUNTAIN »
Snow reliability_The Karwendelbahn (funicular railway) usually opens straight after Christmas and the season can go on until the middle/end of April, depending on snow conditions. Dammkar is sometimes even rideable in spring and early summer, though there's no lift and it's all entirely at your own peril.
'Powder Alarm' is a service provided by the resort which will send you an e-mail about the latest weather and snow conditions as soon as new snow falls at Dammkar. Register at www.karwendelbahn.de or www.dammkar.de

Weather reports
Tel: +49 (0)882 353 96
Funicular railway - Lift
(Ticket Office)
Tel: +49 (0)882 384 80

The resort at Dammkar is continually checked by the Avalanche Commission, and the resort can only be opened after it has given its OK. Whenever required, excessive amounts of snow will be dispersed with explosives to reduce the risk of avalanche. There are no snow making facilities here.
Avalanche reports
Tel: +49 (0) 899 214 1210
www.lawienenwarndienst.bayern.de

Lifts & Piste_One gondola, one long run back down! The *Karwendelbahn* gondola will transport you from *Mittenwald* to the top station at 2244m, which is just below the west summit of the *Karwendelspitze*. This is the only way to get to the top as there are no other lifts in the resort.
From the top lift station you'll need to travel through a 450m long tunnel to get to the start of the off piste run - a 7km run of

pure bliss, in good snow.

Freeriding_With the appearance of new snow and fresh powder you'll have to get there early - there are no secret spots here, Germany's best meeting point for freeriders. Unfortunately, this resort turns into one of the longest mogul runs in the world when the snow fails to fall on a regular basis. Burning calf muscles guaranteed!
Probably the best slopes are below the south face of the Predigstuhls. When this run is tracked out, book a mountain guide and then (and only with said mountain guide!) take a ride down Das Kirchl, an off piste run which is not ridden all that often, and which is not checked by the Avalanche Commision, hence the need for expert local knowledge.
For info about ski guides and mountain guides call Kurverwaltung Mittenwald
Tel: +49 (0) 882 333 981
Vivalpin
Tel: +48 (0) 882 194 30 323,
www.vivalpin.com

Freestyling_Pure park-freestylers won't be too happy here. The wind

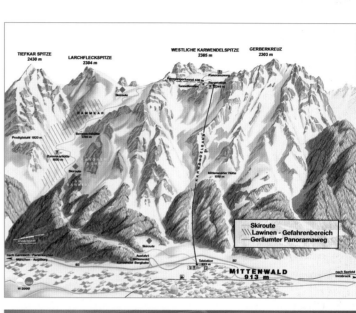

lips on the east side of the hollow allow for some freestyle moves in between the long powder turns. You'll also find a pipe and park in *Garmisch-Partenkirchen,* a short 20 minute drive down the road.

Beginners_*Dammkar* is for experienced riders only. Beginners can take lessons on the nearby *Kranzberg* in *Mittenwald* where the piste is relatively flat.
Snowboard School
Tel: +49 (0) 882 3 8080/4646

Mountain Restaurants_The top lift station has a new self-service restaurant but it isn't cheap. The *Bierstüberl* down at the bottom lift station is a little more relaxing and in addition to its regular menu it also serves light snacks at reasonable prices. The *Dammkarhütte* at 1650m is generally open from the start of the Easter holidays and this is probably the best place for a regenerating feed!

IN THE TOWN »
Accommodation_The youth hostel (Jugendherberge) offers inexpensive overnight accommodation, as do the many private guest houses or pensions. For smaller groups it may be worth your while renting a holiday apartment.
Information and reservations available from Kurverwaltung Mittenwald
Tel: +49 (0) 882 333 981 or Fax: +49 (0) 882 327 01
www.mittenwald.de or
www.mittenwald-info.de

Jugendherberge in the *Buckelwiesen* (near the Tonihof)
Hotel Post and **Hotel Sonnenbichl** (good, double rooms including breakfast €43.00 to €70.00)
Gröbelalm (double rooms including breakfast €62.00 to €87.00)
Hotel Wipfelder (double rooms €30.00 to €34.00)
Pension Nebel (at Mautweg 34, bed and breakfast, simple and cheap, shared shower facilities)

Food_Mittenwalds offers some very fine restaurants, but the choice of cheaper alternatives is not that good. The village supermarket has everything a hungry snowboarder needs, but for those looking for a feast, we can recommend the following restaurants;

"THE RESORT AT DAMMKAR IS CONTINUALLY CHECKED BY THE AVALANCHE COMMISSION."

Alt Mittenwald above the **Disco Pharao** (also caters for vegetarians)
Pizzeria Osteria (excellent Italian cuisine, in the pedestrian area)
Hochland (Bistro)
Alte Mühle (in *Scharnitz,* on the outskirts of *Mittenwald,* 10min away by car. Live music.

Nightlife_There is not much for young people in *Mittenwald* - a *Luftkurort* or health spa where people go to fill their lungs with the bracing air. You'll find a few pubs in the pedestrian area of the town, as well as two discos - *Blacky's* and the *Pharao* - but nothing special.

Alternatives: stay in and party, or travel to *Garmisch-Partenkirchen* or *Seefeld.*

Other Activities_Swimming pool next to the railway station. A trip to *Garmisch-Partenkirchen* or *Innsbruck.*

LOCAL TIP »
In bad weather or poor snow conditions it's worth heading to the Rosshütte/Härmelekopf resort in Seefeld, which is about 20 minutes away by car. It's a nice resort with some good off piste terrain and a funpark.

"CONSIDERED TO BE ONE OF THE BEST FREERIDING AREAS IN GERMANY, AND WELL KNOWN FOR ITS FRIENDLY LOCAL SCENE, OBERSTDORF IS POPULAR WITH SNOWBOARDERS THE WORLD OVER."

OBERSTDORF
GERMANY

»

OBERSTDORF »
www.oberstdorf.de
tourist office tel: +49 (0)83227000
location: Oberstdorf
population: 11000
altitude: 813m

ON THE MOUNTAIN »
season: mid December to mid April
Lifts
vertical drop: 813–2224 m
amount of lifts in total: 28
cable cars: 5
gondolas: 2
chairlifts: 7
drag lifts: 14
Slopes
amount of prepared slopes: 45.8 km
runs w. snowmaking machines: 30
amount of easy runs: 10
amount of intermediate runs: 30
amount of advanced runs: 4
Facilities
night riding: -
amount of halfpipes: 1
amount of funparks: 1
heliboarding: -
Lift-ticket prices in Euro
day: 30
week: 142
season: 343

SNOWBOARD TUITION »
Out of Bounds
Tel: +49 (0)83221729
www.outofbounds.de
Snowboardschule Grenzenlos
Tel: +49 (0)83226594
www.grenzenlos-winterworld.de

SNOWBOARD SHOPS »
Snowboardschule und Shop Alptraum
Tel: +49 (0)83227565
Website www.alptraum.de

GETTING THERE »
Car
Munich – Oberstdorf: 193km
Munich – Landsberg - Kempten - Sonthofen - Oberstdorf
Innsbruck – Oberstdorf: 163km
Innsbruck – A12 towards Landeck – Mötz exit – via Nassereith – Reutte - Nesselwängle - (Au/Ger) - Oberjoch - Sonthofen - Oberstdorf
Zürich – Oberstdorf: 211km
Zürich - via St. Gallen - Lustenau (Switz/Au) - Wildberg (Lindau) - Laufenegg - Oberstdorf
Train
Munich - Oberstdorf approx. 2hours 30min
Air
Munich Airport 203km
Innsbruck Airport 164km

© Obersdorf Tourist office

OBERSTDORF »
Intro_Oberstdorf is in the Allgäuer Alps and is the venue of a good many snowboard contests. Considered to be one of the best freeriding areas in Germany, and well known for its friendly local scene, Oberstdorf is popular with snowboarders the world over. The resort is divided into three areas: the Fellhorn, the Nebelhorn - which includes Germany's longest downhill run (7.5km) - and the beginner's area around Söllereck. Oberstdorf is renowned as a nice relaxing village for older people, which is why most of the action is to be found on the mountain. The nightlife is almost non-existent.

ON THE MOUNTAIN »
Snow reliability_Allgäu is renowned for being an area where you can expect good snow conditions throughout the whole winter and early spring, thanks to the surrounding mountains, which rise to around 2,224m (the Nebelhorn). Depending on snow conditions, the season usually kicks off in December and the resort remains open until Easter. The season on the Nebelhorn can

extend through to the first weeks of May. Most of the snow falls in January and February, and this, combined with snow making facilities, creates one of the longest winter seasons to be found in Germany.

For snow reports
Tel: 0700 / 555 33 666 or
Tel: 0700 / 555 33 888

Lifts & Piste_Weekends and holiday periods in Oberstdorf are generally crowded. This can become particularly obvious at the Nebelhornbahn lift, which is the only mode of transport on to the mountain. (You'll also find yourself waiting for a long time at the middle station, the one that transports riders back down into the village if the snow conditions don't allow you to make a valley descent.) The Fellhorn gondola, which can carry 100 people, is often a faster option, especially as the alternative Fastenoy-Höfle chairlift also takes people as well. Due to the size of the area, people are generally better catered for here in terms of accessing the mountain.

Tip: You can also access the Fellhorn using the Kanzelwandbahn (or funicular railway) and then riding through the Kleinwalser valley, which itself offers additional challenging terrain for snowboarding.

Lift Company Oberstdorf
Tel: +49 (0) 832 296 000

Freeriding_A lot of German freeriders (David Speiser, Flo Weidel & Co.) ride at Oberstdorf. You'll find many riding possibilities here to keep you entertained. The lower lifts on the Fellhorn provide access to some good tree runs which you might consider as an alternative riding area in bad weather conditions or when the higher regions are covered with dangerous amounts of fresh snow. But when the weather and snow conditions are right, you should in fact check out these higher areas which can provide great powder slopes, windlips, cliffs and some real extreme stuff just waiting for good riders. Sven Gittermann's 'Out of Bounds' company is the perfect reference point for information, guided tours, mountain guides and

"ALLGÄU IS RENOWNED FOR BEING AN AREA WHERE YOU CAN EXPECT GOOD SNOW CONDITIONS THROUGHOUT THE WHOLE WINTER AND EARLY SPRING, THANKS TO THE SURROUNDING MOUNTAINS."

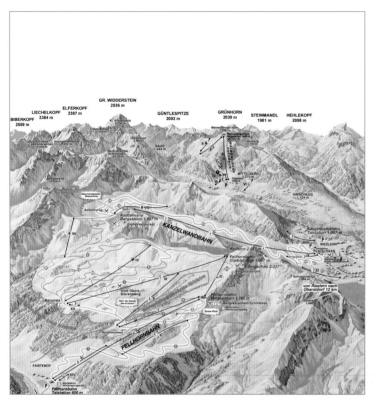

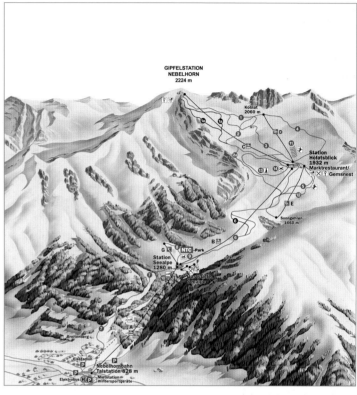

camps and generally educating you on the dangers of avalanches. Tel: +49 (0) 8322 1729

Freestyling_Freestylers haven't been forgotten either. There's a funpark next to the *Kuchenbach* lift on the *Fellhorn*. Offering a range of kickers, gaps, and rails as well as a spine, funbox and corner, the riding standard is generally good. Boardercross riders and half pipe fans will get their money's worth on the *Nebelhorn*. A 100m long Pipe Dragon pipe is located below the *Koblat* chairlift. The boardercross course at *Sonngehren* is open all season and maintained to contest standards. This should come as no surprise though, this is, after all, the home of the snow groomer's World Championships.

Carving_The *Kuchenbach* lift on the *Fellhorn* is open for carving fans and provides an open carving piste.

Beginners_Beginners should attempt their first turns at *Söllereck* or in the area around the *Seealpe* station on the *Nebelhorn,* which is also an ideal learning environment

with a flat tow lift, a rope tow lift and two conveyor belts. You'll also find a small snowtubing park.

Mountain Restaurants_Fellhorn Restaurants (with the traditional umbrella bars) are located at the top and at the middle stations of the lift. The *Obere Alpe Bierenwang* and the *Balzplatz* can be found at the bottom station of the *Möser* chairlift. Tip: eat good schnitzels at the middle station restaurant and keep an eye on the constantly-changing Daily Specials board at the *Bierenwang Hütte*.

Nebelhorn try the *Marktrestaurant* at the *Höfratsblick* station (good fresh food, but expensive), *Edmund Probst Haus, Gemsnest* (Snow Bar at *Höfratsblick*) and the *Gipfelhütte*.

IN THE TOWN »
Accommodation_Oberstdorf has many private rooms, guest houses and hotels available to rent, with prices starting from €14 per night. And there's a youth hostel in *Kornau,* the village on the way to *Kleinwalsertal.*
Information and bookings

Tourist Information Centre
Tel: +49 (0) 8322 7000 or
Fax: +49 (0) 8322 700 236 or at
www.oberstdorf.de

Food_After a day on the *Nebelhorn,* a good option is to head to the *Alpen Sport Cafe,* close to the Valley Station. This is also a good place to meet up in the evening. The Mexican restaurant *Joselitos,* will look after you well, while fans of cheese should try the cheese fondue at the *Alt 168/Käserei Kuhn* (Cheesery). But in fact *Oberstdorf* has something to suit everyone's tastebuds, be it an Allgäuer Gasthaus, or Chinese or Italian cuisine.

Nightlife_The *Walk In* bar is the place to go for music, especially on weekends when it gets packed. However, those looking for a hardcore Après Ski scene or a wild party scene are probably in the wrong resort. The *Bahnsteig 1* village style disco is held at the train station and provides okay music. But the real partying in Oberstdorf only happens at the bigger snowboard events (Oybele-Halle) or at private parties.

"THE LOWER LIFTS ON THE FELLHORN PROVIDE ACCESS TO SOME GOOD TREE RUNS"

Other Activities_The Ice Sport Centre, which has several ice rinks, an indoor climbing wall as well as the new *Kristall-Bad* – a swimming pool with a large sauna landscape - should keep boredom at bay.

LOCAL TIP »
The Allgäuer Gletcher (Glacier) Card provides access to over 30 ski resorts in Allgäu, Kleinwalsertal, and the outer regions of the Tyrol such as the Pitztaler and Kaunertal glaciers. This card is valid for 8 months and costs €378 (kids and students €298). Info: www.allgaeu-gletscher-card.com

"THE INTERMEDIATE RUNS ARE ALWAYS WELL PREPARED, MAKING THIS RESORT A POPULAR DESTINATION, ESPECIALLY WITH FAMILIES."

SUDELFELD
GERMANY

SUDELFELD »
www.sudelfeld.de
Tel: +49 (0)8023648
location: Bayrischzell
population: 1500
altitude: 800m
linked resorts: Wendelstein

ON THE MOUNTAIN »
season: December-March
Lifts
vertical drop: 800-1500m
amount of lifts in total: 20
gondolas: -
chair lifts: 2
drag lifts: 18
Slopes
amount of prepared slopes: 30 km
runs w. snowmaking machines: 6
easy runs: 5 km
intermediate runs: 20 km
advanced runs: 5 km
Facilities
night riding: -
amount of halfpipes: 2
amount of funparks: 1
heliboarding: -
Lift-ticket prices in Euro
1/2 day: 20
day: 22
week: 108
season: 280

SNOWBOARD TUITION »
Skischule Bayrischzell
Tel: +49 (0)8023791
www.skischule-bayrischzell.de
Skischule Sudelfeld
Tel: +49 (0)8023514
Skischule Aib-Ski
Tel: +49 (0)8023809995
www.aibski.de

SNOWBOARD SHOPS »
Aibski
Tel: +49 (0)8062800801

GETTING THERE »
Car
Munich – Sudelfeld: 72km
Munich – Autobahn A8 towards Salzburg - Weyarn or Irschenberg exit then continue on the main road to Bayerischzell - Sudelfeld
Innsbruck – Sudelfeld: 105km
Innsbruck – A12 towards Wörgl/Kufstein – Kufstein Nord exit – in direction of Thiersee (Ger/Au) – Bayerischzell - Sudelfeld
Train
Take the Intercity (IC) or Intercity Express (ICE) - services leave from all major German cities and arrive in Munich. From Munich take the regional train to Bayerischzell - journey time: approx. 1 hour 25 mins. At Bayerischzell change to the Wendelstein-Ringlinie for Sudelfeld.
Air
Munich Airport 110km
Innsbruck Airport 106km

SUDELFELD »
Intro_Sudelfeld is centrally located and easily accessible, and is one of the biggest resorts in Upper Bavaria. Twenty lifts connect the gradually sloping pistes, which run through alpine meadowland. The intermediate runs are always well prepared, making this resort a popular destination, especially with families. As soon as fresh snow begins to fall, you'll find many good riding areas - especially in upper *Sudelfeld*.

ON THE MOUNTAIN »
Snow reliability_Snow can generally be expected from the beginning of December through to mid April. The best time for riding is roughly February and March – plenty of sun and snow. If snow gets thin on the ground, two of the runs are serviced by snow making machines. Snow reports can be found by visiting www.sudelfeld.de or Tel: +49 (0) 8023/428 or /588

Lifts & Piste_Sudelfeld has 16 lifts, mainly tow lifts, a 3 person chairlift, a gondola and there's a quad chairlift currently under construction which will provide a 200 m extension (see Lift Map 2). The *Sudelfeldkopf* T-bar allows you to make the most of your lift pass, offering the optimum combination of a good run and a fast lift.

Freeriding_Tree runs make up the main part of the action, with the exception of a few open powder runs and a small, almost high alpine area in *Upper Sudelfeld*. A few good lines can also be found on the home mountain, the *Wendelstein*.

Freestyling_There's a halfpipe style chute next to the quad chairlift making for a lot of fun. SDF, a local snowboarding club, has helped create a funpark next to the *Sonnenalm*. The park includes 2-4 larger kickers, 4 handrails and a quarter. The halfpipe on the *Walleralm* is not always ideal because the snow conditions tend to be poorer there. The freestyle scene is generally made up of around 15 club members of SDF. Burgi Heckmaier, a member of the '98 Olympic squad, grew up in *Sudelfeld*.

Carving_The best carving runs are the *Herrenabfahrt* and the *Sudelfeldkopflift*.

"TREE RUNS MAKE UP THE MAIN PART OF THE ACTION."

Beginners_Beginners are well catered for on the easy to intermediate runs. The Mittleres Sudelfeld tow lift and the Oberes Sudelfeld tow lift are recommended for those just learning. The runs down to Rosengasse are not suitable for beginners. There are two snowboard schools in the village and one on the mountain.
www.skichule-sudelfeld.de
www.skischule-bayrischzell.de

Mountain Restaurants_Seven mountain guesthouses serve traditional Bavarian fare. The *Schindelberger Alm* is often overcrowded, so head over to the *Waller Alm* in *Oberes Sudelfeld*, where you'll find good food and fewer crowds. Another cosy place is the *Tirolerstüberl*, while the meeting place for the snowboard scene is at the *Sonnenalm*, home of the former World Cup snowboarder, Maikel Wachenfeld. A meal and drink will set you back around €6, pretty cheap for a ski resort.

IN THE TOWN »
Accommodation_The town of Bayerischzell provides overnight accommodation from €25 up to €100. The Gasthaus Wendelstein can be recommended, it has nice rooms and great food. The village is connected to the resort via a chairlift. The youth hostel in the lower lying area of Sudelfeld is owned by very friendly people. For info, log onto www.bayerischzell.de or the administration office (Kuramt) Bayerischzell - Tel: +49 (0) 8023 648

Food_There's a *Tengelman* supermarket and a little corner shop in the village of *Bayerischzell*. You'll also find two pizzerias and a wide range of guesthouses serving traditional Bavarian food. The *Kaminstuben* on the outskirts of the village serves meat cooker over an open fire. The *Lukas Stuben* and *Gasthaus Wendelstein* also serve a full range of Bavarian dishes.

Nightlife_The *Ski Alm Andreas Stüberl* caters for the Après-Ski scene. A visit to the cinema or a few beers in a cosy guesthouse will have to do as the highlight of the evening because there's not much else to do in *Bayerischzell* when the sun goes down.

Other Activities_Try the Snowtub in *Tannerfeld*. Or the bowling alley (kegelbahn) at the *Haus des Gastes*, while across the road there's the *Peterhof Lichtspiele*, a cinema which has a smoking area and where a waiter will bring you a drink while you watch the film. For the more adventurous, try the hang gliding ramp at the *Oberen Sudelfeld*.

LOCAL TIP »
Sudelfeld is a small but beautiful resort with lots of hidden qualities. It's a perfect place to hang out and relax with none of the stresses of some larger resorts. The evenings can be extremely quiet - so bring some friends with you and make your own parties. If you can't live without a disco, you can travel to the Spinnradel at Spitzigsee, about 20 minutes away by car.

"PEOPLE "SPORTS "TRAVEL "CULTURE

We are Chiemsee: Ueli Kestenholz

CHIEMSEE

*49 (0)8661 9888-0

CHIEMSEE.COM

CHIEMSEE AG Chiemingerstrasse19 83355 Grabenstätt Tel. + 49 (0)8661 9888-0 Fax + 49 (0)8661 9888-75 e-mail: info@chiemsee.com

PROS & CONS »
+ Less than an hour from Munich.
+ Shuttle bus to Taubenstein which is where
  you'll find a funpark.

− Some older style lifts and slow tow lifts.
− Weekends are overcrowded.
− Prices don't always reflect the service
  provided.

"IDEALLY SUITED TO LESS EXPERIENCED RIDERS RATHER THAN THOSE LOOKING FOR EXTREME TERRAIN OR A MASSIVE HALF PIPE"

SPITZING
GERMANY

»

SPITZING »
www.spitzingsee.de
tourist office tel: +49 (0)802660650
location: Schliersee
population: 6500
altitude: 780
linked resorts: Stümpfling, Taubenstein

ON THE MOUNTAIN »
season: December–March/April
Lifts
vertical drop: 784-1758m
amount of lifts in total: 13
gondolas:1
chair lifts: 2
drag lifts: 10
Slopes
amount of prepared slopes: 30 km
runs w. snowmaking machines: -
easy runs: 9 km
intermediate runs: 5 km
advanced runs: 6 km
Facilities
night riding: -
amount of halfpipes: 1
amount of funparks: 1
heliboarding: -
Lift-ticket prices in Euro
1/2 day: 18
day: 20
week: 95
season: 253

SNOWBOARD TUITION »
Martina Loch
Tel: +49 (0)80267416
www.snowcamp-martina-loch.de

SNOWBOARD SHOPS »
Martina Loch
Tel: +49 (0)80267416
www.snowcamp-martina-loch.de

GETTING THERE »
Car
Munich – Spitzingsee: 78km
Munich - Autobahn towards Salzburg -
Holzkirchen exit to Rottach via Tegernseer Tal
- Enterrottach - Suttenbahn
or Weyarn exit to Spitzingsee via Schliersee
Innsbruck – Spitzingsee: 121km
Innsbruck - Autobahn Wörgle/Kufstein -
Kufstein Nord exit - in direction of Thiersee
(Au/Ger) - via Heissenbauer - Spitzingsee
Train/Bus
Munich - Holzkirchen - Schliersee - Neuhaus
(approx. 50min)
Munich - Holzkirchen - Tegernsee then by bus
connection to the ski resort
Air
Munich Airport 119km

SPITZING »
Intro_Due to its close proximity to the Bavarian capital, *Spitzingsee-Rottach* is the local resort for the people of Munich. Only 78km separates Munich from this resort and the neighbouring resorts of *Sutten, Stümpfling* and *Taubenstein*. The weekends and holiday periods see a massive influx of locals, while at all other times things are relatively quiet. The resort is ideally suited to less experienced riders rather than those looking for extreme terrain or a massive half pipe. The *Faschings* festival on the *Firstalm*, held in February each year, has added to the popularity of this resort.

ON THE MOUNTAIN »
Snow reliability_The resort starts at 1085m and rises to 1693m, has a gondola, 2 chairlifts, 13 tow lifts and 30km of groomed runs. The winter season generally opens around December, and can continue until April. Snow making facilities are non-existent. The snow in this south facing resort melts quickly, especially in spring, so it's worth checking out the conditions at the resort before you go. Tel: +49 (0) 8026 7099

Lifts & Piste_The bottom stations of the *Stümpfling* and *Taubenstein* lifts can be accessed from the villages of *Schliersee* and *Spitzingsee*. The Sutten lift is accessible from the village of *Rottach-Egern* on *Tergernsee,* and also allows you to access the *Stümpfling* resort. A free shuttle bus travels between *Taubenstein* and *Stümpfling*. Expect long queues at the *Kurven* lift and the *Stümpfling* lift when the sun is shining, particularly at weekends. The *Rosskopf* poma lift is relatively difficult for snowboarders due to its steep gradient.

Freeriding_The freeriding around the *Spitzingsee* is basically reduced to tree runs as a result of the low elevation of the resort. Freeriders can find a few chutes and cliffs among the trees at *Osthang* in the direction of the *Firstalm*. But with a little initiative and a short hike there are some longer runs here - ask the locals.

Freestyling_Freestylers meet up at the *Nordhang* lift. Over the past few years a real scene has

© Peter Mathis *Rider* Mitch Tölderer

developed here and the park has improved. The park currently includes a few jumps of varying sizes, including two larger kickers and a corner. The park still has potential, but Terje & Co., who showed off their talents here at the '94 European Championships, don't seem inclined to build a Freestyle-Mecca. In fact there's still no sign of even a permanent half pipe being built.

Carving_The alpine riders seem to meet quite often on the *Nordhang* for training so this area is often set up with a slalom course. But other slopes are also nice for carving, it's just a little cramped at weekends!

Beginners_Beginners will find suitable terrain on the *Kurven* lift or the even better suited area next to the *3-Tannen* lift. The summit region at *Taubenstein* (*Raukopf* and *Maxelraineralm* lifts) offers easy runs in sunny surroundings. In addition to the Spitzingsee Ski School (which also provides snowboard lessons), the Martina

Loch Snowboard School has been running snowboard courses and camps for all levels for over 12 years. www.snowcamp-martina-loch.de www.skischule-spitzingsee.de

Mountain Restaurants_Your first port of call should be the *Firstalm* (upper and lower *Firstalm*) next to the *Firstalm* lift. This restaurant specialises in meat and cheese platters served with local bread as well as typical Bavarian cuisine like apple strudel. The Firstalm is also the home of the legendary *Fasching* Festival which is held each year in February. On *Fasching* Sunday you'll find hordes of people flocking to the *Alm* to watch an amazing array of unidentified sliding objects constructed to ride down the *Firstalm* slope – very entertaining. Other recommended huts and guesthouse are: the *Stümpflinghaus*, the old *Wurzhütte* or the *Bäckeralm*. When eating at the *Brotzeitstüberl*, located at the bottom of the *Kurven* lift, keep an eye on your gear – it's a popular spot for thieving scumbags.

"THE FREERIDING AROUND THE SPITZINGSEE IS BASICALLY REDUCED TO TREE RUNS AS A RESULT OF THE LOW ELEVATION OF THE RESORT. FREERIDERS CAN FIND A FEW CHUTES AND CLIFFS AMONG THE TREES AT OSTHANG IN THE DIRECTION OF THE FIRSTALM. BUT WITH A LITTLE INITIATIVE AND A SHORT HIKE THERE ARE SOME LONGER RUNS HERE - ASK THE LOCALS."

IN THE TOWN »
Accommodation_ There are a few pads located at *Spitzingsee,* putting you right on the front line. Most of these are the more expensive hotels though. Cheaper accommodation (from approx. €15) such as guesthouses or private rooms can be found in Neuhaus, Schliersee or Rottach. The Schliersee youth hostel offers overnight accommodation and breakfast for around €20.
The villages are all interconnected with a ski bus service.

Information and reservations
Schliersee Information Centre
Tel: +49 (0) 8026 6065 0
Fax: +49 (0) 8026 6065 20
www.schliersee.de

Food_ For those catering for themselves there are a couple of supermarkets in *Schliersee* as well as a number of guesthouses offering traditional Bavarian and international cooking. An *Aldi* supermarket and a McDonalds can be found in *Rottach-Egern.* Tip: The *Bräustüberl* in *Tegernsee* offers a Bavarian version of an

Aprés Ski bar with good beer and traditional food.

Nightlife_ For those snowboarders with enough energy to look for a party, you'll need to be mobile. Most bars and clubs are quite a way away from the resort (the exception being the *Spinnradl* at *Spitzingsee).* Good beer can be found in the *Bräustüberl* in *Tegernsee* - see above. The *Kaktus* in *Rottach-Egern* is a bistro/bar and meeting place for later in the evening. Those who want to dance to cheesy tunes will have to go to the *Moon Club* disco in *Rottach*

Other Activities_ The lake in *Spitzing* is usually frozen over from December to March, and is the ideal place for ice skating or a game of ice hockey. You can also relax after a day's snowboarding at the cinemas in *Hausham* or *Rottach-Egern.*

LOCAL TIP »
A cheaper option for those travelling from Munich by train is the Train-Bus-Ski Pass package which you can buy at the ticket office at the main train station in Munich. www.bahn.de

ITALY
122-151

ITALY MAP

ITALY »

Intro_Many regard Italy as Europe's best-kept secret. Italy has some amazing mountains, some of the cheapest prices in Europe, and doesn't get tracked out as quickly as France. All the spots we've described in this chapter have been picked because they have something exceptional to offer. Whether it be the freeriding in *Courmayeur* or *Alagna*, or the great parks of *Livigno*, *Alleghe* or *Macugnaga*.

The average Italian doesn't tend to go off piste, as the authorities can be strict. Triggering an avalanche is an offence punishable by the state. However, provided you act responsibly and carefully, this means more freshies for you! More good news is that anyone injured here will receive free first aid in any public hospital.

The language barrier can be a problem in Italy, as they only started to teach English in schools a few of years ago. Therefore, it is hard to find anyone over thirty that can speak decent English, even in the tourist villages. Learning a few useful phrases before you come to Italy would be a good idea.

INFORMATION »

Official Name_Repubblica Italiana
Capital_Rome
Population_57,34 Million
Land mass_301.268km2
Language(s)_Italian
Currency_1 Euro = 100 Cent
Highest mountain_Mont Blanc 4807m
International country code_0039
Police_112
Ambulance_118
Fire Brigade_115
Tourist Board_Ente nazionale italiano per il turismo
Tel: +39 06 49711
www.enit.it
Train Info_www.trenitalia.it
Weather Info_www.meteo.it

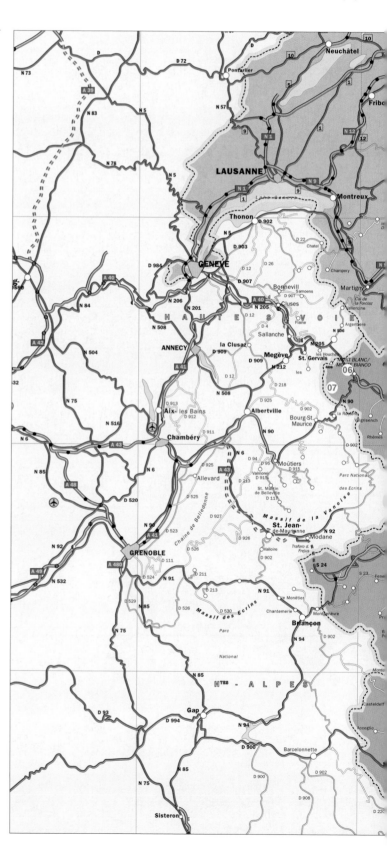

© Pascal Boulgakow **Rider** Laurent Besse

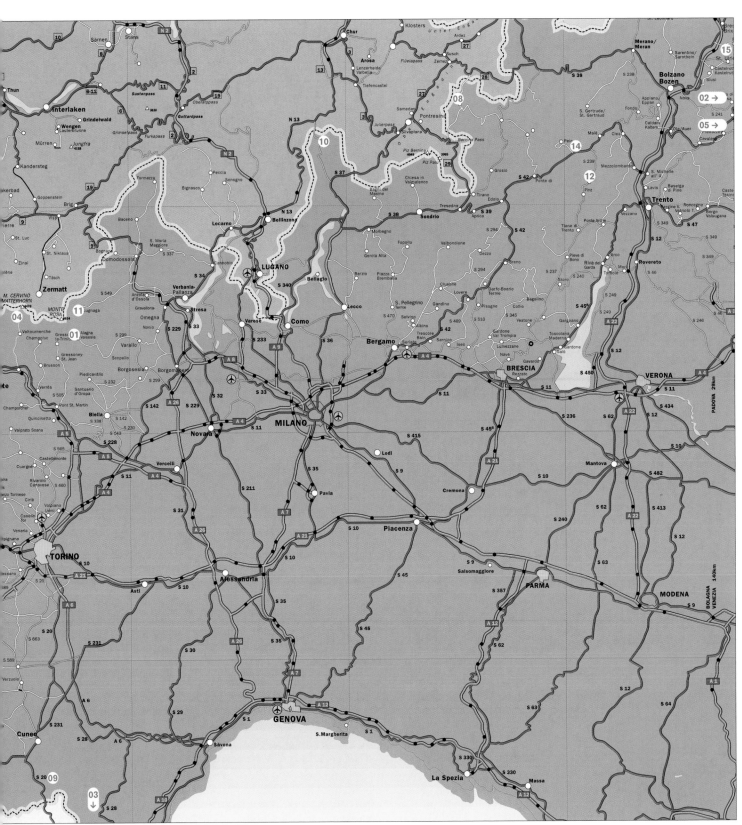

PROS & CONS »
+ One of the best freeride areas in Europe.
+ Breathtaking mountain views.
+ Heliboarding available.

− The resort is not very supportive of snowboarding.
− Very little nightlife.
− Poor for freestylers, carvers or beginners.

"ALAGNA IS WIDELY REGARDED AS ONE OF THE GREAT ITALIAN FREERIDE AREAS, WITH ENDLESS OPPORTUNITIES – GET HERE AS FAST AS YOU CAN!"

ALAGNA
ITALY

ALAGNA »
www.alagna.it
tourist office tel: + 39 0163922988
location: Alagna Valsesia
population: 500
altitude: 1220m
linked resorts: Monterosa Ski area

ON THE MOUNTAIN »
season: December to end of April
Lifts
vertical drop: 1380-3550m
amount of lifts in total: 8
gondolas: 3
chair lifts: 2
drag lifts: 3
Slopes
amount of prepared slopes: 30 km
runs w. snowmaking machines: -
easy runs: 2
intermediate runs: 10
advanced runs: 1
Facilities
night riding: -
amount of halfpipes: -
amount of funparks: -
heliboarding: yes
Lift-ticket prices in Euro
day: 26
week: 60
season: 687

SNOWBOARD TUITION »
Scuola Sci Alagna
Tel: +39 0163922961

SNOWBOARD SHOPS »
Articoli Sportivi Chiara Sport
Tel: +39 016391173
Articoli sportivi Monterosa Sport
Tel: +39 0163922970

GETTING THERE »
Car
Turin - Alagna: 159km
Turin - A4 Biandrate - Romagnano Sesia exit
- SS299 Alagna Valsesia
Milan - Alagna: 144km
Milan - A8 Lainate - A26 Borgomanero -
Romagnano Sesia exit - SS299 Alagna
Valsesia
Geneva - Alagna: 306km
Geneva - (Swiss/Fr) - Annemasse - St.
Gervais les Bain - towards Chamonix - Mont
Blanc Tunnel (Fr/It) - Courmayeur - A5 to
Quincinetto exit - Biella - Valle Mosso -
SS299 Alagna Valsesia
Train/Bus
Milan - Varallo Sesia - 2.5 hrs, 36km away
from Alagna. You'll then need to take a bus
(1 hour journey time) or a taxi (40 minutes) to
Alagna itself. Contact Italian Railways on
www.fs-on-line.com
Air
Milan-Malpensa Airport 108km
Turin Airport 166km

ALAGNA »
Intro_The glacier on the south face of Monte Rosa rises up at the end of the green Valesia valley, creating a dramatic backdrop for the lovely Italian resort of Alagna. The combination of the lovely architecture of the town set amidst such a wild verdant landscape makes this a great place to visit. And if these weren't enough, Alagna is widely regarded as one of the great Italian freeride areas, with endless opportunities – get here as fast as you can!

ON THE MOUNTAIN »
Snow reliability_Depending on the snowfall, Alagna's winter season can run from November to May. If the snow hasn't melted by the end of the regular season, it's not unknown for the lifts around the summit to remain open well into June. This whole area is one big bowl, which allows for great conditions long after the snow has fallen.

Weather and snow reports
www.monterosa-ski.com or
Tel: +39 (0) 125 303 111

Lifts & Piste_The Balma, the queen of the runs in Alagna, is considered to be one of the most beautiful and safest freeride runs on this planet. The run begins at the summit station of the Indren lift at 3200m above sea level, and from here you can ride down the Balma to 2300m. There aren't any significant danger spots, just an infinity of great lines to discover.

Freeriding_Despite the fact that Alagna is one of the best freeride areas in Europe, it has avoided the onslaught of mass tourism - which is great news for us. The best, most pristine terrain is accessible either by lift and a hike, or by helicopter. This is real high alpine terrain - 3550m above sea level - so we won't lead you into the unknown by describing all the possibilities. With the exception of the classic Balma run, we recommend that you use the services of a local mountain guide to help you discover this expansive resort.

For further info
Tel & Fax: +39 (0) 163 91310
Email: guideala@tin.it

Heliboarding in Alagna
www.monterosa-ski.com or
www.guidealagna.com

Freestyling_Although there are one or two great spots to build your own kickers, Alagna doesn't really have much to offer freestylers. There is no park or pipe.

Carving_The terrain here is entirely unsuitable for carving.

Beginners_The lower section of this resort is best for beginners, and is serviced by a gondola. The Balma run is not suitable for learners. On the whole, Alagna is a resort for good freeriders; but beginners will be better served somewhere else.

Mountain Restaurants_Cosy ski huts are plentiful in Alagna. The Guglielmina Hut, Grande Halt Hut, La Baita Restaurant, Gasthaus Indren, Gasthaus Pisse, Bar Wold, Bar Heidi and the Lo Chalet restaurant are all located on the slopes. They all serve food at reasonable prices and the service is friendly. Sundays during high

season can get very lively. One of the best huts is at the valley lift station — the view and the food are both excellent.

IN THE TOWN »

Accommodation_Alagna is a relatively inexpensive town. Prices range from €15 for a simple place to sleep, through to €70 for half board accommodation. The two star Hotel Genzianella is reasonable, and has a house bar, or try Residence Mary.
There are also a good number of holiday apartments available. Further information in English or Italian at www.alagna.it.

Genzianella
Tel: +39 (0) 125 307 156
www.hotelgenzianella.it

Residence Mary
Tel: +39 (0) 163 922 949

Food_Alagna has a few supermarkets, restaurants, pizzerias and the Genzianella Bar — a must after a hard day on the mountain. The prices are fine and there'll be no surprises when you get the bill.

Nightlife_The evenings here are very quiet. You can head to the local guesthouses or bars, but this is no epic party town. Don't be put off though, imagine all those hangover- free early morning snowboarding sessions!

Other Activities_Freeclimbing is available half way down the valley. A fitness centre, sauna, spa, ice rink and basketball court can all be found at the Palazetto dello Sport - Tel: +39 (0) 163 91101

LOCAL TIP »

With the help of a guide, you can access some great freeriding spots within 10 - 20 minutes. Don't go heading out on your own. For further tips ask Andrea Enzio, who can either take you on a tour himself, or at least point you in the right direction. A local mountain guide and snowboarder from Alagna, Andrea is thought to be responsible for a few extra grey hairs on the head of many a freerider.

Info
andrea.enzio@libero.it
Tel: +39 (0) 348 780 0644

"DESPITE THE FACT THAT ALAGNA IS ONE OF THE BEST FREERIDE AREAS IN EUROPE, IT HAS AVOIDED THE ONSLAUGHT OF MASS TOURISM - WHICH IS GREAT NEWS FOR US."

PROS & CONS »
+ One of the best snowparks in Italy.
+ Good tree runs and freeriding potential.
+ Events are held every weekend in the snowpark.
+ Friendly locals.

− Low elevation.
− Busy at weekends.
− Snow base often thin.

ALLEGHE
ITALY

ALLEGHE »
www.infodolomiti.it
Tourist office tel: +39 0437523333
Location: Alleghe
Population: 2500
Altitude: 979

ON THE MOUNTAIN »
Season: December - April
Lifts
Vertical drop: 1000-2200m
amount of lifts in total: 44
gondolas: 2
chair lifts: 7
drag lifts: 17
Slopes
amount of prepared slopes in km: 80
runs w. snowmaking machines: 70 km
of easy runs: 24
intermediate runs: 17
advanced runs: 3
Facilities
night riding: yes
amount of halfpipes: -
amount of funparks: 1
Heliboarding: no
Lift-ticket prices in Euro
Day: 27
Week: 143
Season: 340.86
special deals: night ticket 15,50

SNOWBOARD TUITION »
Scuola Sci Coldai , Corso Italia, 32
Tel: +39 0437723880
scuolascicoldai@dolomiti.it

SNOWBOARD SHOPS »
Ski & snowboardservice
Tel: +39 0437523274
Kiwi-sport
Tel: +39 0437523211

GETTING THERE »
Car
Innsbruck (Au) - Alleghe: 175km
Innsbruck - A12 Brenner - Klausen/Gröden -
St Ullrich (Ortisei) - Arabba - Caprile - Alleghe
Verona - Alleghe: 203km
Verona - Verona Ovest - Brennero/Modena -
Neumarkt (Egna) - Cavalese - Predazzo -
Arabba - Alleghe
Venice - Alleghe: 154km
Venice - Mestre - Belluno - Mas - Agordo -
Taibon Agordino - Alleghe
Train
To get to Belluno take the Padua/Calazo di
Cadore train or the Venice/Belluno service. A
connecting bus then takes you to Alleghe -
journey time approx. 1hr 10min.
Air
Venice Airport 203km
Verona Airport 155km

"ALLEGHE IS A CARVER'S PARADISE. THE PISTES ARE SCRUPULOUSLY MANICURED."

© Ricky Felderer

ALLEGHE »
Intro__Alleghe_ is a beautiful village
in the Italian _Dolomites_ at the foot
of the _Civetta_. Along with its
neighbours, _Zoldo_ and _San Martino
Cadore_, _Alleghe_ is part of the _Ski
Civetta_ ski area. This small, cosy
village is not far from the city of
Belluno and the internationally-
renowned resort of _Cortina_.

ON THE MOUNTAIN »
Snow reliability_ The best time to
visit _Alleghe_, especially for freeriders,
is from the end of December
through to March. If you're more
into the snowpark and just hanging
out with locals, then April is also a
good time.

Lifts & Piste_ The resort is
relatively large, and the modern lifts
are efficient and uncrowded. It is
generally quicker and easier to go by
car up to the lift station rather than
take the gondola from the village.
Once you're up in the resort, you'll
hardly ever have to queue at the
lifts. The chairlift connecting
Alleghe to _Selva_, which is close to
the park, is one of the easiest ways
of getting to the goods. This floodlit
piste also has night boarding.

Freeriding_ When snowfalls are
bountiful, you'll find dream freeride
terrain in _Alleghe_. However, due to
its low altitude, good snow
conditions don't last for long. You'll
find easy and safe off piste run,
though, by turning right from the
summit station of the chairlift that
connects _Alleghe_ with _Sesto_. This
run is visible to the left of the _Piste
Par Della Costa_. A few nice lines
can also be found below the _Col
Dei Baldi_ chairlift.

Freestyling_ Last season, Alleghe
didn't have a pipe, but one is
planned for 2003. The park is one
of the best set-ups in Italy,
featuring two large kickers and six
rails, which all which stay usable
even when there's not much
snow. A snowmaking machine
supplies the park with a
constant snow base. The boys
responsible for its upkeep,
Andrea Codor and Alvar dal Farra,
can keep you posted by email -
contact them at
codoro.andrea@libero.it

Further information
Consorzio di Alleghe
Tel: +39 (0) 437 523 207

Carving__Alleghe_ is a carver's
paradise. The pistes are
scrupulously manicured making
these slopes ideal for the carver,
especially in the morning.

Beginners_ The resort also offers
good terrain for beginners, whether
it be on piste, off piste or in the
park. The modern ski schools offer
both ski and snowboard lessons.
There are no special facilities for
the freestyle beginner, but the
instructors are very helpful and
friendly.

Mountain Restaurants_ There
are a number of bars and
restaurants on the piste itself
where you can get great food. The
meals, ranging from sandwiches
through to local specialities, will
cost you around €5 for a sandwich
up to €15 to €20 for a full-blown
midday meal.

IN THE TOWN »
Accommodation__Alleghe_ has a
range of guesthouses, apartments
and hotels costing between €25
per night and €50 for a four star
hotel. Further information about
accommodation in the Dolomites

"THE RESORT IS RELATIVELY LARGE, AND THE MODERN LIFTS ARE EFFICIENT AND UNCROWDED. IT IS GENERALLY QUICKER AND EASIER TO GO BY CAR UP TO THE LIFT STATION RATHER THAN TAKE THE GONDOLA."

"F40 IS A LOCAL HANGOUT IN BELLUNO, WHERE YOU SHOULD TRY SOME OF THE POLENTA DISHES ALONG WITH A GLASS OF CABERNET OR MERLOT."

© Ricky Felderer *Rider* Giaccomo Kratter

can be found at www.dolomiti.it or www.dolomitisuperski.com .

Food_If you're staying in a holiday apartment, you'll find the price of groceries at the supermarkets are pretty reasonable. But keep an eye on the smaller shops, where the price of local products can get over-inflated. Directly above the car park of the village lift station there are a number of pubs and a good pizzeria, all with decent prices.
F40 is a local hangout in *Belluno*, where you should try some of the polenta dishes along with a glass of Cabernet or Merlot. This place is also highly recommended for its pizzas.

Nightlife_A disco at the lake and a few bars in the village provide the nightlife. For those looking for a little more, head to *F40* in *Belluno*, where there is generally a good crowd.

Other Activities_Close to the pubs in the centre of town is the *Rail Garden* from *Alvaro dal Farra*. There's no skate park, but *Alleghe* does offer freeclimbing and paragliding.

LOCAL TIP »
Alleghe is a stylish village, where even slicing up the pizza is done with great Italian flair! Keep this in mind if you're looking to impress – both in the bars and on the slopes.

© Ricky Felderer

"THE BEST TIME FOR RIDING IS DEFINITELY IN MARCH."

CAMPO IMPERATORE
ITALY

CAMPO IMPERATORE »
www.gransassonline.com
tourist office tel: +39 086222306
location: Campo Imperatore
population: 200
altitude: 1000

ON THE MOUNTAIN »
season: November- May
Lifts
vertical drop: 1000-2100m
amount of lifts in total: 2
gondolas: -
chair lifts: 1
T-bars: 1
Slopes
amount of prepared slopes: 9 km
runs w. snowmaking machines: -
amount of easy runs: 6
amount of intermediate runs: 2
amount of advanced runs: 1
Facilities
night riding: -
amount of halfpipes : -
amount of funparks: 1
Heliboarding: -
Lift-ticket prices in Euro
1/2 day: 17
day: 20
season: 250

SNOWBOARD TUITION »
Gran'Sasso
Tel: +39 0862400012

GETTING THERE »
Car
Rome - Campo Imperatore: 130km
Rome - A24 Torano - L'Aquila - Campo Imperatore
Pescara - Campo Imperatore: 115km
Pescara - Montesilvano Marina - Roseto degli Abruzzi - Villa Vomano - L'Aquila - Campo Imperatore
Train/Bus
By train from Rome to L'Aquila - journey time approx. 3.5 hours - then continue by bus to Campo Imperatore. For further info, log onto the Italian Railways website: www.fs-on-line.com.
Air
Rome Airport: 130km
Pescara Airport: 115km

CAMPO IMPERATORE »
Intro_Who would have thought you could snowboard just 130km from Rome? Campo Imperatore is a small winter village in the Appenines, part of the long range of mountains that stretches from Genoa down to Calabria. Unfortunately, Campo Imperatore is not your typical scenic Italian mountain setting, more a tourist village made up of three hostels and one restaurant/bar. Its position between the sea and the mainland makes for variable weather, but there's usually enough snow for a good freeride session.

ON THE MOUNTAIN »
Snow reliability_Due to the mountain range's ability to hold onto the weather, you'll find it snows here more often than you might expect. Strong winds then create a compacted snow base. The best time for riding is definitely in March, when you'll find plenty of snow and if you're lucky even some friendly weather conditions.

Lifts & Piste_Just two lifts service what is perhaps one of the smallest resorts in this guide. The tow lift, which takes you to the harder slope, is only recommended for experienced riders because the descent is steep. The pistes, which are accessible from the chairlift, vary in difficulty.

Freeriding_The finest freeriding areas are Valloni and Vallefredda. If there's enough snow to carry you down to the lift, you can access two great runs which are considered to be among the best in the Appenines. Both have a vertical drop of over 1000m, and are accessible within a few minutes' walk from the lift. They'll take you through a small valley with lots of cliffs, natural quarters, cornices and tree runs. There are no great danger spots, but following snowfalls, big slabs of snow are sometimes released so you need to take care out there. Both runs are well known, just ask the locals about Valloni and Vallefredda, and hopefully they'll give you a few tips, and even throw in a couple of well kept local secrets too.
    Tip: It's probably not a good idea to be roaming around the village too late at night because that's when the wild pigs come out to forage!

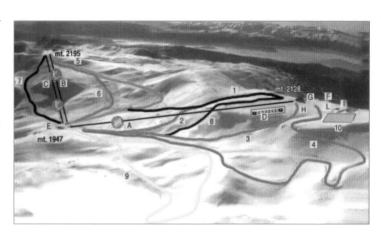

"THE FINEST FREERIDING AREAS ARE VALLONI AND VALLEFREDDA. YOU CAN ACCESS TWO GREAT RUNS WHICH ARE CONSIDERED TO BE AMONG THE BEST IN THE APPENINES."

Freestyling_The park includes a halfpipe, a funbox, rails and a few other hits; some of which are suitable for beginners. Still, don't expect too much... Further info on the current condition of the park is available from the Rad Moves Club, who maintain it:
Tel: +39 (0) 328 326 2734.

Carving_Carving is not really an option because the runs are small and tight.

Beginners_There is one ski school and six pistes that are suitable for beginners, but it's frankly not worth travelling any great distance just to learn here.

Mountain Restaurants_The Hotel Campo Imperatore and L'Ostello are located up on the summit at 2000m above sea level. The local specialities are lamb cooked over a spit or pasta served with a rabbit ragout.

IN THE TOWN »
Accommodation_Overnight accommodation is available at L'Ostello for around 15 euros per night. The choice of hotels is not

great, but then they're not too expensive either - around 25 to 35 euros per night.

Food_Da Maria is the only restaurant in town, but you won't be disappointed. The food is excellent and the prices are cheap. If you want to try somewhere else, you'll need to drive down to L'Aquila where the main square, the Piazza Duomo, has numerous restaurants, including Via Sassa. La Quintana, Magoo, and Al Coloniale.

Nightlife_Unfortunately Campo Imperatore doesn't have any bars or pubs. Here again you'll need to travel to L'Aquila, some 15km away, which has a few bars and pubs. Magoo is one of the better ones.

Other Activities_Yet again, it's a trip to L'Aquila, where there's a small skate park close to the centre of the town.

LOCAL TIP »
If you're in the area, think about a visit to one of the neighbouring resorts - Ovindoli and Campo Felice are both about 20km away.

· · · functional outdoor jeans · · · · functional outdoor jeans · · ·

Outer jeans.
Inner function.

VAUDE DryJeans.

Outside: Cotton for the classic casual denim
look

Inside: CoolMax® for total outdoor performance

The special CoolMax®/Cotton blend is
unsurpassed for sweat management:

• won't stick to skin even during high
activity sports
• transports perspiration quickly away
from body to outer layer
• dries three times faster than ordinary
jeans

VAUDE DryJeans. Providing exceptional
wearing comfort and performance.

www.vaude.de
VAUDE, D - 88069 Tettnang

CoolMax®
WITH
COTTON

Hike   Skate   Bike   Expedition   Travel   Office

VAUDE DryJeans

PROS & CONS »
+ Great pipe.
+ Excellent snow conditions, thanks to the glacier.
+ Lots of professional riders hang out here.

− Often very windy at the summit.
− Not much to do in the village.
− Bad traffic jams on Sunday afternoons.
− No public First Aid Station, only an expensive private one.

"CERVINIA HAS BEEN SWITCHED ON TO THE SNOWBOARD SCENE FOR QUITE A LONG TIME, AND BOTH ITS SPECTACULAR POSITION AND THE HIGH QUALITY PIPE DRAWS MANY SNOWBOARDERS HERE."

BREUIL-CERVINIA
ITALY

CERVINIA »
www.sportepromozione.it
tourist office tel: +39 0166944411
location: Cervinia
population: 800
altitude: 2006m
linked resorts: Valtournenche ,Cervinia ,Zermatt

ON THE MOUNTAIN »
season: all year round
Lifts
vertical drop: 2000-3500m
amount of lifts in total: 36
gondolas: 7
chair lifts: 12
drag lifts: 17
Slopes
amount of prepared slopes: 300 km
runs w. snowmaking machines: 100%
amount of easy runs: 20
amount of intermediate runs: 31
amount of advanced runs: 9
Facilities
night riding: -
amount of halfpipes: 1
amount of funparks: 2
heliboarding: yes
Lift-ticket prices in Euro
day: 33
week: 86
season: 520

SNOWBOARD TUITION »
Scuola di sci del Cervino
Tel: +39 0166949034
Nuova scuola di sci Cieloalto
Tel: +39 0166948451

SNOWBOARD SHOPS »
Point du Sport
Tel: +39 0165236848
Piera Sport
Tel: +39 0166949063

GETTING THERE »
Car
Milan - Cervinia: 189km
Milan - A4 Santhi… - Ivrea - A5 towards Aosta - St. Vincent exit, Ch/tillon - Breuil-Cervinia
Bern - Cervinia: 253km
Bern - towards Fribourg, Lausanne, Geneva - Vevey - Martigny - Grand Saint Bernard Tunnel (Swiss/It) - Aosta - A5 towards Turin - St.Vincent exit, Ch/tillon - Breuil-Cervinia
Lyon - Cervinia: 430km
Lyon - A43 Chambry - Annecy - towards Chamonix-Mont Blanc - Saint Gervais les Bains - Mont Blanc Tunnel (Fr/ It) - Courmayeur - A5 towards Torino - St.Vincent exit, Ch/tillon - Breuil-Cervinia
Bus
Various bus companies run buses to Cervinia from Milan, Turin and Aosta.
Train
Travel on the Milan-Turin line to Chivasso and then on to Chatillon. There are also direct trains from Turin.
Air
Turin Caselle Airport: 118km
Linate Airport: 140km
Milan-Malpensa Airport: 160km

© Ricky Felderer **Rider** Werner Crazzolara

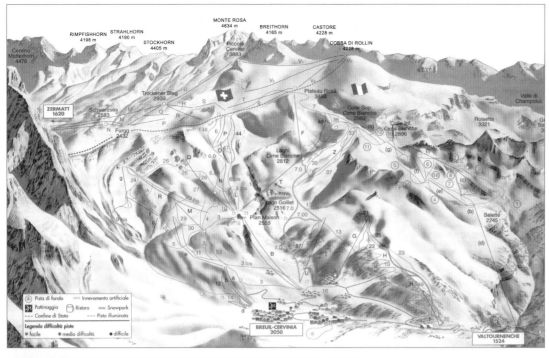

"CERVINIA HAS ONE OF THE BEST PIPES IN EUROPE."

© Ricky Federer

BREUIL-CERVINIA »

Intro_ Up until the 1930s, what is now the town of Cervinia was known as Breuil, but this was considered to be too French-sounding for the Mussolini regime, so the name was changed to Cervinia. In any case, the old name suggested no connection with the local mountain of Monte Cervino, otherwise known as the Matterhorn.

Cervinia has been switched on to the snowboard scene for quite a long time, and both its spectacular position and the high quality pipe (which continues into summer and autumn) draws many snowboarders here.

ON THE MOUNTAIN »

Snow reliability_ Except for the preparation period in May, Cervinia is open all year round. The glacier helps to guarantee good snow, and snowmaking machines are on hand on the lower slopes. For weather and snow reports phone:
+39 (0) 166 949 001

Lifts & Piste_ The International Day Pass is relatively expensive, but it does allow you to travel over the border into Switzerland and to the resort of Zermatt. Don't miss the last lift back to the Italian side of the mountain though - a night in Zermatt can be very expensive. It gets busier during the school holidays and on Sundays, but the waiting periods aren't usually too long. It may be hard to find a parking space though.

Freeriding_ The best terrain has been turned into groomed slopes, but some impressive runs still remain untouched. Many of these depart from Piccolo Cervino, but you'll find that every now and then the runs join the piste before heading into powder again. There are a few runs on the north-facing slopes where the powder remains untouched even weeks after a snowfall. The very best runs are accessible only by helicopter. Popular trips include visits to the summits of Chateau des Dames, Cherillon or Roisette, but it is also possible to fly to Monte Rosa, which, at 4633m above sea level, is the highest helicopter destination in the Alps.

Further info about Heliboarding
Heliski Cervinia
Email: info@heliskicervinia.com
Tel: +39 (0) 166 949 267

Freestyling_ During the summer and autumn months, when the conditions are right, Cervinia provides one of the best pipes in Europe, as well as a fantastic park with rails and jumps. The pipe on the Swiss side is also worth visiting. Ideal kicker building terrain is not easy to find, but the best known spot is next to Plan Maison. Careful though, the rocky terrain can make landing dangerous, so check before you jump.

Carving_ Cervinia often has well groomed, ice hard pistes, with lots of good variation in gradient. The Italians let their edges run hot until late morning, and spend the afternoon enjoying the sunshine.

Beginners_ Beginners will feel at home here in Cervinia, the only disadvantage is the long traverses, which take you from one sector to the other. You'll need good nerves and strong muscles!

Mountain Restaurants_A few huts and rest stations next to the pistes all serve tasty food. It isn't especially cheap here, but if you find Cervinia expensive, don't even bother travelling over to the Swiss side! A popular rest station is the summit station of the glacier lift.

IN THE TOWN »

Accommodation_ Accommodation isn't exactly cheap. Expect to pay around 40 to 45 euros per night. Staying next to the lifts is even more expensive, but rooms further down the valley are a little cheaper - although really cheap is not an option here. Acceptable prices can be found at the 3 star Hotel

Europa - Tel: +39 (0) 166 948 660 or at the 2 star Hotel Marmore - Tel: +39 (0) 166 949 057. A list of hotels and guesthouses can be inspected at www.cervinia.it

Food_ There are many different ways to fill a hungry belly. You can visit the local supermarket, a pizzeria or one of the noble restaurants. There's something for everyone's budget, but pizza and pasta are the best options for the more fragile wallet. The Cucina Valdostana is excellent, and after the great food don't forget to try a Grolla - a hot coffee liquor claimed to aid the digestion.

Nightlife_ There are lots of pubs in the centre of town, and those wanting to party until the early hours will probably find themselves at Etoile - the village disco. Another option is the Casino in St.Vincent. St. Vincent is approximately 20 minutes' drive away, and this is one of the few casinos in Italy. The crowd is quite select, but if you happen to be passing and dressed for the occasion, enjoy the fun. The prices in the Cervinia pubs are okay, the people are sometimes a little too cool - or better said, they think they're cool. Don't let it bother you.

Other Activities_ Activities include ice skating, golf (depending on the season), and in summer there's freeclimbing, swimming, bowling, and a fitness centre.

LOCAL TIP »
After September, you'll begin to meet up with the likes of Gian Simmen and Dani Costandach, in the pipe, as well as the whole North West crew and the boys from the Aosta valley. It's worth asking them what they're up to of an evening.

"THE RECENTLY DEVELOPED FUNPARK CAN BE FOUND AT FALORIA. UNTIL RECENTLY SNOWBOARDERS WERE NOT A CONSIDERATION, AS CORTINA IS TRADITIONALLY A NOBLE SKI TOWN, FULL OF RICH PEOPLE AND LUXURY."

CORTINA
ITALY

CORTINA»
www.infodolmiti.it
Tourist office tel: + 39 0436323123
Location Cortina d'Ampezzo
population: 7000
altitude: 1050m

ON THE MOUNTAIN »
season: December to April
Lifts
vertical drop: 1050-2932m
amount of lifts in total: 51
gondolas: 8
chair lifts: 24
drag lifts: 19
Slopes
amount of prepared slopes: 140 km
runs w. snowmaking machines: 95%
easy runs: 47 km
intermediate runs: 86 km
advanced runs: 7 km
Facilities
night riding: -
amount of halfpipes: -
amount of funparks: -
heliboarding: -
Lift-ticket prices in Euro
day: 31
week: 163
season: 473

SNOWBOARD TUITION »
Scuola Sci Cortina
Tel: +39 04362911
Scuola Sci Azzurra Cortina
Tel: +39 04362694

SNOWBOARD SHOPS »
K2 Sport Lacedelli
Tel: +39 0436870104
Snow Service
Tel +39 0436866635

GETTING THERE »
Car
Innsbruck - Cortina d'Ampezzo 166km
Innsbruck - Brenner - Brixen - Percha -
Töblach/Dobbiaco - Cortina d'Ampezzo
Verona - Cortina d'Ampezzo 258km
Verona - Trevisio - Belluno - Pieve di Cadore -
Cortina d'Ampezzo
Bus
Innsbruck to Cortina by bus - 4 hours
Venice to Cortina - 3.5 hours. Buses travel
daily during the high season. You'll need to
reserve a seat with SE.AM in Cortina -
Tel:+39 (0) 436 867 921 Info: Autolinea
ATVO Tel: +39 (0) 421 59 44
Weekends during winter - a bus from
Autolinea Autostradale from Milan via Brescia,
Bruneck, Dobbiaco to Cortina approx. 6 hours
30 minutes.
Info Tel: +39 (0) 436 867 921
Train
Train line Venezia S. Lucia - Calalzo di Cador,
then continue by the shuttle service to
Cortina. If travelling from the north you will
arrive at Fortezza - Dobbiaco. Change to the
bus service to Cortina. Fortezza to Cortina
takes around two hours.
Air
Innsbruck Airport 163km
Venice Airport 259km
Verona Airport 166km
Taxi service Contac, Cortina
Tel: +39 (0) 436 860 888
From Venice - Taxi to Mestre in approx.
20/30 minutes. 24 hour Funk Taxi service
Tel: +39 (0) 41 936 222
Buses operated by ACTV and ATVO

CORTINA »
Intro_ We are not talking about just any old village here, Cortina, darling, is one of the most exclusive resorts in the Alps. Fortunately the landscapes are as beautiful as the people who spend their holidays here, and the quality and variety of the slopes is excellent, although it is mainly geared towards carvers. A short while ago though, Cortina saw the light in terms of freestyle snowboarding, and even if they aren't there yet, they are at least pretending to head in the right direction.

ON THE MOUNTAIN »
Snow reliability_ The best time to visit Cortina is from mid January through to mid March. Last year saw poor snowfall though, proving the importance of getting informed before you go − check out www.cortina.com/meteo.

Lifts & Piste_ The two areas of Faloria and Tofana are better suited for snowboarders. The Tofana at 3243m is an attraction for carvers and freeriders - with good pistes and some fun off piste runs. At Faloria, a park has recently been developed. Avoid weekends and holiday periods and you'll be able to enjoy the off piste terrain without having to spend most of your time waiting in a lift queue or slicing through other people's tracks and crud.

Freeriding_ The Tofana area has a few interesting runs to discover, but for those really looking for something special, book a guide and head to the places where there aren't any lifts. Lovers of the mountains will definitely have more fun exploring in the Dolomites in this way.

Information
Email: info@guidecortina.it

Freestyling_ The recently developed funpark can be found at Faloria. Until recently snowboarders were not a consideration, as Cortina is traditionally a noble ski town, full of rich people and luxury. The average tourist here isn't on the slopes to try and learn 360's…

Carving_ The carving scene has developed well in the Dolomites and at Cortina in particular, with its wide, well groomed pistes.

Particularly Tofana, but also Faloria, are popular destinations for World Cup champions, and who wouldn't like to share some turns with them?

Beginners_ This resort is ideal for beginners, with excellent instructors and suitable terrain.

Mountain Restaurants_ In total, you will find 56 bars and mountain huts - 'Rifugis' - where a simple panini or a complete midday menu

is available. The prices range between €10 for a panini and a beer through to €40 for a full-on meal including wine.

IN THE TOWN »
Accommodation_ Cortina is one of the most expensive resorts in Italy, but compared with some other Swiss resorts, bearable. Those who can find accommodation outside the village should expect to pay around €30 per night. For

© Ricky Federer **Rider** Andrea Codoro

© Georg Schantl

"THE CARVING SCENE HAS DEVELOPED WELL IN THE DOLOMITES AND AT CORTINA IN PARTICULAR"

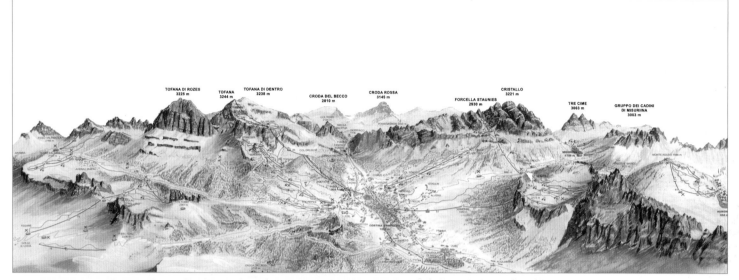

© Georg Schantl **Riders** Harry Putz, Flow Daniaux

something a bit more special, in the village you can lose up to €350 per night. The one star Hotel Fiames is one of the cheapest options - Tel: +39 (0) 436 23 66

Food_A visit to some of the fine restaurants is almost obligatory in Cortina D'Ampezzo. A nice entrée, followed by some fresh pasta in a mushroom sauce and then a game dish cooked in a flavoursome red wine should not be passed up. The Tivoli, Leone e Anna or El Toula are some of the more exquisite restaurants. For the smaller budget, you'll find a lot of good pizzerias such as Cinque Torri or A Passetto.

Nightlife_ Everything you could wish for can be found in Cortina. There are countless discos and bars, from the classic Area to the VIP Club. The Orange is also good for a beer. You certainly won't find it boring.

Other Activities_ The village is very lively and active, especially in regards to cultural events such as exhibitions and concerts. There is also a modern sports centre, an indoor ice rink and other facilities for you to use in your free time.

LOCAL TIP »
Rick Felderer - Editor-in-Chief and photographer for Onboard Italia_"One of the best rails I have ever photographed is located next to the Cristallo chairlift. It is accessible with a car and has 19 perfect steps."

"WE ARE NOT TALKING ABOUT JUST ANY OLD VILLAGE HERE, CORTINA, DARLING, IS ONE OF THE MOST EXCLUSIVE RESORTS IN THE ALPS. FORTUNATELY THE LANDSCAPES ARE AS BEAUTIFUL AS THE PEOPLE WHO SPEND THEIR HOLIDAYS HERE, AND THE QUALITY AND VARIETY OF THE SLOPES IS EXCELLENT"

"THE OFF PISTE RUNS AND HELI ACCESSIBLE BACKCOUNTRY TERRAIN ARE SOME OF THE MOST CHALLENGING AND EXHILARATING RUNS IN EUROPE."

COURMAYEUR
ITALY

COURMAYEUR »
www.courmayeur.net
Tourist office tel: +39 0165842060
Location: Courmayeur
population: 3050
altitude: 1224m

ON THE MOUNTAIN »
Season: December to May
Lifts
vertical drop: 1230-2750m
amount of lifts in total: 17
gondolas: 5
chair lifts: 8
drag lifts: 4
Slopes
amount of prepared slopes: 100
runs w. snowmaking machines: 12
easy runs: 6
intermediate runs: 13
of advanced runs: 4
Facilities
night riding: -
amount of halfpipes: 1
amount of funparks: 1
heliboarding: yes
Lift-ticket prices in Euro
1/2 day: 22
day: 31
week: 182
season: 687

SNOWBOARD TUITION »
Scuola Italiana Sci Montebianco
Tel: +39 0165842477
www.montebianco.maestridisci.com

SNOWBOARD SHOPS »
Snow Blanc
Tel: +39 0165842477

GETTING THERE »
Car
Zürich - Courmayeur 318km
Zürich - Bern - towards Fribourg, Lausanne, Genf - Martigny - Le Châtelard (Swiss/It) – Chamonix - Mont Blanc - Tunnel du Mont Blanc - Courmayeur
Lyon - Courmayeur 250km
Lyon - Chambéry - Annecy - towards Chamonix-Mont Blanc - Saint Gervais les Bains - Tunnel du Mont Blanc (Fr/ IT) - Courmayeur
Milan - Courmayeur 219km
Milan - Santhià - Ivrea - Morgex - Pré Saint Didier - Courmayeur
Train
Pré Saint Didier - 5km from Courmayeur
The train to Aosta is also good. Hop on the busline to Courmayeur from there.
Bus
Connecting bus lines are available from all the larger north Italian cities - Turin, Milan, and Genoa.
Schedules for the buslines from Turin and Milan can be obtained from Autostazione Savda - Tel: +39 (0) 165 842 031
Air
Aosta Airport 40km
Turin Airport 151km
Milan-Malpensa Airport 198km
Geneva Airport 100km
Flight Info for Aosta - Airvallée - Tel: +39 (0) 165 236 966 www.airvallee.com/

© Ricky Felderer **Rider** Rudy Buccolla

COURMAYEUR »
Intro_ The popular resort of Courmayeur is a modern alpine town set in the shadow of Mont Blanc, the fascinating massif blessed with the highest summit in the Alps. Nestling in a large bowl, some 1224m above sea level, surrounded by pine forest, the winter sports resort of Courmayeur is a town that offers lots to do, has an excellent tourism infrastructure and attracts an international crowd of visitors. The area is a paradise for both local Italian and visiting snowboarders, and offers endless off piste possibilities.

ON THE MOUNTAIN »
Snow reliability_ Snow conditions are generally excellent because it snows quite a lot. 50% of the runs have snow-making equipment, should the need arise. Bad conditions are seldom encountered, but the best times to visit are considered to be between February and March.

Lifts & Piste_ Two lifts depart from the centre of Courmayeur and take you to the upper lifts. One of the lifts is located right in the middle of the village and travels to Plan Chécrouit, while the other leaves from Entrèves and goes to Pré de Pascal. The Mont Blanc lift departs from 1306m at La Palud and arrives at Punta Helbronner (3486m), where you can catch amazing views of the French, Italian and Swiss Alps. Courmayeur offers riding terrain for both the beginner and the extreme rider alike. You'll not find any long or flat stretches where you need to walk or push –in fact you'll need to know how to slow your board down! The chutes, powder fields and steep slopes make for nice riding alongside the forested areas in between the piste.

Freeriding_ The off piste runs and heli accessible backcountry terrain are some of the most challenging and exhilarating runs in Europe. We recommend that you don't undertake backcountry tours on your own. Firstly because it's dangerous, but also because you'll have more fun and more powder with a mountain guide who will show you places you'd never find on your own. The run over the Mer de Glace in Vallée Blanche begins in Pont Helbronner and ends down in Chamonix, France, and is a classic tour. The scenery is spectacular but not very challenging if you're a skilled freerider – this is more a photo excursion. The mountain guides generally organise a bus for the return journey to Courmayeur which goes through the Mont Blanc Tunnel, or you could think about sharing the cost of a taxi. More challenging runs include the

"WE RECOMMEND THAT YOU DON'T UNDERTAKE BACKCOUNTRY TOURS ON YOUR OWN."

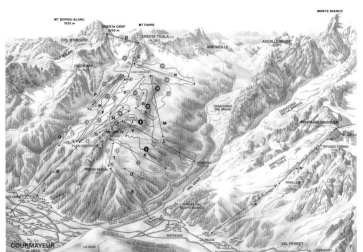

"THE POPULAR RESORT OF COURMAYEUR IS A MODERN ALPINE TOWN SET IN THE SHADOW OF MONT BLANC, THE FASCINATING MASSIF BLESSED WITH THE HIGHEST SUMMIT IN THE ALPS. NESTLING IN A LARGE BOWL, SOME 1224M ABOVE SEA LEVEL, SURROUNDED BY PINE FOREST, THE WINTER SPORTS RESORT OF COURMAYEUR IS A TOWN THAT OFFERS LOTS TO DO AND ATTRACTS AN INTERNATIONAL CROWD OF VISITORS."

Toula run - with a 2000m drop in elevation - or the runs down to Val Veny or La Thuile.

Mountain Guides
Rudy Buccella
Tel: +39 (0) 355 5433 856
Patrick Raspo
Tel: +39 (0) 347 7307 822
Office: Tel: +39 (0) 165 3411 519

Freestyling_Courmayeur has a boardercross course, a park with three rails and a few tables of varying lengths but everything depends on the amount of snow in the resort. Roby Moresi is the park's shaper as well as a damn good rider. A superpark is being planned for the future. For further info regarding the quality and condition

of the park contact Martina Magenta: Email - ttrmag@tin.it

Carving_The pistes are well suited for carving.

Beginners_There are six beginner pistes. The *Chiecco* and *Tzaly* practice lifts can be used, and they're free.

Mountain Restaurants_The quality and the prices in the ski huts are pretty good. *Chamonix*, on the French side of the mountain, is notoriously expensive, and you really should take advantage of *Courmayeur's* fair prices and good food. Christiana at *Plan Checrout* serves great pizzas and for a quick snack, we recommend the *Club Courba Dzeleuna*.

"THE MAIN STREET, VIA ROMA, IS THE PUMPING, PULSING HEART OF THIS TOWN. IT'S SMALL AND WINDY AND FULL OF BUSY SHOPS AND RESTAURANTS/BARS."

COURMAYEUR
ITALY

» IN THE TOWN »

Accommodation_If you want to experience the atmosphere and the tastes of the region, book yourselves into a guestroom at one of the private houses in *Valdigne*. The cost for overnight accommodation and an evening meal is relatively cheap, and you get to experience the traditional lifestyle and hospitality of the locals. There are also endless other possibilities for cheap accommodation. Further info is available from the *Azienda di Informazione ed Accoglienza Turistica Monte Bianco*
Tel: +39 (0) 165 842 060
aptmontebianco@psw.it

Food_The specialities of the region include fontina cheese, smoked ham (speck), polenta, game, etc... And the local red wine is delicious too. *La Terrazza*, *La Pizzeria K2* and the *Red Lion* are all popular restaurants and are all in the *Via Roma*. The prices and the food are great.

Nightlife_The main street, *Via Roma*, is the pumping, pulsing heart of this town. It's small and windy and full of busy shops and restaurants/bars. A lot of younger people meet up at the *Bar Le Privé* or the *American Bar*. For a bit of a dance, most make their way over to the *Disco Le Machis*.

Other Activities_*Centro Sportivo Courmayeur* is one of the best equipped and most spectacular sports centres in Europe, offering a wide range of activities including golf, ice skating, squash, tennis, fitness studio, climbing wall, ice hockey rink and the only indoor curling rink in Italy. Exhilarating dog sledding fun can be organised through www.gjadventures.it
Tel: +39 (0) 165 899 36

LOCAL TIP »

'The eighth wonder of the world' is Europe's highest gondola, which can transport you over the Italian border and down into *Chamonix*. You can depart from *La Palud*. One station is situated next to the Torino Hut and the next station is at *Punta Helbronner* at 3462m. The summer station at *Aiguille du Midi* is 3842m above sea level. On *Punta Helbronner* look out for the spectacular *Terrazza dei Ghiacciai* and the Crystal Museum.

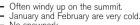

PROS & CONS »
+ Great kicker building terrain.
+ Excellent snow conditions.
+ Good infrastructure.

– Often windy up on the summit.
– January and February are very cold.
– No snowpark.

"LA THUILE ISN'T EXACTLY A BEGINNER'S PARADISE."

LA THUILE
ITALY

LA THUILE »
www.lathuile.it
Tourist office tel: +39 0165884179
location: La Thuile
population: 730
altitude: 1441m
linked resort: La Rosiere

ON THE MOUNTAIN »
Season: December to end of April
Lifts
vertical drop: 1441-2612m
amount of lifts in total: 17
gondolas: 1
chair lifts: 10
drag lifts: 6
Slopes
amount of prepared slopes: 80 km
runs w. snowmaking machines: 10
amount of easy runs: 20
amount of intermediate runs: 14
amount of advanced runs: 6
Facilities
night riding: -
amount of halfpipes: -
amount of funparks: -
heliboarding: yes
Lift-ticket prices in Euro
day: 28.92
week: 181
season: 392.51
special fares: Val d'Aosta season 687

SNOWBOARD TUITION »
Scuola di sci La Thuile
Tel: +39 0165884123

SNOWBOARD SHOPS »
Berthod Sport
Tel:+39 0165884642
www.berthodsport.it

GETTING THERE »
Car
Zürich - La Thuile: 331km
Zürich - Bern - in the direction of Fribourg,
Lausanne, Geneva - Martigny - Le Châtelard
(Swiss/It) - Chamonix-Mont Blanc (Fr/It) -
Pré Saint Didier - La Thuile
Lyon - La Thuile: 264km
Lyon - Chambéry - Annecy - towards
Chamonix-Mont Blanc - Saint Gervais les
Bains - Mont Blanc Tunnel (Fr/ It) - Pré Saint
Didier - La Thuile
Milan - La Thuile: 222km
Milan - Santhià - Ivrea - Morgex - Courmayeur
- La Thuile
Bus
A free bus service runs between La Thuile
and Pré Saint Didier and the connecting train
services back to Milan, Genoa and Turin.
Train
Take a train from Genoa, Turin or Milan to
Aosta, then on to Pré Saint Didier.
Air
Milan-Malpensa Airport 201km
Daily transfers to and from the resort are
available between December and April.

LA THUILE »
Intro_La Thuile is a beautiful and
modern Italian resort. The
characteristics of the terrain mean
you'll be able to build kickers or go
freeriding in any part of it. If the
weather turns bad, take the
connecting lifts and just head
across to the other side of the
mountain, and ride at La Rosiere in
France instead.

ON THE MOUNTAIN »
Snow reliability_Good snow
conditions can be found
throughout the winter, but the best
sessions will normally be had in
spring. Go out freeriding in the
morning and then build a kicker for
an afternoon play session. Should
they be needed, all the main runs
are equipped with snow making
machines.

Lifts & Piste_The resort spreads
out across three different
mountains. *Planibel* often gets
overcrowded on Sundays and
during public holidays. One of the
best slopes is just below the
chairlift that heads up to the
St. Bernhard Pass. If you travel
over the *Col de la Traversette* you'll
end up in the French resort of
La Rosiere.

Freeriding_The area is great for
freeriding and on the *La Thuile*
side you'll find some fantastic tree
runs. If you can spare the money, a
helicopter can take you into whole
new areas, some of which will
remind you of Alaska. The terrain
here is equally challenging. After a
short hike, you can also access
some nice runs on *St. Bernhard* or
go in search of lines at *Rosiere*. If
the conditions at *La Thuile* are less
than ideal, your best solution is to
head over the mountain, where you
can always find a trace of powder.
For further info regarding helicopter
flights Tel: +39 (0) 165 884 4123

Freestyling_Riders from the
North West snowboard crew can
often be found at *La Thuile* in
spring, building kickers on these
ideal pistes. One popular area is
the bowl under the summit station
of the *Kleinen St. Bernhard*
chairlift, which forms a big, fat
quarterpipe. During the spring, the
bowl can also be accessed by
taking a short road journey and a
quick (well, as quick as you are!)
hike to the top.

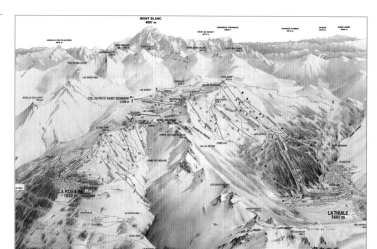

"THE RESORT SPREADS OUT ACROSS THREE MOUNTAINS.."

Beginners_A snowboard and ski
school is available, although *La
Thuile* isn't exactly a beginner's
paradise. There are a lot of difficult
runs and the slopes can get
bulletproof.

Mountain Restaurants_You're in
the *Aosta* valley, home of Fontina, a
cheese that's widely used in the
local cuisine. You can generally get
good food all over the mountain
and the raclette and pierrade are
definitely worth trying. Good pizzas
are served up at *Le Foyer* on the
Piste Chaz Dura. Off-shore, at
the *Belvedere* valley lift station,
serves sandwiches and a range of
hot and cold meals. *Le
Panoramique*, meanwhile, is a self-
service restaurant with seating for
160. It's a classic restaurant with
views across to the fascinating
Ruitor glacier.

IN THE TOWN »
Accommodation_Accommodatio
n prices vary greatly, but start at
around €20 for just a bed. But the
range is fairly diverse, including
holiday apartments either in the
village or on different parts of the
pistes in *La Thuile* - try *Pont
Serrand* or *La Golette* for instance.
The rooms are all of a good
standard, even the cheap ones.

Food_There's a wide range and
you won't be disappointed with any
of it. The *La Lisse* restaurant has a

menu that includes pizza, focaccia,
fresh pasta, home made ravioli and
raviolini, raclette, bourguignonne,
bagna cauda, fondue, plat gourmet
and a wide range of grilled local
specialities. If you're looking for a
great view to eat your food by,
head to *La Granges*, which also
serves up a range of typical
Valdostanish dishes, including
fondue, pierrade, bourguignonne,
raclette and bagna cauda.

Nightlife_A good place to start is
La Bricolette with a glass of 'spritz'.
Then to warm up, head over to the
Bar Ruitor for a few cocktails. *La
Bricole* has live music and a good
range of international beers, and to
finish off the evening dance the
night away at *Disco Fantasia*.

Other Activities_Get a bird's eye
view of the mountains from a
paraglider or hang glider.
Call Jean Claude Cavorsin on
Tel: +39 (0) 166 432 03 or
Marco Letey on
Tel :+39 (0) 166 615 00

LOCAL TIP »
A free ski bus connects with the
nearby resort of Courmayeur. When
in this neck of the woods, try to
spend at least one day on the
biggest mountains in the European
Alps for a bit of freeriding and
enjoy a view of the highest
mountain in Europe. Definitely
worth the effort!

LIVIGNO
ITALY

LIVIGNO »
www.aptlivigno.it
tourist office tel: +39 0324996379
location: Livigno
population: 4700
altitude: 1816m

ON THE MOUNTAIN »
season: November - May
Lifts
vertical drop: 1800-3000m
amount of lifts in total: 32
gondolas: 3
chair lifts: 14
drag lifts: 15
Slopes
amount of prepared slopes: 110 km
runs w. snowmaking machines: 80%
easy runs: 12
intermediate runs: 16
advanced runs: 4
Facilities
night riding: yes
amount of halfpipes: 2
amount of funparks: 1
Heliboarding: -
Lift-ticket prices in Euro
1/2 day: 22
day: 29.5
season: 472
Events
European Open
Italian FSI

SNOWBOARD TUITION »
Scuola Sci Azzurra
Tel: + 39 0342997683
www.azzurrainfo.com
Top Club Mottolino
Tel: +39 0342997408
www.mottolino.com

SNOWBOARD SHOPS »
Adventure
Tel: +39 0342996976
www.zinermann.it

GETTING THERE »
Car
Zurich - Livigno 201km
Zurich - towards Chur - Sargans - Landquart exit - Zernez - Traforo de Munt la Schera (Swiss/It) - Livigno
Milan - Livigno 212km
Milan - Lecco - Colico - Madonna di Tiran (Swiss/It) - approx. 30 min (It/Swiss) - Livigno
Innsbruck - Livigno 162km
Innsbruck - Landeck - Ried - Pfunds - (Aus/Swiss) - Scuol - Susch - Zernez - Traforo de Munt la Schera (Swiss/It) - Livigno
Bus/Train
Milan - Tirano
Then from Tirano to Bormio by bus before changing to the Livigno bus
Zurich - Zernez
then by bus to Livigno (note: this service only runs on Saturdays and Sundays)
Air
Milan Airport 212km
Zurich Airport 201km

LIVIGNO »
Intro_When you're looking to eat well, party hard and access one of Europe's largest snowparks, all without spending too much money, then Livigno is a good place to be. The population of Livigno is estimated at around 5000. The added tourist population can be relatively high in the winter season — this is one of the most resorts in the European Alps. The village is at an elevation of 1816m and stretches over twelve kilometres in a 25km valley. By the way, the practice of tax privileges for the locals, which still exists, dates way back to Neopolitan times and was designed to keep this region alive when the tourist season was over.

ON THE MOUNTAIN »
Snow reliability_The Livigno season normally gets a decent amount of snow, beginning early in December and finishing around the beginning of May. In bad years, such as in the 2001/02 season, snowmaking facilities were able to cover 80% of the piste. In fact, snowmaking facilities were able to artificially create an epic park (from nothing, for the 2002 Burton European Open. Snow reports can be obtained from the Livigno

Tourist Office
Tel: +39 0342 996 379
www.aptlivigno.it info@aptlivigno.it

Lifts & Piste_32 lifts service the resort and are spread out between Mottolino in the east, and Livigno and Costa del Sole in the west. The snowpark can be found at Mottolino and can be accessed by using the Trepalle chairlift, which during really busy periods is often overcrowded. Carosello and Costaccio are good alternatives on busy days. The lower sections around Costa del Sole are our recommendation for beginners. Many of the lifts are positioned next to the easier runs. When a strong wind is blowing, head over to Mottolino.

Freeriding_Following good snowfalls, Livigno is a paradise for freeriding, even if you're in Mottolino, Carosello or at Costaccio. The riding zones from Monte della Neve down to Livigno or to Trepalle are a special recommendation. Carosello has some excellent freeride terrain and

from Costaccio down to Campacc there are some dream runs through the trees.

Freestyling_Livigno has one of the biggest snowparks in Europe. It includes a normal pipe at 4m, a superpipe at 5.3m, a heap of rails built for all levels of difficulty, funbox, 5 tables with jumps from 15 -20m and a sequence of small and middle-sized jumps for beginners. The European Open has been held at Livigno since 2002, and every winter the pros come here to do photo shoots and film videos. A large proportion of the Italian pro riding scene spend their winters riding and training here. The Foscagna Pass and the surrounding areas are ideally suited to kicker building.

Carving_Alongside the snowpark is a boardercross course, which together with the Mottolino, Monte della Neve, Costaccia and Blesaccia pistes provide an ideal carving zone.

Beginners_There are lots of runs lower down the valley which are ideally suited to beginners. Costaccia and Pista degli Amanti are also relatively easy. If you aren't yet confident on your board, you should avoid riding at Monte della Neve.

Mountain Restaurants_Self-service restaurants can be found at Mottolino and Carosello and there's a sandwich bar at Costaccia. A wide range of good pasta can be had in Mottolino, although long queues can often be the case here, especially during the holiday period. It may then be better to head to the bar below the Trepalle chairlift. Good food, including local specialities, can be found at the Tea del Borch hut in Carosello, which is visible from the gondola.

IN THE TOWN »
Accommodation_All categories of accommodation can be found at Livigno, including; apartments, hotels, guest rooms, a youth hostel and even a four star hut. The prices vary depending on the time of the season. Christmas, February and Easter are the most expensive times. On average, the prices range between €23 and €110.
It doesn't really matter where the accommodation is located as

there's a free bus shuttle service that does a complete circuit of the town, including the lifts.

Info and reservations
call APT Livigno on
Tel: +39 (0) 342 996 379

Food_The Co-op supermarkets are generally your cheapest option for food and you'll find two of them located in the middle of the village - one in Via Plan and the other in Via St.Antonio. The Sunday market, on the other hand, is relatively expensive.
Restaurants such as Bait dal Ghet, also offer great food for a fair price. Excellent pizzas and Gnocchi alla Turatello can be sampled at Touring. Reserve a table at Tea da Borch, a fine restaurant, and you'll dine in good company
Tel:+39 (0) 342 997 016
The menu includes specialities such as pizzoccheri, polenta, cheese and salami.

Nightlife_Après Ski bars are a dime a dozen. You can find your way to Tea del Vidal at Mottolino, the ski school in Via Plan and a heap of others just below the lifts. The evening choices for bars include pubs such as; Roxy, Helvetia, Bivio, Galli's, Daphne's or at Cronox, where you'll also find four traditional bowling lanes. Live bands and home brewed beers can be had at Ecos. Marco's disco supplies DJ's and great cocktails. You should also head down to Kokodi or Cielo. The Art Café serves good cocktails and and bar music in a nice environment for those who want it a little quieter.

Other Activities_It's not boring in Livigno! Skidoos - fun on a prepared course - Bormolini Michele via Fontana 64
Tel: +39 (0) 339 573 1987 or
Galli Franco via Rasia
Tel: +39 (0) 342 970 10
Mob: +39 (0) 338 255 90 60
Paragliding - Associazione Volare Livigno c/o Cantoni Flavio via Pontiglia 43
Tel: +39 (0) 342 997 102
Indoor climbing and bowling, Cronox via Rin 39
Tel: +39 (0) 342 970 577
Riding lessons and tours via Bondi
Tel: +39 (0) 335 649 4333
Ice skating San Rocco
Tel: +39 (0) 342 997 244

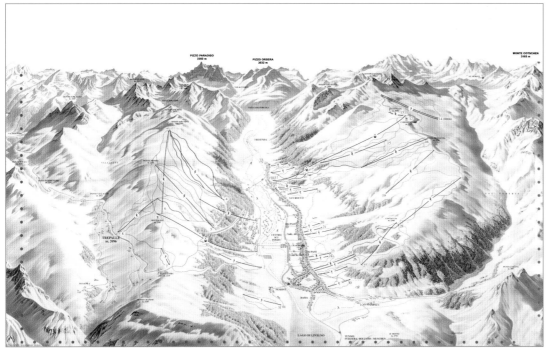

"FOLLOWING GOOD SNOWFALLS, LIVIGNO IS A PARADISE FOR GOOD FREERIDING"

© Ricky Felderer **Rider** Chicco Ciapponi

LOCAL TIP »
After a long day's riding, head off to the Bagni Vecchi di Bormio hot springs, approx. 45 min from Livigno where 26 pools of warm water (35° C to 42° C) will help to regenerate the body and bring about the true sense of living.

Information
www.bagnidibormio.it
Tel: +39 (0) 342 910 1131

"LIVIGNO HAS ONE OF THE BIGGEST SNOWPARKS IN EUROPE. A NORMAL PIPE AT 4M, A SUPERPIPE AT 5.3M, A HEAP OF RAILS BUILT FOR ALL LEVELS OF DIFFICULTY, FUNBOX, 5 TABLES WITH JUMPS FROM 15-20M AND A SEQUENCE OF SMALL AND MIDDLE-SIZED JUMPS FOR BEGINNERS."

"LIMONE PIEMONTE IS NOT AN EXPENSIVE TOWN AND YOU'LL FIND RELATIVELY CHEAP ACCOMMODATION."

LIMONE PIEMONTE
ITALY

LIMONE PIEMONTE »
www.limonepiemonte.it
tourist office tel: + 39 0171929515
location: Limone Piemonte
population:1579
altitude: 1010

ON THE MOUNTAIN »
season: end of November to the end of April
Lifts
Vertical drop: 1010-2050m
amount of lifts in total: 18
gondolas: -
chair lifts: 6
drag lifts: 12
Slopes
amount of prepared slopes: 80 km
runs w. snowmaking machines: 80%
amount of easy runs: 5
amount of intermediate runs: 30
amount of advanced runs: 4
Facilities
night riding: -
amount of halfpipes: -
amount of funparks: 1
heliboarding: -
Lift-ticket prices in Euro
1/2 day: 23
day: 44
week: 118
season: 480

SNOWBOARD TUITION »
Escuela ski Limone
Tel: +39 071927635
www.Limoneweb.com.Scuzlasci

SNOWBOARD SHOPS »
Promo
Tel: +39 0171926459

GETTING THERE »
Car
Turin - Limone Piemonte 122km
Turin - A6 - towards Savona - Fossano exit - Cuneo - SS20 - Limone Piemonte
Nice - Limone Piemonte 96km
Nice - Menton - Ventimiglia (Fr/It) - SS20 - Breil (It/Fr) - N204 - Tende - Col de Tend (Fr/It) - Limone Piemonte
Train
The train between Cuneo and Nice stops at Limone Piemonte, making it easy to get there by rail. There's a bus direct to the lift station from Cuneo.
Air
Torino Caselle Airport 122km
Nice Airport 106km

LIMONE PIEMONTE »
Intro_ Limone Piemonte spreads out over two different slopes in the Ligurian Alps and is just 60km away from the Italian Riviera. The resort gets a good volume of snowfall thanks to its proximity to the Mediterranean. The piste is very rarely overcrowded and there are a heap of jib-able rails in the village, where you'll often meet riders from the local crew, Lemon 8.

ON THE MOUNTAIN »
Snow reliability_ The season runs from the middle of December through until mid March. The beginning of the season generally has poor snow conditions, but when it gets cold enough there is some snow making. Snow reports can be obtained from www.limonepiemonte.it or Tel: +39 (0) 171 929 515

Lifts_ Nothing special to report regarding the lifts here, except that on Sundays you should drive to the lifts at Limone 1400 or Limonetto so as to avoid parking problems.

Freeriding_ Limone is not considered a great freeriding area, but following fresh snowfalls, there are always a few interesting lines, especially as this is a fairly quiet resort. The best chute in the area is on the *Cabanaira* from *Pancani*. Also, departing from the *Alpetta*, you can ride a nice run called the *Valletta*, which travels right down to the valley lift station. Due to the flatter terrain, you'll find it difficult to find a suitable place for a backcountry kicker, except at *Decollater*, which anybody can tell you how to get to.

Freestyling_ At some stage in the season, you'll find a so-called 'park', normally located at *Pancani*, containing kickers and spines, but no pipe. But in town and in the neighbouring villages, you'll also discover a lot of rails. Your best bet is to make contact with Max Galfré and Oliver Mondino from *Lemon 8*, and get a few tips from them.

Beginners_ Limone is an ideal resort for beginners since the snow is generally soft because, the weather is warmer here.

Mountain Restaurants_ Quality

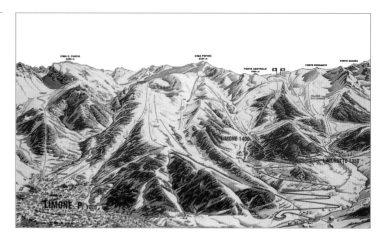

"THE BEST CHUTE IS ON THE CABANAIRA FROM PANCANI. ALSO, DEPARTING FROM THE ALPETTA, YOU CAN RIDE A NICE RUN CALLED THE VALLETTA, WHICH TRAVELS RIGHT DOWN TO THE VALLEY LIFT STATION."

food and service can be found at *Pancani*, the *Alpetto* and at many other bars at the valley lift stations serving Limonetto and Limone 1400. Compared with other resorts, the prices aren't too bad.

IN THE TOWN »
Accommodation_ Limone Piemonte is not an expensive town and you'll find relatively cheap accommodation. If you're not staying near the lifts take advantage of the shuttle service – you don't necessarily need a car here. There's also a camping ground just outside the village - check it out at www.luismatlas.it or phone +39 (0) 171 927 565. Further info about accommodation can be found at www.limonepiemonte.it.

Food_ In addition to the cuisine, which is excellent, you should try the wines in *Limone*. The wine growing area of *Piemonte* produces some of the best vino in Italy, and this is the home of such noble wines as *Barolo* or *Brunello di Montalcino*. The wines from

Langhe are also worth exploring and, considering the quality, the prices are reasonable.

Nightlife_ Limone has a diverse range of pubs and bars. Favourites include *Bocaccio*, La Laterna and the *Puntza*. These are the best places to meet up with the locals and perhaps to enjoy a midnight rail session…

Other Activities_ There's a good skate park around an hour away in *Pinerolo*. Alternatively you can go to the cinema. When the weather on the mountain is bad, you can take a fancy day trip to *Nice or Monaco*, only 100km away.

LOCAL TIP »
The locals are always out for a midnight rail session and on the look-out for the craziest creations. Before they get into swing, you'll find them in the pubs in *Limone*. There's one super rail located above a restaurant - the only one in the village - in *Chinale*, approximately half an hour's drive away.

"MADESIMO IS A GOOD, FUN DESTINATION FOR FREERIDERS."

MADESIMO
ITALY

PROS & CONS »
+ Choice freeriding potential.
+ New lift facilities.
+ Varied levels of difficulty.
+ Pistes are well connected to each other.

− Hard to access by public transport.
− Nightlife isn't too lively.
− Can get very cold.

MADESIMO »
www.madesimo.com
tourist office tel: +39 034353015
location: Madesimo
population: 500
altitude:1550m
linked resorts: Motta , Soste

ON THE MOUNTAIN »
season: December to the end of April
Lifts
vertical drop: 2150-2900m
amount of lifts in total: 15
gondolas: 3
chair lifts: 11
T-bars: 1
Slopes
amount of prepared slopes: 50 km
runs w. snowmaking machines: 22
easy runs: 11
intermediate runs: 13
advanced runs: 4
Facilities
night riding: -
amount of halfpipes: 1
amount of funparks: 1
heliboarding: -
Lift-ticket prices in Euro
1/2 day: 21
day: 28
week: 45
season: 460
Events
Gare nazionali

SNOWBOARD TUITION »
Scuola italiana sci madesimo
Tel: +39 034353049

SNOWBOARD SHOPS »
Olimpic Sport
Tel: +39 034354330

GETTING THERE »
Car
Milan - Madesimo 140km
Milan - Vimercate - Calco - Lecco - Madesimo
Zurich - Madesimo 255km
Zurich - Enge - Sargans - Thusis - Silvaplana - Passo del Maloja - Castasegna (Swiss/It) - Chiavenna - Madesimo
Innsbruck - Madesimo 257km
Innsbruck - A12 towards St.Anton/Bregenz - Fliess/Starkenbach exit - B180 towards Switzerland (Au/Swiss) - Susch Madesimo - Silvaplana - Passo del Maloja - Castasegna (Swiss/It) - Chiavenna -Madesimo
The Spluga Pass in Switzerland is only open in the summer.
Bus
Daily departures from Chaivenna train station. During the winter there's also a direct transfer from Milan two days a week.
Train
Milan - Chiavenna (journey time approx. 2.5 - 3 hours), then from Chiavenna by bus to Madesimo.
Air
Milan-Linate 140km
Milan-Malpensa Airport 166km
Bergamo-Orio al Serio Airport 118km

MADESIMO »
Intro_ This small resort in Val Spulga is a good, fun destination for freeriders. With a few easier powder runs, it is also suitable for the less experienced powder hound – a good place to learn (jumping) the ropes! The town of Madesimo is a quiet little mountain village, with good Italian food, and a chilled-out atmosphere.

ON THE MOUNTAIN »
Snow reliability_ Most of the runs are equipped with snow making facilities, although generally speaking the conditions throughout the season are good. At Canalone dei Camosci, you'll still find powder a few days after a good snowfall. Val di Lei is a real snow trap.

Snow and weather reports
Tel: +39 (0) 343 530 15
www.madesimo.com

Lifts & Piste_ Lifts are located to the west of the village, and the runs are well connected to one another. The lower lying areas of the resort are best for beginners and carvers. During the high season, the Val di Lei lift can get overcrowded, but it's worth it for the view from the top. This is also the starting point for some great backcountry tours.

Freeriding_ Madesimo is ideal for freeriders. There are countless runs alongside the pistes – ideal for less experienced freeriders. Experienced riders will find some testing lines close to the piste at Val di Lei. As well as cliffs and windlips, there are a number of artificial obstacles to test out your skills. The lower part of the resort has a few nice tree runs through the pine forests, but respect the barriers and signs.

Freestyling_ Val di Lei is a great place for freestylers, with its cliffs and other natural obstacles. There's a park at Val di Lei that includes a halfpipe, two kickers (small and large) and two rails.

Carving_ Almost all the pistes are wide, and therefore ideal for carvers. Canalone is one to avoid, though, because more often than not it's a mogul field.

Beginners_ The wide runs offer lots of space to be able to turn,

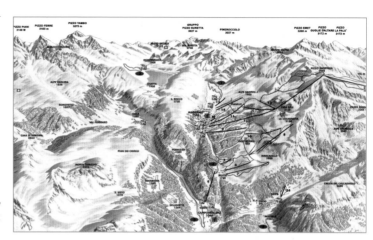

"EXPERIENCED RIDERS WILL FIND SOME TESTING LINES CLOSE TO THE PISTE AT VAL DI LEI. AS WELL AS CLIFFS AND WINDLIPS, THERE ARE A NUMBER OF ARTIFICIAL OBSTACLES TO TEST YOU OUT"

which you'll be glad of when you're learning! The easiest areas are close to the bottom of the piste. Canalone, with its black run, is a definite no-no for beginners. If you're looking to ride the pistes at Val di Lei, just jump back onto the lift and ride down.

Mountain Restaurants_ There is one restaurant at Cima del Sole and one at Pizzo Groppiera. A large self-service restaurant will open soon at Acquerela. The food and drink is good, and reasonably priced.

IN THE TOWN »
Accommodation_ If you're planning to stay a while in Madesimo, it's worth booking an apartment, but otherwise there are plenty of cheap guesthouses to choose from. None are as close to the piste as Mai Tardi at 2000m above sea level. The refuge, Casa Alpina, can be found at Motta, where the accommodation is cheap and there are lots of fun activities to get involved in.

Information
Madesimo Tourist Office - A.P.T Valtellina,

Tel: +39 (0) 343 530 15

Food_A small grocery store provides for self-caterers, but it's pretty pricey. In comparison the restaurants are relatively inexpensive, especially in the nearby villages of Franciscio, Campodolcino and Motta. All three are about 10 minutes drive away, and offer good food at good prices.

Nightlife_ The evenings in Madesimo are not very exciting. The Havana Club is the only pub in town, and it's open from 5pm. The Tender disco is open for late night shenanigans.

Other Activities_ Skidoos are available for hire from Team Deghi at the end of the valley. It's possible to take skidoo trips almost as far as the Swiss border. Alternatively you can opt to ride the skidoo course.

LOCAL TIP »
A visit to the Dogana Vegia in Madesimo is a must and when you get there, try a typical 'grolla' - a warm, alcoholic drink served in a wooden cup, enjoyed in rustic, candle lit surroundings. The boss, Dario, is a friendly host.

PROS & CONS »
+ The snowpark.
+ The parties in Mignon.
+ Snowboarding in May/June.

– Variable weather conditions.
– Very few lifts.
– Poor infrastructure.

"THE MICRO CLIMATE, THE PERFECT SNOWPARK, THE LIVER DESTROYING NIGHTLIFE AND A HEAP OF GOOD RIDERS ALL COMBINE TO CREATE A RESORT WHERE SNOWBOARDERS LOVE TO HANG OUT."

MACUGNAGA

ITALY

»

MACUGNAGA »
www.Macugnaga-online.it
tourist office tel: +39 032465119
location: Macugnaga
population: 2400
altitude:1327m

ON THE MOUNTAIN »
season: end of Nov. to begining of May
Lifts
vertical drop:1327-2900m
amount of lifts in total: 11
gondolas: 2
chair lifts: 3
drag lifts: 6
Slopes
amount of prepared slopes: 40 km
runs w. snowmaking machines: 20
easy runs: 6
intermediate runs: 6
advanced runs: 2
Facilities
night riding: -
amount of halfpipes: -
amount of funparks: 3
Heliboarding: yes
Lift-ticket prices in Euro
1/2 day: 15
day: 22.5
week: 122
season: 398
Events
FSI Italian cup

SNOWBOARD TUITION »
Scuola Sci Macugnaga
Tel: +39 032465217
Scuola Sci Monte Rosa
Tel: +39 032465224

SNOWBOARD SHOPS »
Medley
Tel: +39 0331773224

GETTING THERE »
Car
Torino - Macugnaga: 192km
Torino - Biandrate - Borgomanero - Ornavasso - Piedimulera - Macugnaga
Milan - Macugnaga: 145km
Milan - Lainate - Gallarate - Borgomanero - Ornavasso - Piedimulera - Macugnaga
Zürich - Macugnaga: 284km
Zürich - A4 Steinhausen - Brunnen - Tunnel del Gottardo - Bellinzona - Orselina (Swiss/It) - Domodossola - Piedimulera - Macugnaga
Bus
From Piazza Castello in Milan direct to Macugnaga, in the high season.
Train
To Domodossola (Milan-Brig train line) and from their to Macugnaga.
Air
Milan Malpensa Airport 103km

© Ricky Felder **Rider** Oliver Mondino

MACUGNAGA »
Intro_ Macugnaga is one of the real snowboarding spots in Italy. The micro climate, the perfect snowpark, the liver destroying nightlife and a heap of good riders all combine to create a resort where snowboarders love to hang out. Just to top it all off, the resort is based at the foot of the north face of the amazing Monte Rosa.

ON THE MOUNTAIN »
Snow reliability_ The best time for riding is from the middle of January through to the end of May. More exact info can be obtained from the local snowboarding club MDY - Tel: +39 (0) 331 773 224 or at www.mdysnowparks.com

Lifts_ Most people head to Monte Moro when the weather is fine. Here you can either ride the off piste terrain or to let loose in the park. The alternative is to head into the tree runs at Belvedere, where it is very seldom foggy. In general, waiting times are short.

Freeriding_A good freeriding area is situated below the Pecetto chairlift, but most riders head to the area between Monte Moro and

"THE PARK AND THE KICKER AT PECETTO ARE EXCELLENT. WHEN THE SNOW CONDITIONS ARE RIGHT, YOU'LL FIND AN AMAZINGLY GOOD, NATURAL PARK AT MORO PASSES"

Saas Almgedon. A further attraction is the heli boarding available on Monte Rosa. For a Mountain Guide contact Lacchini Fabio, Tel: +39 (0) 324 651 70

Freestyling_ There is a whole freestyling area which is well set up, and when the weather is bad then you can stick to the rails in the village. The park and the kicker at Pecetto are excellent when the weather is fine. When the snow conditions are right, you'll find an amazingly good, natural park at Moro Passes. Have a chat with the locals, as a tip from the likes of Beto Lacchini, Mario, Pasi Pirali and Gianni Simonini is always helpful.

Carving_ There is no special carving

area but the piste at Belvedere is generally well groomed and good for slicing your edges into.

Beginners_ The beginner area is located at Pecetto. The area at Monte Moro is more difficult. A ski school is available which does snowboarding lessons.

Mountain Restaurants_ Everyone at Moro goes to Dino and his hut, which is situated below the lift. Here you can be served with a small snack of cheese and bread or be treated to the regional pasta specialities such as Pizzocheri. The Restaurant Ghiaccai del Rosa is situated up by the second chairlift at Belvedere and provides a full-blown super meal!

"WHEN YOU FIND YOURSELVES IN MIGNON, ASK FOR THE SPECIAL TREATMENT FROM VITTORIO... IF YOU HAVEN'T EXPERIENCED IT, YOU HAVEN'T EXPERIENCED MACUGNAGA."

© Ricky Felder **Rider** Henry Sankala

IN THE TOWN »

Accommodation_The prices are moderate, unlike other Italian resorts this is not an 'exclusive' village. A bed in a 3 star guesthouse, including half board, will cost you around €15 to €20 per night.

Further info
Tel: +39 (0) 324 651 19

Food_All the restaurants and pizzerias have normal prices, from Glacier through to Cima Jazzi. Great home style cooking, from the filled tortellini through to the risotto and pasta. It's well worth the money to out for a night, but when you want to cater for yourself, you'll find grocery stores in the village.

Nightlife_People usually remain at dinner for quite a long time in Macugnaga, before heading off to Mignon. Live acts and DJ sessions are provided most weekends making Mignon a must for any visitors. This is also the place where all the locals hang out.

Other Activities_An ice rink, a rail park in the village, and a great mini ramp provide for alternative entertainment in Macugnaga. A sports centre is currently in planning.

LOCAL TIP »

When you find yourselves in Mignon, ask for the special treatment from Vittorio... If you haven't experienced it, you haven't experienced Macugnaga.

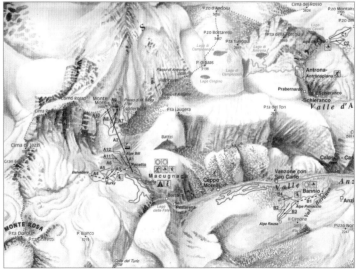

"MADONNA DI CAMPIGLIO IS ONE OF THE BEST KNOWN AND MOST EXPENSIVE RESORTS IN ITALY."

MADONNA DI CAMPIGLIO
ITALY

MADONNA DI CAMPIGLIO »
tourist office tel: + 39 0465442000
location: Madonna di Campiglio
population: 1500
altitude: 1500
linked resorts: Folgarida, Marilleva

ON THE MOUNTAIN »
season: December to April
Lifts
vertical drop: 1520-2450m
amount of lifts in total: 25
gondolas: 5
chairlifts: 13
T-bars: 7
Slopes
amount of prepared slopes: 90 km
runs w. snowmaking machines: 24
easy runs: 29
intermediate runs: 23
advanced runs: 10
Facilities
night riding: yes
amount of halfpipes: 1
amount of funparks: 1
heliboarding: -
Lift-ticket prices in Euro
1/2 day: 23
day: 30
week: 161
season: 465
special fares: www.funiviecampiglio.it

SNOWBOARD TUITION »
Scuola Italiana Sci 5Laghi
Tel: +39 0465441650
www.scuolasci5laghi.com

SNOWBOARD SHOPS »
Sport 3Tre
Tel: +39 0465442353

GETTING THERE »
Car
Innsbruck - Madonna di Campiglio 196km
Innsbruck - Brenner Pass (Au/It) - Bolzano - Fondo - Dimaro - Madonna di Campiglio
Milan - Madonna di Campiglio 225km
Milan - A4 to Brescia exit - Tormini - Madonna di Campiglio
Bus
Connecting buses from Trento. For info (manned Mon - Fri 8.00a.m - 12 noon and 2 p.m - 6p.m) Tel: +39 (0) 461 821 000
Train
The nearest train station is in Trento, 67km away, which also has daily bus connections.

MADONNA DI CAMPIGLIO »
Intro_Set in the heart of the Dolomites, Madonna di Campiglio is one of the best known and most expensive resorts in Italy. Over the years this small mountain village has developed into a modern holiday resort and has invested in snowboarding along the way. A good range of bars and two discos make for a good evening's entertainment, so good in fact, that getting up in the morning can be torture.

ON THE MOUNTAIN »
Snow reliability_The conditions are generally good throughout the whole season, and twenty-four snow making machines are on hand to provide artificial back-up if required. We recommend that you head to Madonna around the end of February/beginning of March, when there's always enough snow and the sun is usually shining. There are generally fewer tourists then too, so things are a little more relaxed at this time of year.

Lifts & Piste_All the runs are connected, and meet up in the village. The fun park is situated on the Gorsté piste, and has two sets of medium difficulty kicker lines. Prado Lago is a good spot for beginners, while Cinque Laghi and Spinale are for more experienced riders.

Freeriding_Campiglio is in one of Italy's National Parks, so heli-boarding is prohibited. Still, there are plenty of great freeriding spots to ride without having to hike too far. Take any of the lifts up and have a look around. There are endless lines to choose from, many of which are suitable for the less advanced rider.
If you're looking for something a little more challenging, seek advice from one of the local mountain guides.

Freestyling_Madonna di Campiglio has a strong local scene, as well as a heap of visiting freestylers. Both the World Championships and the European Championships have been held in Campiglio during the past few winters. This has had a positive effect on the funpark, which at its best consists of six kickers, two quarters, three spines, three fun boxes, a halfpipe, boardercross and a banked slalom course.

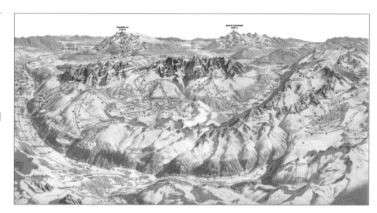

"CAMPIGLIO IS THE OLDEST SNOWBOARD SCHOOL IN ITALY. IT'S AN IDEAL FOR LEARNING, WITH PLENTY OF EASY RUNS."

Carving_Grosté is an ideal piste for testing your edges - it's wide with a varying pitch.

Beginners_Campiglio is home to the oldest snowboard school in Italy. It's an ideal spot for learning, there are plenty of easy runs and the lessons are very professional. Local snowboard schools include; Professional Snowboarding (the first official snowboard school), 5 Laghi, Nazionale and Nardis.

Mountain Restaurants_There are ten or so small restaurants, all of them near the lift stations, and they all serve good food. Boch, the large self-service restaurant on the Grosté is often packed, and should be avoided.

IN THE TOWN »
Accommodation_Madonna di Campiglio is relatively expensive, but the cheapest hotel is Cozzio - Tel: +39 (0) 465 441 083. If you don't want to spend too much money, the neighbouring villages of Pinzolo (13km away), St Antonio di Mavignola (5km), Folgarida and Marilleva (both 10km) all have plenty of accommodation at slightly lower prices.

Food_On the lower section of the Miramonti piste look out for the Ristorante Pizzeria Le Roi. The food is good and the prices are reasonable. Try one of their specialities such as polenta with goulash, venison ragout or sausages with mushrooms. You can also pass a pleasant evening at the Rifugio Montagnoli hut. To make a reservation call +39 (0) 465 443 355

Nightlife_The Stube or the Cliffhanger are considered to be the best pubs, and both are in the centre of town. After closing time, it's off to one of the two local discos, Zangola or Des Alpes. The locals and the boarders often meet up outside Campiglio at La Stella in Campo Carlo Magno.

Other Activities_Campiglio has a wide range of leisure activities, including the following:
Swimming: Spiazzo Rendena Tel: +39 (0) 465 801 019
Tandem paragliding or flight lessons: Aero Club d'Italia - Tel: +39 (0) 465 055 69
Dog Sledding: Scuola di cani da slitta Antartika Tel: +39 (0) 338 234 5425
Mini Golf: Spiazzo Tel: +39 (0) 328 035 0156

LOCAL TIP »
Avoid the Christmas and Easter periods when Madonna Campiglio is way too busy. If you're looking for a quiet resort where you can focus on your riding, then give Campiglio a miss - there are way too many parties and not enough sleep!

PILA AOSTA
ITALY

PROS & CONS »
+ Easy to reach.
+ Well groomed funpark.
+ Modern lifts.

− Weekends are crowded.
− Not a real mountain village.
− Can be very cold.

"THE SEASON LASTS FROM DECEMBER THROUGH TO THE MIDDLE OF APRIL. THE SNOW CONDITIONS ARE GENERALLY VERY GOOD."

PILA AOSTA
ITALY

PILA AOSTA »
www.espace-de-pila.com
tourist office tel: +39 0165521055
location: Pila
population: 80
altitude:1800m

ON THE MOUNTAIN »
season: early December to mid April
Lifts
vertical drop: 579-2709m
amount of lifts in total: 14
gondolas: 4
chair lifts: 8
T-bars: 2
Slopes
amount of prepared slopes: 70
runs w. snowmaking machines: -
amount of easy runs: 2
amount of intermediate runs:14
amount of advanced runs: 3
Facilities
night riding: -
amount of halfpipes: -
amount of funparks: 1
heliboarding: -
Lift-ticket prices in Euro
1/2 day: 19
day: 27
week:147
season: 550
Events
Gare nazionali FSI

SNOWBOARD TUITION »
Scuola Sci
Tel: +39 0165521114
www.scuoladiscipila.com

SNOWBOARD SHOPS »
Point du Sport
Tel: +39 0165236848

GETTING THERE »
Car
Milan - Pila 193km
Milan - Santhià - Ivrea - Aosta - Pila
Bern - Pila 208km
Bern - Fribourg - towards Lausanne,
Montreux - Martigny - Great Saint Bernard
Tunnel (Swiss/It) - Aosta - Pila
Lyon - Pila 294km
Lyon - Chambéry - Annecy - towards
Chamonix-Mont Blanc - Saint Gervais les
Bains - Mont Blanc Tunnel (Fr/ It) -
Courmayeur - A5 towards Aosta - Cogne exit
- Aosta - Pila
Bus
The Turin - Aosta and the Milano - Aosta
express bus services run the whole year
round. The Freccia delle nevi bus service also
operates from Monday to Friday during the
winter, with pick-ups in Bergamo, Milan and
Genoa.
For more info call Zani Viaggi on
Tel: +39 (0) 286 464 854
Train
Take the Turin-Milan / Chivasso - Aosta train.
There's a gondola near the train station in
Aosta which will get you to Pila in about
10 minutes.
Air
Milan-Malpensa Airport 172km
Turin Caselle Airport 125km
An airport taxi service operates between
Milano Malpensa Airport and Pila from
December through to April.

© Daniel Kudernatsch **Rider** Seppi Scholler

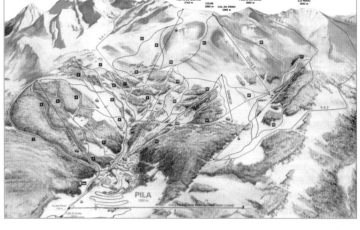

PILA AOSTA »
Intro_ Pila is approximately 11km from Aosta. It is easily accessible and the journey involves no long, winding, mountain roads. The wide and well-groomed slopes are also easy to get to, and there are plenty of them to choose from. There's been a great funpark here for years, and when the snow is good, there are also some great spots for freeriding.

ON THE MOUNTAIN »
Snow reliability_ The season lasts from December through to the middle of April. The snow conditions are generally very good and, as long as it's cold enough, 200 snow making machines provide back up.
Snow Reports
Tel: +39 (0) 165 52 1148 or
Tel: +39 (0) 165 42 1045

Lifts & Piste_ The pistes around *Pila* range from easy to moderate in terms of difficulty, but they're fairly narrow and they often involve tree runs. The *La Couis* lift takes you up to 2700m above sea level, where there are great views of *Mont Blanc*, *Grand Combin*, *Vervino* and *Monte Rosa*. Most of the resort is in the sun.

Freeriding_ Much of the good off-piste terrain is in the forests, where you'll also find plenty of natural jumps. *Chamolé* is one of the nicest runs, and often has good powder. You'll find it to the left of the *Chamolé* chairlift. To reach the fine tree run of *Gorraz*, you'll need to go from the summit station of

the *Chamolé* chairlift, travel a further 200m along the *Du Bois* piste, and then turn off piste. Taking the *Grimondet* chairlift, you can access *Grimondet*, which is a more challenging run.

Freestyling_ The Pila snowpark is next to the Chamolé Traversale. Here you'll find rails, medium and large sized kickers, and a quarter. There is no halfpipe at the moment, but one is in the pipeline, if you'll pardon the pun. Weekly freestyle courses are available, and the Nazca Summer Camps are held here in the summer season, as are a few national contests.

Beginners_ The runs in the forests are tight, and not ideal for beginners. All the runs, from Couis down, are steep and should also be avoided. That just leaves two baby lifts…

Mountain Restaurants_ In Chamolé, try the Chamolé Hut, in Nuova go for the restaurant/bar La Chatelaine, and at the valley lift station, try the popular Hermitage snack bar. On Grimod, we recommend the Gran Grimod Leissé restaurant and at the valley lift station Couis 2 the Lo Baoutson restaurant. But no worries - you can eat well more or less everywhere.

IN THE TOWN »
Accommodation_ If you're travelling in threes or fours, it's worth renting an apartment which will set you back around €400 per week. Guesthouses cost anywhere between €20 and €100. Private rooms are sometimes slightly cheaper.
For more details call the Pila Info Office on +39 (0) 165 52 1148 or log onto www.pila.it

Food_ Take a walk along the main street and you'll have your pick of a good choice of restaurants, pizzerias and guesthouses all offering local specialties.

Nightlife_ There are no discos in Pila, but there are plenty of pubs, some of which stay open until 3am − like the Galenger, Bar mion, Kangu Pub or the Piano Bar Blue Paradise. Otherwise head to Aosta, which has a better selection of nightspots.

Other Activities_ Except for the ice rink, there's not a lot else here. Neighbouring Aosta has a little more going on. The gondola from Pila travels down to Aosta in just ten minutes and operates from 8 a.m to 5 p.m. It takes 15 - 20 minutes to drive there.

"MUCH OF THE GOOD OFF-PISTE TERRAIN IS IN THE FORESTS, WHERE YOU'LL ALSO FIND PLENTY OF NATURAL JUMPS."

"JUST ABOUT ALL OF THE PISTES HAVE SNOW-MAKING EQUIPMENT, AND IN ANY CASE PART OF THE RESORT IS LOCATED ON A GLACIER. THERE ARE RARELY PROBLEMS WITH SNOW CONDITIONS."

PASSO TONALE
ITALY

TONALE »
www.comune.ponte-di-legno.bs.it
tourist office tel: +39 036491122
location: Ponte di Legno - Tonale
population: 1870
altitude: 1258m

ON THE MOUNTAIN »
season: all year round
Lifts
vertical drop: 1258-3100m
amount of lifts in total: 28
gondolas: 1
chair lifts: 13
drag lifts: 14
Slopes
amount of prepared slopes: 21 km
runs w. snowmaking machines: -
amount of easy runs: 5
amount of intermediate runs: 20
amount of advanced runs: 1
Facilities
night riding: -
amount of halfpipes: -
amount of funparks: -
heliboarding: yes
Lift-ticket prices in Euro
1/2 day: 23
day: 26
week: 138
season: 460

SNOWBOARD TUITION »
Scuola pontedilegno tonale
Tel: +39 036491301

SNOWBOARD SHOPS »
Moda sport
Tel: +39 036491562

GETTING THERE »
Car
Milan - Passo Tonale 170km
Milan - A4 towards Venice - Seriate exit - Darfo - Breno -Ponte di Legno - Passo Tonale
Innsbruck - Pass Tonale 200km
Innsbruck - Brenner Pass (Au/It) - Bozen Süd exit - Fondo - Dimaor - Passo Tonale
Zurich - Passo Tonale 314km
Zurich - Sargans - Thusis - Silvaplana - Pntresina - Brusio (Swiss/It) - Tirano - Stazzona - Édolo - Ponte di Legno - Passo Tonale
Bus/Train
The closest major train stations are Milan, Verona, Trento and Brescia. Bus services depart from all of these cities to Tonale, but the most popular service is the one that leaves from Brescia.
Air
Milan-Linate Airport 172km
Trento Airport 86km
Bergamo Airport 122km

© Scalp **Rider** Maggo Strehle

PASSO TONALE »
Intro_Tonale, and its sister village Ponte di Legno, are two of the best-known winter resorts in Italy. The wind-protected and crevasse-free pistes of the Presena glacier are rideable throughout the whole year. The village itself lacks character, but as long as Alpine scenery isn't a priority, you'll feel right at home in Tonale. This resort's best asset is its promise of snow all year round, but it's not really a freestylers' resort.

ON THE MOUNTAIN »
Snow reliability_Just about all of the pistes have snow-making equipment, and in any case part of the resort is located on a glacier. There are rarely problems with snow conditions, then, but for the very latest information call the Tourist Office on
+39 (0) 364 903 838

Lifts & Piste_There are three areas, *Ponte di Legno*, close to the valley, *Passo del Tonale* and the Presena glacier. All three are fine, but the glacier is best. The village is easily accessible and there are lots of places to stay there.

However, weekends in the high season do get very busy.

Freeriding_The *Presena* glacier is the best place for *freeriders*. The classic run is situated below the gondola, so you can study it on your way up. If you're looking for something a little more challenging, try the *Cantiere* run. Looking up from *Presena* to the top of the mountain, head left and take the run down to *Tonale* and the road that leads to *Val di Sole*. But remember you'll need to hitchhike back to the lifts unless you have return transport *oganised*. You may run into *Emilio Previtali*, one of Europe's best *freeriders* (see Extreme *Verbier*). They also do *Heliboarding* here.

Freestyling_Although the resort is not equipped with a snowpark or anything like one, there are heaps of places to build a kicker.

Carving_The pistes at *Passo del Tonale* are well groomed and wide, making them ideal for carvers.

Beginners_*Tonale* is the area

most suitable for learning those first few turns.

Mountain Restaurants_The food on the slopes is good, and although the fast food at the pass is not really recommended, it's at least cheap and it's certainly fast. Two local dishes - *pizzoccheri* and the *polenta taragna* - won't knock a hole in your pocket and will satisfy your hunger far better. Another local speciality we recommend you try (influenced by Southern *Tyrolean* cooking) is a *"sengalini"*, a sandwich filled with smoked bacon and cheese.

IN THE TOWN »
Accommodation_In both *Passo del Tonale* and *Ponte di Legno* you'll find everything from campsites to luxury hotels. Prices vary, but on average, half board accommodation costs between €50 to €60 per day. Ask the Tourist Office for details of any special package deals available. You can call them on
Tel: +39 (0) 364 903 838
or visit there website:
www.pontedilegnoturismo.it

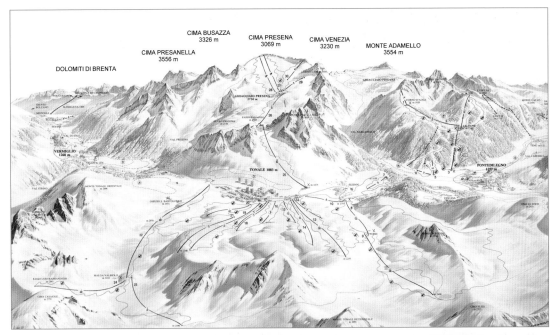

"TONALE
IS THE
AREA MOST
SUITABLE FOR
LEARNING"

© Ricky Felderer

"IF YOU'RE LOOKING FOR SOMETHING A LITTLE MORE CHALLENGING, TRY THE CANTIERE RUN. LOOKING UP FROM PRESENA TO THE TOP OF THE MOUNTAIN, HEAD LEFT AND TAKE THE RUN DOWN TO TONALE AND THE ROAD THAT LEADS TO VAL DI SOLE. BUT REMEMBER YOU'LL NEED TO HITCHHIKE BACK TO THE LIFTS UNLESS YOU HAVE RETURN TRANSPORT OGANISED."

Food_In addition to the polenta taragna and the pizzoccheri, you might also want to try real local specialities like casola, gnoc de la cua and strangulaprecc. You've come a long way so while you're here, why not give everything a try! The best pizzeria is La Toretta and for those who like pasta, head to Palla di Neve.

Nightlife_In Ponte di Legno and Passo del Tonale you'll find a wide range of discos, pubs and restaurants. Our tips though are: Heaven and Antares, which are generally lively and the music is not too bad. Those who just want to rave all night can dance until the early hours to some of the best DJs at the Brescia disco.

Other Activities_No skatepark unfortunately, but there's lots else to do, including a swimming pool, sauna, spa, and ice rink.

LOCAL TIP »
There's a disused wartime tunnel at the end of the Cantiere run, which will save you a walk, but if there's a lot of snow you'll need to know where to look. Best ask a local.

"THERE DEFINITELY ISN'T ENOUGH SPACE TO WRITE ABOUT ALL THE LIFTS AND RUNS AVAILABLE. THE DOLOMITI SUPER SKI PASS GIVES YOU ACCESS OVER 1220KM OF PISTE."

GRÖDNER TAL (VAL GARDENA)
ITALY

VAL GARDENA »
www.valgardena.it
tourist office tel: +39 0471795122
location: Semlva Val Gardena
population: 2500
altitude: 1563
linked: resorts Alpe di Siusi

ON THE MOUNTAIN »
season: end of Movember to end of April
Lifts
vertical drop: 1500-2500m
amount of lifts in total: 76
gondolas: 8
chairlifts : 33
draglifts: 35
Slopes
amount of prepared slopes: 175 km
runs w. snowmaking machines: 65%
amount of easy runs: 58
amount of intermediate runs: 100
amount of advanced runs: 17
Facilities
night riding: -
amount of halfpipes: 1 (Alpe di Siusi)
amount of funparks: 1 (Alpe di Siusi)
heliboarding: -
Lift-ticket prices in Euro
day: 31
week: 154
season: 390

SNOWBOARD TUITION »
Scuola di Sci e Snowboard Selva Gardena
Tel: +39 0471795156
Scuola di Snowboard e Sci "2000"
Tel: +39 0471773125

SNOWBOARD SHOPS »
Alex Giorgi
Tel: +39 0471794212

GETTING THERE »
Car
Verona - Selva 193km
Verona - towards Trento, Bolzano, Brennero - Bolzano Ponte Gardena - Exit Chiusa - Val Gardena - Selva
Innsbruck - Selva 115km
Innsbruck - Brenner (Aust/It) - Exit St.Ulrich (Ortisei) - Chiusa (Klausen) - Selva (Wolkenstein)
Bus
A busline travels from Genoa - Savona - Sestri - Piacenza - Cremona to Val Gardena. Check with STAT Turismo
Tel: 0142 781 660 - or the tourist offices in Val Gardena.
Train
Bolzano and Bressanone are stopping stations for the Intercity Express Trains. Buses depart from these stations to Val Gardena. Some hotels offer a pick up service from the station.
Air
Bolzano Airport 47km
Innsbruck Airport 115km
Verona Airport 193km

© Ricky Felderer

VAL GARDENA »
Intro_ Selva di Valgardena (Wolkenstein), together with Ortisei (St.Ulrich), is one of the most fascinating places in the Dolomites, and, some say, one of the most beautiful regions in the whole of Europe. The locals speak both Italian and German, and you'll find that English is also fairly widely spoken, especially amongst the younger generation. Val Gardena is the departure point for one of the most impressive tours that can be undertaken in the European Alps - Sella Ronda. The village itself is a beautiful and very typical south Tirolean farmer's village, with a relaxing atmosphere.

ON THE MOUNTAIN »
Snow reliability_ Selva is situated in the Dolomites. December and January can be very cold and have very little snow. The best times for riding are between February and March and even in April, when new snowfall often finds its way into the region. There are snow making facilities.

Lifts_ There definitely isn't enough space to write about all the lifts and runs available in this region.

The Dolomiti Super Ski Pass enables you to access over 1220km of piste. Even passionate freestylers who find their way to Selva should consider taking the Sella Ronda tour, which guides you amongst some of the most beautiful mountains in the world. The pistes offer something for everyone and there are almost no restrictions for boarding. Queues often form on the weekends and during the high season.

Freeriding_ There is a lot of challenging freeriding terrain in the Dolomites. The only problem is the relatively low elevation and low annual rainfall, which do not make for ideal snow conditions. If and when the snowfall has been good, you'll discover endless great tree runs. Forcella del Sassolungo provides a great freeriding area, or make your way to the Marmolada glacier or Schlern, where you'll also find some good runs. You will need a mountain guide, however, who can be found at info@catores.com or booked at the office - Piazzadella Chiesa, 39046 StÜllrich -

Tel: +39 (0) 471 798 223

Freestyling_ The area at Selva is mainly for carvers. Freestylers head to Seis, where you'll find a well maintained pipe, a reasonable park, and plenty of spots to build kickers. Keep your eyes open for pro riders such as Lukas Goller and Danny Morandini.

Carving_ Alpine riders will be happy here, where the pistes are perfectly suited to long, powerful carving turns. The runs are well groomed and the hard, compact snow draws hard booters from all over Europe. The competition scene is also well developed, with the local event, the South Tirol Cup being well known throughout Europe.

Beginners_ The resort is suitable for all levels of riders, whether you are a beginner or pro. The region is so big that there's something for everyone.

Mountain Restaurants_ Hey, waddayamean? This is Italy! Local restaurants, both on and off the mountain, are first class. All the eateries offer great food and drinks for a fair price, and we can recommend them all. Just to name

"THE AREA AT SELVA IS MAINLY FOR CARVERS. FREESTYLERS HEAD TO SEIS, WHERE YOU'LL FIND A WELL MAINTAINED PIPE, A REASONABLE PARK, AND PLENTY OF SPOTS TO BUILD KICKERS."

a couple of huts, Daniel hut and the Raiser hut are very popular and can be found in the Seceda zone. A rest stop in one of the huts is always relaxing, even if it is just for a small snack of bread, smoked ham and a beer.

IN THE TOWN »
Accommodation_Traditional south Tirolean hospitality is available both in Val Gardena and Selva for a fair price. You'll find guesthouses and rooms to rent,

with prices ranging from around €15 upwards. A 2 star guesthouse in South Tirol often matches a 3 star anywhere else in Italy.

Food_Regional cuisine combines the best of Tirolean and Italian flair. On offer are schlutzkrapfen, speckknödel, pasta and polenta… and then come the desserts! In Val Gardena, where the locals speak German and Italian, you'll find fantastic food at a good price. You'll not be disappointed if you go

on a gastronomic tour through the many restaurants and pizzerias.

Nightlife_Val Gardena is home to a rather impressive number of bars and pubs, all providing good quality service and prices - unfortunately they don't stay open for very late. For those wishing to stay out a little later, then try Dalí in Selva, or jump in the car and head to Mauriz disco pub in St.Ulrich. The real parties in Selva basically happen in the Après Ski bars.

Other Activities_Plenty, from free climbing to curling, from hockey and bowling to paragliding.

LOCAL TIP »
It is possible that the guesthouse or pension where you are staying will lock its doors relatively early on in the evening. Its always a good idea to check with the owner before going out for the evening – you don't want to be spending a night on the porch as it can be very cold!

"IF AND WHEN THE SNOWFALL HAS BEEN GOOD, YOU'LL DISCOVER ENDLESS GREAT TREE RUNS. FORCELLA DEL SASSOLUNGO PROVIDES A GREAT FREERIDING AREA, OR MAKE YOUR WAY TO THE MARMOLADA GLACIER OR SCHLERN, WHERE YOU'LL ALSO FIND SOME GOOD RUNS. YOU WILL NEED A MOUNTAIN GUIDE."

DONUTS

Donuts 2 Place de l'Industrie CH. 1180 ROLLE SWITZERLAND.www.donut

PHOTO:M.NINGHETTO/CREA:GERALD ★ SHAPE BY T.K

SCANDANAVIA
154-178

GEILO
HEMSEDAL
NARVIK

TRYSIL
VOSS
ÅRE

RIKSGRÄNSEN
SÄLEN
TÄNNDALEN

YLLAS
RUKA
TALMA

SCANDANAVIA MAP

SCANDANAVIA »

Intro_Although not as popular as the rest of Europe, Northern Europe can be a great destination for snowboarders – especially park fiends. Like the Americans, the Scandinavians realised quickly that well shaped parks and pipes count for a lot in the absence of good freeride terrain. So, even though the mountains are far smaller than the Alps, and the resorts tiny, a huge snowboard scene has developed here, which includes many of the world's best freestylers.

The midnight sun of May and June is an amazing experience, and allows you to participate in round the clock kicker sessions. The natural environment is impressive and quite different to that of middle Europe. The Scandinavians themselves seem to be a race of their own. First impressions may suggest that they are reserved and calm in character, but anyone who has partied with Scanners will tell you a different story. Disadvantages include the long travelling time needed to get to resorts, and the high cost of living – you'll soon think twice about buying a beer after riding here.

Having said all that, an adventure in the Scandinavian Alps is one that you, and your bank manager, will never forget.

INFORMATION »
NORWAY
Official Name_Kongeriket Norge
Capital_Oslo
Population_4,48 Million
Land mass_323.877km2
Language(s)_Norwegian
Currency_1 Krone = 100 øre
Highest mountain_Glittertind 2.470m
International country code_0047
Police_112
Ambulance_113
Fire Brigade_110
Tourist Board_Norges Turistråd
Tel: +47 (0)24 14 46 00
www.visitnorway.com
Train Info_Tel: 815 00 888
www.nsb.no
Weather Info_www.dnmi.no

SWEDEN
Official Name_Konungariket Sverige
Capital_Stockholm
Population_8,892 Million
Land mass_449.964km2
Language(s)_Swedish
Currency_1 Krone = 100 Ore
Highest mountain_Kebnekaise 2.111m
International country code_0046
Police_112
Ambulance_112
Fire Brigade_112
Tourist Board_Sweden Tourism
Tel: +46 (0) 8 789 24 80
www.visit-sweden.com
Train Info_Tel: +46 (0)771 757575
www.samtrafiken.se
Weather Info_www.smhi.se

INFORMATION »
FINLAND
Official Name_Suomen Tasavalta
Capital_Helsinki
Population_5,165 Million
Land mass_338.145km2
Language(s)_Finish
Currency_1 Euro = 100 Cent
Highest mountain_Haltiatunturi: 1.328m
International country code_0035
Police_112
Ambulance_112
Fire Brigade_112
Tourist Board_Finnish Tourist Board
Tel: +358 (0)9 417 6911
www.finland-tourism.com
Train Info_www.vr.fi
Weather Info_www.fmi.fi

LOCATIONS »
01 **GEILO**
02 **HEMSEDAL**
03 **NARVIK**
04 **TRYSIL**
05 **VOSS**
06 **ÅRE**
07 **RIKSGRÄNSEN**
08 **SÄLEN**
09 **TÄNNDALEN**
10 **YLLAS**
11 **RUKA**
12 **TALMA**

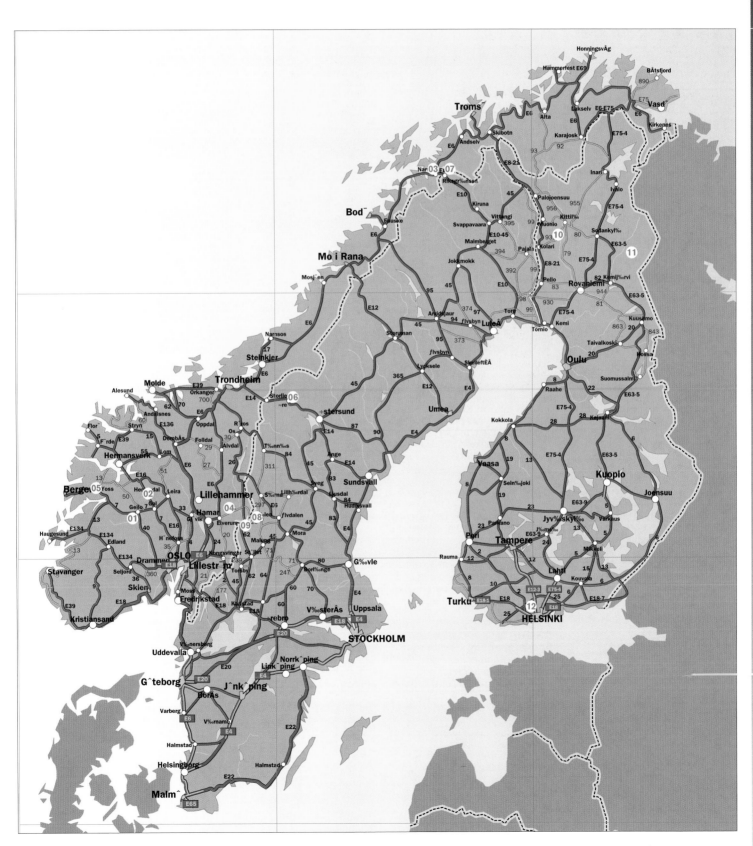

"WHAT MAKES GEILO A TOP-NOTCH DESTINATION, THOUGH, IS ITS INCREDIBLE SNOWPARK. NTG (THE NORWEGIAN SPORTS HIGH SCHOOL) IS LOCATED HERE, HOME OF RIDERS SUCH AS JP SOLBERG AND EIRIK HAUGO."

GEILO
NORWAY

GEILO »
www.geilo.no
tourist office tel: +47 (0)32095900
location: Geilo
population: 2500
altitude: 789-1178m

ON THE MOUNTAIN »
Season: End November – May
Lifts
vertical drop: 1300-2000m
amount of lifts in total:17
gondolas: -
chairlifts: 4
T-bars: 13 (5 for children)
Slopes
amount of prepaired slopes: 28 km
runs w. snowmaking machine: 20
amount of easy runs: 6
amount of intermediate runs: 22
amount of advanced runs: 5
Facilities
night skiing: yes, until 8 pm
amount of halfpipes: 1
amount of funparks: 3
heliboarding:-
Lift-ticket prices in Euro
1/2 day: 29 (190 Nkr)
1 day: 35 (260 Nkr)
week: 160 (1195 Nkr)
season: 413 (3100 Nkr)
special deals: weekend: 2 days 60 (450 Nkr)
 weekend: 3 days 82 (615 Nkr)

SNOWBOARD TUITION »
Per Bye
Tel: +47 (0)32090650
www.geilo.no
Slaatta Skiskole
Tel: +47 (0)32091710
www.geilo.no

SNOWBOARD SHOPS »
Vestlia
Tel: +47 (0)32095515
www.geilo.no

GETTING THERE »
Car
Bergen – Geilo: 229km
Bergen – 540 – Rv7 – Geilo
Oslo – Geilo: 236km
Oslo – Rv7 – Geilo
Train
3 hours from Oslo
3.5 hours from Bergen
Check out fares and timetables at
Norwegian railway: www.nsb.no/EN/
Air
Oslo Airport: 236km
Bergen Airport:230km
Dagali Airport: 27km – Sun Air flies to Dagali from Copenhagen, Denmark, from December until the end of the season.

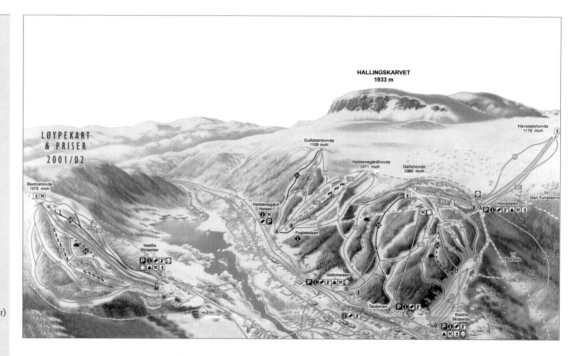

LØYPEKART & PRISER 2001/02

HALLINGSKARVET 1933 m

GEILO »
Intro_ Geilo is what you might call a 'high-class' resort, popular with the upper classes from Bergen and Oslo.
Although there are 17 ski lifts here, the mountain itself is rather flat and the vertical drop is a joke compared with resorts like Hemsedal and Voss.
What makes Geilo a top-notch destination, though, is its incredible snowpark. NTG (the Norwegian Sports High School) is located here, home of riders such as JP Solberg and Eirik Haugo. Valuable feedback from these guys has helped Geilo to become one of the most attractive winter destinations for freestylers in little over three short years.

ON THE MOUNTAIN »
Snow reliability_ Geilo is situated just east of the border between the western/eastern Norwegian mountain range. This means it gets more sunshine with a longer winter season but a little less snow than out west.
Geilo opens up in November and doesn't close until May. Late January, February and March are the best times to visit and also the months when the park is at its best. In April the snow starts to get slushy and warm.
Expect a solid snow base from mid to late December. It can rain in

all the resorts out west, but it always snows at Geilo, thanks to its high altitude.

Lifts & Piste_17 lifts, mostly high-speed chairs and some T-bars. Geilo consists of two separate mountains, Geilo and Vestlia. Vestlia has a chairlift and a T-bar. The park here is usually mellow and in better shape towards the end of the season.

Freeriding_ Hardly worth mentioning, the trees (mainly birch) grow so close together that tree runs are out of the question; the only exception would be at the Halstengaard lift.
The uppermost lift on the far right hand side, Havsdalen, does offer some windlips and kicker-building spots at the very top, but don't expect too much...

Freestyling_ Now this is a different story: Geilo actually hosts no less than three snowboard parks, one of which is for advanced riders only.
The beginner park is in Havsdalen, where you'll find a small halfpipe (3-3.5 metre walls), a 10-12 metre funbox and two friendly plastic rails.
Across the valley, in Vestlia, there's another park with some fun speed bumps, mellow kickers, rails,

a small pipe and usually a hip. Finally, when you've outgrown these parks and are ready to step it up, head over to Fugleiken. This is perhaps the best park in Norway. Don't be surprised to see JP Solberg spinning way above you, as he actually lives here, when he's not touring the world.
The super pipe is one of a kind in the whole of Scandinavia − 5 metre plus walls and a length of 150 metres - minimum. The pitch is 15 degrees plus.
In addition, there's also a big-jump fluctuating between 15-17 metres in size, two fun boxes and loads of rails in various shapes and sizes, flat bars, as well as curved and kinked ones. Right next to the park there is also a permanent Boarder Cross course.
Don't miss out on this park − even if it's only to see what you could be riding if you keep practising!

Beginners_A wide variety of mellow, daily groomed slopes make sure that beginners won't feel out of their depth.

Mountain Restaurants_ Four. Three on the Geilo side and one at Vestlia.
Try the soups and "Kjöttkaker", Norwegian meatballs.
The Today's Special is always a

© Chris Holter **Rider** Halvor Lund

© Chris Holter **Rider** Per Lohren

Nightlife_Geilo can go off at night, especially in the holiday season. Don't be surprised if some young, luscious (but spoiled) CEO's daughter wants to elope with you after rubbing her in with your life-enhancing milk.

JP and Eirik Haugo recommend the following spots:

Lille Blaa: This is where all snowboarders hang out. Quiet at times, then going off the next night. Frequent live bands.

Bukkespranget: A party pub filled to the rafters every weekend, but quiet during the week.

Après-Ski:
Taubanekroa
Recepten Pub at Dr. Holms

Other Activities_Not many, perhaps a movie or a snowmobile safari. Hopefully an indoor skatepark will be built soon.

"DON'T BE SURPRISED TO SEE JP SOLBERG SPINNING WAY ABOVE YOU, AS HE LIVES HERE, WHEN HE'S NOT TOURING THE WORLD."

safe bet for those with a big appetite.

IN THE TOWN »
Accommodation_Remember, Geilo is an expensive place. Best-case scenario would be to hook-up with riders living here, attending the Snowboarding High School and crash on their couch. If that doesn't work out, try the following:

Geilo Camping & Cabins.
For info phone: +47- 3209 5940
E-Mail: booking@geilo.no

Geilo Apartment Hotel, 56.
bedrooms with cable TV sleeping 4-6. For info phone:
+47-32095948,
Email: geiloapartment@skiinfo.no

Dr. Holms Hotel, built in 1909.
One of the most exclusive hotels in Norway.
Info: www.drholms.com,
Email: post@drholms.no.
For info phone: +47-32095940

Food_Peppes Pizza, where the

pizza is great and the beer flows freely. Table reservations:
+47- 32091815
Sidespranget Restaurant, excellent steaks and huge servings. Great place to visit after a hard day on the mountain. Table reservations:
+47- 32090500
Hallingstuene Restaurant is THE place if you want to try venison or moose. Table reservations:
+47- 3209 1250
Another great restaurant is the one at Dr. Holms Hotel. Bring a thick wallet.

LOCAL TIP »
Rookie of the Year, JP Solberg_"Geilo is where I usually ride when I'm home. It's cool 'cause it has three terrain parks, most of the kickers are small, and so are the rails. This is where I learn all my shit when I'm not out filming". JP rides for Burton, Volcom, Dragon, Nixon, Gravis, and Base.

PROS & CONS »

+ The best snowboard park in Norway, from beginning of the season to the end.
+ A nightlife and Après-Ski unheard of in this religious, Puritan country.
+ Incredible backcountry.

− Can be too cold in December/January (-20°C and colder not uncommon).
− Crowded during Winter/Easter break.

"THE HEMSEDAL SNOWBOARD PARK IS CONSIDERED TO BE ONE OF THE BEST IN EUROPE AND IS KNOWN FOR ITS HIGH STANDARD."

HEMSEDAL
NORWAY

»

HEMSEDAL »
www.hemsedal.com
tourism-office tel: +47 (0)32055030
location: Hemsedal
population:2000
altitude: 625m
linked resorts: Solheisen

ON THE MOUNTAIN »
season: November – beginning of May
Lifts
vertical drop: 640-1497m
amount of lifts in total: 18
gondolas: 0
chair lifts: 5
drag lifts: 13
Slopes
amount of prepared slopes: 38 km
runs w. snowmaking machines: 14
amount of easy runs: 21
amount of intermediate runs: 10
amount of advanced runs: 7
Facilities
night riding: 4
amount of halfpipes: 2
amount of funparks: 1
Heliboarding: -
Lift-ticket prices in Euro
1/2 day: 25 (260 Nkr)
week: 148 (960 Nkr)
season: 475 (2400 Nkr)
Events
Big Air at Easter

SNOWBOARD TUITION »
Hemsedal Aktiv
Tel: +47 (0)32055390
www.hemsedal.com

SNOWBOARD SHOPS »
Totten Skiservice
Tel: +47 (0)32062390
www.hemsedal.com
Hemsedal Sport
Tel: +47 (0)32062110
www.hemsedal.com

GETTING THERE »
Car
Hemsedal is approximately 230km from Oslo. Depending on the traffic, it will take you somewhere between 3 -3.5 hours to drive up from Oslo.
Other Distances:
Hemsedal–Bergen: 280km
Hemsedal–Göteborg: 540km
Hemsedal–Karlstad: 440km
Hemsedal–Stockholm: 740km
Hemsedal–Geilo Airport: 110km
Hemsedal–Fagernes Airport: 90km
Train
Another alternative is to take the train from Oslo Central Station to Gol (25km from Hemsedal) and then take the local bus for the final leg. Check out the times on www.nsb.no or call them on: +47 815 00 888
Air
Our best tip is to fly in to Oslo, then jump on the Norway Express direct to the Hemsedal bus at Oslo Central Station.
Check www.nor-way.no for times and fares or call them on: +47-815 44 444.

HEMSEDAL »
Intro_Hemsedal is by far the biggest and most innovative resort in the whole of Norway, if not Scandinavia. Whether you're a technical jibber in search of triple kink rails, a Craig Kelly clone, pipe rat, kicker specialist or even an absolute beginner, Hemsedal won't disappoint you. It's a melting pot/salad bowl of freaks of nature. How many resorts around the world can rightfully brag about possessing the irresistible combination of epic riding and the craziest partying known to man?

ON THE MOUNTAIN »
Snow reliability_Hemsedal gets dumped on when the winds are blowing either from the east or the south. Unfortunately, most of the heavy winter storms come from out west, caused by strong areas of low pressure in the North Atlantic. These storms dump the majority of their precious, white gold on the western side of the Norwegian mountain chains. Hemsedal, situated on the east side, understandably gets less. Nevertheless, consistent winter temperatures enable Hemsedal to be one of the first resorts to open

every season, usually as early as mid-November. Late January and February are great months for freeriding; snow cover is usually thick by this time.
March offers great light conditions for shooting pictures/freestyle riding, and by late April you can ride/hike until 8-9pm.
Extensive use of snowmaking machines if needed. 65% of the slopes can be covered with artificial snow.

Lifts & Piste_16 lifts. 6 chairlifts (4 express ones) and 6 T-bars. Total lift capacity is 22 600 persons per hour.
Vertical drop of 810 metres, way more if you hike.
32 runs
Permanent, high standard snowboard park.
1 Ski School, and 2 on-hill rental locations.

Freeriding_There are so many backcountry runs to choose from that deciding where to start is a tough choice. Hemsedal covers such a big backcountry area that pow can sometimes be found weeks after it last snowed. Try

these runs for starters:
- "Analen". A super steep and narrow chute. Head up to Reidarskaret with the top lift, then ask your way from there. Not recommended without local knowledge. Transceivers are a must.
"Lille Matterhorn". Take the Ronin lift or the new Skarsnuten lift and then hike. You'll recognise the peak; the resemblance to the real Matterhorn is striking.
"Tottenskogen". Epic tree runs, with little or no hiking needed.

Freestyling_The Hemsedal snowboard park is considered to be one of the best in Europe and is known for its high standard throughout the season.
The park is 600 metres long, 50 metres wide and was designed by Daniel Franck and Lars Eriksen. It consists of two halfpipes, several rails, fun boxes, jumps in various sizes, a hip and a corner. Jumps are made in all sizes, from beginner to expert.
This year the resort invested in a new Pipe Dragon, and plans on maintaining a Super Pipe from early to late season. The shooting stars Andreas Wiig and Sondre

"THE INFAMOUS QUARTER PIPE ON TOP OF FJELLHEISEN USUALLY WORKS TOWARDS THE END OF THE SEASON AND DOWN BY THE BOTTOM RESTAURANTS THERE'S THE WOODEN RAIL, INFAMOUS FOR ALL ITS VIDEO APPEARANCES."

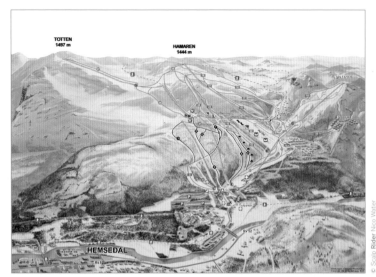

© Scalp Rider Nico Walter

Hylland provided valuable feedback on how to build a park to match the needs of the best riders.

Seven big jumps are at your disposal and five of those can be hit in one line, providing variation only rarely found elsewhere. There will also be two regular-sized pipes and a bunch of rails, starting with flatbars for beginners, moving on to rainbow rails for advanced jibbers and culminating with triple-kink and huge curved rails for the real Tech dogs.

There's lots to be found outside the park too. The infamous Quarter pipe on top of Fjellheisen usually works towards the end of the season and down by the bottom restaurants there's the wooden rail, infamous for all its video appearances.

Search and you will find!

Beginners_A variety of wide open and perfectly groomed slopes await beginners.

There are secluded slopes for kids only, and because not all slopes will be groomed instantly after a heavy snowfall, even those riders who are not yet ready to head out into the backcountry will get the chance to enjoy real powder. We recommend you try the following runs:
"Gummiskogen". Nice tree run with great powder, friendly pitch.

"Tindenheisen". Great run above the tree line. Wide runs and incredible views.

"Breidalen". Means "Wide Valley" in English. Sweet run when coming down from Tinden!

IN THE TOWN »
Accommodation_ Almost too much to choose from. We recommend the following three, though, depending on your budget:

Moen Camping and Cabins. Popular with snowboarders spending the entire season here. Inexpensive cabins. Call them at +47-3206 0136

Norlandia Skogstad Hotell. Skogstad Hotel has everything, including an excellent nightclub, and the Hemsedal Café, THE place to see and be seen in is just across the street.
Phone: +47-3206 0333
www.norlandia.no

Mölla Sportell. Has 56 apartments close to the base of the mountain. 2-6 person bedrooms. Check prices at www.molla.no or call them on: +47-3206 2252

For more options in all price ranges visit:
www2.skiinfo.no/hemsedal/page.php3?Mid=1&id=3

Food_ Eating out in Norway in expensive and Hemsedal is certainly no exception. Nevertheless, you can still find great meals at an affordable price. We recommend the following:
-Amanda Gresslök, popular with the snowboarding crowd, great burgers, rice, chicken and Wok-meals.
Dinners from 75-175 NOK.
Phone: +47-3206 0555

Hemsedal Café, best Chicken Burgers in town. Gets crazy around Après- Ski hours. The place to scope for girls.
Phone: +47-3205 5410

Oxen Bar & Restaurant, great place for steaks and salads. Within walking distance from the lifts.
Phone: +47-3205 5853

Nightlife_ Die-hard Hemsedal fans claim that the party scene and nightlife up here is even better than down in Oslo. I won't argue with them. Every year it seems that more and more people come up here just to party. The closing week in May is unbelievable. Don't be

"PERFECTLY GROOMED SLOPES AWAIT BEGINNERS."

surprised if you see naked people running around the streets or skinny-dipping in the river after steaming, outdoor jacuzzi sessions. Girls of all ages, often wearing expensive designer-dresses, provide sexually malnourished snowboarders with just what they need. Try the following clubs for easy muff access:
Hemsedal Café, Anytime of the day or night will do...Forget going there if you plan on staying, or don't want to get your clothes wet.

Skogstad Nightclub, where everyone goes when Skogstad closes

Hemsen Night Club, a fairly new night club, where bands often play. Great place to score, right by the lifts.

Garasjen, a nice place to enjoy a few beers but gets packed on special occasions.

Remember that there are many more to choose from.

Other Activities_ Fitness gym, bowling, winter golfing, golf simulators, snowmobile safaris, paragliding, ice climbing and most of all, partying!

LOCAL TIP »
Rene Hansen, Burton's Global

Team Director, on Hemsedal_"We've chosen Hemsedal as the location for our biggest European shoot simply because we wanted to work with one the most professional ski resorts in Europe, and their late-season snow conditions. They listen to snowboarders and us in general, and try to improve their service towards riders year by year.

Personally I like to visit Hemsedal for the sheer natural experience, and the snowboarding possibilities, of course. I'm not much of a party-animal, but if that is what you are after, then Hemsedal is definitely the place".

Mads Jonsson- Burton Team Rider and Hemsedal local_"If you're going to Hemsedal, you should go there in the mid- season. Around February/March. This is the time when you'll most likely find some good powder up there. The park is also for sure up and running. And then you have some jibs to do too.

If you want to stay for a longer time, you ought to get in touch with local riders, you could get some apartments for less money than the hotels, and perhaps they'll even show you their sisters and secret-spots. Have fun up there.
PS: The parties can be really fun on the weekends"

PROS & CONS »
+ Narvik with great snow in May, is like
   Chamonix, La Grave or Alagna in January.
+ Riksgränsen is only 40 minutes away so it is
   a good way to kill two birds with one stone.

– Early season can be dark, and the peak lifts
   don't open until the end of March.
– Norway has never been an ideal country to
   visit for budget travellers.

"VARIOUS SKI AND SNOWBOARD COMPANIES HAVE HELD THEIR PHOTO SHOOTS IN NARVIK, AND THE NUMBER OF FILM CREWS HAULING NORTH EVERY SPRING IS MULTIPLYING YEAR BY YEAR."

NARVIK
NORWAY

»

NARVIK »
www.narvikinfo.no
tourist office tel: +47 (0)76943309
location: Narvik
population:18500
altitude: 0m

ON THE MOUNTAIN »
season: December to the end of May.
Lifts
vertical drop: 0-1272m
amount of lifts in total: 5
gondolas: 1
chair lifts: 1
T-bars: 3
Slopes
amount of prepaired slopes: 12 km
runs w. snowmaking machines: 4
amount of easy runs: 5
amount of intermediate runs: 7
amount of advanced runs: 2
Facilities
night skiing: yes
amount of halfpipes: 0
amount of funparks: 0
heliboarding: yes 47 km away
Lift-ticket prices in Euro
1/2 day: 30 (130 Nkr)
week: 128 (960 Nkr)
season: 320 (2400 Nkr)
special deals: 160 Euro (1125 Nkr) for 2
nights in double room at Grand hotel with
liftpass Saturday and Sunday

SNOWBOARD TUITION »
Hojdpunkten
Tel: +47 (0)76959487

SNOWBOARD SHOPS »
Bergswkkski & surf
Tel: +47 (0)76951390

GETTING THERE »
Narvik has frequent communication with the
outside world.
There's a direct train from Stockholm,
Sweden, and the Evenes International Airport
is only one hour away. From there, Oslo is
only a 1 hour and 20 minutes direct flight
away. A return flight will cost you around
2100,- NOK. Check www.sas.no for prices
and flight schedules.
The airport bus to Narvik runs around the
clock and costs around 120,- NOK one-way.
The cheapest rental car will cost around
1000,- NOK, when picked up Friday morning
and returned Sunday night. Check at the
airport for offers.

© Jeff Webb

NARVIK »
Intro_ If you think the winter is
over in May, you're wrong. This is
when it begins in Narvik. High
season starts around Easter, and
runs until June 1st.
   Peaks similar to those found in
the Alps surround this lovely
harbour town of Narvik. Add
powder snow, fjords and midnight
sun, and you'll be one step closer
to the ultimate snowboard-
adventure.
   The city itself, with about 19,000
inhabitants, is rather ugly, but
beautifully situated at the base of
the Fagernes Mountain, which rises
directly from the fjord. The lifts are
only a 10-minute walk from the
centre of town.
What makes Narvik unique is the
mountain, the riding and the view.
When dropping in from the top
elevation, you get the feeling that
you are diving right into a fjord.

ON THE MOUNTAIN »
Snow reliability_ Narvik is
exposed to a maritime climate,
which means that temperature
ranges fluctuate rapidly, based
upon what the Golf Current and
North Sea brings.
   The months of April and May are
just as snow reliable as any, but

always check with www.skiinfo.no
for the latest updates on weather
and snow conditions. If Narvik isn't
faring well, then head on to
Riksgränsen, which is usually open
until June 24th.

Lifts_5 lifts. 1 Gondola, 1 chair
and 3 t-bars. 14 marked slopes.
Narvik is not known for its vast
amount of lifts, capacity or wide,
well-groomed family slopes. All that
counts up here is vertical drop and
easily accessible out-of bounds
terrain.
   Vertical Drop: 875m. If you hike a
little, you get a vertical drop of
1150 metres, second to none in
Scandinavia.

Freeriding_ Ski and snowboard
magazines have contributed greatly
to the exposure of Narvik over the
last few years. Various ski and
snowboard companies have held
their photo shoots in Narvik, and
the number of film crews hauling
north every spring is multiplying
year by year. In spite of all this,
Narvik still remains a quiet,
desolate pearl.
   When disembarking the chair,
you'll find yourself at about 1000
metres over sea level, and
everything is within easy reach. To

your right, from Linken there is a
black groomed run - the only
groomed run descending from the
peak. Should you decide to go out
off bounds instead, head left, and
you'll find a wind lip reaching all
the way down to the tree line,
holding endless possibilities for
kicker and quarter pipe
constructions. This run also goes
under the name of Turisten,
because it rapidly turns into a
mogul run after a heavy snowfall.
The Tourist is the first and smallest
bowl of the Fagernes Mountain. If
you want to access the real candy,
you need to hike to the summit.
Arriving at the 2nd bowl, Mörkhola,
which means The Dark Hole in
English, you will most likely be too
stunned by the sheer beauty of the
view to do anything but sit down.
Cliffs, chutes, and the sea surround
you. Too many riders drop in here,
tempted as they are by this
magnificent run, not knowing that
only 10 minutes more of hiking
would bring them to a bowl even
gnarlier, steeper and scarier than
The Dark Hole. This third bowl is
found 1280 meters above sea
level. It remains steep until the tree
line, approximately 600 vertical
metres lower, and when the snow
base is sufficient, you can ride all

"NARVIK LIKES TO COMPARE ITSELF WITH CHAMONIX"

the way down to the waterfront. Always check with the locals/ski patrol before you drop in. And wear a transceiver! The avalanche danger can be extremely high around the peaks.

Freestyling_ Every year a couple of kickers and tables are built, and, although there has been talk about a pipe for years, if your coming here looking for a sick park, you'll end up disappointed. The fact of the matter here is that the riders themselves always build the best kickers.

Narvik has bred many respected riders over the years. They're not necessarily known for technical tricks, but rather a smooth style, combined with going bigger than anyone else.

If you are into rails, then we recommend cruising around downtown Narvik, where some crazy rails and architecture is to be found.

Beginners_ Narvik likes to compare itself with Chamonix, which pretty much explains that this is not an ideal mountain for beginners. Nevertheless, beginners will still find groomed slopes. In case Narvik turns out to be too

steep for you, jump on a train bound for Riksgränsen, only 40 minutes away on the Swedish side of the border, and the slopes are more forgiving.

Mountain Restaurants_ Only one, Fjellheisrestauranten, at the top of the Gondola.

Nice meals, not too expensive. Some sweet rails can be found here too, if you fancy a little jibbing as an appetiser.

IN THE TOWN »
Accommodation_ Narvik's vast range of accommodation will suit every wallet.

One of the most popular will cost you 700 NOK, -, for a two-night stay, including breakfast and ski pass. Or how about a camping-cabin with ski pass for 445 NOK,-? For detailed information and reservations, go to: www.narvikinfo.no/overnatting Recommended alternatives:
- BREIDABLIKK Guest House: Downtown Narvik, rooms from 185-650,- NOK per night, with breakfast. Phone: +47 76941418
- NARVIK YOUTH HOSTEL: A very high standard hostel with kitchen and TV, washing machine and dryer with room prices ranging

from 150-415,- Tel: +47 76 99 22 00, E-Mail: ssin@ssin.no
- Norlandia Narvik Hotel: An excellent hotel right next to the gondola, Prices upon request. Tel: +47 76 96 48 00

For more options, visit; www.narvikinfo.no

Food_-Napoli Pizzeria, downtown Narvik. Inexpensive Italian-style pizza, as recommended by Daniel Astrup-kjelleren.
For a big night out. Address: Kinobakken 1, 8500 Narvik Table reservation:
+47- 76 96 04 02
Fu Lam Chinese Restaurant. Address: Dronningens gate 58, 8500 Narvik
Table reservation:
+47 76 94 40 35
Mat & Vinhuset Restaurant. Pricey, but well worth a visit. Address: Brugata 3, 8507 Narvik
Table reservation:
+47 76 94 42 90
For further options, go to: www.narvikinfo.no

Nightlife_ Narvik locals are as infamous for their partying and drinking, as they are for their riding. There are not that many bars and nightclubs to choose from, but Malmen Disco often popular. The month of May is by far the craziest partytime of the year. The sun finally returns, long days of 24-hour sunshine is just around the corner, and all high-school seniors celebrate their final days of compulsory tuition like there was no tomorrow - by indulging in sex and drinking orgies yet unknown to

the rest of the civilised world. Every Saturday, the age limit at the door drops to 18, so expect heaps of sexually insatiable 16-17 year-old blondes with fake id longing for out of town lovesticks.

A more mature alternative is Telegrafen, a nightclub/bar combo filled to the brim every weekend. If you're more into quiet pubs, then Peacock is well worth a visit. Here you'll probably meet many of the mountain regulars. Not a bad place to ask around for "classified info"…

Other Activities_ Golfing, mountain biking, mountain climbing Killer whale safaris, wreck-diving and Para-gliding. My best tip would be: Bring your surfboards and head out to the Lofoten Peninsula. The waves there need no further comment, just check out Chilli Video's Y2K.
Contact Narvik Aktiv at:
+47-76960494

LOCAL TIP »
Wise words from almost local ripper and Burton Rookie Daniel Mikkelsen_"Narvik has some of the sickest terrain I've ever ridden, but don't go there before spring comes around. You won't see too much during the dark season. The city of Narvik is rather small, but all the locals and students (the sexually insatiable girls) make sure that Narvik sparkles every weekend. Check out the inexpensive pizza at Napoli, then move on to Malmen Disco (my personal favourite) and Telegrafen Night Club. You won't be disappointed". Good luck and enjoy!
Daniel Mikkelsen.

TRYSIL
NORWAY

"TRYSIL IS THE PLACE FOR BEGINNERS. THE MAJORITY OF THE RUNS ARE BLUE OR GREEN, AND THE RESORT TAKES GREAT PRIDE IN GROOMING."

PROS & CONS »

+ Sick park/pipe.
+ Long season.
+ Lots of sunshine and epic park sessions in April.

− Expensive.
− Super cold in the early season.
− Limited freeriding.

TRYSIL »
www.trysil.com
tourist office tel: + 47 (0)62453000
location: trysil
population: 3000
altitude: 351m

ON THE MOUNTAIN »
Season: late november to late April
Lifts
vertical drop: 351 - 1132
amount of lifts in total: 26
gondolas: -
chairlifts: 5
drag lifts: 21
Slopes
amount of prepared slopes: 65
runs w. snowmaking machines: 18
amount of easy runs: 21
amount of intermediate runs: 32
amount of advanced runs: 11
Facilities
night riding: yes, 5 pistes
amount of halfpipes: 2
amount of funparks: 1
heliboarding: -
Lift-ticket prices in Krona
day: 280
week: 1200
season: 3560

SNOWBOARD TUITION »
Sports service
Tel: +47 (0)62448500

SNOWBOARD SHOPS »
Jules sports shop
Tel: +47 (0)62457950

GETTING THERE »
Car
Oslo – Trysil: 210km
Oslo – E6 towards Trondheim – take the exit before Hamar – Highway 25 to Elverum/Trysil
Stockholm – Trysil: 470km
Stockholm – E4 towards Uppsala – Highway 72 towards Sala – Highway 70 towards Borlänge/Mora – Sälen – Rörbäcksnäs - Trysil
Air
Stockholm Airport: 470km
Oslo Airport: 210km

TRYSIL »
Intro_ Trysil is by far Norway's largest ski resort. 26 lifts, 64 runs and a massive snowpark all provide a multitude of choices for the picky rider. Less than a three-hour drive from Oslo, Trysil lies in the middle of deep forests in the heart of Scandinavia. No other Scandinavian resort is further away from the ocean than Trysil. This means stable weather and guaranteed white winters. Should, however, the white gold refuse to fall, Trysil´s 248 snow making machines will ensure that there's sufficient cover for a November opening.

ON THE MOUNTAIN »
Snow Reliability_ Lack of snow is never usually an issue in Trysil. Although the resort doesn't receive the same quantities as resorts in the more westerly mountains, constantly cold pre-season temperatures ensure the build-up of a nice solid base. In April, when spring comes around, it can turn surprisingly warm due to the interior climate. This of course causes rapid meltdown, but usually allows for at least a week of fun, spring slush, t-shirt days in the park. Snow conditions: +47-62450599

Freeriding_ Don't expect too much if you're used to the Alps. There are, though, a few runs that will get the hearts of even the most experienced freeriders pumping faster. Try the 75 R: a short but 45° steep run near the top of the mountain. Follow your eyes and you can't miss it.

Freestyling_ This is another story altogether. Trysil is a major contributor to the development of snowboarding. Here you will find a snowpark to please both novice and advanced riders. You can't miss it when you get to the top of the "Knetta" chair.
The park consists of a sweet halfpipe at the top, followed by tables and rails of various sizes on the way down. There's usually a rainbow rail, and to your left you'll see the most challenging kicker in the park. Depending on the season, and whether there's been a contest or not, it varies in size anywhere from 13-20 metres. Those hungry for natural rails won't be disappointed either. Check out Heikki Sorsa in the upcoming Standard flick, and you'll know what to look for.

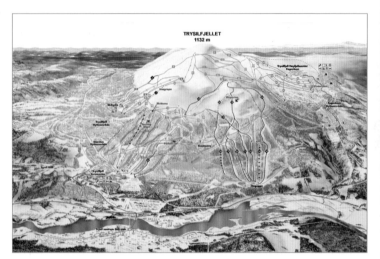

Beginners_ Trysil is THE place for beginners. The majority of the runs are either blue or green, and the resort takes great pride in grooming. Besides, there are tons of people from Denmark here trying to snowboard for the first time ever, so you won't feel out of place.

Mountain Restaurants_ Try the following:
Knettsetra Best around lunch, after 11:00. The Gulasch is a must
Stallen Après-ski starts as early as 14:00, Tapas and beer.
Vaffelstua Insane waffles with jam

IN THE TOWN »
Accommodation_ It's not cheap to stay around here. Remember that people like Michael Schumacher have their winter homes in Trysil. But here are some reasonably priced options:

Klara Camping
Tel: +47 6245 1363
Trysil Gjestegård Panorama
Tel: +47 6245 0850
www.trysil-gjestegard.no
Trysil Hyttegrend Øråneset
Tel: +47 6245 0000
www.trysilhytte.com

Trysil Booking
Call Trysil Booking for information, particularly if you're looking for somewhere inexpensive to stay.
Tel: +47 6245 0000
www.trysil.com

Food_
Heiskroken Great pizza and mellow atmosphere.

Tel: +47-62 452365
Sams Snowboarder hangout. Try the chicken wings.
Glasset A la Carte, expensive, but worth it. Tel: +47-62 450541
Laaven The Barn, worth visiting just for the hot blondie who works there!

Nightlife/Party_
Ski Pub (Girls, cheap beer, 18 year entry, girls, girls with blurry vision)
Heiskroken Bar A popular place to start off the night. Situated at the bottom of the hill.
Glasset Night Club Après dining, this fine cuisine clears out all tables, so that snotty upper-class females, cougars and teenagers alike can burn off their dad's hard-earned cash on super-expensive drinks. Do not underestimate your chances of scoring a bed in an exquisite mountain cabin here.

Other Activities_ Not a lot. Golfing, rafting and fishing during spring & summer months. Bowling? Drinking is one of the most popular past times here.

LOCAL TIP »
Sverre Selheim, national Forum and Session BoardShop rider offers the following tip_"When attempting to reach the park on busy days avoid the main chair. Walk another 200 metres to your right, and you'll find the Knetta chairlift. It's a little slower than the main chair, but you'll actually end up logging more runs if you ride this lift all day rather than standing in line with all the other tourists."

PROS & CONS »
+ Some of the best snow in Norway.
+ Great powder runs through the trees, similar to those found in Austria.
+ Incredibly friendly locals.
+ Varied terrain and challenging freeriding.

− Lack of sunshine in the early season.
− Lack of a proper snowpark.
− Usually closes after Easter, in spite of the fact that the snow base is still 3m + deep.

"THE Z, WHICH LIES A HIKE ABOVE THE SUPERBODEGA, IS FOR EXPERT RIDERS ONLY. CATCH AN EDGE HERE AND IT MIGHT BE THE LAST TIME YOU EVER SNOWBOARD."

VOSS
NORWAY

VOSS »
www.2skiinfo.no/voss-fjellheiser
tourist office tel: +47 (0)56511212
location: vossewangen
population: 2000
altitude: 0m
linked resorts: none

ON THE MOUNTAIN »
deason: from–until mid December to mid April
Lifts
vertical drop: 0–945m
amount of lifts in total: 10
gondolas: 1
chairlifts: -
drag lifts: 9
Slopes
amount of prepared slopes: 42 km
runs w. snowmaking machines: yes
amount of easy runs: 4
amount of intermediate runs: 8
amount of advanced runs: -
Facilities
night riding: -
amount of halfpipes: 1
amount of funparks: 1
heliboarding: -
Lift-ticket prices in Krona
1/2 day: 180
day: 240
week: 1070

SNOWBOARD TUITION »
Voss ski & surf
Tel: + 47 (0)56610032

GETTING THERE »
Car
Driving to Voss will take you just over an hour from the airport
Bus/Train
Alternatively, jump on one of the buses or trains that leave at frequent intervals from the downtown Bergen train and bus station. Departure times available on request at: www.nsb.no or phone: +47-55 96 69 00
Air
Nearest airport is in Bergen: Daily international flights to the UK, Denmark and the Netherlands.

© Chris Holter **Rider** Lassic

VOSS »
Intro_ Voss, the mountain that rightfully claims to be the best powder resort in the whole of Norway. In terms of snow conditions, only two other Norwegian mountains come anywhere close; Röldal and Strandafjellet. But, considering everything else Voss has to offer, it's the place to go.

Powder days are just as common here as rainy days in Bergen. And to cap it all, Voss is full of cute girls. What more could a single male snowboarder possibly need?

ON THE MOUNTAIN »
Snow Reliability_ The early season (Nov-Jan) tends to be unpredictable due to Voss's maritime climate, the result of its proximity to the North Sea and the warm Gulf Stream. Voss usually opens around Christmas, although this varies from year to year. A 50-80 cm fall of fresh snow overnight followed by rain and warmer temperatures is not uncommon during these early months. By January, though, the cold stabilises

and once February comes around, the snow cover tends to be 3-4 metres deep.

Lift_10 lifts. 1 Gondola, 4 chairs and 5 t-bars. Vertical drop of 800 metres. Add another 100 if you don't mind hiking. 40km of groomed slopes, snowmaking machines and a kiddie-lift. A snowboard park is in the pipeline, but don't hold your breath.

Freeriding_ Three runs are highly recommended: the Bodega, the Superbodega and the Z. All of them are at the top right hand side of the mountain. At the Bodega and the Superbodega you'll find the steepest slopes combined with the deepest snow. But always be aware of the danger of avalanches round here, and never drop in without a properly functioning transceiver.

The Z, which lies a hike above the Superbodega, is for expert riders only. Catch an edge here and it might be the last time you ever snowboard. The name "Z" reflects the shape of this narrow

chute that can only be ridden 5-10 days a year. Check with the locals or the ski patrol before attempting to conquer this brutal descent. During a snowfall, on foggy or other low visibility days, head down to the Bavallen Forest, where you'll find epic tree runs and pillow runs similar to those in the Alps. Start out right under the chairlift and work your way through the goodies. Be aware of the cliffs on your right hand side.

The sweetest cliff drop in the area is called Sukkertoppen (The Sugar Top), offering 5-19 metre drops. It's fairly easily accessible, and not really prone to avalanche danger.

Ask a local to point it out to you while you're on the Slettafjellet T-bar.

Freestyling_ The Admin at Voss Mountain have been promising locals a proper snowpark for years, but so far the talk has been cheap – to date the efforts have been less than impressive. The locals have more or less given up lobbying, and these days they put their efforts

© Chris Holter **Rider** Suerr

"ONE SECRET TIP FOR FREESTYLERS IS LYKKEDALEN."

"DURING A SNOWFALL, ON FOGGY OR OTHER LOW VISIBILITY DAYS, HEAD DOWN TO THE BAVALLEN FOREST, WHERE YOU'LL FIND EPIC TREE RUNS AND PILLOW RUNS SIMILAR TO THOSE IN THE ALPS."

into shovelling instead. Given the diversity of the easily accessible terrain, there's really not much work needed in order to build sick jumps. The mountain does construct some half-hearted kickers and rails around Slettafjellet, which provide basic fun…

One secret tip for freestylers is Lykkedalen (or Lucky Valley): Take the T-bar at Slettafjellet, then ride towards Horgaletten. As soon as the slope starts pitching downwards, take a sharp left and hike for 5-10 minutes and you'll come across an epic quarterpipe for regular-footers, and heaps of cornices and wind lips. Don't forget to bring shovels.

Beginners_40km of groomed slopes caters for all levels and abilities. Stick around Slettafjellet and Horgaletten, where you'll find plenty of wide and open slopes that are not too steep. A kiddie lift/tow rope is situated right next to the restaurant.

Mountain Restaurants_ Three, one at the bottom in Bavallen, next

to where you buy your pass, a second at Slettafjellet, by the towrope, and the third at the top of the Hangur Gondola. No particular local dishes, but all of these restaurants serve big juicy burgers. Local snowboarders tend to hang out at the Slettafjellet Restaurant.

IN THE TOWN »
Accommodation_ Options available in all price categories, but we recommend the following:
Fleischers Hotel & Apartments The best hotel in Voss for those on an unlimited budget. An epic breakfast buffet and a nice late hour Jacuzzi in the basement.

Fleischers Hotel & Apartments
Evangervegen, 5700 Voss
Tel: +47 56 52 05 00
Fax: +47 56 52 05 01
Hotel@fleischers.no
www.fleischers.no

Jarl Hotel A cosy mid-priced hotel with a nightclub in the basement

Jarl Hotel
Elvegata, 5700 Voss
Tel: +47 56 51 19 33
Fax: +47 56 51 37 69
booking@jarlvoss.no
www.jarlvoss.no

Voss Youth Hostel For those on a budget. Daniel Franck used to sneak in here way back when…. A bed will cost you around 200-250 NOK per night, with an all-you-can-eat breakfast included.

Voss Youth Hostel
Evangervegen, 5700 Voss
Tel: +47 56 51 20 17
Fax: +47 56 51 08 37
voss-hostel@voss.online.no
www.vandrerhjem.no

Haugo Apartment Rental
Apartments rented out by the Haugo Family, the most snowboard supportive family in Voss, ever. Double rooms 195 NOK per night. Single rooms 250 NOK per night. Eirik Haugo is the new Norwegian shooting star, and these days rides for the Norwegian Halfpipe Team. If you stay here, the Haugos will make sure you're never bored. Triple trampoline and miniramp action nearby.

Haugo Apartment Rental
Gamle Bordalsvegen 54, 5700 Voss
Tel/fax: +47 56 51 23 50

Food_ Try the local Kebab; locals claim it's the best in Norway.

Hotel Jarl The restaurant here serves great meat balls, a Norwegian speciality

Stallen the place for pizza and cheap (by Norwegian standards) beer

Ringside shows snowboard movies and offers all-you-can-eat pasta.

Fleischer has great à la carte.

If you get the chance to try "Smalahove", don't pass it up. It's a typical dish from Voss and means "Sheep Head" in English, so not recommended for vegetarians!

Nightlife_ Try the disco at the Hotel Jarl for an unbelievable girl to boy ratio. Pentagon, in the basement of the Park Hotel suits the more mature crowd better. Expect visitors to be wearing everything from tuxedos to sandals. Want to blend in with the local 30+crowd? Try the Top Spot Bar at Hotel Fleischer with live music provided by Bulgarian bands. Rondo is a fun bar, and girls, the bartender looks just like Lorenzo Lamas…

Other Activities_ Skateboarding, rafting, paragliding, skydiving, mountain hiking, sick road gaps at the nearby Vika fjellet in the late season (May-June), ice-skating, bowling and more.

LOCAL TIP »
Björn Mortensen, Transworld and Onboard cover boy_"Try the pow under the Hangur single chair as a warm up run. There won't be anybody there… Rails in downtown Voss: A nice double kink right by the retirement home, and a mellow 12-stair curved rail right across the road from the Shell station. Be careful with the local girls, they might not be what you expect them to be…"
Björn rides for Burton, Anon, Analog and Base.

Eirik Haugo, riding for O'Neill, Vans, Smith, Da Kine, and Extrem_recommends a visit to the local skatepark, just 50 metres across the street from the Voss Train Station. Opening Hours:
Mon-Fri: 17:00-22:00
Sat-Sun: 12:00-22:00

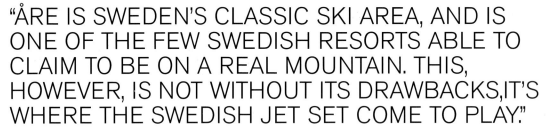
"ÅRE IS SWEDEN'S CLASSIC SKI AREA, AND IS ONE OF THE FEW SWEDISH RESORTS ABLE TO CLAIM TO BE ON A REAL MOUNTAIN. THIS, HOWEVER, IS NOT WITHOUT ITS DRAWBACKS,IT'S WHERE THE SWEDISH JET SET COME TO PLAY."

PROS & CONS »

+ Wide variety of terrain.
+ Excellent celebrity spotting potential.
+ Easily accessible by train or bus.

− Notoriously unpredictable weather.
− Expensive and snobbish.
− Overcrowded slopes and lift.

ÅRE
SWEDEN

ÅRE »
www.skistar.com/are
Tourist office tel: +46 (0)64717720
location: Åre
population: 1000
altitude: 380m
linked resorts: Duved, Are Bjornen, Tegefjall and Rodkullen

ON THE MOUNTAIN »
season: December – mid May
Lifts
vertical drop: 380-1274m
amount of lifts in total: 39
Funicular: 1
gondolas: 1
chair lifts: 6
drag lifts: 31
Slopes
amount of prepared slopes: 100 km
runs w. snowmaking machines: 21
amount of easy runs: 51
amount of intermediate runs: 39
amount of advanced runs: 10
Facilities
night riding: yes 4days a week until the end of february when there is daylight all through the evenings. (in the end of june it is daylight 24 h/day)
amount of halfpipes: 1
amount of funparks: 4
heliboarding: yes
Lift-ticket prices in Euro
day: 31 (290 Skr)
week: 158 (21530 Skr)
season: 387 (3405 Skr)
Events
12-15 december 2002 Free snowboard testing
17-19 april 2003 Red Bull Big Air

SNOWBOARD TUITION »
Are Skischool
Tel: +46 (0)64717700
www.skistar.com/are

SNOWBOARD SHOPS »
Skidakarna
Tel: +46 (0)64717700
www.skistar.com/are

GETTING THERE »
Car
Östersund – Åre: 101km
Östersund – E14 – Åre
Stockholm – Åre: 612km
Stockholm – Uppsala – Mehedeby – Gävle – Ljusdal – Ytterhogdal – Svenstavik – Mattmar - Åre
Train
From Stockholm: 7-9hours
From Östersund: 1hr 20min
Air
Östersund Airport: 92km
Stockholm-Arlanda Airport: 580km

© Red Bull/Grill Ulrich

ÅRE »
Intro_Åre is Sweden's classic ski area, and is one of the few Swedish resorts able to claim to be on a real mountain. This, however, is not without its drawbacks because this means it's where the Swedish jet set come to play. Members of Royalty are frequently sighted here, prices are shockingly high, and in certain places, the atmosphere can make you want to start a revolution. But the village is as cosy as it is beautiful, the mountain has everything you could hope for, and the nightlife can be great too.

ON THE MOUNTAIN »
Snow reliability_Early season is very unpredictable. There's just no telling when it will start to dump. It always does eventually though! The best thing to do is either go late in the season or, if you really must go earlier, at least check the snow reports.

Lifts_The main areas are the World Cup lift, and the area just below Hummeln. Avoid them if you can, they can get very busy. The Olympia lift is fun, but just as crowded. The upper regions of the resort are best, and the little eggs that take you from the halfway point to the top are highly efficient, delivering you to one of the funnest runs in the country. The gondola is always crowded, so taking the Olympia and then the egg up is often faster. The minor areas are a bit flatter, but less crowded.

Freeriding_Freeriding in Åre can be great when the conditions allow. There are a number of routes down from the top. Ask around for specific and up to date information. There might even be guided tours to different hikes and runs. Powder can be found and accessed easily, but be quick, as the locals are early risers. Respect restrictions as the fluctuating temperatures make avalanches an ever-present hazard.

Freestyling_If you like parks and pipes you're in the wrong place. Åre is a thoroughly conservative place and you sometimes get the feeling they don't even want snowboarders around. Saying this, there is a park and it has been greatly improved lately. A pipe can be found at the bottom of the World Cup slope, but there's no guarantee it will be in good condition. A number of good riders have come out of Åre, and this is where the Swedish freeriding scene is at its strongest.

Carving_Swedish carvers flock here – Åre boasts long runs with efficient lifts back to the top. The slopes are thick with people though, so they tend to get really bumpy after lunch. The top area is always a popular spot.

Beginners_The main sections of Åre are fairly steep, so stay away if you don't want to get run over. For a more mellow ride check out the peripheral lifts like Duved or Tegefjäll. Lessons are widely available.

Mountain Restaurants_For lunch or dinner, head down to the village, as it offers a wide variety of food without the extortionate prices of the mountain. The mountain restaurants are packed out by fat people with fat wallets, and your best bet is to stay away, unless you're in possession of a fat wallet of your own…

IN THE TOWN »
Accommodation_Many cabins and apartments are situated a long way from the lifts, so be sure to find out where they're putting you before you sign up. Åre is usually sold out by October time, so book ahead. If you don't, you may not find anywhere at all.
   Prices are high. Expect to be charged anything from 200 Euros onwards for a week in a shared cabin. Check out www.skistar.com/are/ or +44 (0)647-177 00 for booking or information.

Food_Downtown offers a plethora of places offering eats of all sorts. Budget travellers grab hot dogs at the stand by the square, while big spenders dine at the Hotel Diplomat. A good alternative is to cook for yourself – there are supermarkets in the town, they're fairly big and have most things you need.

Nightlife_There's a thriving nightlife here and the bars are top notch. There's really no way of telling where's good till you get there and check things out.

"FREERIDING IN ÅRE CAN BE GREAT WHEN THE CONDITIONS ALLOW. THERE ARE A NUMBER OF ROUTES DOWN FROM THE TOP. ASK AROUND FOR UP TO DATE INFORMATION. THERE MIGHT BE GUIDED TOURS TO DIFFERENT HIKES AND RUNS."

»

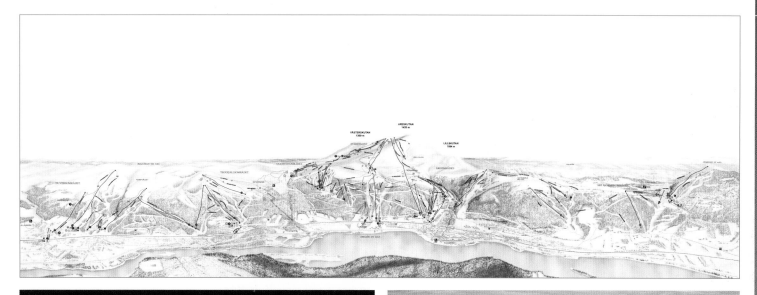

Nightclubbing will inevitably be a tormenting experience of the cheesy disco variety.

Other Activities_There is a skatepark, or at least an indoor mini. Browse the local board brand Extrem's products in store, go on snowmobile cruises or hit the streets with a snowskate.

LOCAL TIP »
Fredrik Sarvell, pro snowboarder and former local_"If the snow is good, go to Duved. Get all the way up, and then hike a little bit further still. It only works if you think it's really fun to hike and even better if you love to snowboard."

"A PIPE CAN BE FOUND AT THE BOTTOM OF THE WORLD CUP SLOPE, BUT THERE'S NO GUARANTEE IT WILL BE IN GOOD CONDITION."

PROS & CONS »
+ This mountain was built for snowboarding.
+ The natural scenery – it's as close as you'll ever get to walking on the moon.

– It's a very isolated place.
– The weather can screw things up badly.
– Getting there is a hassle.
– Expensive.

"RIKSGRÄNSEN IS THE ULTIMATE PROOF THAT GOD IS A SNOWBOARDER – THE TERRAIN IS ABSOLUTELY PACKED WITH NATURAL KICKERS, WINDLIPS AND EVERYTHING ELSE."

RIKSGRÄNSEN
SWEDEN

» »

RIKSGRÄNSEN »
www.riksgransen.nu
tourist office tel: +46 (0)98040080
location: Riksgränsen
population: 35
altitude: 500m

ON THE MOUNTAIN »
season: Febuary - June
Lifts
vertical drop: 500-910m
amount of lifts in total: 6
gondolas: -
chair lifts: 2
drag lifts: 2
Slopes
amount of prepared slopes: 21 km
runs w. snowmaking machines: -
amount of easy runs: 4
amount of intermediate runs: 16
amount of advanced runs: -
Facilities
night riding: yes, natural light May-June
amount of halfpipes: -
amount of funparks: -
heliboarding: -
Lift-ticket prices in SEK
1/2 day: 200
day: 250
week:1230
season: 2190

SNOWBOARD TUITION »
Riksgränsen
Tel: +46 (0)98040080

SNOWBOARD SHOPS »
Schmedjan
Tel: +46 (0)98040080

GETTING THERE »
Car
Kiruna – Riksgränsen: 214km
Kiruna - Nordkalott Highway E10 – Riksgränsen
Train
There's an 18 hour sleeper from Stockholm.
www.sj.se -
Air
Fly to Stockholm (1370km away from Riksgränsen) and take a domestic flight to Kiruna Airport (214km)

RIKSGRÄNSEN »
Intro_Riksgränsen is just about as far north as you can get. It's a spot that earned its fame from various film sections during the nineties, including Ingemar Backman's legendary backside air. But it's been a popular place for a lot longer than that among dedicated riders and skiers. The name Riksgränsen literally translates as 'National Border' – it lies a (girl's) stone's throw from the border with Norway. The resort consists of a handful of lifts, a hotel, a few cabins and a whole lot of space. The atmosphere is strange, but homely. Some employees have been there longer than you've been alive and it takes about two hours in the bar to get to know everyone.

The reason why people brave the journey is the riding. Riksgränsen is the ultimate proof that God is a snowboarder – the terrain is absolutely packed with natural kickers, windlips and everything else. And then there's the enchanting Midnight Sun. Riksgränsen is unlike anywhere else you've ever been, and if you're going to just one place in Sweden, go there.

As it lies above the Arctic Circle, the sun never sets during the summer months and the lifts often stay open later than your average nightclub.

ON THE MOUNTAIN »
Snow reliability_The lifts don't open until February and close again around mid June. Early season riding means immense amounts of powder. Late season means kicker heaven and slushy snow. Riksgränsen is always good. Lately the winters have been shorter so check the snow report before booking your room.

Get information at
www.riksgransen.nu
reservation@riksgransen.nu
Tel: +46–(0)980-400 80
Fax: +46–(0)980- 431 25

Lifts_Everyone starts their day at the main lift. Thereafter you can stay, move up a section or go over the top and down the other side. That's it. Two chairs and a bunch of T-bars. The slopes facing the hotel are a bit steeper than the ones on the backside. Cruise around and find your spot.

© Vincent Skoglund **Riders** Björn Lindgren

Freeriding_Freeriding is what Riksgränsen is all about. You can access a number of drops and lines without walking a step. There's an infinite number of lines and the terrain is full of surprises. Everywhere you turn you'll see something tempting. Standing at the top you can see Norddalsfjället, which is an hour's hike but well worth it. The entire resort is above the tree line so the snow soon gets windpacked.

Freestyling_The highway gap, the train tunnel, the quarters in Norgesvängen and the Norddals kicker. They're all classic photo spots, seen a hundred times in a hundred magazines and videos. Riksgränsen has the natural terrain needed for any kind of kicker or hit you want. Natural lines are usually formed down the slopes and are sooooo much fun. If you're feeling ambitious, take the chair to the top, hike up to the little hut on your right and marvel at the view from up there. You're in Norway now and this area is known all over the world for the sick natural terrain. To return, you have to hike back along the train tunnel, a very sketchy walk as you might fall through, but people usually hike the same kicker for hours. If there's an event

"EARLY SEASON RIDING MEANS IMMENSE AMOUNTS OF POWDER. LATE SEASON MEANS KICKER HEAVEN AND SLUSHY SNOW."

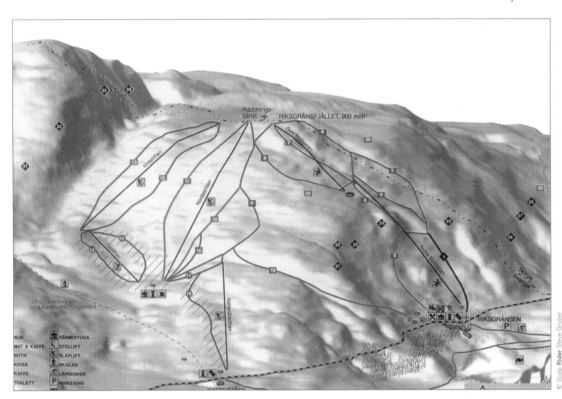

"NATURAL LINES ARE USUALLY FORMED DOWN THE SLOPES AND ARE SOOOOO MUCH FUN. IF YOU'RE FEELING AMBITIOUS, TAKE THE CHAIR TO THE TOP, HIKE UP TO THE LITTLE HUT ON YOUR RIGHT AND MARVEL AT THE VIEW FROM UP THERE. YOU'RE IN NORWAY NOW AND THIS AREA IS KNOWN ALL OVER THE WORLD FOR THE SICK NATURAL TERRAIN. TO RETURN, YOU HAVE TO HIKE BACK ALONG THE TRAIN TUNNEL, A VERY SKETCHY WALK."

on or something similar they might build a park but, hey, that's not why you're here…

Carving_ Sure. Great snow and some fairly long runs down the backside. You'll have great fun trying to outrun the skiers and telemarkers who have mad skills when it comes to going fast.

Beginners_ Beginners really don't need to go to Riksgränsen. Björkliden, about 30 kilometres closer to Kiruna, have perfect mellow runs and anything else you might need to learn.

Mountain Restaurants_ Just like

there's one hotel, there's just one restaurant. But the food is top notch and usually just what you're craving for after an exhausting day.

IN THE TOWN »
Accommodation_ There's only one option for accommodation – the hotel. Prices vary with the season and depending on what kind of room you're looking for. Riks is a remote spot – be prepared to lay down some big bills for the privilege. However, Swedish pro rider Jacob Söderqvist used to sleep in the laundry room for weeks at a time without paying a penny. For more info contact: reservation@riksgransen.nu or

Tel: +46–(0)980-400 80

Food_ Either go to the restaurant or get groceries in the little store in the lobby.

Nightlife_ Towards the end of the season the veranda opens but before that you're restricted to the cellar bar – the Grönan. This is okay though because everybody goes there. You don't go to Riksgränsen for the nightlife, but when spirits are high spontaneous outbursts are known to happen, including the occasional riot!

Other Activities_ There's a spa, and if the Finns are around you

can challenge them to a sauna-endurance contest. There's also a small mini-ramp at the back of the hotel. It's a bit kinky but the sessions are always fun.

LOCAL TIP »
- Peter Ström, Allian Pro and long time Riksgränsen, local_"When you go to Riksgränsen, you go because you want to ride the mountain. Not to hang around a pipe or a park or anything like that. Go into Norway. There are so many little transitions to land in or take off from. It's not the biggest mountain in the world but most days you spend riding natural lines down it and try to adapt to them."

"IF YOU HOOK UP WITH SOME LOCALS THERE'S AN ENDLESS NUMBER OF SECRET LITTLE TREE RUNS AND HIDDEN RAVINES. THE AREA AROUND THE VÄGGEN LIFT IN HUNDFJÄLLET IS A GOOD HINT…"

SÄLEN
SWEDEN

SALEN »
www.salen.com
Tourist office Tel: +46 (0)28018700
location: Sälen
population: 1600
altitude: 400m
linked resorts: Lindvallen-Högfjället & Tandådalen/Hundfjället

ON THE MOUNTAIN »
season: November to end of April
Lifts
vertical drop: 600-930m
amount of lifts in total: 79
gondolas: -
chair lifts: 8
drag lifts: 71
Slopes
amount of prepared slopes: 110
runs w. snowmaking machines: 60
amount of easy runs: 41
amount of intermediate runs: 50
amount of advanced runs: 19
Facilities
night skiing: 27 pistes
amount of halfpipes: 3
amount of funparks: 7
heliboarding: -
Lift-ticket prices in SEK
1/2 day: 225
week: 1135
season: 3405
Events
5-8/12 world cup snowboard.

SNOWBOARD TUITION »
Lindvallens & Högfjällets skidskola
Tel: +46 (0)28086000
www.skistar.com/salen
Tandådalen & Hundfjället Fjällvärdar
Tel: +46 (0)28084000
www.skistar.com/salen

SNOWBOARD SHOPS »
Lindvallen
Tel: +46 (0)28086066

GETTING THERE »
Car
Stockholm – Sälen: 396km
Stockholm – Sollentuna – E18 Enköping – Sälen
Oslo – Sälen: 273
Oslo – E06 Jessheim – Ausfahrt Elverum – Elverum – Innbygda – Nybergsund (N/S) – Sälen
Göteburg – Sälen: 463km
Göteburg – Trollhättan – Nysäter – Vålberg – Malung - Sälen
Air
Flughafen Stockholm: 376km
Flughafen Oslo: 284km

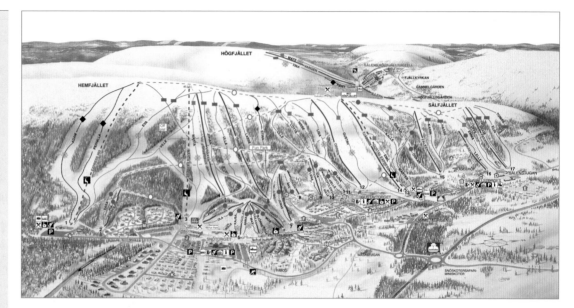

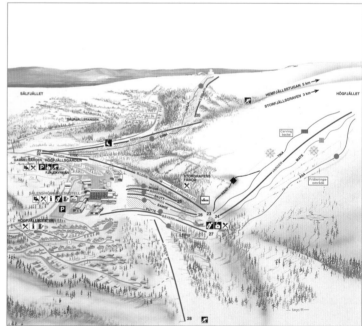

SÄLEN »
Intro_Sälen is the southernmost 'big' resort in the country, and as a result it's the one that receives the most visitors. When a Norwegian chap suggested building a ski resort here in 1936, the locals all thought he was nuts. No one's complaining now however, as the place has become a veritable goldmine.

The resort is made up of several smaller areas, though they aren't all interconnecting. Starting from the south, heading north, the first area you get to is called Kläppen, which lies about half an hour from Lindvallen. Lindvallen is then linked with Högfjället followed by Hundfjället, which is connected to Tandådalen, and a little further down the road there's Stöten. (Stöten and Kläppen are separate areas not connected in any way with the others.)

The village is a little far away, but the mountains are scattered with apartments and cabins for rent. Because Sälen attracts a lot of visitors from the cities the nightlife flourishes throughout the season, culminating in their season finale, 'Ski & Rock'.

ON THE MOUNTAIN »
Snow reliability_ Coinciding with the decline in the amount of snow that falls naturally, the resort's snow-making system has had a timely upgrade. These days, all that is needed are some sub-zero conditions and the machines can take care of the fine white cover.

Early season, November and December are only for die-hards who crave anything that slides. The rest of the season is usually good and the snow is very reliable.

One thing cannot be stressed enough –avoid the main holiday periods. During Easter both slopes and the lifts suffer from a very bad case of overcrowding. Further info from: +46-(0)280-88 000
www.skistar.com/salen/
+46-(0)280-96 200

www.klappen.se
+46-(0)280-750 00
www.stoten.se

Lifts_ As the mountains are so small, the slopes are basically side by side. This makes riding a bit dull, but getting around extremely simple. Try to avoid the main lifts and search out peripheral slopes and lifts, especially in Lindvallen. The area around Väggen in Hundfjället is usually well worth scoping out.

© Vincent Skoglund

© Vincent Skoglund **Rider** Emilio Previtali

"FREESTYLING IS THE BUSINESS AROUND HERE. TANDÅDALEN HOLDS THE COUNTRY'S OFFICIAL WORLD CUP PIPE"

The Kläppen and Stöten systems are rarely as populated as the central areas. Make sure you don't miss the transfer lifts back home at the end of the day.

Freeriding_Freeriding, in the true sense of the word, isn't really possible in Sälen. Having said this, if you hook up with some locals there's an endless number of secret little tree runs and hidden ravines. The area around the Väggen lift in Hundfjället is a good hint… If the snow is plentiful and you have the energy for a short hike, then Sälen can also be a lot of fun.

Freestyling_Now this is what you're looking for. Freestyling is The Business around here. Tandådalen holds the country's official World Cup pipe whilst other resorts dig out the occasional ditch. In order to keep pesky snowboarders out of trouble they have tried to focus all the snowboarding around Tandådalen, which now sports two parks known as Black Magic and White Magic. The parks have tabletops, rails, bumps, and everything else that you could hope to find. Also, last season the Kläppen park attracted a lot of people, and it's probably going to be even better this season. Despite the great parks, the essence of freestyle in Sälen is the various ravines, which, if you're prepared to bring a shovel, are great for kickers and quarters. Högfjällshotellet has easily accessible ravines but these are usually crowded and packed. Keep your eyes peeled from the chair or the road and you'll be sure to scope some out. Huck your heart out!

Carving_As the entire resort is state of the art and top of the line, the slopes are groomed every day. Early risers can always satisfy their cravings for corduroy. The slopes are almost all very short and have a tendency to level out.

Beginners_You have definitely come to the right place. Slopes are smooth and gentle enough to spend those first shuddery days on. There are some steep spots, but a brief look at the map should help you steer clear of these.

Mountain Restaurants_There are lots of restaurants sprinkled around the area, ranging from cheap McDonald's and similar fast food joints to classier joints. Lunches usually consist of a main course and some serve-yourself salad. They're often a good deal, and a lot healthier than the deep-fried burger food. If you're riding on a budget, don't forget your sandwiches.

IN THE TOWN »
Accommodation_There are cabins and apartments around every separate area, usually within a few minutes' walk from the lift. If you plan ahead, booking one of these shouldn't be a problem. This has to be your best bet, and in fact there really aren't any other options available. A bed in an apartment or cabin varies from around 50 to 150 Euro per week. bokning@salen.com or +46 (0)280-88 000

Food_All cabins and apartments come equipped with a kitchen. To save funds you may want to do your shopping before getting to Sälen as the supermarkets there tend to over charge. Apart from cheap prices, anything you might wish for is available on the mountain. Prices vary very little between the food stores, but groceries are usually more expensive at the gas stations. Important – the sale of alcohol is state monopolised in Sweden. It can't be purchased after 6pm, and before that only in special stores called Systembolaget. Stock up!

Nightlife_The aprés ski partying is the main reason people come here. Every single bar is stuffed from 3pm until 6am, and they are all playing the same old songs. If Creedence Clearwater covers are your cup of tea, you can drink yourself silly every day. For clubbing go to H.C or Aqua bar. Sundays are the employees' night out and usually a decent alternative. Entrance fees can be up to 20 Euros if there's a concert on or similar. Read the posters! Foreigners are popular pickings for the locals. Tell them you're a pro – everybody else does… Because this place is so spread out, taxis or a designated driver are necessary, as the police come down heavily on drink drivers in Sweden. Drunken people die walking home every year – don't be one of them.

Other Activities_The Sälen area is mainly aimed at families. Hence, you have a choice between bowling, pinball or a dip in a pool.

LOCAL TIP »
Andreas Åvik, national team coach and ripper, born and bred in the area_"Lately the snowboard park in Kläppen has been really, really good. It now has its own lift, is shaped everyday, and has a chill section at the bottom. If you want to go out head for Aqua near Sälfjällstorget."

"JUST CRUISING AROUND HERE IS GREAT. SCOPE THE PLACE OUT AND HIT ANYTHING THAT LOOKS NICE."

TÄNNDALEN
SWEDEN

TÄNNDALEN »
www.tanndalen.com
tourist office tel: +46 (0)68416410
location: Tänndalen
population: 240
altitude: 750m
linked resorts: Funäsdalen/Ramundberget

ON THE MOUNTAIN »
season: late November – early May
Lifts
vertical drop: 750-1083m
amount of lifts in total: 18
gondolas: 1
chair lifts: 1
drag lifts: 16
Slopes
amount of prepaired slopes: 34 km
runs w. snowmaking machines: 6
amount of easy runs: 15
amount of intermediate runs: 21
amount of advanced runs black: 5
Facilities
night riding: no
amount of halfpipes: 1
amount of funparks: 2
heliboarding: -
Lift-ticket prices in Euro
1/2 day: 24
day: 26
week: 110
season: 310

SNOWBOARD TUITION »
Kjaergaads - Skidskola
Tel: +46 (0)6841330
www.kjaergaards-skidskola.se

SNOWBOARD SHOPS »
Svansjöliftarnas uthyrning
Tel: + 46 (0)68422105

GETTING THERE »
Car
Oslo – Tänndalen: 445km
Oslo – Jessheim – Stange – Røros – Fjällnäs (N/S) – Tänndalen
Stockholm – Tänndalen: 577km
Stockholm – Uppsala – Mehedeby – Gävle – Ljusdal – Älvros – Sveg – Tänndalen
Air
Flughafen Oslo: 456km
Flughafen Stockholm: 545

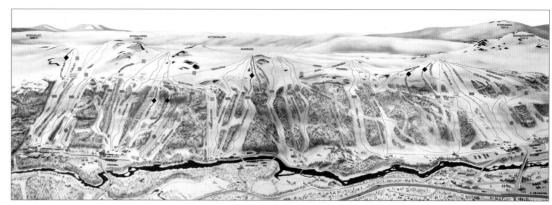

"ONE OF THE MOST UNSPOILED AREAS IN THE NORTH, THE RIDING IS ALMOST ALWAYS SUPERB."

TÄNNDALEN »
Intro_Tänndalen is made up of a string of small, interconnected areas. As far as the Swedish mountains go, this one is an absolute pearl and well worth the visit. It's one of the most unspoiled and unexploited areas in the north, and the riding is almost always superb. Tänndalen has always been a popular place to hang out among good riders. Known mainly for being the home of Jacob and his untamed brother Jonas Wilhelmsson and the park in Hamra that their father shapes daily. It is, however, not a place to live out one's vices. The focus is set on the riding in Tänndalen, and, after a trip there, you usually come home with a handful of new tricks and a feeling of balanced interior harmony. There's no other way of putting it – Tänndalen is the shit!

The resort sprawls out along the road and there really isn't anything remotely resembling a village within 20 kilometres. You'll need a car and someone who can drive it to get there and to get around.

ON THE MOUNTAIN »
Snow reliability_Natural snow is rarely a problem. Tänndalen is usually one of the first to open and one of the last to close. They also have an extensive snow making system. Early to mid season might be chilly, but the spring is usually blessed with bluebird days and perfect conditions all-round. Snow report: www.snorapporten.nu

lift_Each area has its own parking and a main lift, where you usually

start off. The area is small and rarely gets crowded. The lifts are T-bars in most cases, but efficient enough for the cause. You'll probably be hanging around the main lift in Hamra and that's not a bad choice as it allows you to go either all the way up or get off by the kicker you fancy the most.

Freeriding_Just cruising around here is great. Scope the place out and hit anything that looks nice and fluffy. There are too many tree runs to even try to explain. From the top you can access a number of smaller peaks if the weather's good. Explore and enjoy.

Freestyling_Hamra is the place for freestyling. The park is without doubt the best in the country, shaped with the precision of a genius and immaculately maintained. There's a pipe but the state of it varies immensely. The scene is kicking – this is the home of the Wilhelmsson brothers. Their friends come here to hang out and there are a number of really good locals who'll be stomping all the tricks from the movies. As opposed to most other areas the obstacles are usually big.

Carving_Hard boots are still spotted here from time to time as the snow is great and the runs are groomed to perfection. Steeps and long cruisers can all be had.

Beginners_If you're just starting out Tänndalen is a good choice. You rarely have to deal with bone-breakingly hard man-made snow

here and there are a number of perfect slopes. Your best picks are the eastern areas like Svansjön and Tännporten. Lessons are available everywhere.

Mountain Restaurants_Restaurants are few and far between, but they do exist. Just don't expect to be able to be picky. The bottom of every main lift has its own little place usually featuring some lunch deal and a bit bigger selection for the evening meal. The food is usually traditional with small eruptions of spontaneity like Tex-Mex or Japanese stuff. Prices are reasonable but nowhere near cheap.

IN THE TOWN »
Accommodation_When browsing for accommodation you should also check out Funäsdalen down the road from Tänndalen. Finding a place shouldn't present any major difficulties but don't expect to be able to strap in by the front door.

Find out more
www.tanndalen.com
info@tanndalen.com
+46-(0)684-22 105
+46-(0)684-221 00
+46-(0)684-230 00
+46-(0)684-221 94

Food_See Mountain Restaurants. For groceries and anything else you usually need to go back down the road to Funäsdalen.

Nightlife_Bring your Playstation…

Other activities_Girls or playstation…

PROS & CONS »
+ Beautiful landscape, especially in the spring.
+ Sunset – it's a dream for photographers.
+ The Northern Lights can be seen in mid-winter.
+ Snowboarder-friendly.

– Very cold.
– Only very intermediate freeride terrain.
– Terrible nightlife.

"IN THE LOCAL HOTELS, THE MENU FEATURES SUCH TRADITIONAL DISHES AS SALMON AND REINDEER."

YLLÄS
FINLAND

YLLAS »
www.yllas.fi
tourist office tel: +35 (0)8165105100
location: Kolari, Lapland
population: 5000
altitude: 255m
linked resorts: Iso-Ylläs and Ylläs-Ski

ON THE MOUNTAIN »
Season: mid Nov. to the begining of May
Lifts
vertical drop: 255-718m (highest in finland)
amount of lifts in total: 19
gondolas: -
chair lifts: -
drag lifts: 19
Slopes
amount of prepared slopes: 39
runs w. snowmaking machines: 7
amount of easy runs: 25
amount of intermediate runs: 8
amount of advanced runs: 4
Facilities
night riding: yes
amount of halfpipes: 2 (1 superpipe)
amount of funparks: 3
heliboarding: yes
Lift-ticket prices in Euro
1/2 day: 26
week: 115
season: 275

SNOWBOARD TUITION »
Iso-Ylläs skischool
Tel: +35 (0)8165103500
www.iso-yllas.fi
Ylläs Skischool
Tel: +35 (0)816553171
www.laplandhotels.com

SNOWBOARD SHOPS »
Sport shop
Tel: +35 (0)816569099

GETTING THERE »
Car
Ylläs is 980km north from Helsinki. The drive takes around 17 hours.
Train
Train from Helsinki to Kolari, 40km to the south of Ylläs
Air
Fly from Helsinki to Kittilä

YLLÄS »
Intro_ At 150km north of the Arctic Circle, Ylläs is Finland's highest resort. The landscape here is pure Lapland, and its unique atmosphere is as palpable at the top of the resort as it is in the hotels and bars. Ylläs consists of two resorts, Iso-Ylläs and Ylläs-Ski, which together offer 37 slopes. Ylläs has a reputation for taking care of snowboarders, and the terrain offers a few nice bowls and natural quarter pipes. This resort is an ideal destination for snowboarders wanting to session natural hits or to build a few of their own. However, there's not much for jibbers here, and like the rest of Finland, even less for the adventurous freerider.

ON THE MOUNTAIN »
Snow reliability_ In Finland, most of the snow falls in the north-east, but winter is at its purest in Lapland. Ylläs is an exceptionally cold place mid winter, so the best time for riding is spring, when the sun shines and the temperature rises to a more bearable zero. Polar night lasts from November to March, and this is when the beautiful Northern Lights are at their brightest and best.

Lifts_ Most of the lifts are T-bars, which is OK as long as the wind isn't blowing too fiercely. If you are good enough, stick to the black runs, as these tend to be the least crowded. It's much quieter mid winter, when the only person you're likely to bump into is Santa Claus…

Freeriding_ There are some nice bowls with natural hits in-between Iso-Ylläs and Ylläs-Ski, and crews from Finnish snowboarding magazines can often be found on photo-shoots there. However, you'll not find anything that even comes close to epic, this is Finland - notorious for its lack of freeride.

Freestyling_ Despite the resort's best efforts, the parks here aren't particularly good by Finnish standards, but the natural freestyle terrain more than makes up for it.

Beginners_ Like all Finnish resorts, the terrain is ideal for beginners. Children are well taken care of, and the nursery slopes are near all the main services such as bars and ski rental shops.

"HERE ARE SOME NICE BOWLS WITH NATURAL HITS IN-BETWEEN ISO-YLLÄS AND YLLÄS-SKI, AND CREWS FROM FINNISH SNOWBOARDING MAGAZINES CAN OFTEN BE FOUND ON PHOTO-SHOOTS THERE. HOWEVER, YOU'LL NOT FIND ANYTHING THAT EVEN COMES CLOSE TO EPIC, THIS IS FINLAND - NOTORIOUS FOR ITS LACK OF FREERIDE."

Mountain Restaurants_ Last year a slab avalanche carried one small restaurant 100 metres down the hill! There are still, however, several other little cafes dotted around the resort and these all serve nice traditional food, coffee and pastries. At bigger restaurants, such as those in the local hotels, the menu features such traditional dishes as salmon and reindeer. Prices for dinner start from 6€ upwards, depending on what your order. For a full list of local restaurants log onto www.yllas.fi.

IN THE TOWN »
Accommodation_ You basically have two options: small, wooden self-catering cabins, or a hotel. You may need a car to get to some of the cabins, alternatively check into a hotel near the lift. The nearest city is Kolari, 40km to the south. Ylläs is currently undergoing re-development, with a number of big hotels due for completion this year. Check out the latest info at www.yllas.fi.

Food_ There are numerous restaurants and supermarkets in the Ylläs area. The food on offer ranges from a hamburger to seven course à la carte. Reindeer and salmon are both recommended.

Nightlife_ The nightlife here is pretty dubious. Ladies Night finds the bars filled with dirty old men, and there's little to appeal to the youth.

Other Activities_A Snowmobile trip can take you far from civilisation, while hiking with snowshoes can take you to places where no one but you and a few reindeer have ever been before. Communing with Nature is the main activity here!

LOCAL TIP »
Jaakko Kantola, snowboard photographer for Slammer magazine_"A good place for hand shaping a quarterpipe lies between the resorts near Iso-Ylläs in Keskinen. Great for a photo shoot at sundown!"

"THE WORLD CUP SUPER-PIPE, BUILT FOR FIS CONTESTS, IS THE TRAINING GROUND FOR WELL-KNOWN RIDERS LIKE MARKKU KOSKI."

RUKA
FINLAND

RUKA »
www.ruka.fi
Tourist office tel:+ 35 (0)888600200
location: Kuusamo
population: 18000
altitude: 280m
linked resorts: Pyhä

ON THE MOUNTAIN »
season: from November until May
Lifts
Vertical drop: 280-496m
amount of lifts in total:18
gondolas: -
chair lifts: 4
T-bars: 14
Slopes
amount of prepaired slopes: 20 km
nu of snow canons: 50
amount of easy runs: 11
amount of intermediate runs: 11
amount of advanced runs black: 6
Facilities
night riding: yes
number of halfpipes: 2
number of funparks: 1
heliboarding: -
Lift-ticket prices in Euro
1 day: 27
week: 125
season: 350

SNOWBOARD TUITION »
Ruka Ski School
Tel: + 35 (0)888681430
www.ruka.fi

SNOWBOARD SHOPS »
Ruka ProSop
Tel: +35 (0)888600236

GETTING THERE »
Car
Ruka lies 800 kilometres north of Helsinki
Bus/Train
Take train from Helsinki to Oulu and then by coach to Kuusamo
Air
Take flight from Helsinki to Kuusamo, which is 25km south of Ruka

RUKA »
Intro_Ruka is the oldest skiing area in Finland. Although people began to ski here in the thirties, the first lift wasn't built until 1955. Since then Ruka has become Finland's leading ski resort, and a pioneer in snowmaking and snowboard park design. Big halfpipes, jibs and kicker lines, combined with guaranteed snow between October and May make Ruka a big hit in Finland. Furthermore, a wide choice of accommodation, efficient transportation from Kuusamo city, and some very good riders make Ruka a serious contender for a snowboarding trip north.

ON THE MOUNTAIN »
Snow reliability_The snow making here is probably the best in Scandinavia. The north-eastern climate helps when, in October, Ruka starts to make snow for the season ahead. Almost every slope in Ruka consists of man-made snow. Of all the finish resorts, Ruka opens first and closes last, with the season running from the end of October through to mid May. For the park rider, spring is definitely the best time to come. Before then the snow is icy and hard. The super-pipe opens in November. Check snow conditions at www.ruka.fi

Lifts_The lift system serves the area well and there are no bottlenecks. Winter here can be fierce, so choose your slopes and lifts according to wind direction.

Freeriding_No…

Freestyling_If you like good park and pipe, you'll like Ruka. Pipes, rails and tables – it's all here. The World Cup super-pipe, built for FIS contests, is the training ground for well-known riders like Markku Koski. Five of the seven Finns who went to the Salt Lake City Olympic games were Ruka locals. The scene is not as big as in Southern Talma, but the quality of jumps and pipes is equal. Like the rest of Finland, freestyle is all that matters here. Numerous jumps and three different sizes of halfpipe, all shaped every day, make this a breeding ground for top freestyle riders, with plenty of ex-pros around to coach you.

"RUKA IS A FAMILY ORIENTATED RESORT. THE SNOWBOARD SCHOOL COACHES BEGINNERS AND EXPERTS ALIKE. SLOPE MAPS ARE CLEAR AND SIMPLE TO FOLLOW."

Beginners_Ruka is a family orientated resort. The Snowboard School coaches beginners and experts alike. Slope maps are clear and simple to follow, and there is nothing very dangerous here because the mountains are so small.

Mountain Restaurants_On the western side of Ruka, traditional Finnish food like reindeer is served in the numerous restaurants. On the eastern side, you'll find familiar 'Alps' fare, such as fondue at Ski Bistro. Over ten restaurants and bars offer a wide variety of foods, from hamburgers to a la Carte.

IN THE TOWN »
Accommodation_Both young people and families tend to stay in rented wood cabins. It's comfortable, and the authentic Lapland way to enjoy your holiday. Some of the cottages are close to the town, but for others you may need a car. A Ski bus serves the main cabin areas. The cabins are well equipped, with cooking facilities, televisions and, of course, your very own Sauna!

Go to www.ruka.fi to find all the necessary booking information.

Food_There's a small supermarket 1.5km down from Ruka, and a couple of the bars also sell groceries. Big supermarkets and cheap foreign pizzerias are all in Kuusamo City, 25km south of Ruka.

Nightlife_Young people over 18 (or 20 - depending on the season) go to Restaurant Piste, a nice club with a cosy atmosphere. The Finnish holiday period is the best time for partying here, when it is generally packed.

Other Activities_Take a Sauna in your hotel or your cabin, or go to Rukaklubi, which has gyms, golf simulators, hot tubs etc. Hot baths called Rukan Tropiikki lie 15km south. A Snowmobile Safari is good way to experience Finnish nature.

LOCAL TIP »
Talk to the locals if you have any specific requests for jumps, rails or pipe. Teemu Lahtinen: "Anything is possible here, whether you are snowboard photographer, pro or an unknown ripper" Teemu who shoots for Northlightpictures and rides his own Icon Snowboards pro model, is one of the park's designers.

"LYING 20KM NORTH OF FINLAND'S CAPITAL, HELSINKI, TALMA IS ONE OF THE SMALLEST SKI RESORTS IN THE WORLD."

TALMA
FINLAND

TALMA »
www.talmaski.fi
tourist office tel:+35 (0)892745410
location: Talma
population:16.000
altitude: 55m

ON THE MOUNTAIN »
season: November - April
Lifts
vertical drop: 55m
amount of lifts in total: 6
gondolas: -
chair lifts: -
drag lifts: 6
Slopes
amount of prepared slopes: 3 km
runs w. snowmaking machines: 8
amount of easy runs: 3
amount of intermediate runs: 3
amount of advanced runs: -
Facilities
night riding: -
amount of halfpipes: 1
amount of funparks: 3
heliboarding: -
Lift-ticket prices in Euro
1/2 day: 16
day: 18
season: 255

SNOWBOARD TUITION »
Talski
Tel: +35 (0)8503668145
www.talmaski.fi

SNOWBOARD SHOPS »
Talma Ski Shop
Tel: +35 (0)892745410

GETTING THERE »
Car
20 kilometres drive from the centre of Helsinki.
Bus
City bus from Helsinki to Talma.
Train
City train to Kerava and from there city bus to Talma.
Air
Fly to Helsinki, Finland.

TALMA »
Intro_Lying 20km north of Finland's capital, Helsinki, Talma is one of the smallest ski resorts in the world. However, in terms of the riders it has produced, it is probably the biggest... Jussi Oksanen, Heikki Sorsa, Joni Malmi, Wille Luoma, Eero Niemelä, and Henri Sankala, to name just a few...

This is a freestyle paradise. Fast and short draglifts take riders to the top in a jiffy. The whole resort is full of jumps and rails, and the halfpipe and kickers are shaped to perfection, daily.

ON THE MOUNTAIN »
Snow reliability_Winter in Helsinki is similar to central European winter weather, only colder. You never really know if the snow will fall or not. However, despite this changeable weather, snowmaking ensures a consistent base.
Call +358 9 2745410 for resort opening dates and times.

Lifts_Four of the six lifts are high-speed drags. The place is bursting at the seams with snowboarders in the evenings and at weekends, and queuing here resembles the scramble for the first gondola in Chamonix, the morning after a big dump. So be prepared, your nice new snowboard won't look so nice after a session here...

Freestyling_If you've ever wondered why Finland produces so many top riders, come to Talma. Only 30 minutes from the town centre, kids come here by bus every day after school, and do more jumps in a couple of hours than you'll do in a week anywhere else.

Huge hips, tables, rails, all sessioned by beginners and pros alike — it is no wonder the progression here is so rapid. By 9pm the resort closes and the jumps are rutted. The best time to ride is in the afternoon before the kids arrive, as it gets hectic afterwards. The website www.talmaski.fi will give you an idea of what to expect.

Beginners_Talma is a resort for freestyle snowboarding pure and simple. The three parks have jumps of all sizes, so there is something to suit riders of all standards. However, beginners need to keep their wits about them, and remember to get out of the landing area fast if you fall, else you'll get landed on.

IN THE TOWN »
Accommodation_The nearest accommodation is in Kerava City (www.kerava.fi), but you may prefer to stay in Helsinki, which has much more to offer in the way of accommodation and nightlife. Visit the Helsinki City Tourist website: www.hel.fi. Here you'll find info on the best entertainment and accommodation, which starts at 25 euros.

Food_Helsinki is the capital city, so you'll find every kind of food under the sun, from Finnish restaurants to Japanese, Chinese, Nepalese... The list goes on.

Nightlife_Nightlife in Helsinki varies, often depending on what clubs have got going on at any one

© Jaakko Kantala **Rider** Teemu Lahtinen

time. Safe bets include Bar Jump In on Fredrikinkatu and Restaurant Vanha's Club Kajal on Mannerheimintie on Saturday. For a better idea, ask a snowboarder while you're in Talma.

Other Activities_Besides horse riding, there are no other activities in Talma. Everyone heads back to Helsinki to party, socialise, sleep and skate... Helsinki has two indoor skateparks, one in the centre and one in Kontula. The city is also full of nice handrails, ready to jib if there's snow on the ground — that is if you've got any energy left after Talma!

LOCAL TIP »
Jussi Oksanen_"When in Finland, I like riding Talma most. Riding there with friends is so fun that you want to go every day."

"IF YOU'VE EVER WONDERED WHY FINLAND PRODUCES SO MANY TOP RIDERS, COME TO TALMA. ONLY 30 MINUTES FROM THE TOWN CENTRE, KIDS COME HERE BY BUS EVERY DAY AFTER SCHOOL, AND DO MORE JUMPS IN A COUPLE OF HOURS THAN YOU'LL DO IN A WEEK ANYWHERE ELSE. HUGE HIPS, TABLES, RAILS, ALL SESSIONED BY BEGINNERS AND PROS ALIKE."

SCOTLAND

180-189

SCOTLAND MAP

SCOTLAND »

Intro_Scotland is a country well worth the visit. A land full of culture, hospitable people, rugged and beautiful scenery, whisky, and men who wear skirts. It is not, however, one of Europe's premier alpine destinations. Compared to the mountains to be found in central Europe, Scotland has only hills. Many of the lifts are primitive, and lift tickets are expensive. The weather is unpredictable, and you are just as likely to meet with howling gales, fog and horizontal rain as you are with blue sky.

Having said all this, the place has its moments. The season of 2000/01 saw Scotland blessed with huge dumps of snow late into the season while the rest of Europe struggled. Each resort has its own thriving snowboard scene, with die-hard locals and regular commuters from Glasgow, Edinburgh and Aberdeen. When the snow is good, even the most hardcore freeriders can find steep, challenging terrain if they are prepared to hike for it. Headworx hosts a series of fun contests throughout the season, and in the evenings the partying is amongst the best you'll find anywhere.

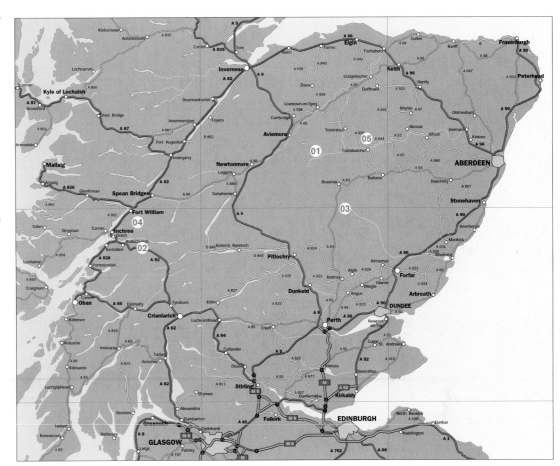

INFORMATION »
Official Name_United Kingdom of Great Britain and Northern Ireland
Capital_London
Population_59,2 Million
Land mass_244.100km2
Language(s)_English
Currency_1 Pounds = 100 Pence
Highest mountain_Ben Nevis 1.344m
International country code_0044
Police_999
Ambulance_999
Fire Brigade_999
Tourism_Scottish Tourist Board
Tel: +44 (0)131 332-2433
www.visitscotland.com
Train Info_Scottish Tourist Board
Tel: +44 (0)131 332-2433
www.rail.co.uk
www.visitscotland.com
Weather Info_Tel: 08457 48 49 50
www.meto.govt.uk

LOCATIONS »
01 **CAIRNGORMS**
02 **GLENCOE**
03 **GLENSHEE**
04 **NEVIS RANGE**
05 **THE LECHT**

CAIRNGORM
SCOTLAND

CAIRNGORM »
www.cairngormmountain.com
tourist office tel: +44 (0)14791479861261
location: Aviemore
population: 0
altitude: 637m

ON THE MOUNTAIN »
season: December to end of April
Lifts
vertical drop: 637-1097m
amount of lifts in total 16
gondolas: -
funicular: 1
chair lifts: 2
drag lifts: 13
Slopes
amount of prepared slopes: 37 km
runs w. snowmaking machines: -
easy runs: 6 km
intermediate runs: 29 km
advanced runs: 2 km
Facilities
night riding: -
amount of halfpipes: 1
amount of funparks: 1
heliboarding: -
Lift-ticket prices
1/2 day: £24
week: £134
season: £320
special fares: Weekday £21.60(not including Bank Holidays, Christmas, New Year, Half Term and Easter)

SNOWBOARD TUITION »
CairnGorm Snowsports School
Tel: +44 (0)1479861261
www.cairngormmountain.com

SNOWBOARD SHOPS »
North 57
Tel: +44 (0)1479810310

GETTING THERE »
Car
Take the A9 south from Inverness (36 miles), M90 and A9 north from Edinburgh (146 miles), or the M8/M0/A9 from Glasgow (158 miles).
Bus
A bus service runs from Aviemore to the mountain base. Telephone +44 (0)1479 811211.
CityLink run buses to Aviemore from lots of places in Scotland. Check them out at: http://www.citylink.co.uk
Air
Fly to Inverness from London. Alternatively, there are plans for more international flights to Glasgow or Edinburgh. Check out Easyjet.com and Ryanair.com - both often have bargains available.

CAIRNGORM »
Intro_ Cairngorm, which lies just 10 miles from the party town of Aviemore, has seen some big updates in the past couple of years. After seemingly endless debates between environmentalists and mountain capitalists (the capitalists won (don't they always?) and Cairngorm now has a rather convenient new funicular railway to provide fast and easy access to the Scottish snow. The year 2002 saw the British Champs head home to Cairngorm for their annual snowboard comp and piss up. Check out thebsa.co.uk for dates if you fancy your chances in future years!

ON THE MOUNTAIN »
Snow reliability_ The 2001 season saw a huge snowfall that lasted all the way into May – so it does have potential for some of the good stuff. However, remember this is Scotland, and even if the snow does fall in abundance, the wind may be hot on its tail ready to blow it all away. There are no snowmaking facilities.

At the lift_ The long-awaited funicular railway makes travel up the mountain far more reliable and it can still travel up the mountain in higher winds the old chair could. You can travel the total 1200m from the car park up to the Ptarmigan restaurant in less than 7 minutes – all this for a reasonable £7.50.

Freeriding_ In terms of terrain Cairngorm doesn't offer a huge range of natural features. The toughest, most challenging ride will be found in the one and only black run, the so-called West Wall. However, don't expect any rushes of adrenaline, and watch out for your base if the snow isn't deep – the rocks have sent many a boarder to hospital.
In good snow and good weather a short hike up to the summit from the Ptarmigan T over to the head wall of the Coire Cas, could provide a few moments of fun. Another spot to hunt down is Aladdins. This is where some of the most gnarly and steep chutes in Scotland can be found, but as there's a 200ft cliff to fall off if you go wrong, you really need to go there with an experienced local.

Freestyling_ If you get lucky there'll be a funpark between the Crossover and Fiaciall Ridge drag lifts. If park riding is your main concern, though, your best bet would be to phone the resort before you set out. Nothing can be guaranteed with the Scottish weather being as temperamental as it is. If you think the resort might not give you a totally honest answer as to whether the park is good or not, you may want to contact the chaps at the North 57 snowboard shop – they will tell it as it is!

Carving_ For on piste carving your best bet would be the imaginatively named runs 1 and 2. But don't blink – the run to the bottom will be over before your eyes are open again.

Beginners_ Despite the slopes not being very exciting for advanced riders, they're scarcely ideal for beginners either, with any areas that would be suitable often being clogged up with ski schools or moguls. However, if you insist, I'd recommend you head up to the Ptarmigan or Coire Na Cist T-bars on the summit and try your luck up there.

Mountain Restaurants_ Food prices on the mountain, as in many European resorts, are shocking. The T-Bar restaurant is in the day lodge, while the Shieling and the Ptarmigan are at the top.

IN THE TOWN »
Accommodation_ The nearby resort of Aviemore has all sorts of accommodation available, from hostels to posh hotels. Contact aviemoretic@host.co.uk for more info.

Food_ If you've survived on packed lunches all day, Aviemore has plenty to offer your stomach in the evenings. Restaurants abound, but Cafe Mambo, Hamblett's, Littlejohn's, PH22, McKenzie', La Taverna and The Bridge Inn all offer pukka tucker.

Nightlife_ In nearby Aviemore you'll probably want to check out Chevvy's Bar and Mambo's, both of which are popular with sideways sliders. Chevvy's is easy to find as it festers under the North57 snowboard shop, and there's a ramp and other obstacles to play on between pints. N57 is also the best place to hire boards.

Other activities_ For shopping Aviemore has its own branch of The Snowboard Asylum, as well as the aforementioned local snowboard shop, North57, where you'll find the skate ramp.

LOCAL TIP »
Basil Allan_ Go to the top of the Ptarmigan T-bar, then hike off to the left for about 150m. You'll come across a place called Ciste Meredith which is a small bowl that collects most of the snow and keeps it right into the summer. We were camping up there in July last year with a kicker right next to us and a barby on the go – brilliant.

CHAIRLIFTS AND TOWS
1 Funicular
2 Car Park T-Bar
3 Fiaciall Ridge Poma
4 Shieling Platter Lift
5 Fiaciall T-Bar
6 Coire Cas T-Bar
7 M1 Poma
8 White Lady T-Bar
9 Coire na Ciste
10 Coire na Ciste Chairlift
11 West Wall Chairlift
12 Aonach Poma
13 Coire na Ciste T-Bar
14 Ptarmigan T-Bar
15 West Wall Poma
16 Link Poma
17 Day Lodge Poma

Lifts valid for use with Beginner Ticket

Very Difficult
Difficult
Intermediate
Easier
Patrol Boundary

Tickets
Toilets
First Aid
Snack Bar
Bar
Restaurant
Equipment Hire
Shop
Bus Stop
Public Phone
Snowsports School
Slow Areas
Terrain Park

PROS & CONS »
+ Said to be the best resort in Scotland with some of the gnarliest terrain.
+ Friendly people with a good local atmosphere.
+ On a clear day the views across Scotland are breathtaking.

− Lift passes are expensive.
− Near the west coast - this makes the conditions extremely variable.
− Strong winds can blow the powder away faster than it can fall.

"THE BRITISH MAGAZINE "SNOWBOARD WORLD" PROUDLY HAILED GLENCOE (ALBEIT IT 7 YEARS AGO IN 1995) AS 'WITHOUT DOUBT, ONE OF SCOTLAND'S BEST SNOWBOARDING AREAS'."

GLENCOE
SCOTLAND

GLENCOE »
www.ski-glencoe-co.uk
tourist office tel: +44 (0)1855834226
location: south of Glencoe village
population: none
altitude: 305m

ON THE MOUNTAIN »
season: December - late April
Lifts
vertical drop: 305–1108m
amount of lifts in total: 7
gondolas: -
chairlifts: 2
T-bars: 2
pomas: 3
Slopes
amount of prepared slopes: 20km
runs w. snowmaking machines: -
amount of easy runs: 4
amount of intermediate runs:13
amount of advanced runs: 2
Facilities
night skiing: -
amount of halfpipes: -
amount of funparks: -
heliboarding: -
Lift-ticket prices in £
1/2 day: 14.50
week: 102
season: 170
special fares: Advantage Card £40 entitles card holder to 40% off list pass at glenshee & glencoe every day

SNOWBOARD TUITION »
Glencoe Ski Centre Snowsports School
Tel: +44 (0)1855851226
www.ski-glencoe.co.uk

SNOWBOARD SHOPS »
No shop at center

GETTING THERE »
Car
Glencoe is on the A82, 26 miles south of Fort William and 23 miles north of Crianlarich.
Glasgow – Glencoe: 90miles
Glasgow – M8 – A 82 – Glencoe
Prestwick – Glencoe
Prestwick – Kilmarnock – A77 – M77 – A82 – Glencoe
Inverness – Glencoe
Inverness – A82 – via Spean Bridge - Glencoe
Bus
The nearest station is Fort William which is serviced by a daily Scottish Citylink service from Glasgow. This service stops at White Corries, the access road to the Glencoe Ski Centre. For further info contact:
Scottish Citylink, Tel: 08705 50 50 50 or National Express, Tel: 08705 80 80 80
Train
The nearest stations are Bridge of Orchy and Fort William. For further info call the National Rail Enquiry Service on 0845 748 49 50 or log onto www.nationalrail.co.uk.
Air
Glasgow Airport: 90miles
Prestwick Airport: 115miles
Inverness Airport: 80miles

Note: it's worth checking offers with the following budget airlines:
Easyjet - www.easyjet.com
Ryan Air - www.ryanair.com
British European - www.british-european.com
Go - www.go-fly.com

GLENCOE »
Intro_The tiny resort of Glencoe is in the Western Highlands of Scotland, 74 miles north of Glasgow. It was Scotland's first commercial ski area and the first ski-lift was opened there in 1956. The British magazine "Snowboard World" proudly hailed Glencoe (albeit it 7 years ago in 1995) as "without doubt, one of Scotland's best snowboarding areas." Thankfully little has changed since then and visitors to the resort still sing its praises both for its comparatively impressive terrain and its friendly attitude towards visiting snowboarders.

ON THE MOUNTAIN »
Snow reliability_A freak season in 1993 saw massive snowfalls which buried lifts and extended Glencoe's winter right through to June. However, the key word there is "freak". Snowfalls in Scotland are far from reliable and Glencoe's geographical location does little to improve matters. Its proximity to the sea also means that the powder is rarely dry and the place is often swathed in mist with a strong wind blowing.
 In 2002, the season only got started on 6 February due to the lack of snow. The best time to visit is typically February -March, since this is when the snow is generally at its best. If you plan to make the trip, make sure you check the local conditions first. There are no snow making facilities.

Lifts_There are seven lifts and nineteen runs in total. These are: 2 Chairlifts, 2 Pomas, 2 T-Bars, and one 1 Trainer tow. If you're a beginner you'd be wise to spend your first few days avoiding the upper drag lifts. The Cliffhanger Chairlift is often the worst for queues.

Freeriding_If you're looking for day after day of virgin powder, Scotland is probably not your best bet. However, the resort of Glencoe is the proud possessor of the steepest on-piste black run in Scotland, The Fly Paper, which can be fun, although saying that it's often icy or closed due to the risk of avalanche. Head slightly off the beaten track to either side of this run and, on the right day, you may just find the freeride you were looking for. The Canyon is promoted as the snowboard area.

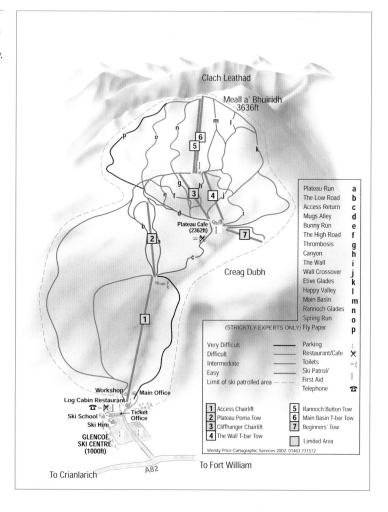

If there's a big dump the snow tends to gather in the Cliffhanger gully and around The Wall next to the lower T-Bar tow. If that fails, because of the sheer nature of the Scottish weather, your best bet would be to ask the locals where to head on any particular day. They are very friendly and may just take you there themselves!

Freestyling_Although the changeable weather in Scotland makes the building of a decent half pipe virtually impossible, Glencoe does boast a variety of natural hits and spines that will keep any freestyler happy – in fact many of the riders visiting Glencoe are freestyle orientated.
 The Canyon run, right in the middle of the resort, has a natural halfpipe, as does the terrain just off the Thrombosis. Haggis Trap has a great big gully jump and in general

the resort has lots of spines and wind lips to keep you entertained.
 If you're itching for a decent kicker to hurl yourself off, you'd be wise to have some friendly words with the management. At best they may help you create just what you had in mind. At worst, they'll hand you a shovel to do it yourself.

Carving_For those of you hopping around in hard boots looking for some piste to shred we recommend heading to Etive Run, which is often well prepared and lies at the top of the highest ski tow.

Beginners_As with most of the Scottish resorts, there's plenty of short runs within easy reach for the beginner to tackle. Avoid the ball breaking T-bars higher up the mountain - the tracks can be steep and irregular.

"THE RESORT OF GLENCOE IS THE PROUD POSSESSOR OF THE STEEPEST ON-PISTE BLACK RUN IN SCOTLAND, THE FLY PAPER, WHICH CAN BE FUN, ALTHOUGH SAYING THAT IT'S OFTEN ICY OR CLOSED DUE TO THE RISK OF AVALANCHE."

Mountain Restaurants_There's the Base Restaurant and the Plateau Cafe on the mountain. The Plateau Cafe is reasonably priced for what it is (take-away food like sausage rolls, bacon rolls, toasties etc). The Base Restaurant is also pretty good value and makes delicious home made soups.

IN THE TOWN »
Accommodation_As with most Scottish ski areas there is no accommodation in the actual resort, but there is the nearby Glencoe Youth Hostel. This is a YHA hostel so discounts are available to YHA members. There's also the Red Squirrel Camping Ground nearby. Both are probably around 9-10 miles from the Ski Centre.

Food_Being Scotland, it would be rude of us not to mention Haggis! You can also get some really top notch salmon up here. There isn't much in the way of 'restaurants' in the area. All the local pubs serve bar meals and popular spots include the Glencoe Hotel, the Clachaig Inn (a popular spot with climbers) and the Loch Leven Hotel which serves some mean Cantonese dishes.

Nightlife_Unlike every other European resort, nobody has ever attempted to sell Glencoe as 'the Winter Ibiza'. This is because most night time activities centre around small local pubs – good places for getting drunk with the locals and for meeting 'interesting' characters.

Other Activities_This is quite a small area. Most of the other activities on offer involve climbing and walking on the mountains. Just use your imagination - you'll never get bored.

© Vernon Deck

GLENSHEE
SCOTLAND

»

GLENSHEE »
www.ski-glenshee.co.uk
Tourist office tel: +44 (0)1339741320
location: south of Braemar
population:450
altitude: 650 m

ON THE MOUNTAIN »
season: December to April
Lifts
vertical drop: 650–1068m
amount of lifts in total: 23
gondolas: -
chair lifts: 2
drag lifts: 21
Slopes
amount of prepared slopes: 40 km
snowmaking machines: 4
amount of easy runs: 10
amount of intermediate runs: 13
amount of advanced runs: 15
Facilities
night riding: -
amount of halfpipes: -
amount of funparks: 1
heliboarding: -
Lift-ticket prices in £
1/2 day: 15.50
week: 112
season: 170
special fares Snowboard Packages – includes
full area lift pass, equipment hire and 2 hrs
instruction per day (example 2 day adult
–£75
Advantage Card – 64e (£40) entitles card
holder to 40% off list pass at glenshee &
glencoe every day

SNOWBOARD TUITION »
Glenshee Ski Centre Snowsports School
Tel: +44 (0)1339741320

SNOWBOARD SHOPS »
None at centre

GETTING THERE »
Car
From the south-west follow the M74 to
Glasgow, change to the M73 then the M80 to
Stirling. From here take the A9 to Perth. At
the Broxden Roundabout follow the signs for
Braemar. Drive over the Friarton Bridge and
take a left into Perth. From here follow the
A93 to Blairgowrie. Follow the A93 through
Blairgowrie to Braemar. Glenshee is
signposted from here.
From the south-east take the A1 to
Edinburgh, then the north-bound M9, across
the Forth Bridge to Perth. Continue as above.
Bus
The nearest stations are Aberdeen, Perth and
Dundee. For further information on bus travel
to these stations contact:
Scottish Citylink 08705 50 50 50,
National Express 08705 80 80 80.
Unfortunately, there are no connecting bus
services direct to the ski centre, although
local bus services do run to Braemar (9 miles)
and Blairgowrie (9.25 miles).
Train
The nearest stations are Aberdeen, Perth,
Dundee or Pitlochry.
Information from the National Rail Enquiry
Service on 0845 748 49 50
www.nationalrail.co.uk.
Air
The nearest airports are:
Aberdeen: 01224 722331
Edinburgh: 0131 333 1000
Glasgow: 0141 887 111
Dundee: 01382 643242
Easyjet: 0870 600 0000
Ryan Air: 08701 569 569
Go: 0845 605 4321

GLENSHEE »
Intro_Glenshee, which spans three valleys and boasts 26 lifts, is Scotland's largest snowboard area. The name originates from the romantic Gaelic name of Gleann Shith or "Glen of the Fairies".The weather and snow conditions here can be unreliable but this is a vast expanse of mountain, so explore a bit and you're bound to find something fun to ride. While you're there, try to find time to visit the neighbouring Caenlochan National Nature Reserve - Britain's second richest site for rare arctic-alpine flora.

ON THE MOUNTAIN »
Snow reliability_The snow comes in fits and starts. In a good winter the conditions can be great. In a poor one you'll want to take out insurance for 'base shred'. Late season is often the best time to catch the good snow up here.

Lifts_As this is Scotland's largest resort the access lifts can get incredibly busy but there's no way of avoiding this unless you only go riding on white-out storm days. Do this and you're guaranteed a whole mountain and lift network all to yourself. Another problem with the lifts in Glenshee is that they often require a lot of hopping and skating to clear the flat before the run down.

Freeriding_On a good day there's some good off piste powder but you'll want to head over to the Glas Moal to find this. Be careful in bad weather - whiteouts can be sudden and you don't want to get stranded. There can be some huge windlips forming on the bowl to the right hand side of the Glas Maol tow which are nice to drop into, but watch out as the danger of an avalanche is always looming when there's been fresh snow. So if you're planning to do this wait until the end of the day - it's a protected area and the ski patrol may pull your pass. Weather permitting, Meall Odhar also has potential as a good freeride playground with cornices and natural drop-offs. One good cornice to throw yourself off is on the right side of the Tiger, on the way to Claybokie. If you're up for a short hike, just 10 minutes, then head over to Maell Odhar where there's often a fairly large cornice. Here's another good tip for experts: go up to the top of the Cairnwall T-Bar (the race tow) and

when you reach the top walk for about 20 metres til you get to the Cairn and look at the cliffs behind. Pick a line and get it clear in your head. You then need to walk for another 300-400 metres along the ridge that brings you to the top of the cliffs and find the same spot that you saw from the opposite side. This area has loads of choice and some sweet lines with some big drops, but only do it when the

snow is good, as the rocks are sometimes only covered by a couple of inches of snow. The hike back out is an absolute killer especially in deep snow but I guarantee you that you will come back smiling. Do not go there unless you are experienced and fit as the potential for injury or avalanche is very high.

Freestyling_In the past attempts

© Vernon Deck

"IF IT'S ON PISTE CARVING YOU'RE AFTER YOU CAN GATHER SOME SPEED DOWN THE CAIRNWALL. DON'T GATHER TOO MUCH THOUGH - YOU'LL BE AT THE BOTTOM BEFORE YOU REALISE YOU'VE EVEN STARTED."

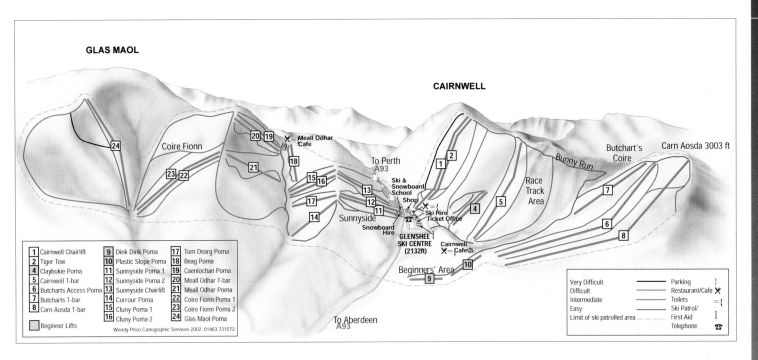

GLAS MAOL

CAIRNWELL

Coire Fionn

Meall Odhar Cafe

To Perth
A93

Butchart's Coire

Carn Aosda 3003 ft

Bunny Run

Ski & Snowboard School Shop

Race Track Area

Sunnyside

Ski Hire Ticket Office

Snowboard Hire

GLENSHEE SKI CENTRE (2132ft)

Cairnwell Cafe

Beginners' Area

1	Cairnwell Chairlift	9	Dink Dink Poma	17	Tom Dearg Poma
2	Tiger Tow	10	Plastic Slope Poma	18	Beag Poma
4	Claybokie Poma	11	Sunnyside Poma 1	19	Caenlochan Poma
5	Cairnwell T-bar	12	Sunnyside Poma 2	20	Meall Odhar T-bar
6	Butcharts Access Poma	13	Sunnyside Chairlift	21	Meall Odhar Poma
7	Butcharts T-bar	14	Corrour Poma	22	Coire Fionn Poma 1
8	Carn Aosda T-bar	15	Cluny Poma 1	23	Coire Fionn Poma 2
		16	Cluny Poma 2	24	Glas Maol Poma
	Beginner Lifts				

Wendy Price Cartographic Services 2002. 01463 731572.

To Aberdeen
A93

Very Difficult — Parking
Difficult — Restaurant/Cafe
Intermediate — Toilets
Easy — Ski Patrol/
Limit of ski patrolled area — First Aid
Telephone

have been made to construct both a half pipe and a park. These attempts were largely unsuccessful due to early thaw. However, this does prove that the resort was willing, even if the mountain wasn't able. Give them a call before you go, perhaps this year will be the year Glenshee gets some good luck and the park comes together. Don't hold your breath though. One spot that is worth checking out, though, is directly opposite the Butcharts T-Bar. If you go to the bottom of the T-bar and look behind you you'll see a natural gully that almost forms a halfpipe type affair – this is one of the best spots in Glenshee to build jumps as it seems to hold the fresh snow. Over at the lower end of the Glas Maol you may also notice the fun natural halfpipe – but don't expect to be able to pull your first McTwist – this is for mellow fun only.

Carving_If it's on piste carving you're after you can gather some speed down the Cairnwall. Don't gather too much though - you'll be at the bottom before you realise you've even started.

Beginners_Out of the 26 available lifts, 12 are rated as beginner's lifts, so you should have no problem getting up the mountain. There are also plenty of easy runs (in close proximity to the café) so learning should be no major chore in Glenshee. Also there are lots of areas where you can learn without even having to purchase a lift pass.

Mountain Restaurants_The usual Scottish munchies are available at three different mountain restaurants. However, if you are on a tight budget you'll want to bring a packed lunch. Beginners will be pleased to note that one of the cafes is based at ground level.

IN THE TOWN »
Accommodation_The nearest accommodation to Glenshee is either in The Spittle of Glenshee (Perth side) or Braemar (Aberdeen side) both of which are about 9 miles away. Prices start from £7.50 a night for Bunkhouse accommodation behind The Mews Shopping Arcade and go up to £50+ at the Invercauld Arms and the Fife Arms. For details call into the local Tourist Office (also located in The Mews) or call them on 01339 741600. Their full address is The Mews, Mar Road, Braemar, AB35 8AY.

Book ahead as Braemar, like Aviemore, attracts a lot of winter climbers so it tends to get very busy at weekends. There is also a Youth Hostel on the road out of

Braemar towards Glenshee (on the left hand side as you leave the town) and a campsite on the right, but you'd have to be brave or stupid (or both) to be camping midwinter in Braemar. Braemar holds the record for the UK's lowest temperature at -28°!!

Best places to stay are the Bunkhouses, where the accommodation is very cheap and they provide full cooking and washing facilities, we usually book out the whole bunkhouse, that way you don't get any snotty climbers/walkers moaning if you are still up at 10pm drinking.

There are a few of these bunkhouses around and you can get info from any of the locals, who are usually very helpful. Another thing, if you are gonna stay in the bunkhouses do not say you are a snowboarder as they sometimes have a small minded attitude and will say they are full when they have loads of space.

Food_In Braemar there is a local chip shop in the town centre. The local store is just an Alldays and it's the only place you can buy food.

Other than this, two of the main hotels do food, but they tend to be expensive (the Invercauld Arms and the Fife Arms)

Nightlife_Almost non existent,

there are only two bars that I know of and these are again in the two hotels. The Fife Arms is right in the centre of the village and on Friday nights they put on a disco (super cheesy music).

Other Activities_If the weather is good then there are some good mountain bike trails along the Lynn of Dee and the rock climbing at the Pass of Ballater is superb. You can hire bikes from the local Outdoor Shop (also in the village centre).

LOCAL TIP »
Basil Allan_There is a place called Lochnagar about 20 miles from Glenshee near Balleter, now this is not for the faint hearted as it requires a 6 mile hike in and the same, back out but it is one of the best things I have done in Scotland. Best to camp out at the car park as you will need to start early. You will need to hike right to the summit for this one and I would suggest you do what we did and get the ice axes and crampons out, and hike the gully first, as this is the best way to check out the conditions. The best gully to start with is The Black Spout, it is very steep and can have huge windlips at the top edge so once again it is best to do this one late season as the ice climbers have usually cut a route out the top.

PROS & CONS »
+ Scotland's most modern resort.
+ Easiest access to off-piste.
+ Highest altitude resort in Scotland.
+ Variety of good terrain.

− Exposed part of the country: weather can get very harsh.

"THE NEVIS RANGE IS A GREAT PLACE IF YOU'RE SIGHTSEEING AS IT PROVIDES A GREAT VIEW ACROSS TO BRITAIN'S HIGHEST PEAK, BEN NEVIS"

NEVIS RANGE

SCOTLAND

NEVIS RANGE »
www.nevis-range.co.uk
Tourist office tel: + 44 (0)1397705825
location: Fort William
population: 10000
altitude: 1221m

ON THE MOUNTAIN »
deason: End of December – Mid-April
Lifts
vertical drop: 650-1221m
amount of lifts in total: 12
gondolas: 1
chairlifts: 3
drag lift: 8
Slopes
amount of prepared slopes: 19 km
runs with snowmaking machines: -
amount of easy runs: 8
amount of intermediate runs: 23
amount of advanced runs: 5
Facilities
night riding: -
amount of halfpipes: -
amount of funparks: 3
heliboarding: -
Lift-ticket prices in £
half day: 15.50
full day: 22.00
week: 99.00
season: 235

SNOWBOARD TUITION »
Nevisport
Tel: + 44 (0)1397704921
www.nevisport.com

SNOWBOARD SHOPS »
Tel: +44 1397706220
www.snowboard-asylum.com

GETTING THERE »
Car
From Glasgow, drive 2 hours up the A82, or take the A9 from Inverness and turn off to Fort William.
Bus
A bus service runs from Fort William to the base of the Nevis Range. The CityLink public buses run from all over Scotland to Fort William: Check them out at http://www.citylink.co.uk
Train
Fort William is well served for train connections. For info log onto: www.scotrail.co.uk
Air
The best airport to fly to is Glasgow, although Inverness is also an option.

NEVIS RANGE »
Intro_Having first opened on the slopes of Oanach Mor as recently as 1989, Nevis Range could be considered the baby of the five main Scottish resorts. Because it's so new the resort has plenty of up-to-date lifts, including a gondola. The Nevis Range is a great place to visit if you're sightseeing in Scotland and it provides a great view across to Britain's highest peak, Ben Nevis, as well as being an area of great natural beauty. If hikin' and bikin' are your cup of tea, Nevis Range is also a great summer destination. So much so that many of the scenes from the movie Braveheart were shot here. On that note, keep an eye out for the Braveheart chair, which provides access to the back of the mountain, and some the areas best off piste terrain.

ON THE MOUNTAIN »
Snow reliability_As with the rest of Scotland, snowfall is unpredictable to say the least. Also, as this is one of the more exposed mountains, any fresh snow is prone to becoming quickly windswept, or even swept away… There are no snow-making facilities.

Lifts & Piste_Most of the resort is served by one modern gondola, so queues are small and the ride up is fast. However, high winds can wreak havoc.

Freeriding_Up until 1998 the resort consisted of one main basin. But the building of the Braveheart lift off the back of the mountain has opened up The Corries, which now provide some of the best off-piste Scotland has to offer, as long as the snow is good. The fact that the resort is based around one large basin means there are lots of different lines to explore down to the bottom. The most challenging terrain is to be found a short hike from the summit around the area known as The Spikes.

Freestyling_Depending on snow conditions, the area has a few spots to leave the ground, especially with the help of a bit of shovelling. There's also a few different spots where funparks exist or have existed, with tables, gaps and rails. Last year's park was sponsored by Boardwise and featured 3 different rails, hips, a big

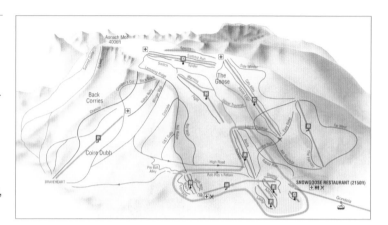

"MANY OF THE SCENES FROM THE MOVIE BRAVEHEART WERE SHOT HERE."

kicker and a table. The rails cater for all standards and range from a short double to a monster 30ft double, and when the snow is good they'll build as big a table as possible too.

Carving_The main area offers a relatively large selection of wide pistes, all served by the main gondola, although these tend to get very narrow when snow is in short supply.

Beginners_There are plenty of blue runs to choose from, as well as some greens at the base. Nevis Range also helps out with cheap lift tickets for bunny slope access. Once you can handle button lifts there's plenty more for the beginner at the top, plus a long blue under the Quad chairlift.

Mountain Restaurants_The Snowgoose Mountain Restaurant. Hot meals cost £5 on average.

IN THE TOWN »
Accommodation_Fort William offers plenty of places to stay for the budget conscious, starting at £8 per night at The Smiddy.
Ben Nevis Bunkhouse:
Tel: 01397 702240
Glen Nevis YHA:
Tel: 01397 702336
Farr Cottage Bunkhouse:
Tel: 01397 772315

The Smiddy Bunkhouse:
Tel: 01397 772467
Backpackers:
Tel: 01397 700711
There are also several bargain B&Bs from £12 upwards (prices are per person per night), as well as plenty of campsites in the area.

Food_There are plenty of eateries, from Chinese, Indian, Fish & Chips or Bar Meals. All of them are on the High St. Favourites include the Grog & Gruel for real ale & Mexican meals, or Nevisport for generous, good value bar meals.

Nightlife_Although Fort William isn't the most happening spot in the world, there are a few good pubs and plenty of good beer to be drunk.

Other Activities_There is a small cinema, a new climbing wall, a leisure centre (with pool, gym, sauna, squash etc), Go-Karting, 10 pin bowling, white water rafting, clay pigeon shooting, mountain biking and, of course, plenty of castles to visit!

LOCAL TIP »
Basil Allan_If you're going to find powder anywhere in Scotland this is the place to go. Last year we even managed to go into the back Corries, jump off the wind lip, ride to the bottom, have a beer, a toot, a swim in the river and back up for more.

LECHT
SCOTLAND

LECHT »
www.lecht.co.uk
tourist office tel: +44 (0)1339741600
location: A939 6 miles South of Tomintoul
population: 0
altitude: 640m

ON THE MOUNTAIN »
season: December until April
Lifts
vertical drop: 640-820
amount of lifts in total: 14
gondolas: -
chair lifts: 1
T-bars: 13
Slopes
amount of prepaired slopes: 6 km
snowmaking machines: 12
amount of easy runs: 7
amount of intermediate runs: 13
amount of advanced runs: 1
Facilities
night skiing: -
amount of halfpipes: 1
amount of funparks: 1
heliboarding: -
Lift-ticket prices in £
1/2day: 13
day: 17
5 days: 73
season: 200
special 5 day lift pass, hire and 10 hours instruction: 150

SNOWBOARD TUITION »
Lecht Ski and Snowboard School
Tel: +44 (0)1975651412

SNOWBOARD SHOPS »
Boarderline
Tel +44 (0)1224626996

GETTING THERE »
Car
It's 60 miles from Aberdeen along the A939 through Royal Deeside. Don't forget to wave to the Queen as you pass Balmoral. From Aviemore or Inverness take the A9 / A938 / A939.
Bus
No public transport to the resort.
Air
Fly to Aberdeen.

"FREERIDING IS LIMITED AS THIS IS SUCH A SMALL RESORT. AN INTERMEDIATE RIDER WILL HAVE MOST OF THE PLACE COVERED IN A MORNING."

LECHT »
Intro_The Lecht is the smallest of the five Scottish resorts included in this Guide. It lies on the north east side of the country in the Grampian Mountains. Although The Lecht is small compared to other Scottish winter sports resorts, it has a great personality and whatever it lacks in size it makes up for in friendliness and the efforts it goes to in respect of snowboarders, especially beginners.

ON THE MOUNTAIN »
Snow reliability_Relatively speaking The Lecht fares reasonably well for snow. Beware of heading out there too early in the season though. Because there are so few rocks on the hill The Lecht is notorious for opening before the snow is really deep enough for a decent ride. Don't assume that the fact the is 'open' means there's a decent covering of snow – make sure you know there's enough. Having said that, even if there really is no snow, you can still go for 'a day out on the hill' because the site includes a 200m dry slope. And oh yes, The Lecht has snowmaking facilities too.

Lifts_There are a total of 13 lifts in The Lecht. But most of these are surface lifts – only one is a chairlift, so stay too long and you'll be going home with massive thighs from all the drag lifts!

Freeriding_Very limited as this is such a small resort. An intermediate rider will have most of the place covered in a morning. There are a handful of relatively steep runs to give your legs a workout – check out the Falcon and Harrier runs, for example. As for off piste, don't expect much, although there is a hike over the back to be had if the snow is good. If you head to the top of the Grouse poma then walk directly over the back you will see a long gully in the background. This can be amazing as it seems to collect all the snow that gets blown off the rest of the mountains and it piles up in to big windlips which make for some nice hip jumps and lines.

Freestyling_Although there is very little to get excited about in terms of natural freestyle terrain, the resort is showing some commitment to snowboarding by providing a halfpipe and a funpark.

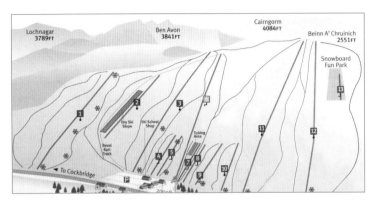

"THERE IS VERY LITTLE TO GET EXCITED ABOUT IN TERMS OF NATURAL FREESTYLE TERRAIN, BUT THE RESORT IS SHOWING SOME COMMITMENT TO SNOWBOARDING BY PROVIDING A HALFPIPE AND A FUNPARK."

Of course the quality of the pipe and jumps (and whether they actually exist) will depend very much on the snow conditions. Nick, the owner's son has really made an effort to get things done and this shows in the rail park that's been set up under the Snowy Owl chairlift. As it stands they have a funbox, a 15ft double rail, a 25ft kinked double rail and an elevator rail which are usually set up so you can hit one after another, which keeps the flow going.

Carving_Providing you go at times of decent snow you'll have plenty of chances to carve with the skiers down the groomed pistes – but if you are at any level higher that beginner or intermediate you'll soon get frustrated with the lack of terrain.

Beginners_Beginners will be in their element here. There are lots of bunny slopes for you to find your legs and once you get more confident the larger longer pistes are all within a stone's throw.

Mountain Restaurants_The average meal on the mountain should set you back about a fiver.

IN THE TOWN »

Accommodation_The Lecht itself doesn't actually have any accommodation on the hill. However, there are small B&Bs and hotels within a twenty minute drive to the east or west towards Tomintoul or Strathdon. Try the Allargue Arms for a good deal.

Food_The Craigendarroch Country Club is recommended.

Nightlife_If you're here for the boozing, you can forget The Lecht. Even the neighbouring places where you'll be staying offer very little in terms of pub crawl territory. In fact the nearest major piss up, unless you organise your own, is in Aberdeen, sixty miles away on the east coast.

Other Activities_Not exactly the centre of the party universe, but there are a few castles to visit and of course distilleries and 'whisky trails'.

LOCAL TIP »
Basil Allan_Do not hire your equipment from The Lecht because it's not great quality. Get it before you come up the hill. Also, if you're just planning to do rails in the park don't bother buying a lift pass as it's only a short hike to the park.

SPAIN AND ANDORRA

190-207

ASTUN/CANDANCHU
BAQUIERA BERET

BOÍ TAÜLL
CERLER

FORMIGAL
SIERRA NEVADA

SOLDEU

SPANISH PYRENEES MAP

SPAIN »

Intro_If you look at a clear satellite photo of Europe, Spain looks much browner than the rest of the continent. This is a dry country, sunny and hot. You'd be forgiven then, for thinking of Spain purely as a good place for a week by the pool with a frosty Sangria. But it also has the Pyrenees, the mountain range between France and Spain, stretching over 600 km from the Mediterranean sea to the Atlantic coast, with peaks over 3000 meters. And then of course, far south there's the Sierra Nevada, one of the most exotic places to board in Europe, with an amazing view reaching as far as Morocco. As Spain is not famous for it's snowparks and pipes (although they are getting better), to temp you down they offer the cheapest heli-flights in Europe. Spain is an affordable experience you will never forget.

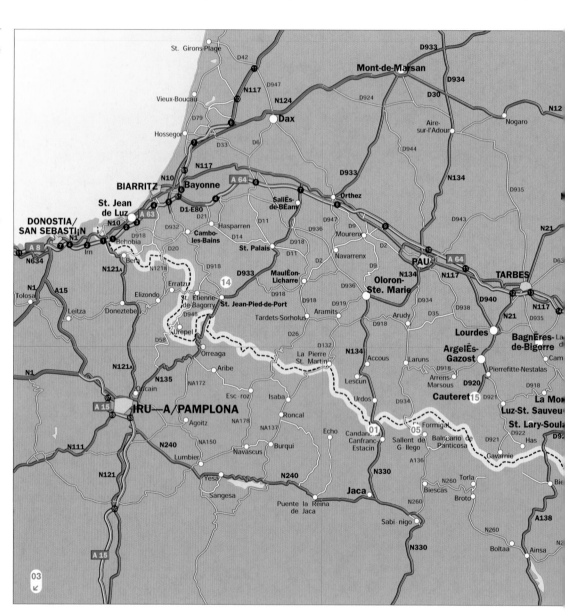

INFORMATION »
Official Name_Reino de España
Capital_Madrid
Population_39,63 Million
Land mass_505.992 km2
Language(s)_Spanish
Currency_1 Euro = 100 Cent
Highest mountain_Mulhacen 3.482m
International country code_0034
Police_092
Ambulance_092
Fire Brigade_080
Tourist Board_www.tourspain.es
Train Info_www.renfe.es
Weather Info_www.inm.es

LOCATIONS »
01 **ASTUN/CANDANCHU**
02 **BAQUIERA BERET**
03 **BOÍ TAÜLL**
04 **CERLER**
05 **FORMIGAL**
06 **SIERRA NEVADA**
07 **SOLDEU**

FRENCH PYRENNES
14 **ARTOUSTE**
15 **CAUTERETS**
16 **LES ANGLES**
17 **SAINT LARY**

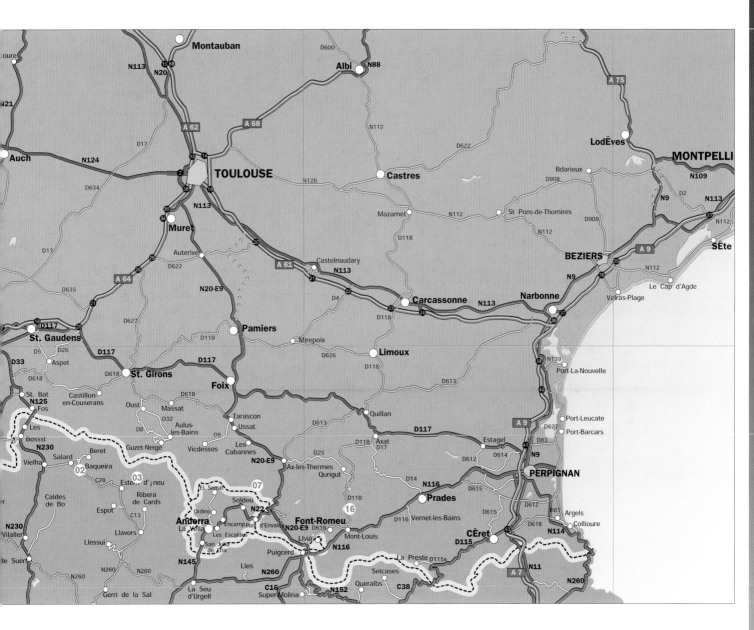

Montauban

N113 · N20 · 10 68

Albi · N88 · D600

A 75

N21

A 62 · A 68

D17 · N112

LodÉves

Auch · N124 · D634 · D622 · D908 · Bdarieux · MONTPELLI

2 · 33 · 14 · TOULOUSE · N126 · Castres · N109

36 · 19 · D2 · N9 · N113

35 · N113 · Mazamet · N112 · St Pons-de-Thomires · D909 · 33 · N112

Muret · D909 · SÉte

Auterive · D118 · N112 · BEZIERS · A 9

D17 · 28 · D622 · 20 · A 61 · Castelnaudary · N113 · N9 · 35 · Le Cap d'Agde

A 64 · 26 · D635 · N20-E9 · 21 · 22 · D4 · Carcassonne · Narbonne · Valras-Plage

D627 · 23 · 24 · N113 · 36 · 37

31 · D118

18 · D117 · 20 · D118 · N139

St. Gaudens · Pamiers · Port-La-Nouvelle

D5 · D26 · D117 · Mirepoix · 35

D33 · Aspet · D117 · D119 · Limoux · 40

D618 · D618 · St. Girons · D626 · D613 · Port-Leucate

St. Bat · Castillon- · Foix · D618 · D118 · Quillan · Port-Barcars

N125 · en-Couserans · Oust · D613 · D117 · Estagel · A 9 · D627

Fos · Massat · D32 · Tarascon · Axat · D614 · 41 · D83

Les · D8 · Aulus- · Ussat · D613 · D17 · D612 · N9

Bossst · N230 · Salard · Guzet-Neige · les-Bains · D8 · Les · D25 · D14 · PERPIGNAN

Vielha · 02 · Beret · Vicdessos · Cabannes · N20-E9 · N116

C28 · Baqueira · Ax-les-Thermes · D118 · Prades · D612 · D81

Esteri d'¡neu · 03 · Qurigut · D14 · D615 · Argels

Caldes · Ribera · 07 · El Serrat · D118 · D116 · Vernet-les-Bains · D615 · Collioure

de Bo · C13 · Soldeu · 16 · Font-Romeu · D618

Espot · de Cards · Ordino · N22 · CÉret · N114

N230 · Llavors · Encamp · Port d'Envalira · Llivia · Mont-Louis · 33

Vilaller · Andorra · La Presta · D115A · D115 · N11

Llessui · La Vella · Les Escaldes · Puigcerd · N116 · A 7 · N260

le Suert · San Juña · Lles · N260 · Setcases · N260

N145 · de Dia · N260 · Queralbs · C38

N260 · Gerri de la Sal · La Seu · C16 · N152 · Super Molina

d'Urgell

PROS & CONS »

"LOOKING FROM THE ATLANTIC COAST, CANDANCHÙ IS THE FIRST BIG SKI AREA YOU COME TO IN THE SPANISH PYRENEES, AND THE FIRST RESORT TOWN TO BE BUILT IN THE REGION."

ASTÚN/CANDANCHU
SPAIN

»

ASTUN/CANDANCHU »
Web address www.candanchu.com
Tourist office tel +34 974373194
www.astun.com
Tourist office tel: + 34 974373088
location Candanchu
altitude 1530 m
Location: Astun
altitude 1700 m

ON THE MOUNTAIN »
season December to April
Lifts
vertical drop: 1700 - 2324 m
amount of lifts in total: 39
gondolas: -
chair lifts: 11
drag lifts: 28
Slopes
amount of prepared slopes: 40 km
snowmaking machines: 215
amount of easy runs: 13
amount of intermediate runs: 59
amount of advanced runs: 22
Facilities
night riding: -
amount of halfpipes: -
amount of funparks:1
Heliboarding: -
Lift-ticket prices in Euro
1/2 day: 19
day: 27
week: 100
season: 450

SNOWBOARD TUITION »
Escuela esqui Y snowboard de astun
Tel +34 974372000
Escuela de esqui de candanchu
Tel +34 974372033

SNOWBOARD SHOPS »
Astun sport
Tel +34 974373296
desporte roldan
Tel +34 974373122

GETTING AROUND »
Car
Zaragoza - Astún 170km
Zaragoza - N 330 (E-7) - Huesca - Castiello de Jac - Canfranc – Astún/ Candanchù
Toulouse - Astún 338km
Toulouse - A64 - Muret - Exit Soumoulou - Idron - Oloron/Sainte Marie - Col du Somport - Aisa (Fr/Sp) - Canfranc – Astún/ Candanchù
Barcelona - Astún 370km
Barcelona - A2 (E-90) - Exit Martorell/Lleida - N2 - Jorba - Granyanella - Lleida - La Luenga - Huesca - Canfranc – Astún/ Candanchù
Bus
Alosa buslines www.alosa.es run from Madrid and Barcelona to Jaca. A bus also runs from Pau to Jaca.
Mavaragon buslines www.mavaragon.com /mancobus.htm travel fron Jaca to Candanchú and Astún.
Train
Trains travel from Madrid, Zaragoza and Barcelona.
www.renfe.es
Air
France:
Pau Airport 82km
Toulouse Airport 338km
Spain:
Pamplona Airport 141km
Zaragoza Airport 183km
Barcelona Airport 388km

© Jorge Dominguez

ASTÚN/CANDANCHU »
Intro_ Looking from the Atlantic coast, Candanchù is the first big ski area you come to in the Spanish Pyrenees, and the first resort town to be built in the region. The reasons for visiting then, were the same as they are now: the beauty of the surrounding landscape and its mountain scenery. The summit is more than 2400m high and forms a majestic silhouette. Lying in the same valley just a few kilometres away, is the town of Astún. There's quite a difference, however, especially with regards to the atmosphere and even the weather.
  The heart of every freerider will glow like a Spanish fire when they first set eyes on those steep, inviting runs.

ON THE MOUNTAIN »
Snow Reliability_ From the beginning of January you'll generally be treated to good snow conditions. Good powder can often be had, especially between January and March. Weather and temperature changes are frequent and the snow conditions can change rapidly. Snow report www.astun.com, www.candanchu.com

Lifts/Piste_ Astun: The most important access lift is La Raca (fast moving quad chairlift), which can be taken from the valley station to the highest point in the resort. You then make your way to the main runs and the fun park. Two alternative lifts are available when queues are too long, the chairlifts Debutantes and Pastores.
  On the other side you can take the Truchas chairlift to the top. You won't find as many people on this side, but the double chairlift is relatively old and slow. The Truchas does provide access to the longest run on the mountain and also the second of the two fast moving quad chairlifts, Canal Rolla.

Candanchù: If you want to get to La Olla or one of the higher sections of the resort, use one of the three valley stations: Tobazo I, Tobazo II or Alto Aragón. When everything's tracked out or if the chairlift's overcrowded, an alternative is the Navarros T-bar. The fast moving chairlift known as La Tuca Blanca takes you up to 2400m, the highest point in the resort.

Freeriding_ The freeride terrain isn't extensive, but what freeriding there is, is extremely good. In the area close to La Raca, you will find good off piste terrain that is plenty steep. But, on a good day, this run will also be tracked out very quickly. A wide chute with great banks can be found running between the Canal Rolla chairlift and the Anayet T-bar.
  Good runs with variable gradients can be found in the Truchas area. For those looking for really long runs, try the following two runs; The El Ruso run and the Los Tubos run. They both begin on the summit of La Raca and start on the piste heading towards Candanchú. This excellent freeriding and freestyling terrain is located in between pine forest and rock faces. The runs are not sign posted and have a few tricky sections which should be inspected from below, or, better still, take a local with you. The runs end up on the road and your only option is to hitch back to the lifts, so be warned!
  Freeriding is at the heart and soul of Candanchù. Leaving the relatively flat piste for the off-piste, you'll find the stuff that dreams are made of…deep, dry powder! Leaving the Navarros lift, you'll find an unprepared area running

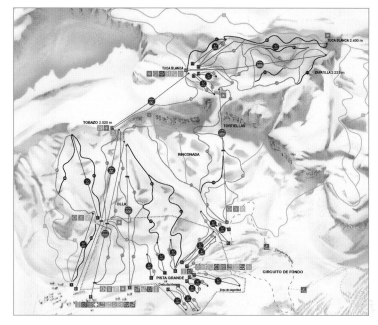

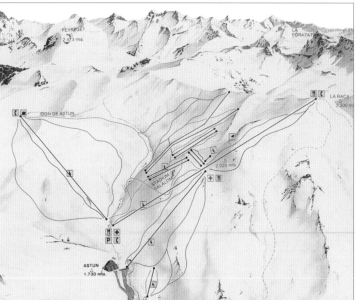

© Jorge Domínguez **Rider** Eduardo

THE FREERIDE TERRAIN ISN'T EXTENSIVE, BUT WHAT FREERIDING THERE IS, IS EXTREMELY GOOD. IN THE AREA CLOSE TO LA RACA, YOU WILL FIND GOOD OFF PISTE TERRAIN THAT IS PLENTY STEEP. BUT, ON A GOOD DAY, THIS RUN WILL ALSO BE TRACKED OUT VERY QUICKLY."

through a cleared pine forest immediately above the village. There won't always be heaps of snow but as soon as the conditions are right, head up for a run before the locals track it out. In the Rinconada area, down in a small valley, you'll not find much in the way of prepared piste. Instead you'll find a heap of possibilities for freeriding and freestyling. Rinconada can be accessed via La Olla. In El Tuvo de la Zapatilla you'll find the best off piste run from Candanchù. It can be accessed from the Tuca Blanca piste, but this too will be tracked out by locals as soon as the snow is good. The run finds its way down a 10m wide channel protected by large rock faces, and in places the gradient is as steep as 42°. The last, and biggest freeriding area is Loma Verde. To access it from the upper section of the Tuca Blanca piste, ride down the north-facing slope until you arrive at the Tortiellas chairlift. The snow quality is variable.

Freestyling_Below the big jump, you'll find a permanent fun park. (A rare phenomenon on a south facing slope in the Pyrenees!) For almost two years now, Mauricio Peñerolla, one of Spain's best known freestylers, has taken it on himself to make sure that the park is constantly improving. Candanchù has no park.

Beginners_In Astun, the main area for beginners is called Prado Blanco. This can be accessed by the Debutantes and Pastores chairlifts. The area is very high up and for those of you not comfortable with your turns, you should probably ride the chairlift back down, rather than testing your luck on the home runs. For complete beginners, close to the car parks is a small piste with its own lift -Manantiales. In Candanchù, go to Pista Grande.

Mountain Restaurants_There are two restaurants, the Pista Grande and the Tuca Blanca. El

Destajo is a new coffee shop-cum-bar which has been opened at the top station of the Tobazo. You can buy snacks there too.

IN THE TOWN »
Accommodation_Rooms, apartments and *, ** and *** hotels can all be found in the town. For info and reservations:

www.candanchu.com
or ring Etuksa on:
Tel +34 (0) 974 373194
or +34 (0) 974 373263
Fax +34 (0) 974 373348

LOCAL TIP »
The season pass for Candanchù is also valid in Sierra Nevada, Spain's southernmost ski resort.

PROS & CONS »
+ Fast lifts.
+ Snowboard guides available.
+ Heli-boarding.
+ Great snowboard vibe.

− Spain's most expensive lift tickets.
− Often overcrowded.
− No snowpark, halfpipe sporadic.

© Jorge Dominguez **Rider** David Pujol

"DESPITE THE FACT THAT A SNOWPARK HAS BEEN INCLUDED ON THE RESORT MAP, THERE IS NO SNOWPARK."

BAQUEIRA-BERET
SPAIN

BAQUEIRA BERET »
web address: www.baqueira.es
tourist office tel: +34 973639010
location: Baqueira
population: 300
altitude: 1500
linked resorts: no

ON THE MOUNTAIN »
season: begining of Decermber - end of April
Lifts
vertical drop: 1500-2510 m
amount of lifts in total: 26
gondolas: 0
chair lifts: 17
drag lifts: 9
Slopes
amount of prepared slopes in km: 75
snowmaking machines: 244
easy runs: 32 km
intermediate runs: 32 km
advanced runs: 7 km
Facilities
night riding: no
amount of halfpipes: 1
amount of funparks: 0
heliboarding: yes
Lift-ticket prices in Euro
1/2 day: 20
day: 33
week:122
season: 195

SNOWBOARD TUITION »
Escuela de snowboard Val D'Aran
Tel: +34 973646083

SNOWBOARD SHOPS »
Mombi Surf
Tel: +34 973645081

GETTING THERE »
Car
Barcelona - Baqueira 28km
Barcelona - Enlace A18/E9 - Cadi Norte - Sort - Esterri d'_neu - Baqueira
Zaragoza - Baqueira 275km
Zaragoza - Huesca - Barbastro - Benabarre - Vielha - Baqueira
Toulouse - Baqueira 174km
Toulouse - towards Bayonne, Pau, Tarbes - Saint Gaudens exit - Montrejeau - Barbazan (Fr/Sp) - Vielha - Baqueira
Bus
Ribagorza Buses operate a regular service from Barcelona to Baqueira.
Check it out at www.ribagorza.com
Taxis are also available
Tel: +34 (0) 973 640 196
Train
Trains travel to Lerida (Spain), 184km away from Baqueira or to Montrejeau (France), 60km away.
Air
Toulouse (France) Airport 166km
Zaragoza (Spain) Airport 290km
Barcelona (Spain) Airport 286km

© Jorge Dominguez **Rider** Carlos Rumeu

BAQUEIRA-BERET »
Intro_Baqueira is one of the main snowboard areas in Spain, mainly because it boasts some of the best snow conditions in the Pyrenees. Consequently, this is also where you'll find some of Spain's best riders.

ON THE MOUNTAIN »
Snow reliability_When a northern low-pressure system meanders over the Iberian peninsula, you're pretty much guaranteed great snowfall. Snow-making machines are on hand in all areas, except Bonaigua. Check out the latest snow report for yourself at www.baqueira.es .

Lifts & Piste_There are five valley lift stations - Baqueira at 1500m above sea level, Beret 1850m, Orri 1850m, Tanau 1700m and Bonaigua 2072m. All of the runs are connected, and it's possible to ride them all in a day. The chairlift from Baqueira to Beret is long and slow, and the run rather arduous. Most visitors stay in Baqueira, but the Mirador quad chairlift and the Pla de Baqueira six-person chairlift quickly help disperse any long queues. Beret is the second main

lift station in the resort and also has two fast chairlifts, the Blanhiblar quad, and the Dera Reina six-person chair. The areas of Orri and Bonaigua have slower lifts, but get less crowded as a result.

Freeriding_Baqueira has two completely different freeride areas to choose from. The first is Cara Norte; the slopes next to the Luis Aria tow lift. There are a good number of lines running down to the valley lift station at Orri. They are relatively steep, and there are a few dangerous cliffs lurking in the shadows. Although there are some easier lines here, it's really an area for experienced riders.
The second is located on both sides of the Teso Dera Mina chairlift. A couple of short, easier chutes can be found on the north side; and these are generally well covered with snow. However, because they're easy to access they get tracked out quickly. You can ride right down to the Bonaigua chairlift from the south side - it's a little steeper and a good long run. The only real danger here is straying too far to the right and

ending up on the road - you'll have a tiring walk back to the lift.
Other good runs (that may not necessarily end up at a lift station) include the one from Tuc deth Dossau to the ghostly village of Montgarri; or from Cap de Blanhiblar to the village of Bagergue; or from Pla de Baqueira to the road after Bonaigua - close to Baqueira

Heliboarding_Spain offers the cheapest heliboarding flights in Europe, but you also have to hire a mountain guide.

Baqueira Beret Heliport
25598 Salardu Leirida
Tel: +34 (0) 973 645 797

Freestyling_Despite the fact that a snowpark has been included on the resort map, there is no snowpark, and only an occasional halfpipe. Freestylers at Baqueira spend a lot of time building their own kickers, or playing on the natural jumps on the side of the Os and Isard pistes. They generally build their kickers around Tuc de la Llana. The locals have also built a great little rail park

"FREESTYLERS AT BAQUEIRA SPEND A LOT OF TIME BUILDING THEIR OWN KICKERS, OR PLAYING ON THE NATURAL JUMPS ON THE SIDE OF THE OS AND ISARD PISTES. THEY GENERALLY BUILD THEIR KICKERS AROUND TUC DE LA LLANA."

© Jorge Dominguez **Rider** Bona Dominguez

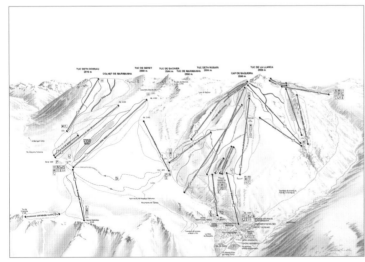

"BAQUEIRA IS ONE OF THE MAIN SNOWBOARD AREAS IN SPAIN, MAINLY BECAUSE IT BOASTS SOME OF THE BEST SNOW CONDITIONS AROUND THE PYRENEES. WHEN A NORTHERN LOW-PRESSURE SYSTEM MEANDERS OVER THE IBERIAN PENINSULA, YOU'RE ALMOST CERTAINLY GUARANTEED GREAT SNOWFALL."

de Baqueira (2200m), Pla de Baqueira (2400m), Asrgulls and Bonaigua (2072m). All serve sandwiches and hot meals.

IN THE TOWN »

Accommodation_Baqueira has some three to five star hotels, and a large choice of holiday apartments. Eleven villages are dotted along the 13km that constitute the length of the entire valley, and you'll find everything from 4 star hotels to holiday apartments and guesthouses.

Info and reservation
Tel: +34 (0) 973 639 000 or www.centralderervas.net
Tourist Info, Tel: +34 (0) 973 649 110 or www.baqueira.es

Food_Finding a good restaurant in the village won't be a problem, as there's a huge choice of places to eat in the Aran Valley. Try Ma's Pasta, Eth Rastrille, Montagut and El Jardi dels Pomers, where you can eat good food while chatting with the owners and the locals about the mountain - if you understand Spanish! La Sidreria and Urtau - fantastic food - fast.

Nightlife_Things don't really kick off here until around 10pm or 11pm. Bars such as Era Crin in Escunhao or La Luna in Arties are good places to check out. You can also party into the early hours of the morning at places such as Pacha or Tiffanys. Things really fire up at weekends and during holidays.

where the roads to Orri and Beret intersect, near the train station.

Beginners_There are two areas that are suitable for beginners. In Baqueira: the Rabada, Pastores I and Pastores II tow lifts. These are 1800m above sea level and are accessible via the Bosque or Esquiros tow lifts.

In Beret: a bigger area for beginners, comfortably serviced by the double chairlift, Pla de Beret. A lift ticket is available for just this lift, to save beginners a little cash.

Mountain Restaurants_There are nine restaurants on the piste at Beret (1850m), Dossau, Cap de Blanhiblar, Orri (all at 1850m), Pla

"OPEN POWDER FIELDS, STEEP RUNS AND A FEW CHUTES CAN ALL BE HAD AT 'TUC DEL MUNTAYON' AT 2600M, A GREAT PLAYGROUND FOR ANY RIDER, BUT ESPECIALLY THOSE WHO LIKE IT EXTREME."

BOÍ TAÜLL
SPAIN

BOÍ TAULL »
Web address: www.boitaullresort.es
Tourist office tel: +34 934146660
Location: Boi-taull
Population: 0
Altitude: 1700

ON THE MOUNTAIN »
Season: December to April
Lifts
vertical drop: 1700- 2750 m
amount of lifts in total: 15
gondolas: 0
chairlifts: 6
drag lifts: 9
Slopes
amount of prepared slopes: 43 km
snowmaking machines: 118
amount of easy runs: 8
amount of intermediate runs: 25
amount of advanced runs: 8
Facilities
night riding: no
amount of halfpipes: 0
amount of funparks: 1
heliboarding: no
Lift-ticket prices in Euro
1/2 day: 20
day: 26
week: 160
season: 510.86
SNOWBOARD TUITION »
Escuela valle de Boi
Tel: +34 973297001

GETTING THERE »
Car
Toulouse - Boí Taüll: 219km
Toulouse - A64 - Muret - Montrejeau exit - Tarbes - Galie - Canejan (Fr/Sp) - Arres - Montanuy - Vilaller - Boí Taüll
Barcelona - Boí Taüll: 291km
Barcelona - Marorell - N2 - Jorba - Lleida - Tolva - Sopeira - Bonansa - Boí Taüll
Bus
'Ribagorza' run a bus service from Barcelona www.ribagorza.com
Train
There are trains from Lleida (Spain), Baqueira (France) and Montrejeau (France), all of which are about 124km away.
Air
Toulouse Airport (France) 266km
Zaragoza Airport (Spain) 255km
Barcelona Airport (Spain) 310km

© Jorge Domínguez **Rider** Prieto

BOÍ TAÜLL »
Intro_ Boí Taüll is a MUST for all snowboarders visiting the Pyrenees. Not only is it the highest winter sports resort in the Pyrenees, it also has an amazing freeride area with endless possibilities and long, steep slopes. There are also lots of chutes and natural kickers for you to discover. And if these three reasons are still not enough, you'll be pleased to know that its position in the west Pyrenean Alps guarantees optimum snow conditions. This valley has an interesting history too, not only because it was occupied by the Romans, but because there are

traces of the earlier snowboard scene to be found.

ON THE MOUNTAIN »
Snow reliability_ When a low-pressure system accompanied by a southerly wind arrives, you'll find the best conditions in the whole of the Pyrenees. The best time to visit is between January and March. Snow making facilities are on hand.
Info: www.boitaullresort.es
For snow reports, phone:
+34 (0) 973 696091

Freeriding_ This wide open resort is relatively steep and perfect for long powder runs. The cliffs and

natural jumps provide plenty of variation for adrenaline junkies. There are some good spots up on 'Puig Falcón' at 2750m. 'Vaques' at 2300m provides an impressive variety of natural fun. Open powder fields, steep runs and a few chutes can all be had at 'Tuc del Muntayon' at 2600m, a great playground for any rider, but especially those who like it extreme. Awaiting you off piste at Xtra there's a beautiful downhill run with stunning panoramic views of the mountain, although access involves a 15 minute hike. It begins with soft powder, drops down into a steep chute between

"IN THE 2001/02 SEASON A SNOW PARK WAS BUILT AROUND THE 'VAQUES' AREA. THE FIRST SEASON SAW THE INCLUSION OF 3 BIGGER JUMPS AND A SERIES OF SMALLER JUMPS, A PYRAMID AND A JUMP WITH A GAP."

© Jorge Dominguez **Rider** Jorge Burillo

© Jorge Dominguez

"THE REGION IS PROUD OF ITS REPUTATION FOR HOSPITALITY AND GENERALLY SPEAKING YOU CAN EAT WELL EVERYWHERE."

rocks, and runs out through a wide open tree area.

Freestyling_ Freestylers are catered for every bit as well as freeriders. In the 2001/02 season a snow park was built around the 'Vaques' area. The first season saw the inclusion of 3 bigger jumps and a series of smaller jumps, a pyramid and a jump with a gap. You'll also find a 5m straight rail and two curved rails. Next season there are plans to build a new snow park in the 'Chicolla' area which will be equipped with snow making facilities and a lift specifically for the park.

Accommodation_ Unfortunately, you'll not find any accommodation close to the piste. The nearest rooms are 8km away. Hotels (2-3 star) and holiday apartments can be found throughout the valley. A car is a must. Reservations: +34 (0) 934 146660 www.boitaullresort.es

Food_ The region is very proud of its reputation for hospitality and generally speaking you can eat well everywhere. In Boí there are two restaurants, the *Ca la Pepa* (a Crêperie, though it also serves lots of other tasty dishes too) and the pizzeria *Casós,* where you'll find

wonderful pizzas and delicious cutlets that will fill even the hungriest belly. Expect to pay more at restaurants such as *La Coma* in Taüll or *La Llebreta* in 'Barruera'..

Nightlife_ There's not much nightlife here. Your best bet would probably be La Ferradura, though it's a bit off the beaten track in the historical part of 'Boí'. La Cova is under new management and has recently been renovated. La Perera, previously a classic, has now closed down, unfortunately. Chillin' with friends or travelling down to Pont de Suert approximately 20km away are

your only other options.

LOCAL TIP »
Marco Bajona_ Boí Taüll is a town with immense freeride potential and is becoming ever more interesting for freestylers. I'd recommend a visit to 'Tubo de Vaques', 'Santi's Paradise', 'Pic de Cerbí', 'Vista Aneto' and 'Puig Falcó'. On these runs you can often find undiscovered snow to ride. For some runs, though, you'll need a snowmobile. 'Coliflor', the Snowboard Camp organisers also offer tours in these areas.
For infoTel: +34 (0) 973 690055
Fax: +34 (0) 973 690155

CERLER

SPAIN

CERLER »
www.cerler.com
Tourist office tel: +34 974551012
Location: Cerler
Population: -
Altitude: 1500

ON THE MOUNTAIN »
Season: December - April
Lifts
Vertical drop: 1500- 2630m
amount of lifts in total: 18
gondolas: -
chairlifts: 9
drag lifts: 9
Slopes
amount of prepared slopes: 52 km
snowmaking machines: 200
amount of easy runs: 8
amount of intermediate runs: 30
amount of advanced runs: 7
Facilities
night riding: -
amount of halfpipes: -
amount of funparks: 1
Heliboarding: -
Lift-ticket prices in Euro
1/2 day: 21
day: 26
week: 145
season: 451

SNOWBOARD TUITION »
Escuela cerler
Tel: +34 974551553

GETTING THERE »
Car
Barcelona - Cerler approx. 300km
Barcelona - A2 or N II - Lleida - C 139 - Cerler
Zaragoza - Cerler 250km
Zaragoza - N 123 - N 240 - C 139 - Cerler
Bus
From Barcelona to Lleida, Barbastro via the Alto Aragonesa line
From Lleida, Barbastro to Benasque via local buses. Info: www.ribagorza.com
Air
Barcelona Airport approx. 300km
Zaragoza Airport 250km
Madrid Airport 600km

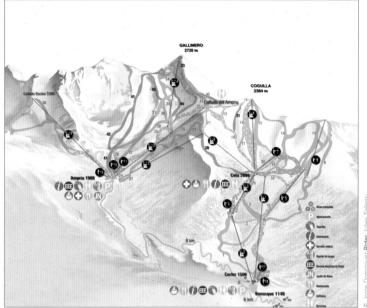

CERLER »
Intro_In the heart of the Aragonese Pyrenees, situated between the National Parks of Posets and Maladeta, is the lovely village of Cerler. At 1500m above sea level, Cerler is the highest inhabited village in the region and home of the resort known as Cerler Valle de Benasque.

The resort spreads out over two mountainsides and is split into two sections, Cerler and Ampriu. The second highest chairlift in the Pyrenees is in Ampriu, the Gallinero quadlift which transports visitors up the to the summit of Gallinero at 2728m. Cerler, meanwhile, has 35km of piste in all, although none of it is anywhere near as interesting as the off piste potential this resort has to offer.

ON THE MOUNTAIN »
Snow reliability_The best snow conditions can be experienced between January and March, which is when you'll find a good snow base. The winds are sometimes very strong, blowing away much of the snow that falls up on the summit. Some of the more exposed lifts are often closed. The snow in the upper reaches is often very hard while in the lower areas it can be quite slushy. Snow making facilities are available.

Snow reports
www.cerler.com
Tel: 974 55 11 11

Lifts & Piste_There are two valley stations that allow access to the resorts. The *Molino* chairlift in *Cerler* and the *Ampriu* chairlift in *Ampriu*. The most popular lift is the Cogulla chairlift, which leaves from the cafeteria at 2000m, and heads up to the summit station at 2384m. This also connects both sides of the resort. The *Basibé*, a 6 seater chairlift, is fast and efficient while the *Gallinero* quad chairlift provides access to the highest point in the resort. This is where you'll generally

"CERLER IS THE HIGHEST INHABITED VILLAGE IN THE REGION."

find the fewest people and the best snow conditions.

Freeriding_Cerler certainly has a lot of freeriding terrain, and indeed it's the main draw of this resort. The northern slope of *Pico Gallinero* is the place to ride when the snow in other parts of the resort is poor. *Canal Amplia* is a great chute where the snow often holds its quality right throughout the day. The south side provides a lot of good terrain which often goes untouched. But be on your guard for avalanches in this area, which are always a real risk. And don't forget to traverse to the right in good time to get back to *Ampriu*. More experienced freeriders should drop in to the north face of *Cibolles*, north of *Pico Gallinero*. The walk takes around 30 minutes from Gallinero, but it's well worth the effort.

Freestyling_There's a small snowpark on the *Cogulla* piste which you can see from the chairlift. Two jumps, 2 handrails and a box make for a basic snowpark.

Beginners_The best choice for beginners is to ride at *Ampriu*, where you'll find flatter sections connecting with the I and II tow lifts. The *Basibé* also services a flatter slope. The lower area of *Cerler* is equipped with a tow lift and a conveyor belt.

Mountain Restaurants_There's a restaurant with a cafeteria at 2000m, plus a self-service restaurant in *Ampriu*, and a small bar where they make the best burgers in the world!

IN THE TOWN »
Accommodation_In *Cerler* try

the *Hotel Edelweiss* and *Hotel Monte Alba*.
There's a bigger choice 8km away in *Benasque* ranging from private rooms to luxurious hotels.

Further information
Benasque Tourist Office
Tel: 974 55 12 80 or
974 55 12 89

Food_After a day on the mountain in *Cerler*, most people go to *La Cabana* which serves tasty sandwiches - 'bocatas' - and crêpes. If you're looking for something a little more substantial, head to *El Buixo* for pizzas at a fair price.
Benasque caters for all tastes, including a number of supermarkets.

Nightlife_During the week the resort is very quiet, but on weekends you'll find good music at the *Las Arcades* bar. Surcos is a place where the riders like to go and it has Internet access. The places to go in *Cerler* are *La Border del Mastín* or *El Paralelo* for a game of table football.

Other Activities_No skate park, no cinema, only the mountain, so after you've finished snowboarding there's not really much to do. Members of the Spanish Alpine School can use the climbing wall for €2. You can also go mountain biking or on a trekking tour in the *Valle de Benasque*.

LOCAL TIP »
David Pujol_"I'm a freerider and in this valley I'm in my element. Not only because of the freeriding terrain, but also because of the people. It may not be the most luxurious town in the Pyrenees, but it does have one of the best vibes!"

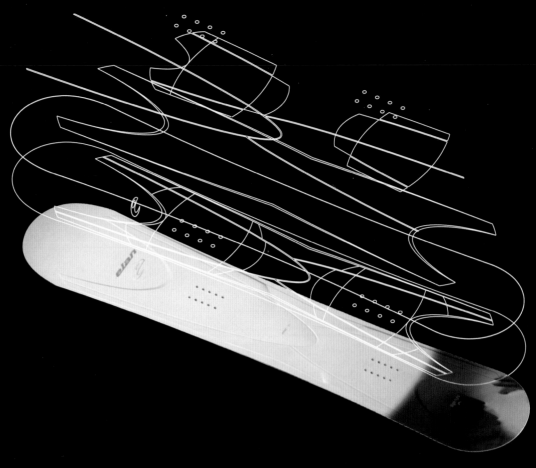

vertigo ◐

superior. performance.

elan®
snowboards

Elan snowboards are manufactured with superior engineering knowledge and technology, offering you the optimum personal riding performance and durability. Experience them.

PROS & CONS »
+ Long and variable pistes.
+ Good freeriding spots for the not-so-experienced snowboarder.
+ Friendly crowd.
+ Nightlife can go wild.

− Snow quality can deteriorate by end of season.
− Like many Spanish resorts, pipes and parks are generally not worth the drive.
− A few older, slower lifts.

FORMIGAL
SPAIN

»

FORMIGAL »
www.formigal.com
tourist office tel: +34 974490000
location: Sallent de Gallego
population:300
altitude: 1150m

ON THE MOUNTAIN »
season: December- end April
Lifts
vertical drop: 1510−2250m
amount of lifts in total: 22
gondolas: 1
chairlifts: 5
drag lifts: 16
Slopes
amount of prepared slopes: 57 km
runs w. snowmaking machines: 13
amount of easy runs: 4
amount of intermediate runs: 37
amount of advanced runs: 11
Facilities
night riding: yes
amount of halfpipes: -
amount of funparks: -
Heliboarding: -
Lift-ticket prices in Euro
1/2 day: 20
day: 25
week: 116
season: 427

SNOWBOARD TUITION »
Spanish ski school
Tel: + 34 974490135

SNOWBOARD SHOPS »
Intersport
Tel: +34 974490138

GETTING THERE »
Car
Pamplona - Formigal: 168km
Pamplona - Jaca - Sabiñánigo - Biescas - Formigal
Barcelona - Formigal: 365km
Barcelona - N2 towards Igualada - Cervera - Lérida N240 - Huesca - Jaca, Sabiñánigo N260 - Biescas A136 - Formigal
Toulouse - Formigal: 295km
Toulouse - towards Tarbes - via Lannemezan - Bielsa Tunnel (Fr/Sp) - Escalona - Sarvisé - Biescas - Formigal
Air
Toulouse Airport: 299km
Pamplona Airport: 163km
Barcelona Airport: 359km

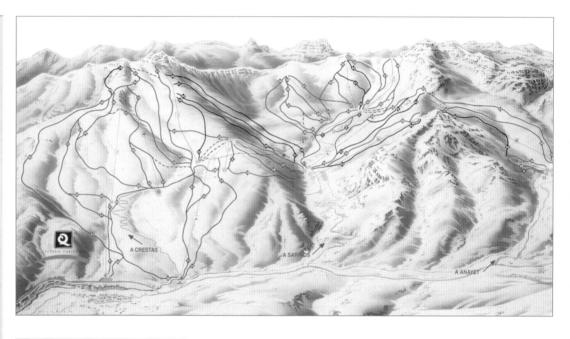

FORMIGAL »
Intro_Formigal is not well known outside Spain, but all that is about to change. The resort is already quite popular with intermediate and beginner riders, and the town has plenty of nightlife. The area has some nice open terrain, which makes it easy to find your way around. Following a good dump, the many powder runs are rideable for even powder beginners. This resort is not really suited to extreme freeriders, but it's a great alternative for those who are looking for an inexpensive resort with a lot of variation in terrain and a good nightlife.

ON THE MOUNTAIN »
Snow reliability_The snow conditions here are relatively good because this is where eastern frontal systems meet cold air streams. The snow is at its best in the colder months of January and February, and occasionally even into March. There is generally very little snow in December and the warmer weather arrives around April. But there are lots of high and low-pressure snow-making machines on hand to help Mother Nature out if needs be.

Lifts & Piste_The lift system is relatively efficient, thanks to the strategic positioning of the lifts around the resort. The most popular lifts are the chairlifts, even though a couple of them are quite

slow, but there are lots of tow lifts too. The Sallent tri chairlift is one of the longest and slowest on the mountain, but it does connect the end station of the gondola with the rest of the resort. And you can avoid this lift if you're willing to take a few tow lifts instead.

Freeriding_Freeriding is not Formigal's biggest draw, but there are still a few good spots when the snow conditions are right. The mountains are fairly open and there are no forests, which makes it easy to see where all the runs are located. The special topography of the resort offers endless accessible spots that are ideal for the not-so-experienced freerider. To the right of the Collado chairlift there's an ideal slope for riding, but the chutes at Canatal and Izas can also be fun.

Freestyling_Formigal has a snowpark with a halfpipe and a few jumps, but unfortunately it's not always kept in good condition. There are plans to incorporate a few rails in the park, which would be a good start.

Beginners_There are four slopes for beginners in the area of Cantal, Izas and Anayet. All of them easily accessible and all of them supported by a good infrastructure. The beginner lifts are easy and the runs are flat. The area around Crestas is not recommended for

beginners as it's strictly red and black runs here. The ski school at Formigal also offers snowboard lessons.

Mountain Restaurants_Formigal has a mountain restaurant, two self-service bars and five cafeterias. Chocolaterías are well worth a visit - try the ones on Sarrios and Anayet. There's also a picnic area there. The food is excellent and the prices are kept under firm control. Local specialities such as grilled meat dishes or pastries can be expensive, though.

The Gemsbock, the only mountain restaurant, is built in the Tyrolean style - no sign of Spanish flair here. It offers a dish of the day, fondues and meat cooked on a stone griddle. The food is quite good and if the budget stretches to it, we'd recommend you go there for an evening meal, where the specials menu (weekends only) is a must.

IN THE TOWN »
Accommodation_Prices in Valle del Tena range from €14 to €450 per night, depending on where you stay. A nice option is accommodation in Formigal itself, but it won't be cheap. The town is made up of nothing but 2 - 4 star hotels. For those with the cash, you can spend a very comfortable night at the ***Eguzki Lore. In Valle del Tena all sorts of accommodation is available.

"THIS RESORT IS NOT REALLY SUITED TO EXTREME FREERIDERS, BUT IT'S A GREAT ALTERNATIVE FOR THOSE WHO ARE LOOKING FOR AN INEXPENSIVE RESORT WITH A LOT OF VARIATION IN TERRAIN AND A GOOD NIGHTLIFE."

© Jorge Dominguez. **Rider** Igor Dominguez

One of the cheapest options would be to stay at either *Albergue Foratata* in *Sallent de Gállego* or at *Camping Escarra* in *Escarilla*. *Formigal* has a central reservations office Tel: +34 (0) 974 490 000 or www.centralreservaformigal.com Which can help you access 68 hotels as well as the ski school.

Information about the area generally or accommodation can also be obtained from the *Valle del Tena* Tourist Office.
Tel: +34 (0) 974 490 196
www.valledeltena.com

Food_Both the prices and the service in the restaurants here are very good. For those on a tight budget, we'd recommend either the *Pizzeria Bocateria* which serves great sandwiches as well as good pizzas, or the *Frankfurt Aragón* whose menu includes sandwiches, tapas etc. The town has its own supermarket, a bakery and a butcher. If you can afford it, head to the *Gemsbock* at the weekend for dinner. *La Tosquera* in the *Peña*

"THE PIPE IS SHAPED TWICE A WEEK ENABLING IT TO BE USED THROUGHOUT PIPE IS SHAPED PIPE IS SHAPED PIPE IS SHAPED PIPE IS SHAPED PIPE IS SHAPED THE WHOLE DAY AND EVEN ON SOME NIGHTS. IT'S STEEP, DEEP AND ONCE YOU'RE USED TO RIDING IN IT, YOU'LL FLY."

Blanca building is a super tip for anyone looking for regional cooking and it has a good wine list too. Regional specialities based on grilled or braised game make for a memorable eating experience.

Nightlife_The nightlife in *Formigal* is lively and colourful, but then it's good everywhere in the *Valle del Tena*. The first port of call is the *El Duende* pub (D.N.D) for a few beers or a glass of wine and then on to Mojitos and Caipiriñas later in the evening - a little bit of the

Caribbean in the Pyrenees. *La Cueva* pub is also a good warm-up bar where the drinks are reasonably priced, and from there you can move on to *Tres Hombres* where.depending on what mood you're in, you can dance all night or just play table soccer and billiards. The *Collins* and *Slalom* discos are best reserved for the midnight hours! The music in most of the bars is a flashback to the 80's and 90's disco scene, though you might hear the odd techno beat.

Other Activities_While you won't find a skatepark, we did find a good church with a few stairs and some good rails. For those of you who haven't had enough fun in the snow, you can rent a snow scooter or hang off the back of a dog sled.

Gorgol
Tel:+34 (0) 974 487 626
Naturaleza y Aventura
Tel: +34 (0) 974 490 046

Film freaks will enjoy the cinema in *Sabiñánigo*, 40km away.

PROS & CONS »
+ All night partying.
+ Lots of sunshine.
+ Spring snow.

− Miles from any other resort.
− The rideable area is small.
− Not much powder.

© Pierre Canweng

"ON A CLEAR DAY MOROCCO BECKONS FROM THE OPPOSITE SIDE OF THE MEDITERRANEAN."

SIERRA NEVADA
SPAIN

SIERRA NEVADA »
www.sierranevadaski.com
Tel: +34 958249100
location: Pradollano
population: 11000
altitude: 2100m

ON THE MOUNTAIN »
season: end of Nov. -until beginning of May
Lifts
altitude of resorts: 2100-3102m
amount of lifts in total: 20
gondolas: 2
chairlifts: 13
T-bars: 5
Slopes
amount of prepaired slopes: 66 km
runs w. snowmaking machines: 35
amount of easy runs: 4
amount of intermediate runs: 46
amount of advanced runs: 4
Facilities
night riding: yes
halfpipe: 1
funparks: 1
heliboarding: -
Lift-ticket prices in Euro
1/2 day: 25
day: 30
week:150
season: 510

SNOWBOARD TUITION »
Surfin Escuela
Tel: +34 958481190
www.surfinsnowboard.com

SNOWBOARD SHOPS »
Surfinsnowboarding
Tel: +34 958480125
www.surfinsnowboard.com

GETTING THERE »
Car
Madrid – Sierra Nevada: 453km
Madrid - N-IV - Ocaña - Bailén N323 - Jaén - Granada - Sierra Nevada
Malaga – Sierra Nevada: 156km
Malaga – N331 Villanueva de Cauche - Estación de Salinas A92 – Granada - Sierra Nevada
Bus
Granada – Sierra Nevada: 8am, 10am, 5pm
Sierra Nevada – Granada : 9am, 4pm and 7.30pm Tel: 0958273100
Train
Take the train to Granada, then continue by coach. Spanish railways: www.renfe.es
Air
Granada Airport: 32 km
Malaga Airport: 160 km

© Jorge Dominguez; **Rider** Xavier Lasagabaster

SIERRA NEVADA »
Intro_Situated high in the mountains just inland from the southern Spanish coast, the Sierra Nevada is different from any other resort in Europe. On a clear day Morocco beckons from the opposite side of the Mediterranean and this, combined with Andulucian hospitality, creates a heady atmosphere, panoramic views and days of blissful t-shirt riding. This is primarily a freestyle resort with a busy funpark. Locals sleep in the morning, snowboard in the afternoon, and party all night.

ON THE MOUNTAIN »
Snow reliability_Being one of Europe's highest resorts, you'd expect a lot of snow here, but this isn't really the case. When the snow falls, the dumps are never normally that big, so powder riding is only good in the early part of the following morning, before the sun has taken its toll. The best time to go is from February onwards. This is when the snowfall tends to be at its best, rather than early season. When the white stuff is sparse, there are over 30kms of piste with snowmaking equipment.

Lifts & Piste_The lifts fan out in three directions from the main resort, with most of them heading

to Borreguiles and the beginner's zone and the connecting lifts to the upper slopes. The gondolas that travel direct to Borreguiles get extremely busy at weekends and at holiday times.

To get round this bottleneck, take the Jarra chairlift and connect onto the Montebajo or Momachil chairlifts. From Borreguiles you can use a combination of lifts: the Valeta peak (views down to the Mediterranean and across to Morocco); cross over to the Laguna de Las Yeguas for freeriding, or make your way up to the snowpark and halfpipe just above Borreguiles. This is a small resort and most of the riding is intermediate, with only a few black runs.

Freeriding_There are plenty of open slopes for freeriding, but not enough large dumps in a season to be able to take real advantage of them. La Laguna de las Yeguas and the Vallée de San Juan are the main freeride areas. La Laguna de las Yeguas is a large open area with no trees, few cliffs and plenty of small hits. To get toVallée de San Juan, keep to the right from Valeta, take the Aguila piste and then drop off further to the right for the Barranco de San Juan route. Finish off with the Ventlsquero Moron route back to

the resort - a good last ride of the day. But be careful. Go too far down the Vallée de San Juan and it's a hike out. For a big day out, hire a guide, and go over the top at Valeta and take the La Alphurras route. Just make sure you organise a taxi or a friend to pick you up, as there's no lift back.

Freestyling_This is Freestyle City with large numbers of snowboarders hanging out and using the halfpipe and fully equipped funpark above Borreguiles. The easiest way to access it is via the Veleta and Veleta II lifts. The funpark has rails, tabletops and a spine, as well as a number of kickers. The halfpipe and funpark are still rideable at the end of the season. Away from this, the Montebajo lift provides access to the best area for high-speed freestyling. It has natural hits on the way back to the resort, in particular the face of the Ascensor, which is fast and north facing – good for a blast down.

Carving_Not a carver's paradise. None of the snowboard shops in the resort sell hard boots. That's probably a pretty fair indication of the attraction of and attitude towards carving in the Sierra Nevada!

"THE NEARBY BEACHES ADD YET ANOTHER DIMENSION. THEY MAY NOT BE THE PRETTIEST SPOTS BUT IT'S HARD TO BEAT A MORNING'S SNOWBOARDING FOLLOWED BY AN AFTERNOON'S BODYSURFING."

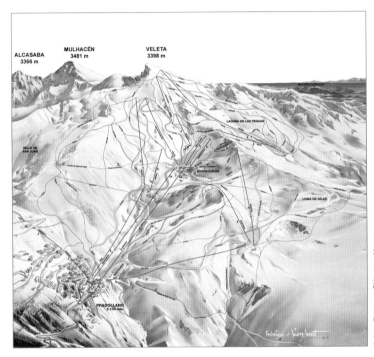

© Jorge Domínguez **Rider** Hugo Morales

Beginners_ This is a beginner-friendly resort, with a large learning area at Borreguiles. Lots of sun, so you stay warm as you learn, lots of nightlife when you're fed up with falling over, and there's little risk of getting lost, even in bad conditions. There's gondola access to the learning zone and some of the cheapest snowboarding lessons in Europe.

Mountain Restaurants_ The mountain restaurants are not your average romantic Alpine experience. Think more fast food takeaway with quick service and cheap prices. Most of them are at Borreguiles which during theSpanish lunchtime/siesta (which lasts from 2 'till 5) is the place where everybody who isn't on the slope hangs out.

IN THE TOWN »
Info_ This is a very dense, purpose-built, modern resort with most facilities within walking distance of each other. Not the most beautiful place in the world, but it has that Spanish party spirit. Part of the resort is built on a steep slope with access via a chairlift or buses that run till midnight. Most things are open until late but might be closed for the midday siesta from two till five.

Accommodation_ Make sure you organise your accommodation before you arrive, particularly if you're staying over the weekend, as the place is often packed out. It's a long way back to Grenada! Most snowboarders tend to stay in the four apartment blocks, which are cheaper if you cram enough people in, and you're then free to do what you want. The best of these is Apartamentos Monachil: Tel: +34 958481450 in the centre of town. For budget accommodation, there's the Youth Hostel/Albergue Juvenil at 18 euros a night: Tel: +34 958481241. And at the top of the resort there's the University hostel: Tel: +34 958249238. Central room reservations: Tel: +34 902708090 or agencia@cetursa.es

Food_ Spanish food is generally cheap and simple and includes such well-known specialities such as Paella and Rabo de Toro. Eating is a huge social event, so you could be waiting for hours if you don't book a table in advance. After riding, most locals consume vast quantities of tapas and beer. The Snowbar, right at the bottom of the main piste, and the Cartujano are the most popular hangouts. Later on in the evening, the favourite places to eat are the

"LOTS OF SUN, SO YOU STAY WARM AS YOU LEARN."

Pizzeria Floren (good and cheap), La Carreta for meat and fish Spanish style, the Midas if you want to impress your taste buds (and shock your wallet), and Tia Maria for Texmex. There are three supermarkets in the town.

Nightlife_ This is a party town with lots on offer. Don't go out early, though, because nothing really kicks off before midnight. Look out for Sticky Fingers for a game of pool, the popular tourist hangout La Cheminée, Chicle for dancing and girls, and the Snowlunch if you still need a drink at 5am in the morning. If you're having no luck on the dance floor then night boarding is an option. Normally open Friday and Saturday nights between 7.30 and 11pm. Ask at the lift office which nights the lights are on as the schedule can vary.

Other Activities_ For a bit of variety, try snowmobiling with a guide (36 Euros for 30 minutes) or a dog sled ride - 30 Euros for 40 minutes. There's a cinema, an ice skating rink and the health spa

will cure whatever ails you. For those who have not had enough excitement, you can even try hang gliding.

The nearby beaches add yet another dimension. They may not be the prettiest spots but it's hard to beat a morning's snowboarding followed by an afternoon's bodysurfing. And then in Grenada there's the Alhambra, an old Moorish Palace, and probably the most stunning building in Europe. Grenada is also a large university town ensuring that partying is an all night thing...

Thanks to_ Jura and the rest of his crew at Surfinsnowboards. If you're in town drop in and buy him a beer, but not too many! And Jesús Rada at Frost Rice, who doesn't mind what you buy him.

LOCAL TIP »
Go with the vibe! Ride on the spring snow in March and April between 1 and 5 in the afternoon then go for tapas and beer, a quick rest, something more substantial to eat, and then check out the bars and clubs till 6am. The best of both worlds.

"THE COUNTRY IS HOME TO SIX SKI RESORTS, SOLDEU BEING THE BIGGEST AND THE BEST KNOWN. THE LOW PRICES AND THE EASY TERRAIN MAKE ANDORRA A POPULAR PLACE FOR BOTH BEGINNERS AND INTERMEDIATES"

SOLDEU EL TARTER
ANDORRA

SOLDEU »
Web address: www.soldeu.ad
Tourist office tel: +376 890500
location: Soldeu
population:
500
altitude: 1710 m
linked resorts: el Tarter, Canillo

ON THE MOUNTAIN »
season: December - end of April
Lifts
vertical drop: 1710 – 2560m
amount of lifts in total: 32
gondolas: 2
chair lifts: 13
drag lifts: 17
Slopes
amount of prepared slopes: 90km
runs w. snowmaking machines: 32km
amount of easy runs: 3
amount of intermediate runs: 32
amount of advanced runs: 10
Facilities
amount of prepared slopes: 90km
runs w. snowmaking machines: 32km
amount of easy runs: 3
amount of intermediate runs: 32
amount of advanced runs: 10
Lift-ticket prices in Euro
1/2 day: 21
day: 29.5
week: 157.5
season: 555

SNOWBOARD TUITION »
Soldeu el Tarter
Tel: +376 890 591 Website

SNOWBOARD SHOPS »
Pic Nagre
Tel: +376 851441
Calvo
Tel: +376 851251

GETTING THERE »
Car
Toulouse - Soldeu 167km
Toulouse - A620 -Foix Roques Labathe exit - Foix - L'hospitalet pres l'Andorre - Pas de la cas (Fra/And) - Soldeu
Barcelona - Soldeu 211km
Barcelona - E9 - Terrassa Nord/Manresa exit - Navas - Sant Corneli - Urus - La seu d'urgell (Sp/And) - Sant Julia de Loria - La Vella - Soldeu
Air
Toulouse Airport 170km
Barcelona Airport 219km,

SOLDEU EL TARTER »
Intro_The tiny Principality of Andorra is situated between France and Spain, right in the heart of the Pyrenees. The official language is Catalan, but most of the locals also speak Spanish and/or French. In the more touristy areas you'll also be able to get by with English. The currency is the Euro and Andorra is a tax-haven. The country is home to six ski resorts, Soldeu being the biggest and the best known. The low prices and the easy terrain make Andorra a popular destination for both beginner and intermediate snowboarders.

ON THE MOUNTAIN »
Lifts & Piste_Canillo (1500m above sea level), El Tarter (1700m) and Soldeu (1800m) all have access lifts. From El Tarter you'll have to take a chairlift to get to the top, whereas from Soldeu and Canillo, you can travel on the 8-person gondolas. Getting to the main areas takes a little longer when travelling from Canillo, but your reward is a direct entry into a beautiful area known as Pic de la Portella.

Freeriding_For those searching for steep and extreme lines, you'd be better off somewhere else. The slopes at the top are short, exposed and not particularly steep. But there are more challenging sections, such as any one of the do-able lines between Pic d'Encampadana and Riba Escorxada, or the chutes between Teixo and Flop. Below 2200m the

"THERE'S A HEAP OF DIFFERENT SORTS OF RAILS AND BOXES SCATTERED ALL OVER THE PARK, SO YOU HAVE A GOOD RANGE TO CHOOSE FROM. SERIES OF RAMPS ARE FEW AND FAR BETWEEN, NORMALLY THEY'RE ALL BUILT NEXT TO EACH OTHER. YOU'LL ALSO FIND A BOARDER-CROSS COURSE."

areas between the piste runs are forested and the tree runs are wild, especially in the upper sections, although there is enough room for fast long turns in between the trees. The lower down you travel, the more trees you'll find. Don't bother riding all the way through the forest to the lift.

Freestyling_Riding the Tosa Espiolets 6-person chair lift or the Font Roiges T-bar will take you to the Riba Escorxada piste. From here you can find the funpark.
The park's halfpipe is progressively shaped but when the weather starts to get a bit warmer (from April onwards) they sometimes close it after midday so that it doesn't get too trashed. There's a heap of different sorts of rails and boxes scattered all over the park,

so you have a good range to choose from. Series of ramps are few and far between, normally they're all built next to each other. You'll also find a boarder-cross course.

Beginners_All three resorts have areas suitable for beginners. In Riba Escorxada and El Forn the ski school has a conveyor belt, but very little piste. There's a good piste for beginners in Espiolets, while the piste at Os is very long and travels right down to Soldeu.

Mountain Restaurants_The mountain has a restaurant in each of the three main areas: Espiolets at 2250m, Riba Escorxada at 2100m and El Forn at 2000m. You can order at the bar or take your pick from the buffet.

"YOU'LL FIND VERY FEW NIGHTCLUBS, BUT LOTS OF PUBS. THE ASPEN COLORADO OR FAT ALBERTS IN SOLDEU ARE BOTH ENGLISH-SPEAKING BARS AND THE CLOSEST THINGS TO NIGHTCLUBS IN THE AREA."

© Jorge Dominguez **Rider** David Maurell

IN THE TOWN »

Accommodation_ Hotels (2 to 5 star), hotel apartments and holiday apartments are plentiful throughout the entire Canillo Valley. For further info and to make a booking visit www.vdc.ad

Food_ La Cort delpopaire is a good place to eat in Soldeu. The menu features every type of food that can be cooked over a grill and the meat is the best you'll eat for miles around. Prices are around 18 euros, not including wine. There is also a very good Indian restaurant which is slightly more expensive - expect to pay around

30 euros a head. Near the gondola look out for the Sol i Neu, which is cheap and fast. Between Soldeu and Tarter, El Canario has a good menu and fantastic service. For evening meals in Mosquit you'll find the price and quality are both excellent. But if you just want a snack, sandwiches are available at a fair price near the car park at Barset. Between Tarter and Canillo look out for La borda del horto where they serve paellas and fideuas, regional specialities based on rice or pasta, for around 20 euros per person. Lulu's in Canillo is the best place for pizza fans.

Nightlife_ You'll find very few nightclubs, but lots of pubs. The Aspen Colorado or Fat Alberts in Soldeu are both English-speaking bars and the closest things to nightclubs in the area. But our tip would be the Capital.

Tarter is a better bet for a night out. La Gen Sana has the best DJs, a choice of fine cocktails and probably the most relaxed atmosphere in the whole town. Start the evening off with a bevvy at Arzurs.

In Canillo there's really only the Camping Café, where you can have a game of darts or table football.

LOCAL TIP »

Jordi Font_"Soldeu el Tarter is a town that has really made an effort to provide for snowboarders. Here, you'll find a free area and funpark with a pipe, rails, jumps, a rainbow, boxes, music and a good vibe.

On weekends, when the weather is right, you can take a ride on the snow grooming machines up to Pico de Encampadana and enjoy the free runs back down without having to walk a centimetre. This service is included in the price of your lift tickets. In the freeride area, there are two huts where you can get overnight accommodation for free. Ask the lift personnel."

GIAN
SIMMEN

SWITZERLAND
210-247

FOUR VALLEYS
ADELBODEN
ANDERMATT
DAVOS

ENGELBERG
GRINDELWALD
LAAX/FLIMS

LES DIABLERETS
PORTES DU SOLEIL
SAAS FEE

ST MORITZ
VERBIER
ZERMATT

SWITZERLAND MAP

SWITZERLAND »

Intro_What this small, landlocked country lacks in beaches, it certainly makes up for in other ways, including its rich supply of glaciers and mountains. First impressions of the Swiss Alps could lead you to think that it is just one compact mountain range, but the reality is more complicated. The Alps are separated by glaciers and deep valleys, creating a number of very different regions. Although the topographics of the land may be similar, each region seems to have its own microclimate. These differences cannot only be seen in the land. The Swiss people and their languages are also very diverse. Switzerland has four official languages; German, French, Italian and Ratoromanic – creating different cultures from region to region. Switzerland is original Heidi country – clean, beautiful, cultured… and often expensive.

INFORMATION »

Official Name_Schweizerische Eidgenossenschaft, Confédération Suisse, Confederazione Svizzera
Capital_Bern
Population_7,16 Million
Land mass_41.293km2
Language(s)_Swiss German, French, Italian, reto-romanic
Currency_1 SFR = 100 Rappen
Highest mountain_Duffourspitze 4634m
International country code_0041
Police_117
Ambulance_144
Fire Brigade_118
Tourist Board_Switzerland Tourism
Tel: +41 (0)1 288 11 11
www.myswitzerland.com
Train Info_www.sbb.ch
Tel: +41 (0)512 20 11 11
Weather Info_www.meteo.ch

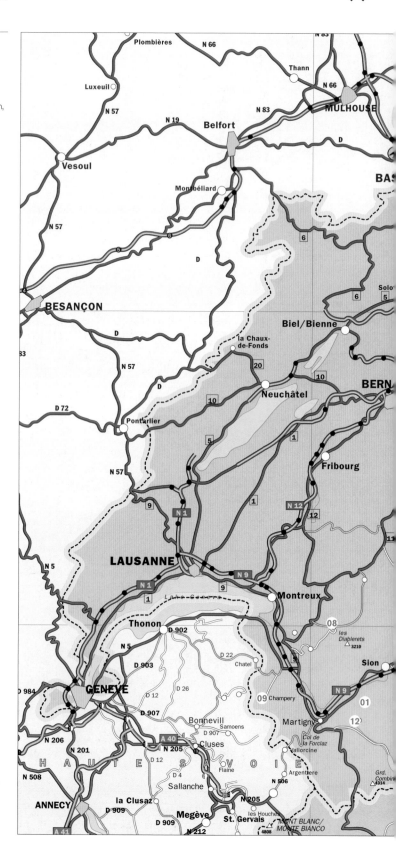

PROS & CONS »
+ Freeriding in Nendaz and Mayens de Riddes.
+ The Snowpark at Thyon.

− Connecting trails are often flat and very tiring.
− Icy conditions often prevail.

"LES QUATRE VALLÉES (THE FOUR VALLEYS) INCLUDES THE REGION AROUND THYON WHICH IS WHERE YOU'LL FIND THYON 2000, LES COLLONS 1800, LES MASSES 1600, VEYSONNAZ, NENDAZ AND VERBIER."

THE FOUR VALLEYS
SWITZERLAND

THE FOUR VALLEYS »
www.thyon-region.ch
tourist office tel: +41 (0)27 281 2727
location: Thyon
population: 80
altitude: 2000 m
linked resorts: Nendaz, Veysonnez, Verbier, La Tzoumaz, Mayens de Riddes

ON THE MOUNTAIN »
season: end October − beginning of April
Lifts
vertical drop: 821-3330 m
amount of lifts in total: 95
gondolas: 17
chair lifts: 32
drag lifts: 46
Slopes
amount of prepared slopes: 331 km
amount of easy runs: 135 km
amount of intermediate runs: 170 km
amount of advanced runs: 26 km
Facilities
night riding: -
amount of halfpipes: 1
amount of funparks: 1
heliboarding: yes
Lift-ticket prices in Euro
1/2 day: 33
day: 40
week: 234,5
season: 814

SNOWBOARD TUITION »
École Suisse de Ski
Tel. 027/281 2738
Les Collons-Thyon 2000
www.leweb.ch/essthyon/

SNOWBOARD SHOPS »
Theyaz Sports
1988 Les Collons
Tel: +41 (0)27 281 13 56

GETTING THERE »
Car
Geneva - Thyon: 181km
Geneva - A1 towards Lausanne - Montreux - A9 towards Martigny - Sion - Thyon
Milan - Thyon: 265km
Milan - A8 towards Domodossola (It/Swi) - through Brig - Sion - Thyon
Train
Train to Sion, then transfer to the Post bus to Nendaz or Veysonnaz (runs every hour up to 9.00 pm), or take the Theytaz bus as far as Thyon (runs four times a day).
Air
Geneva Airport 179km
Milan Airport 265km

© Jul **Rider** Joel Strecker

"ON THE PISTE BETWEEN TRACOUET AND NENDAZ THERE ARE COUNTLESS JUMPS AND NATURAL QUARTERS THOUGH YOU MAY SOMETIMES NEED TO DO A LITTLE SHAPING WITH A SHOVEL TO BRING THEM UP TO STANDARD."

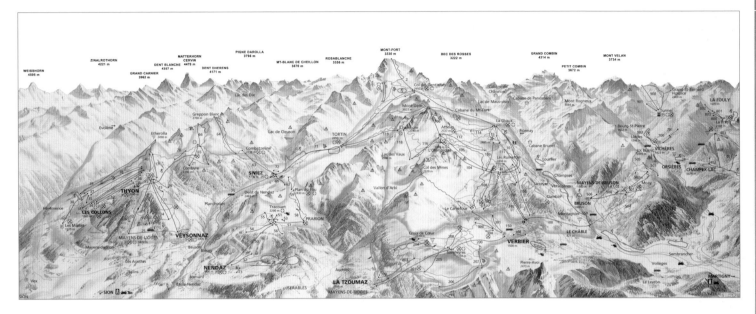

THE FOUR VALLEYS »

Intro_ The Four Valleys includes the region around Thyon which is where you'll find Thyon 2000, Les Collons 1800, Les Masses 1600, Veysonnaz, Nendaz and Verbier. Together, these resorts form one of the largest winter sports areas in Europe, with over 100 lifts and 400km of piste, offering both freeride and freestyle terrain par excellence. Even though Verbier is part of Les 4 Vallées, this guide also contains a dedicated listing for the resort.

ON THE MOUNTAIN »

Snow Reliability_ Les 4 Vallées holds the record for having the most snow cannons, although the north facing slopes ensure that the snow usually remains in good condition without having to resort to these. Snow reports can be obtained at the Ticketing and

Tourism Office
www.nendaz.ch
www.thyon-regio.ch
www.veysonnaz.ch
Lifts
Nendaz www.telenendaz.ch
Tel: +41 (0) 272 895200
Veysonnaz: +41 (0) 272 085544
Thyon: +41 (0) 272 811919

Lifts & Piste_ In Prinzte 4 Vallées you can purchase all-inclusive tickets that either cover all four areas or just a single one (Thyon/Veysonnaz, Nendaz or

Verbier). In Thyon and Veysonnaz you won't find long queues at the lifts. In Thyon you can ride the Collons chairlift, the Thyon 1800 tow lift, or the direct connection to the piste on Thyon 2000. In Veysonnaz you can ride the somewhat older gondola which leaves from the village, or the gondola over the Piste de l'Ours. Most of the lifts at Thyon or Veysonnaz are tow lifts. For those wanting to get to the Nendaz piste, there are two options - your car or the shuttle buses from Siviez. Be warned! The small tow lift behind the Plan du Fou, which takes you from Siviez back to Haute Nendaz, will be packed to the roof after 3.30pm. You'll have the same problem with the Noveli chairlift and the Greppon Blanc chairlift from Siviez to Veysonnaz and Thyon. During the Christmas and February holidays the Matzepiste is floodlit and stays open from 6.30pm until 10.00pm.

Freeriding_ Mayens de Riddes and Nendaz are good starting points for freeriders. For those of you who like high alpine terrain you'll find everything you need at Mt. Fort and Mt. Gelé - powder, couloirs and steeps. But avalanches are a real danger on all these slopes, so if you value your life, get information from a competent guide before entering one of these areas. On the summit of Thyon leaving from Etherolla

"THYON IS THE BEST SNOWPARK IN SWITZERLAND, SO YOU'LL COME ACROSS NUMEROUS PRO-RIDERS SUCH AS THE STRECKER BROTHERS, EMILIEN BADOUX AND DAVID LAMBERT, AS WELL AS HORDES OF PHOTOGRAPHERS. DON'T BE SHY IN THE PIPE - YOU COULD END UP ON FILM!"

you'll discover some excellent chutes, ending with tree runs finishing in an easterly direction. Crêtes in the direction of Veysonnaz offers similar terrain, but with more trees.

Freestyling_ The snowpark at Nendaz is ideal for both beginners and better riders alike. And on the piste between Tracouet and Nendaz there are countless jumps and natural quarters though you may sometimes need to do a little shaping with a shovel to bring them up to standard. The village of Nendaz also has riding possibilities, but the snowpark itself, which has been developed by experts, is at Thyon. The only criticism of the

park is that some of the bigger jumps and landings overlap each other. The park has two hips, a table with two kickers, two gaps (one small, one big), rails, and a quarter. The Snowpark is well used and maintained, receiving a reshape at least once a week. Plans have been put forward to build a snowskate-park for 2003. Thyon is the best snowpark in Switzerland, so you'll come across numerous pro-riders such as the Strecker Brothers, Emilien Badoux and David Lambert, as well as hordes of photographers. Don't be shy in the pipe - you could end up on film! Alongside the riding, you can chill out to reggae and enjoy a BBQ in the snowpark hut.

"THERE ARE 15 OR SO RESTAURANTS THAT FEED AND WATER THE MASSES. UNLIKE THE RESTAURANTS IN VERBIER, YOU'LL FIND THE FOOD HERE IS WITHIN A NORMAL PRICE RANGE. A GOOD PLACE TO EAT IN NENDAZ IS THE PLAN DU FOU"

THE FOUR VALLEYS
SWITZERLAND

© Pilitpo Berclaz **Rider** David Vincent

» **Carving**_For all our hardbooter friends, we recommend the Piste de l'Ours. An icy, rock hard, steep run. Sharpen those edges! In Nendaz we recommend the piste at Tracouet for some great carving. After expending all that energy riding you can then head to the Bars to rejuvenate: Try the Bouton d'Or in Veysonnaz, the Tipi and the Igloo on the Thyon piste, Luge or Joyce's in Collons, or Cactus Cantina (which serves snacks) and Bodega in Nendaz.

Beginners_The best place for beginners to head to is Thyon 2000. Snowboard lessons run by the Ecole Suisse de Ski in Thyon or Veysonnaz can be had between the Piste de l'Ours and the village,. Tel: +41 (0) 272 813330 www.ess-thyon.ch David Lambert can provide you with information about freestyle lessons in the snowpark. Baby lifts for use by beginners are located at Nendaz

and Tortin in Siviez .

Ecole Suisse de Ski
Tel: +41 (0) 272 882975
www.skinendaz.ch
Neige Adventure
Tel: +41 (0) 272 883131
www.nendaz-info.ch info@cactus.ch

Mountain Restaurants_There are 15 or so restaurants that feed and water the masses. Unlike the restaurants in Verbier, you'll find the food here is within a normal price range. A good place to eat in Nendaz is the Plan du Fou, which has a restaurant on the first floor and a self-service restaurant on the ground floor. Located between Nendaz and Veysonnaz is Les Chottes, an old style service restaurant which is well worth a visit. A great menu for a good price. Those of you based at Thyon/Veysonnaz will find a wide range to choose from.

IN THE TOWN »
Accommodation_Overnight accommodation in 4 Vallées costs on average around Sfr40 to Sfr50 (€27 to €34) per night. The Auberge des Cleusis, which has shared toilet and shower facilities, is in Nendaz: Tel +41 (0) 272 887880. The Auberge les Clèves offers overnight accommodation right next to the slopes. The Auberge des Collons is in Thyon: Tel+41 (0) 272 811296. For further information visit: www.nendaz.ch www.veysonnaz.ch www.thyon-region.ch .
Renting an apartment or a studio is often the best bet when it comes to accommodation, and can work out cheaper than hotels – especially if you pack 'em in.

Food_Every town has countless supermarkets and grocery stores. The supermarket down in the valley at the Tranbanta (Thyon) lift station, is very handy for shopping during the day. Non-

veggies will find food to their liking at the Metzgerei Mariettoz in Nendaz. Restaurants combining good prices with good service are: the Pinnochio in Thyon, Relais des Mayens in Veysonnaz, Pizzeria La Luge in Collons, the Pizzeria des Flambeaux, the Cantina, Mondial Food, and the Thai Food Take Away, all in Nendaz. Excellent, traditional dishes are served at La Cabane, again in Nendaz.

Nightlife_Every town has its own scene, but no town really differs from any other. The Cactus Saloon in Nendaz is one of the most popular bars and often puts on concerts and events. The Bar Bodega is well known for its generous measures. The Caribou or the Bal are considered the best places to stomp your feet. Joyce O'Sullivan's Pub in Thyon is a great spot for a few beers. For dancing, head to the Cosmos or the

"EVERY TOWN HAS ITS OWN SCENE, BUT NO TOWN REALLY DIFFERS FROM ANY OTHER. THE CACTUS SALOON IN NENDAZ IS ONE OF THE MOST POPULAR BARS AND OFTEN PUTS ON CONCERTS. THE BODEGA BAR IS WELL KNOWN FOR ITS GENEROUS MEASURES."

Underground (Collons). In Veysonnaz try Night Town or the Vague à l'me.

Other Activities_ The sports centre in Nendaz has a range of facilities, including an indoor climbing wall. An ice rink and an ice climbing tower are located in the village. You can also visit the thermal pools in Saillon, not too far from Les 4 Vallées.

LOCAL TIP »
Creppon Blanc has a great freeride run which heads down to the village of Mâche. In earlier days, it was a wild run only used by the locals. Today, the run is generally safe from the danger of avalanche and open to those who dare when the conditions are right. Take the shuttle bus to get back to Nendaz. Bus timetables and details about the availability of transfers can be obtained at the Télé-Thyon ticket office.

PROS & CONS »
+ Extensive stretches of off piste riding.
+ Well known snowpark - GMP.
+ Lift tickets are cheaper than at most other resorts in Switzerland.

− Resort is some distance away from the village itself.
− Impractical connections.
− Expensive parking.

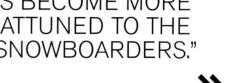

"OVER THE PAST FEW YEARS, THIS FORMER TRADITIONAL SKI RESORT HAS BECOME MORE AND MORE ATTUNED TO THE NEEDS OF SNOWBOARDERS."

ADELBODEN
SWITZERLAND

ADELBODEN »
www.adelboden.ch
Tourist office tel: +41 (0)336738080
Location: Adelboden
Population: 3500
Altitude: 1353m
linked resorts: Lenk

ON THE MOUNTAIN »
Season: December to April
Lifts
Vertical drop: 1353 −2357m
amount of lifts in total: 56
gondolas: 12
chair lifts: 9
drag lifts:35
Slopes
amount of prepared slopes in km: 200
runs w. snowmaking machines: 0
amount of easy runs: 24
amount of intermediate runs: 34
amount of advanced runs: 5
Facilities
night riding: yes
amount of halfpipes: 2
amount of funparks: 1
Heliboarding: no
Lift-ticket prices in Euro
Day: 33
week: 171
season: 490

SNOWBOARD TUITION »
Swiss Snowboard School
Tel: +41 (0)336733000
www.crazy-sports.ch

SNOWBOARD SHOPS »
Name: Crazy Sports Ltd.
Tel: +41 (0)336733000
www.crazy-sports.ch

GETTING THERE »
Car
Zürich - Adelboden: 184km
Zürich - A1 towards Bern - A6 towards Thun - Adelboden
Geneva - Adelboden: 230km
Geneva to Bern on the A1 - then the A12 (Interlaken -Thun) - as far as Adelboden
Milan - Adelboden: 341km
Milan - Chiasso (It/Switz) - Gottard Tunnel - Hergiswil - Brienzwiler - towards Thun/Interlaken - Spiez - Frutigen - Adelboden
Train
Take the Zürich to Bern service, change to the train for Brig and get off at Frutigen. Continue by the AFA bus to Adelboden.
Take the Geneva to Bern or Brig service, change at Brig and continue via Lötschberg to Frutigen
Swiss Rail Service www.sbb.ch
Air
Zürich Airport 189km
Geneva Airport 228 km

ADELBODEN »
Intro_ Adelboden is a variation on the German 'Adlerhorst' or 'Eagle's Nest', an apt name for a village that lies in a deep valley surrounded by high peaks. Over the past few years, this former traditional ski resort has become more and more attuned to the needs of snowboarders and Adelboden now offers a snowpark, good freeride terrain, and even a few spots for freestylers.

ON THE MOUNTAIN »
Snow reliability_ Despite its lower altitude -1800/1900m - the geographical formation of the surrounding mountains, especially the Wildstrubel (3,243m) and the Plaine-Morte-Glacier, form an impenetrable barrier to clouds. While this doesn't stop the snow from melting, it does protect it from direct sunlight which means the snow remains in better condition for longer. January and February are the best months for powder, while March is a better month for the pipe and park. In bad weather it isn't possible to return down to the village from Geils or Sillerenbühl. The run from Geils to Hahnenmoos is serviced by snow making machines, and is open the minute the season starts. Up-to-date information about local snow conditions can be obtained from the Tourist Office or from the lift operators.

Engstligenalp
+41 (0) 336 733 270
Chuenisbärgli
+41 (0) 336 731 447
Tschentenbahnen
+41 (0) 336 731 106
Sillerenbahnen
+41 (0) 336 733 568
www.silleren.ch

Lifts & Piste_ The resort at Adelboden comprises five sections - Engstligenalp, Tschenten, Chuenisbärgli, Sillerenbühl and Hahnenmoos. The winter sports village of Lenk is accessible via a connection over the Hahnenmoos, although you'll need to be careful because the route sometimes strays onto the mountain road. The trip on the gondola up to Sillerenbühl is amazingly long. An alternative to riding the gondola is to take the bus to Geils. Access to Sillerenbühl or Hahnenmoos is much easier from Geils. Engstligenalp and Tschenten, on

the other hand, can be accessed via the gondola, and in fact if you want to avoid the crowds this can sometimes be a better option, especially during the school holidays. Once you're there, getting back to Adelboden is not a problem, because even when there's not enough snow, you can always take the ski bus. One problem you might have, though, is trying to get back up to the top of the Sillerenbühl.

Freeriding_ Parts of all five sections of the resort often stay untracked. A number of lines take you towards the village, starting from the Sillerenbühl. These runs are relatively safe and travel over alpine meadows and through a small section of forest. There's a wicked slope just below the Laveygrat chairlift, but if you want to ride it untracked, you'll have to get up early in the morning. Leaving the summit station of the Luegli chairlift, you take a short hike and then you're rewarded with a great ride down into the Bütschi valley. This run has varying terrain combined with loads of little gullies. Because it faces north, the bowl-style Engstligenalp is an ideal spring location where the snow stays in relatively good condition. If you're willing to take some short hikes, you can access many more slopes that will provide you with some interesting descents. Tschenten, due to its flatter gradient and south-facing exposure, is not so good for freeriding, although there are still a few good lines, especially up along the ridge.

Freestyling_ The piste below the Laveygrat chairlift is ideal freestyle terrain. It's not groomed, but it's relatively steep and has a number of breaks in the slope, creating a perfectly natural funpark. The real funpark, Grand Masta Park, is situated at Hahnenmoos and lives up to its name. Three lines have been developed in the park: one for beginners (4 jumps and 1 hip); one for intermediate and more experienced riders (4 jumps); and one with rails (2 rails, 1 kink and a rainbow). The boys from GMP have also set up a little snack bar, which pumps out good tunes and is an ideal spot to chill or meet up with friends. The GMP crew are well motivated, organising contests

and jams every year. More info at www.gmp.here.de
   The pipe is located opposite the park and its size varies depending on the snow conditions. The lift company made a whole piste available when the park was built so that lines wouldn't overlap. Another perk is the tow lift that runs alongside the park. You won't, however, find any lifts close to the pipe, so you'll just have to hike it if you want to ride it. Finally, the lift company has built a boardercross park and a few smaller jumps on the Engstligenalp.

Carving_ The north-east facing Luegli-Gleis piste is ideally suited for carving: steep and hard. You'll discover similar runs at Sillerenbühl.

Beginners_ Beginners' courses are run at Hahnenmoos to take advantage of the easy gradient of the piste. Beginners and less experienced riders should also be able to handle the slopes on the Engstligenalp and the Tschenten. Sillerenbühl, however, requires more expertise.

Mountain Restaurants_ There are eight restaurants in Silleren and Hahnenmoos, one in Tschenten and six in Engstligenalp. The restaurant on the Sillerenbühl is built completely out of wood and includes a self-service section and a pizzeria. The self-service section dishes up good food at a reasonable price, as does the Geilsbrüggli in Geils.

IN THE TOWN »
Accommodation_ The town of Adelboden spreads out over both sides of the valley so you should check the location of your accommodation, otherwise you could end up having to trek a fair way into the town centre. Of the many attractive Pensions, our favourite is the Bodehüttli which is located directly on the piste (www.bodehuettli@bluewin.ch). A room here costs around 55 to 65 SF (€37 to €44) per night - Tel: +41 (0) 336 733 700. Coming a close second is the Ruedy-Hus on the edge of the village, where a room will set you back from 45 to 70 SF per night (€30 to €48). Also recommended is the Pension Skiheim, at 52 SF (€35) per night. Price includes breakfast, but there

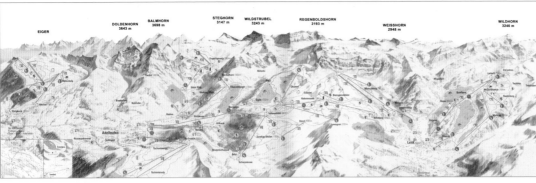

Rider Urs Kropfli | © Stefan Hunziker

are no shower facilities.
Tel: +41 (0) 336 731 044.
Email: pensionskiheim@bluewin.ch.
The cheapest option - apart from a
holiday apartment - is to book
shared accommodation, and there's
lots to choose from.

Food_ The supermarkets, grocery
stores and bakeries are all in the
middle of the village and are ideal
for a quick breakfast on your way
to the lift. The *Crystal* restaurant is
one of the cheaper options in
Adelboden and serves a range of
vegetarian dishes and a special menu
for low budget tourists. Pasta and
pizza are available at the *Trattoria-
Pizzeria Alfredo* (10% discount for
take-away). The *Alpenblick* offers
more substantial meals, including
specialities from the *Bern Oberland*
region, including Spätzli, Rösti and
meat dishes. The *Bären* restaurant
offers a similar menu and has an
extensive wine list.

Nightlife_ The Alpenrose is the

meeting place for Aprés Ski parties
or for a drink in the evening. Next
door to the *Party Pub* is a
Spielothek or games arcade where
you can play darts, billiards, pinball
or a variety of computer games.
Another alternative is the *Bern Bar*.
Younger people and music fans
meet at the Taverna club which has
a DJ or gig every weekend.

Other Activities_*Adelboden* has
a public swimming pool, a fitness
centre, and tennis, badminton and
squash courts. If you're looking for
a more regional experience, then
pay a visit to the mineral water
factory. The *Rex Kino* (cinema)
shows films in their original
language with English, German or
French subtitles.

LOCAL TIP »
A freeride tour from the Wildstrubel
is organised every Friday between
January and March (minimum 3
riders). You can also go ice
climbing from January to March.

"THE PISTE BELOW THE
LAVEYGRAT CHAIRLIFT IS
IDEAL FREESTYLE TERRAIN.
IT'S NOT GROOMED, BUT IT'S
RELATIVELY STEEP AND
HAS A NUMBER OF BREAKS
IN THE SLOPE, CREATING
A PERFECTLY NATURAL
FUNPARK."

© Christian Stadler

© Philipo Berclaz

ANDERMATT
SWITZERLAND

ANDERMATT »
www.andermatt.ch
tourist office tel: +41 (0)418871454
Location Andermatt
population:1500
altitude: 1444m

ON THE MOUNTAIN »
season: December – April
Lifts
Vertical drop: 1444 –2963m
amount of lifts in total: 12
gondolas: 2
chair lifts: 4
drag lifts: 6
Slopes
amount of prepared slopes in km: 56
runs w. snowmaking machines: 0
easy runs: 6.5 km
intermediate runs: 26.1 km
advanced runs: 23.4 km
Facilities
night riding: no
amount of halfpipes: 2
amount of funparks: -
Heliboarding: no
Lift-ticket prices in Euro
day: 36
week: 130
season: 450
SNOWBOARD TUITION »
Skischule Andermatt
Tel: +41 (0)418871240
www.skischuleandermatt.ch
Mountain Guides:
Tel: +41 (0)418831728
www.alpine-sportschule.ch

SNOWBOARD SHOPS »
Snowlimit Boards
Tel: +41 (0)418870614
Snowvirus
Tel: +41 (0)418870866

GETTING THERE »
Car
Zürich - Andermatt: 109km
Zürich - A3 Chur - Richterswil -
Gotthard/Altdorf - A2 Gotthard/Lugano -
Göschenen - Andermatt
Geneva - Andermatt: 348km
Geneva A1 - Bern A1 - Zürich A1
Milan - Andermatt 181km
Milan - Chiasso (It/Swiss) - Gottard Tunnel -
Göschenen - Andermatt
Train
From Zürich to Göschenen, then change
trains to Andermatt. From Geneva to Zürich
or Brig then take the Andermatt train.
Air
Zürich Airport: 145km
Geneva Airport: 345km

ANDERMATT »
Intro_Andermatt is situated in
Kanton Uri, home of the most
famous freedom fighter in Swiss
history, Wilhelm (William) Tell. This
small, traditional village lies at the
foot of the Gemsstock, a mountain
famous for its dream powder runs.
Those looking for kicking parties
and kick-ass kickers are in the
wrong place. However, freeriders
and mountain lovers treasure this
part of the world.

ON THE MOUNTAIN »
Snow reliability_The *Ursern* valley
is well protected from the wind and
stays relatively cold throughout the
whole winter. This allows the snow
conditions to remain in an excellent
state right through to the end of
the season. The geographical
formation of the surrounding
mountain range encourages low-
pressure systems. These sweep in
from all directions, build up around
the resort and drop their precious
cargoes of snow. With the
exception of the *Nätschen/Gütsch*
area, the slopes all face north. In
spite of this, the sun still seems to
find its way through and into the
valley. The season at *Andermatt* is
especially long, beginning in
November and ending in the early
part of May. Avalanche and weather
reports are posted up at every lift
station and can also be obtained
from: Tel: +41 (0) 418 870 181
The lift company also provides
reports - *Nätschen/Gütsch*:
+41 (0) 418 870 366

Lifts & Piste_*Andermatt* is divided
into two main sections, one around
Gemsstock and one around
Gütsch/Nätschen. The two areas
are relatively different and are not
linked to each other. Hospental
and Realp are two smaller areas
that are accessible by using the
Furka-Oberalp lift. The *Gemsstock*
(summit station: 2963m) has nice
terrain, excellent for freeriding. The
groomed runs can be reached by
taking the gondola, and if you
continue up on the bigger
gondola you'll end up on the
summit. The middle area is
serviced by a further chairlift and
two tow lifts. The bigger gondolas
can very quickly get overcrowded
at the height of the season. At
these times, it's often better to stay
around the Hospental area, where
you'll find similar riding conditions
but with fewer people. Despite the

fact that there's only one tow lift
and one chairlift, you'll generally
find that you can reach the top
much quicker. This is a favourite
area amongst the locals during the
busy period. *Gütsch/Nätschen* is
the place for families because the
runs are easier. People here don't
seem to get the most out of their
lift tickets – it's a pretty relaxed
environment. You'll only find one
tow lift servicing Realp.

Freeriding_*Gemsstock* is an ideal
location for freeriding. Following
fresh snowfall, next to the runs
travelling to *Gurschen* (middle
station), there are excellent, open,
steep off-piste runs. But a word of
caution! Wait until the chute has
been inspected by the ski patrol
before you go riding here. You can
get a map of the resort from the
Tourist Office and this will show
you where to find some
signposted off piste runs. These
runs, though, will not necessarily be
monitored by the ski patrol, so be
careful! The first run is known as
the *Oberer Geissberg*. Turn right
from *Gemsstock* onto the glacier
piste, towards the *Lutersee* tow lift
bottom station. The descent takes
you through rock faces onto steep
slopes. The second run is known
as the *Felsental*. Heading right
from *Gemsstock* along the *Sonnen*

piste towards the pipe, drop into
the small hollow. You can vary the
run by remaining above the hollow,
where it's not so steep and more
open. Be careful not to ride directly
beneath the avalanche zone. The
runs end at *Hospental,* as you
come out of the tree runs. The
longest route, involving a drop in
elevation of around 1490m and
stretching for more than 13km, is
the *Guspital* run. Heading south
from *Gemsstock* along the flat
section, you'll need to climb up to
Gefallenlücke. From here you can
descend into the long valley which
makes its way towards the lake.
Make sure you keep riding left
from the waterfall. This run also
finishes at *Hospental*. For safety's
sake, you should always ride with a
qualified guide or well informed
locals. The added advantage is that
this will allow you to enjoy the
terrain to the full and discover all of
its secrets. When *Gemsstock* is all
tracked out, you can still find
interesting lines in *Hospental*. Ideal
runs with some good couloirs
await you.

Freestyling_The freeride terrain is
definitely the main attraction at
Andermatt. For freestylers, there's
a pipe at *Gemsstock* on the
St. Anna glacier. Unfortunately, it's
not serviced by a lift, so a good

"THIS SMALL, TRADITIONAL
VILLAGE LIES AT THE FOOT
OF THE GEMSSTOCK, A
MOUNTAIN FAMOUS FOR ITS
DREAM POWDER RUNS."

"THE URSERN VALLEY IS WELL
PROTECTED FROM THE WIND
AND STAYS RELATIVELY COLD
THROUGHOUT THE WHOLE
WINTER. THIS ALLOWS THE
SNOW CONDITIONS TO REMAIN
IN AN EXCELLENT STATE RIGHT
THROUGH TO THE END OF
THE SEASON."

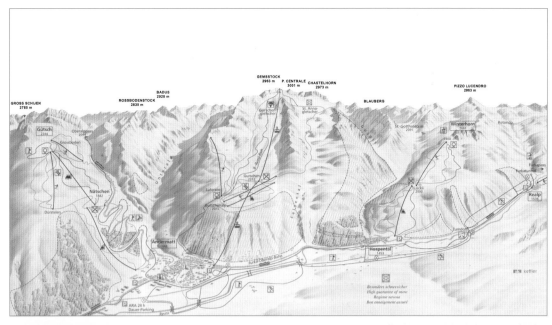

© Phillipo Berdaz

beds and cooking facilities about two kilometres out of *Andermatt* in the village of Hospental. www.youthhostel.ch Email: hospental@youthhostel.ch

Food_You'll find a few shops and a Co-op mini market in Andermatt itself. Light meals and snacks can be had at the *Tea Room*. A pizza and salad will cost you around 10 to 20 SF. (€6.80 to €13.50) at the restaurant *Sypcher*. Other good options include the *City Bar* and the *Snack Pot*. For those of you looking to fill your belly but not empty your wallet, head to the *Hotel Schweizerhof* for Italian; the *Gasthaus Altkirch* for Röstis; or the *Gasthof Ochsen* for a good fondue.

Nightlife_*Andermatt* is a quiet, small, mountain village and what nightlife there is is restricted to the weekends and school holidays. Aprés-ski can be found at the *Piccadilly Pub* (billiards and darts) or at the restaurant/bar *Spycher*. Later in the evening people head to the *Barry Bar, La Curva,* the *City Bar* or the *Barokko Bar*. But in the end everyone ends up at the Gotthard, where the local DJ works his turntables until the early morning.

Other Activities_A fast sledding run can be found at *Nätschen/ Gütsch*. But don't go too fast or you'll end up on the railway track! A fitness centre, sauna and solarium can also be found in the area. To really relax, you can take a trip down to the Roman Hot Springs at Göschenen, approximately 6 km from *Andermatt*.

LOCAL TIP »
Andermatt is blessed with some great backcountry routes. One of the best is the tour from Gemsstock out towards Gotthard. After a couple of hours snow- shoeing, you'll be rewarded by an amazing panoramic view across untouched country before descending a quality run.

warm up hike is required. A snowpark has been built at *Gurschen,* but it's obvious the park and the boardercross course have been built by people who've never been on a snowboard. If you're still looking for a freestyle kick, you'll find something to shape at *Felsental* and *Hospental*.
Carving_The piste at *Gemsstock,* made famous by the 70's ski star Bernard Russi, is ideal for carvers. The run is steep, hard and long. The downhill run on the other side of *Gemsstock* won't disappoint those looking for a challenge either.

Beginners_Beginners will find the conditions at *Gütsch* ideal because the runs are quite easy there. There's only one ski school in

Andermatt - the Swiss Ski School.

Information
Tel: +41 (0) 418 871 240 or www.skischuleandermatt.ch

Mountain Restaurants_*Gemsstock, Gütsch/Nätschen* and *Hospental* are all well catered for by restaurants and snack bars. The restaurant at *Gurschen (Gemsstock),* for example, serves a range of local sausages and there are two set menus every day, one for 18 SF (€12) and the other for 12 SF (€8).

IN THE TOWN »
Accommodation_Private houses offering bed & breakfast are

probably your cheapest option for accommodation. Expect to fork out around 30 to 50 SF (€20 to €34) per person per night. A list of rented accommodation and hotels can be found at www.andermatt.ch. The Pension Bonetti is located close to the Gemsstock gondola. For half board in a holiday apartment you can expect to pay around 50 to 70 SF (€34 to €48) Tel: +41 (0) 418 871 960 www.bonettiag.ch
   Another option is the Gasthof Tell right in the middle of the village - Tel: +41 (0) 418 871 520 www.gasthaus-tell@bluwin.ch Or try the rustic Herberge Sternen Tel: +41 (0) 418 871 130 sternen.andermatt@bluewin.ch There's a youth hostel with 65

PROS & CONS »

+ Four ideal areas promising variations in terrain.
+ Good snow, thanks to the elevation.
+ Excellent halfpipe in the middle of town.
+ Great nightlife plus lots of other activities.

– Almost a city atmosphere.
– Overcrowded during the usual holiday periods.
– Relatively ugly architecture.

"BECAUSE OF ITS ELEVATION, STEEP GRADIENTS AND THE UNDERLYING SCREE, DAVOS IS CONSIDERED TO BE MORE DANGEROUS THAN MANY OTHER SWISS RESORTS.."

DAVOS
SWITZERLAND

DAVOS »
www.davos.ch
Tourist office tel: +41 (0)814152121
Location: Davos
Population:13000
Altitude: 1540m
linked resorts: Jakobshorn,
Parsenn/Gotschna, Pischna, Rinerhorn

ON THE MOUNTAIN »
Season: November – end of April
Lifts
vertical drop: 1540-2844 m
amount of lifts in total: 54
gondolas: 15
chairlifts: 10
T-bars: 29
Slopes
amount of prepared slopes: 320 km
runs w. snowmaking machines: 30
easy runs: 96 km
intermediate runs: 128 km
advanced runs: 96 km
Facilities
night riding: yes
amount of halfpipes: 2
amount of funparks:1
Heliboarding: -
Lift-ticket prices in Euro
1/2 day: 27
day: 42
week: 210
season: 646

SNOWBOARD TUITION »
Schweizer Schneesportschule Davos
Tel: +41 (0)814162454
www.ssd.ch
Top Secret Snowboardschule
Tel: +41 (0)814134043
www.topsecretdavos.ch

SNOWBOARD SHOPS »
Top Secret Snowboard-Shop
Tel: +41 (0)814134043
www.topsecretdavos.ch

GETTING THERE »
Car
Zurich - Davos: 150 km
Zurich - A4 towards Chur - A13 exit:
Landquart - Davos
Innsbruck - Davos: 183 km
Innsbruck - Landeck - through Pfunds
(Aut/Ch) - Davos
Milan (Mailand) - Davos: 238 km
Milan - A8 towards Varese (It/Ch) - A2
towards San Bernadino - A13 towards
St.Moritz/Davos - through Suraya - Davos
Air
Zürich Airport 158 km
Innsbruck Airport 180 km

© Stefan Hunziker **Rider** Martina Tscharner

DAVOS »
Intro_ Davos is a real snowboard realm that can cater for all tastes, centrally located between four riding areas situated at such a high elevation that good snow conditions are ensured. On the Jakobshorn you might well run across the ISF Finals or the Snowboard Jam contests. The off piste terrain is held in high regard by many freeriders and the perfectly prepared super pipe near the Jakobshorn base station in the middle of town is a dream for all freestylers.

ON THE MOUNTAIN »
Snow Reliability_ Davos has an elevation of 1560m and its highest point is the summit of the Weissfluh at 2844m. The town's position, north of the main Alpine range, ensures good snow conditions. In fact its position is so ideal it's the home of the Swiss Avalanche Research Institute. Before we go any further,

though,be warned: *Davos is an extreme avalanche danger zone.* There are avalanches every year at Davos and every season they claim a number of lives. Because of its elevation, steep gradients and the underlying scree, Davos is considered to be more dangerous than many other Swiss resorts.

If the snowfalls don't match expectations, the resort is equipped with snow making facilities to guarantee fun on the piste. The winter season starts at the end of November and goes on until around the end of April. The best time to visit Davos is generally between January and March, but saying that, it can also be great in December or April depending on how much snow there's been. Up-to-date snow and avalanche reports can be found in English, German and Italian by visiting www.slf.ch.

Lifts_ The biggest of the four

Davos areas is *Parsenn* which is connected via a long traverse to *Gotschna (near Klosters and the neighbouring Madrisa)*. The resort is equipped with modern lifts and the crowds are evenly distributed throughout so generally speaking you won't be faced with too long a wait in a queue to the access lifts. In two of the areas outside Davos, *Pischa* and *Rinerhorn,* you'll find a more relaxed atmosphere and fewer people. The short bus ride is rewarded by two great areas containing lots of cornices and lots of variation in the piste.

The *Jakobshorn* is generally accessed by the lift which starts from the base station, although when it's really busy it's probably better to take the chairlift which is located to the right of the halfpipe. Most of the lifts are very comfortable chairlifts, which is why so few people use the *Brämabüehl* T-bar. Those with strong legs and »

"THE TOWN'S POSITION, NORTH OF THE MAIN ALPINE RANGE, ENSURES GOOD SNOW CONDITIONS. IN FACT ITS POSITION IS SO IDEAL IT'S THE HOME OF THE SWISS AVALANCHE RESEARCH INSTITUTE."

© Christian Stadler **Rider** Xaver Hoffmann

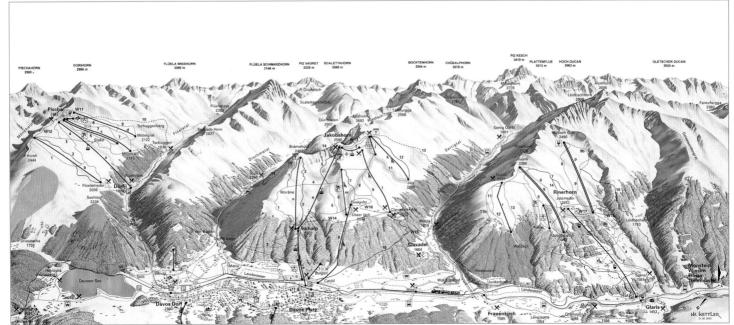

"THE PIPE IS SHAPED TWICE A WEEK WHICH MEANS IT CAN BE USED THROUGHOUT THE WHOLE DAY AND EVEN AT NIGHT SOMETIMES. IT'S STEEP, DEEP BUT ONCE YOU'RE USED TO RIDING IN IT, YOU'LL FLY."

DAVOS
SWITZERLAND

© Christian Stadler **Rider** Dani Constandache

» the stamina will be able to get to the top of some nice variable slopes that are ideal for freeriding and natural freestyling.

Freeriding_ All of the mountains around Davos offer great freeriding terrain, but none is without its dangers. In *Parsenn,* you'll discover challenging couloirs at the summit of the *Weissgluh.* On the *Jakobshorn,* the north run (Nordabfahrt) is worth a ride, while those looking for tree runs should head to *Gotschna* and take the valley run down into *Klosters.* You'll find numerous off piste and touring possibilities in all of the areas around Davos, of course, but these require a lot of experience and local knowledge of the terrain. It's very easy to lose your way and ride into

an extreme avalanche danger area or even get to a point where you can't go any further. Many slopes in Davos start off by being open and with a normal gradient, but soon change into a tighter, steeper run. You should only go riding off piste with a guide or with an experienced freerider from Davos. There are some off piste runs which are signposted and only open when the Avalanche Commission thinks they're safe enough to use.

Freestyling_ The *Jakobshorn* is the place to be if you're a freestyler. At the foot of the Bolgenhang there's an impressive superpipe. The pipe is shaped twice a week which means it can be used throughout the whole day and even at night sometimes. It's steep, deep

but once you're used to riding in it, you'll fly. Even when you come across a lot of Pros and very good riders, you'll have no problem riding on in as a beginner without feeling that you don't belong. Thierry Brunner, twice runner-up World Cup rider says, "My favourite pipe is at Davos. It rocks, there aren't too many people and there's a restaurant close by."

A smaller fun park and natural terrain for freestyling can also be found in the upper section of the *Jakobshorn.* The best cornices and windlips can be found at *Pischa* and *Rinerhorn.* Depending on the snow, snowparks can generally be found in both areas.

Carving_ Most runs are well prepared making them very suitable

for carving. Carving on Parsenn is child's play - wide, flat and smooth as a baby's bottom. If you start to get bored with the piste, go riding on the more variable Jakobshorn runs, which hang a little towards the right.

Beginners_ The best place for beginners is the *Bolgenhang,* next to the half pipe. When you can turn your board left and right, we'd recommend riding on *Parsenn.* The runs back down the valley are not suitable for beginners, but you can take the lift to ride back down.

Mountain Restaurants_ Wherever you go, you'll find enough to eat. On the *Jakobshorn,* there's a *Jätzhütte,* where the dish of the day is cooked

"MY BEST OFF PISTE RUN IN DAVOS IS STILL
THE TEUFI. THIS RUN HEADS DOWN INTO A
SMALL SIDE VALLEY FROM THE SUMMIT OF
THE JAKOBSHORN."

224 | **225**
DAVOS
SWITZERLAND

© Stefan Hunziker **Rider** Martina Tscharner

© Stefan Hunziker **Rider** Florian Weisner

in a giant frying pan. For good pizza, go down to the *Chalet Güggel*. The *Parsennhütte* in *Parsenn* is a very popular restaurant…
Prices are relatively high everywhere on the mountain.

IN THE TOWN »
Accommodation_Davos has hotels and pensions to suit every purse. *The Snowboard Palace* (tel: +41 (0) 814 149020) is good value at €84.00 for bed and breakfast and a two day ski pass. Or check out the *Snowboardhotel Bolgenschanze* - www.bolgenschanze.ch. More info at www.davos.ch.

Food_You'll find all of the bigger supermarkets in Davos and groceries cost as much here as

they do anywhere else in Switzerland. The main street is full of restaurants - all next door to each other. A visit to the *Restaurant Scala* or the *Restaurant Grand Cafè* is worth the effort. And there's even a McDonalds directly opposite the *Parsennbahn* base station. But if you're looking for good coffee and a *Gipfeli* (better than a Big Mac!), try the *Cafè/Bäckerei Weber* next door to McDonalds.

Nightlife_Snowboarders are generally hangin' out at the *Bolgenplaza* - www.bolgenplaza.ch , next to the halfpipe. You'll find live concerts or known DJ's creating the sound most weekends at the *Bolgenschanze*. Music styles vary from Punk, HipHop, Funk and Drum'n Base. Other happenin' bars

include the *Chämibar* or the Ex-Bar, which are both open until six in the morning. Don't bother with the *Cabanna* or the *Carlos Bar*. Those living in Davos and who are into Hardcore/Punk should take a look inside the *Val Halla*.

Other Activities_Ice hockey fans should try to catch a game featuring the Swiss champions, HCD - Hockey Club Davos. There are lots of sled runs to choose from, excellent cross country skiing trails, an indoor swimming pool, indoor tennis courts, cinema and casino.

LOCAL TIP »
Martina Tscharner, born in Davos, 1999 world halfpipe champion, now concentrating

more on freeriding_"My best off piste run in Davos is still the Teufi. This run heads down into a small side valley from the summit of the Jakobshorn. From the top, follow the path and then drop left. The first slope is steep, a really good drop. After the drop there are a couple of good cornices to jump off and then lower down you pass through the tree runs. It's a signposted run and you need to follow it, otherwise you end up in the shit and not in the relaxed restaurant. In the restaurant you can eat really well and then catch a bus back to Davos. The bus costs around SFR 5 (€3.45). The best time to ride the Teufi is in the morning, but look at the shields before you drop in, as it can be closed off."

"ONCE A SLEEPY SWISS VILLAGE, OVER THE PAST FEW YEARS ENGELBERG HAS TRANSFORMED ITSELF INTO A FREERIDING MECCA."

ENGELBERG
SWITZERLAND

ENGELBERG»
www.engelberg.ch
tourist office tel: +41 (0)639 77 77
location: Engelberg
population: 3300
altitude: 1050m

ON THE MOUNTAIN »
season: December – June
Lifts
vertical drop: 1050–3060m
amount of lifts in total: 24
cable car: 1
gondolas: 7
chair lifts: 5
drag lifts: 11
Slopes
amount of prepared slopes: 82 km
runs w. snowmaking machines: 5
easy runs: 25 km
intermediate runs: 55 km
advanced runs: 2 km
Facilities
night riding: 2
amount of halfpipes: 1
amount of funparks: 1
heliboarding: -
Lift-ticket prices in CHF
day: 49,-
week: 240,-
season: 470

SNOWBOARD TUITION »
Skischule Engelberg Titlis AG
Tel: + 41 (0)416395454
www.skischule-engelberg.ch

SNOWBOARD SHOPS »
Okay Snowboard- und Telemark-Shop
Tel: +41 (0)416370777

GETTING THERE »
Car
Milan - Engelberg 247km
Milan - A8 towards Lugano - Como (It/Swiss) - A2 towards San Bernadino - Gotthard Pass - via Stans - Engelberg
Zurich - Engelberg 88km
Zurich - A4 towards Gotthard Lucerne 20km - A14 towards Gotthard Lucerne 14km - A2 to Engelberg
Munich - Engelberg 398km
Munich - towards Lindau (Ger/Aut) - towards St. Gallen (Au/Switz) - Zurich Ost - towards Luzern - A2 to Emmen exit - via Stans - Engelberg
Air
Zurich Airport 99km
Bern Airport 148km

© Stefan Hunziker **Rider** Thomas Wyder

ENGELBERG »
Intro_ Once a sleepy Swiss village, over the past few years Engelberg has transformed itself into a freeriding Mecca. Close to Lucerne, this resort was first discovered by Scandinavian telemarkers. Telemarkers, skiers and snowboarders of all nationalities can now be regularly seen blazing trails through Engelberg's challenging and playful terrain. Snowboard freestylers also arrive in the summer for the yearly Ice Ripper Summer Camp up on the Titlis glacier.

The village itself has a cosy little centre, which is so nice and relaxed in the low season that you can say goodnight to the foxes and rabbits when the sun goes down. But as soon as the snow begins to fall, the masses begin to arrive - and not only to go hard on the mountain…

ON THE MOUNTAIN »
Snow reliability_ The snow conditions are generally very good, thanks to the high altitude. Engelberg is 1050m above sea level and the summit station is 3020m. The 15 snow making machines - in use between 1st

November through to 28th of February - guarantee good conditions on-piste.

Snow Information
Engelberg-Titlis Tourist Office
Tel: +41 (0) 41 639 77 77
Email: tourist.centre@engelberg.ch
www.engelberg.ch or www.titlis.ch
Email: titlis@titlis.ch

Weather and piste info
Tel: +41 (0) 41 637 01 01

Lifts/Piste_ The six-person gondola departs from Engelberg and travels through the Gerschnialp up to Trübsee, where the rest of the lifts branch out. On your left, you'll see the main resort area of Stand-Titlis. Taking the chairlift above Trübsee brings you to the lower part of the Jochpass. This is where you'll find Engslenalp, a popular area with snowboarders because of the park and the natural kickers which litter the area. The beginning of the 2002/03 season should see the phasing out of drag lifts, the plan being to replace these with nine brand new chairlifts. A connecting lift from Jochpass across to Stands is also

in the planning stages.

The crowds spread themselves out well and it's not likely you'll have to queue for a lift. The best time to visit is definitely the end of the season, when snowboarders seem to dominate the resort.

Day tickets are expensive, and weekends even more so. The only positive thing is the hourly reduction rates. Tip: The Spring season price (Mar - Jun) comes down to 150 SFr (Kids 90 SFr) - a much more reasonable price.

Freeriding_A good off piste run starts from the Titlis summit station. Ride over the glacier and down to Tr_bsee - a 1200m drop in elevation. As you look down at the tracks from the Rotair lift you'll quickly see this is no secret run, however. The sign posted piste normally takes you via Rotegg, but on a good powder day there'll be more people riding the glacier than the piste. When you see the glacier with its big wide powder fields, assorted cliffs and steep drops, you'll understand why. Don't be too cocky though, this run has claimed more than its fair share of victims. Consider making your first

"IN MAY 2002, WE HAD OVER A METRE OF FINE POWDER, RIGHT DOWN TO TRÜBSEE - 1800M - AND THERE WAS NO ONE HERE! AFTER RIDING ALL DAY, WE DROVE DOWN TO LUCERNE AND CHILLED OUT ON THE BANKS OF THE LAKE. IT'S PERFECT HERE!"

226 | 227
ENGELBERG
SWITZERLAND

run with a guide or a local.

On the Jochpass side, you'll find some great freeriding terrain. The run from Jochstock summit station, ending at Tr_bsee, is a fantastic descent, but you could be faced with a few massive, and dangerous, rock faces. It pays to plan your lines before running them.

One final tip: try the glacial descent from the Galtiberg, which goes from Titlis all the way down to the valley. It's over 2000m in elevation and is definitely worth doing.

Freestyling_ There's a freestyle area on the Jochpass, where you'll find an average halfpipe and funpark. The Engstlen run may offer more freestyle terrain from the 2002/03 season onwards.

A pipe and park (as well as a snowskate park) can be found on the Titlis glacier in the summer. The pipe is shaped every day during the summer camp period, and is well looked after by 10 camp shapers. Check it out at www.iceripper.com

Carving_ Good carving pistes can be found between Stand and Trübsee.

Beginners_ There's a slope that's ideal for beginners next to the Gerschnialp lift. The Jochpass area is not recommended for beginners, though, as it is relatively tight and steep. The south side of Stand is a better option for those riding in the main area of Titlis- Stand.

Snowboard lessons
www.skischule-engelberg.ch
Email: info@skischule-engelberg.ch

Mountain Restaurants_ There's a wide choice of restaurants here, but as is the case in the rest of Switzerland, they don't come cheap. The best prices/service are at El Burro Loco Restaurant (TexMex Restaurant/Bar) at the Station Stand. It's a bit off the beaten track, there's no sunny terrace, but it does have a great view of the glacier, good food and fair prices. Other restaurants include:

Titlis
Panaroma Restaurant Titlis - self-service and à-la-carte, - Titlis summit lift station. *Pizzeria Mamma Mia* - Titlis summit lift station. *Ofenbar* - Titlis summit station. *Golden Bamboo* - Asian food, Titlis

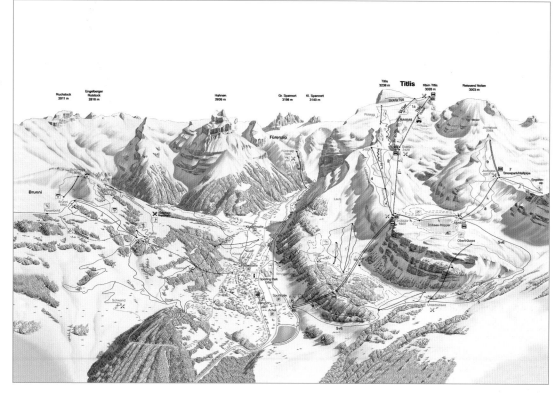

summit station, (only open in winter). *Sunnäblüemli Bar* - cool drinks and snacks, valley station Iceflyer, (only open in summer). *Restaurant Stand* - with terrace in the sun, Station Stand. *Stern Bar* - open air or under a canopy, drinks and snacks, Station Stand.

Trübsee
Sporthotel Trübsee - Pizzeria, self-service and bar, Station Trübsee. *Alpstübli* - self service, Trübsee. *Bärghuis Jochpass* - sunny terrace, self service, Jochpass station. *Jochpass Stübli* - bar, comfortable atmosphere, noble a-la-carte menu. *Jochpass Zelt* (tent) - snacks and drinks. *Restaurant Untertrübsee* - Meringue turn, Untertrübsee. *Restaurant Ritz* - Gerschnialp Linie 8 and Salamon Station.

IN THE TOWN »
Accommodation_ Tight budget: Jugi Engelberg -
Tel: +41 (0) 41 637 12 92
www.familienherberge.ch
Email: info@familienherberge.ch

Mid price range:
Hotel Bellevue
Tel: +41 (0) 41 639 68 68

bellevue.engelberg@bluewin.ch

Astronomical:
Hotel Terrace
Tel: +41 (0) 41 639 66 66
www.terrace.ch Email:
terrace@terrace.ch

Food_ Everything a self-caterer needs to survive can be found either in the Migros Co-op Supermarket in Klosterstrasse, or in the village store in Dorfstrasse. There are plenty of restaurants here, from takeaways to traditional village guesthouses, where you must sample the roasted cheese Röstis. You can down a few beers and tuck into a bowl of Mexican chow after a hard day's snowboarding opposite the train station at the Yucatan.

Nightlife_ If you can't wait till you get back to town, stop for a drink or two at the Salamon Station next to the Engelberg valley lift station. The Yucatan, opposite the train station, is the usual meeting place for snowboarders. Happy hour is from 5pm to 6pm. Fine girls are hard to find, but later in the evening...

Tip for the boys: At around 2am the girls working at the local hotels start to show up at the Spindel or Yucatan - so hang on in there!

Other Activities_ There's a skatepark at the Sportplatz Wyden, but it's not all that good. For those on the adrenaline trip, head to Adventure Engelberg and try a spot of rafting, bungee jumping, and extreme climbing, amongst other things.
www.adventure-engelberg.ch
Don't forget there's also a casino!

LOCAL TIP »
Flo & Claus Zimmermann - founders of the Ice Ripper Summer Camps_"During our first days in the resort, we underestimated the freeriding potential of this area. But now, after a few seasons living here, we've discovered that the area is a freeride paradise. In May 2002, we had over a metre of fine powder, right down to Trübsee - 1800m - and there was no one here! After riding all day, we drove down to Lucerne and chilled out on the banks of the lake. It's perfect here!"

PROS & CONS »

+ An excellent superpipe, always well groomed.
+ Interesting freeride terrain.

– The south west facing slopes mean that the snow won't last as long as in some resorts (but it's sunny).
– The lower elevation means a shorter season.

"A DIRECT VIEW OF THE EIGER AND ITS FAMOUS NORTH FACE."

GRINDELWALD
SWITZERLAND

GRINDELWALD »
www.grindelwald.ch
tourist office tel: +41 (0)338541212
location: Grindelwald
population: 4250
altitude: 1035m
linked resorts: First, Kleine Scheidegg, Männlichen, Muerren-Schilthorn

ON THE MOUNTAIN »
season: mid November to end of April
Lifts
vertical drop: 960 – 2971m
amount of lifts in total: 44
gondolas: 2
chair lifts: 16
drag lifts: 14
Slopes
amount of prepared slopes: 213 km
runs w. snowmaking machines: 34
amount of easy runs: 28
amount of intermediate runs: 37
amount of advanced runs: 14
Facilities
night riding:
amount of halfpipes: 2
amount of funparks: 3
heliboarding: yes
Lift-ticket prices in Euro
1/2 day: 28.60
day: 37.40
week: 212
season: 544

SNOWBOARD TUITION »
Private Ski & Snowboardschule
Tel: +41 (0)338533353
www.grindelwald.ch/buri-sport
Schweizer Ski und Snowboardschule Kleine Scheidegg
Tel: + 41 (0)338551545

SNOWBOARD SHOPS »
Backdoor
Tel: +41 (0)338530970

GETTING THERE »
Car
Zürich - Grindelwald 140km
Zürich - A4 to Chur - A14 to Lucerne - A2 to Sarnen/Interlaken - Grindelwald
Geneva - Grindelwald 243m
Geneva A1 - Bern A1 - Interlaken/Thun A12 - Interlaken – Grindelwald
Milan - Grindelwald 276km
Milan - Chiasso (It/Swiss) - Gotthard Tunnel - Wassen exit - via Brienzwiler - Interlaken Sud exit - Interlaken - Grindelwald
Train
Train to Zürich or Bern, then on to Interlaken, where you change for the Grindelwald train. Train from Geneva to Bern, then to Interlaken and Grindelwald.
Air
Zürich Airport 153km
Geneva Airport 241km

GRINDELWALD »
Intro_The small village of Grindelwald is surrounded by picturesque mountain scenery, including a direct view of the Eiger and its famous North Face. The views alone make Grindelwald a worthwhile place to visit. Add a well-prepared superpipe and great variation in the freeriding terrain, and Grindelwald has to be one of the top spots in the Berner highlands.

ON THE MOUNTAIN »
Snow reliability_Grindelwald is fortunate that the surrounding mountains of the Eiger, Mönch, and Jungfrau form a barrier which holds up the weather coming in from the north. The massive mountains rise up to 4000m and overshadow the resort itself, which is situated between 1034m and 2501m. Snow problems arise because of the high temperatures and the warmer winds which melt the snow, especially later on in the season. The middle section of the resort is well equipped with snow making facilities. The best powder months are January and February.

Snow reports/Piste conditions
First: +41 (0) 338 545 054
www.gofirst.ch
Kleine Scheidegg:
+41 (0) 338 554 433
or at the tourist office

Lifts & Piste_Grindelwald is made up of two unconnected resorts - First and Kleine Scheidegg. The valley lift station serving First is located at Oberdorf. The gondola transports you past two mid-stations on its way to the top. During high season, it's better to get an early night and be at the lift before the masses. Long lift queues are not unusual. The other resort, Kleine Scheidegg-Männlichen, is accessible from either the lift at Unterdorf, which feeds directly to Kleine Scheidegg, or with the longer Europa gondola to Männlichen. The summit stations are both located at the highest points of the sectors, making heading from one side to the other simple. You'll also find a connection to the neighbouring village of Wengen. If you do end up here, make sure you leave time to head back to Kleine Scheidegg or Männlichen.

Freeriding_At First, you'll find many excellent lines leaving from Schreckfeld, Bort or Hohwald, which head down to the village. These lines extend over big areas of moguls and at times through the trees. When the middle section is tracked out, you can run a few lines between upper areas of Oberjoch or Schilt to First and Unterlager. The runs here are a little steeper, with a few grippy couloirs requiring a higher level of riding expertise. In any case, you should always heed the warnings put out by the ski patrol because the south west facing flanks can be dangerous. Kleine Scheidegg/Männlichen provide pure freeriding. The runs under the chairlifts from Männlichen and Gummi are steep and include a few cornices. You should stay away from the forest at Kleinen Schiedegg and Männlichen. They're out of bounds, and with good reason. The gradient and the more mature trees combine forces to create a danger that can be easily underestimated. If you have to

travel through the forests, only do it with people who have good local knowledge.

Freestyling_Natural freeriding terrain with rolling hills and natural pipes can be found at Schreckfeld in First. The snowpark is on the summit at Oberjoch. There are three rideable lines – one for more experienced riders (3 tables and 1 hip), an easier line with 3 jumps, and a line with small jumps for beginners. The jumps are all well shaped, the only problem being that the terrain is relatively flat, so don't brake too much. The superpipe is located at Schreckfeld and has real superpipe dimensions and timber supports for the drop-ins. The superpipe attracts a lot of pro riders and locals such as Pascal Imhof use it as a training base. The greatest mistake this resort ever made was not installing a lift near the pipe. You need to ride the piste and take a long chairlift after every run, unless you have the energy to hike.

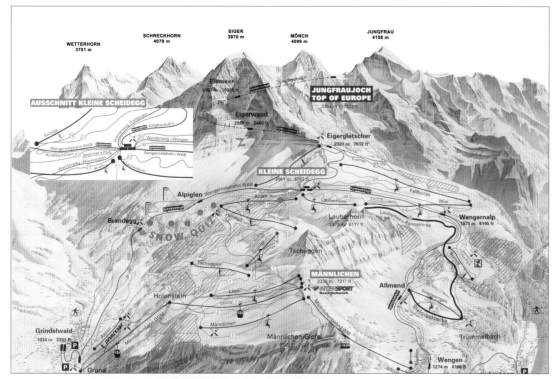

»

€34.50) for bed and breakfast, depending on the number of people sharing a room. Jugenherberge Tel: +41 (0) 338 531 009 or www.youthhostel.ch.
There are also lots of holiday apartments for rent. Further information about apartments and hotels can be obtained from the local Tourist Office.
Tel: +41 (0) 338 541 212 or at www.grindelwald.ch.

Food_ Supermarkets are well represented in the village, and there are a few bakeries and smaller grocery stores too. Onkel Tom's Pizzeria has good pizzas. Fajitas, tacos and tortillas are available at Restaurant Mescalero in Grindelwald. There's also a sushi bar, Kabuki Sushi. Don't be worried about the raw fish, the mountain air does them good! Traditional food can be eaten at the Swiss Chalet in the Hotel Eiger, where the specialities include cheese and meat fondues. Tuesdays are the best day to eat there which is when they put on the Farmer's Buffet (Bauernbuffet). The Latino-Bar Ristorante serves great Italian food.

Nightlife_ The Tipi Bar in the village is an Aprés Ski bar which often has live music. A good place to chill, meet people and sink a few beers is at the Espresso Bar. Two other popular bars are the Pinet and the Gepsi. Save the discos at Plaza or at Mescalero for later on at night - both have a real Majorca feel. If you've got money to burn, head to the casino in Interlaken.

Other Activities_ Grindelwald is a haven for sledders. There are six different sled runs and one of them is a speed run. A sports centre located in the centre of town offers an impressive array of activities, including: pool, sauna, fitness, curling, table tennis, billiards, cinema and Internet.

LOCAL TIP »
The views from the summit of the Eiger - Jungfrau - Mönch are absolutely fantastic. There are two ways to get there; one is to climb the north face of the Eiger to the top, the other is to catch a gondola to the top of the Jungfrau at 3454m, the highest lift station in the world. www.jungfrau.ch

© Stefan Hunziker

THIERRY BRUNNER, TWICE RUNNER-UP WORLD CUP RIDER SAYS, "MY FAVOURITE PIPE IS AT DAVOS. IT ROCKS, THERE AREN'T TOO MANY PEOPLE AND THERE'S A RESTAURANT CLOSE BY."

Carving_ Honnegg is a great carving piste at Kleine Scheidegg. When that's not enough, head to the Lauberhorn run, which should help you enjoy your day.

Beginners_ The shorter Bodmi lift just above the village is ideal for beginners. Grindelwald is basically an intermediate level resort, and the only really steep slope is the Lauberhorn run. Lessons are available from the Swiss Snowboard School Tel: +41 (0) 338 551 545 or Buri Sport +41 (0) 338 533 353

Mountain Restaurants_ First has 8 restaurants, a couple of which are self-service. Next to the Bergrestaurant Schreckfeld is a small snack bar serving cheap food. You can also listen to live music from the restaurant terrace. Just to warn you though, we use the word 'music' in the very loosest sense… The restaurant Kleine Scheidegg caters for every budget, from specialities such as fondues and röstis, etc to a simple burger.

IN THE TOWN »
Accommodation_ In Grindelwald, it's still possible to find accommodation at a reasonable price. You'll have a choice of countless guesthouses. In the middle of the village, there's Lehmann's Herberge. A single room here costs around 45 SF (€30) per night but the price goes down if you stay for longer.
Tel: +41 (0) 338 533 141
A room at the Glacier Touristenlage, near the railway station, costs around 35 SF (€24), half board available on request. Tel: +41 (0)338 531 004 or www.glacierhotel.ch
   Next to the gondola valley station at Männlichen is the Mountain Hostel, where you'll pay between 34 and 44 SF a night (€23 and €30). You'll need to bring a sleeping bag or rent a blanket.
Tel: +41 (0) 338 533 900 or visit www.mountainhostel.ch.
   Grindelwald also has a youth hostel which charges between 29.50 and 50.50 SF (€20 and

PROS & CONS »
+ Perfect, regularly reshaped superpipe.
+ A lot of variation in the Crap Sogn Gion park.
+ Good freeriding spots.
+ Short waiting periods, thanks to modern lift facilities.

− The mountain is relatively flat.
− High season becomes overcrowded.
− Too big, too many people, too hectic.

"FLIMS/LAAX IS SAID TO BE THE BEST FREESTYLE SNOWBOARD RESORT IN ALL OF SWITZERLAND. THIS RESORT WAS THE HOME OF THE FIRST PIPE DRAGON IN SWITZERLAND, AND SO WAS AN EARLY SWISS PIONEER OF GOOD HALFPIPES."

LAAX/FLIMS
SWITZERLAND

»

LAAX/FLIMS »
www.alpenarena.ch
tourist office tel: +41 (0)819209200
location: Flims Laax, Falera
population: 4544
altitude: 1000m

ON THE MOUNTAIN »
season: late November to late April
Lifts
vertical drop: 1100–3018m
amount of lifts in total: 29
gondolas: 7
chair lifts: 7
drag lifts: 11
Slopes
amount of prepared slopes: 220
runs w. snowmaking machines: 12.9 km
amount of easy runs: 25
amount of intermediate runs: 21
amount of advanced runs: 13
Facilities
night riding: -
amount of halfpipes: 3
amount of funpark: 2
heliboarding: -
Lift-ticket prices in Euro
1/2 day: 33.50
day: 59
week: 230
season: 650
Events
05.-08. December 2002 UBS Take Off Laax 2002
27.-30. March 2003 BoarderX Laax
09.-13. April 2003 Spring Session

SNOWBOARD TUITION »
Snowboard Fahrschule
Tel: +41 (0)819277156
Boarderschool Touch
Tel: +41 (0)788305960

SNOWBOARD SHOPS »
Chopp Snowboardshop
Tel: +41 (0)819115315
www.chopp.ch

GETTING THERE »
Car
Geneva (Genf) - Laax/Flims 428km
Genf - Bern - Zürich - Chur - Reichenau - Laax/Flims
Munich - Laax/Flims 302km
Munich - Lindau (Ger/Aut) - Bregenz (Aut/Swiss) - Chur - Reichenau - Laax/Flims
Milan - Laax/Flims 226km
Milan - Varese - Chiasso - San Bernadino - Piazza - Reichenau - Laax/Flims
Train
Train to Zürich, then on to Chur, then with a bus to Laax/Flims. www.ssb.ch
Air
Zürich Airport 154km

© Christian Stadler **Rider** Marco Schwab

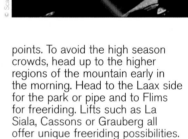

© Scalp

LAAX/FLIMS »
Intro_Flims/Laax has been said to be the best freestyle snowboard resort in all of Switzerland. This resort was the home of the first Pipe Dragon in Switzerland, and so was an early Swiss pioneer of good halfpipes. It has also been a favourite location for ISF contests, the Swatch BoardX final and the Spring Session comp, acquiring itself a great reputation along the way. The two superpipes are always freshly shaped, as is the park at Crap Sogn Gion, which includes kickers, rails, and boxes.

The villages of Flims and Laax are cosy, yet also offer a great nightlife. You'll have the choice of five different clubs, countless bars, pubs and (expensive) restaurants.

ON THE MOUNTAIN »
Snow reliability_Whether the snow is natural or artificial, winter in this place will always be white. The piste is well supplied with snow and exceptionally well groomed. www.laax.ch - your internet address for weather, snow and piste reports.

Information numbers
Automatic Information
+41 (0) 81 927 7000
Information Flims
+41 (0) 81 927 7201
Information Laax
+41 (0) 81 927 7001

Lifts & Piste_Flims, Laax or Falera are all have resort access

points. To avoid the high season crowds, head up to the higher regions of the mountain early in the morning. Head to the Laax side for the park or pipe and to Flims for freeriding. Lifts such as La Siala, Cassons or Grauberg all offer unique freeriding possibilities.

Freeriding_The mountains here are not as steep as in the Engadine but there is still a lot of fun to be had testing out the many natural kickers, cliffs and windlips. The freeriding areas are shown on the panorama map, and the runs are marked but not groomed. The tree runs are not really recommended because, as a non-local, it is very easy to get lost in this large expanse of mountain. For high-speed powder turns we recommend the Vorab run, accessible via the Vorab lift or the Cassons lift on the Flims side.

Freestyling_There are two superpipes and a few kickers at Vorab and at Crap Sogn Gion.

Riders such as Nicolas Müller, the Buvoli Brothers, Marco Schwab, Fadri Jecklin, Alex Schauwecker and Marco 'Heavy' Widmer ensure that the riding standard is brought to the highest level. The park and superpipes are regularly shaped and kept in great condition. Those looking for a course in freestyle should head down to the snowboard school - www.snowboard-fahrschule

Carving_The best known area for carving is on the piste next to the 6 person chairlift Plaun at Crap Sogn Gion, mainly due its exposure at the ISF World Cup Take Off comp. This run is exceptionally well groomed every morning, so that your edges will run hot. Not only the alpine riders will relish this one.

Beginners_If it were just down to the characteristics of the mountain, this would be an ideal place to begin snowboarding. The problem is that the pistes are generally overcrowded. You would probably

"THE MOUNTAINS HERE ARE NOT AS STEEP AS IN THE ENGADINE BUT THERE IS STILL A LOT OF FUN TO BE HAD TESTING OUT THE MANY NATURAL KICKERS, CLIFFS AND WINDLIPS."

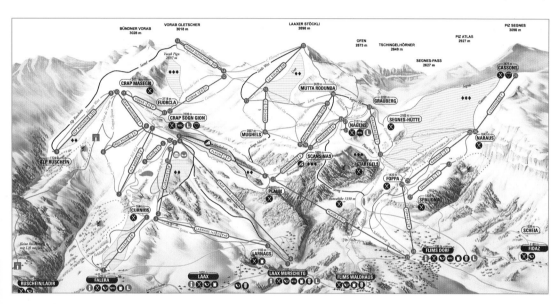

"THERE ARE TWO SUPERPIPES AND A FEW KICKERS AT VORAB AND AT CRAP SOGN GION. RIDERS SUCH AS NICOLAS MÜLLER, THE BUVOLI BROTHERS, MARCO SCHWAB, FADRI JECKLIN, ALEX SCHAUWECKER AND MARCO 'HEAVY' WIDMER ENSURE THAT THE RIDING STANDARD IS BROUGHT TO THE HIGHEST LEVEL. THE PARK AND SUPERPIPES ARE REGULARLY SHAPED AND KEPT IN GREAT CONDITION."

have more fun making your first few turns in a quieter resort.

Mountain Restaurants_ There are four large restaurants at Vorab, Crap Sogn Gion, Nagens and Curnius. The food is quite edible in all restaurants and the prices are all a little on the expensive side. For those able to dig a little deeper into their pockets, head down to Stargels, at the Grauberg valley lift station. A fine, flame grilled BBQ meal is waiting on their terrace.

IN THE TOWN »
Accommodation_ The Laax homepage is a good source of information regarding the different accommodation on offer - www.laax.ch. You can access telephone numbers, e-mail addresses and prices of accommodation from low budget to fine hotels. We recommend the Gutveina Backpackers in Flims - www.gutveina.ch for the not so 'well to do' and the Riders Palace at Laax, a high tech hotel with

multi media rooms, equipped with DVD players, video beamer, PSII and a sound system. Not the cheapest of places, but for those who like to chill out in deluxe style, take a closer look - www.riderspalace.ch

Food_ Laax doesn't have very much to offer in the way of cheap restaurants. You'll need to fork out around Sfr 20 (€14) for a decent meal. The stupidly named Crap Bar can supply you with OK burgers. We can recommend the Pizzeria Pomodoro, located on the main street of Flims - a large salad buffet with great specials on pizzas and Italian dishes. Capuns is the place to go for traditional cooking. Many of the restaurants will offer traditional meals such as a meat dough mixture wrapped in a silver beet leaf. Yum.

Nightlife_ The first place to visit is the Angel nightclub in Flims. There is generally a day of the week that will suit everyone's musical tastes. The Angel parties are wild and very amusing, but expensive. Best thing to do is head to the Pub in Flims first - next to Angel - and drink a few beers. The Riders Palace Club is open on weekends.

Other Activities_ There are many things to do in bad weather when you don't want to head up the mountain.
Sport Centre Prau la Selva in Flims – has an ice rink and fitness studio in winter and tennis, a skatepark and minigolf in the summer. Tamins, approx. 10min towards Chur is an indoor Go-Kart track. Super hot springs can be found in the other direction at Vals www.therm-vals.ch.

For those who want to go shopping or catch a film, you'll need to drive for 15mins to Churs.

LOCAL TIP »
Fadri Jecklin, sponsored by Head, West Beach, Iris and Laax_ Tip 1: "When there are too many people on the mountain and you want to go freeriding, head to the Grauberg lift on the Flims side. Travel up with the gondola and looking out, you'll discover some cool runs. There are cliffs, natural corners, and quarters and some good spots to build a kicker. Except for a few locals, you'll not find many people there."
Tip 2: "The locals, Marco 'Heavy' Widmer and Gian Bundi, run a snow and skateboard shop Chopp Snow, 100m from the valley lift station at Flims. A good location to hook up with some of the locals!"

PROS & CONS »
+ Glacier open all year round.
+ One of the best summer camps in Europe.
+ Snowboarder friendly.
+ Very hospitable.

- Glacier is relatively flat
- Always crowded

"THE HIGH ALTITUDE AND GLACIAL TERRAIN MAKE FOR SOME GOOD FREERIDE TERRAIN. RUNNING FROM THE GLACIER DOWN TOWARDS OLDENALP IS THE COMBE D'AUDON, A WIDE GULLY WITH STEEP WALLS AND LOTS OF CORNICES."

LES DIABLERETS
SWITZERLAND

LES DIABLERETS »
www.diablerets.ch
tourist office tel: +41 (0)2449233 58
location: Les Diablerets
population: 1350
altitude: 1200m
linked resorts: Villars-Gryon

ON THE MOUNTAIN »
season:
Isenau and Meilleret: mid Dec. –mid April
Glacier: Mid June - end July, October - April
Lifts
vertical drop: 1200–3000m
amount of lifts in total: 24
gondolas: 4
chairlifts: 6
T-bars: 14
Slopes
amount of prepared slopes: 65 km
runs w. snowmaking machines: -
amount of easy runs: 22
amount of intermediate runs: 42
amount of advanced runs: 1
Facilities
night riding: -
amount of halfpipes: 1
amount of funparks: 1
heliboarding: yes
Lift-ticket prices in Euro
day: 52
week: 246
season: 890
Events
Glissclub Snowboard Camp www.glissclub.ch
Jame's B Summer camp (October)
Longboard Contest in May

SNOWBOARD TUITION »
Ecole Suisse de Ski et Snowboard
Tel: +41 (0)244922002
www.diablerets.ch/skischool

SNOWBOARD SHOPS »
Holiday Sport
Tel: +41 (0)244923717
Jacky Sport
Tel: +41 (0)244923218
www.jackysports.ch

GETTING THERE »
Car
Milan - Les Diablerets 196km
Milan - Santhià - Ivre - exit Aosta - Colle del
Gran San Bernardo (It/Swiss) - Martigny -
towards Lausanne - exit Bex, Saint Maurice -
Aigle - Le Rosex - Les Diablerets
Zürich - Les Diablerets 240km
Zürich - Bern - Fribourg - Vevey - towards
Grand St Bernard/Martigny - exit Villeneuve -
Aigle - Le Rosex - Les Diablerets
Geneva - Les Diablerets 123km
Geneva - Lausanne - towards Grand St
Bernard/Martigny - exit Villeneuve - Aigle -
Le Rosex - Les Diablerets
Train
By train to Aigle, then with the regional ASD
train - Tel: +41 (0) 244 923 115. The local
bus completes the connection from Gstaad
Air
Geneva Airport 123km

LES DIABLERETS »
Intro_ Les Diablerets was once considered to be a dangerous and cursed place, hence the 'diabolical' name. A local legend tells of once lush green fields transformed into a desert of stone, when a heartless shepherd wouldn't help some hikers who were in desperate need of help.

ON THE MOUNTAIN »
Snow reliability_ Apart from the glacier, the resorts of Les Diablerets - Isneau and Meilleret - are at a relatively low elevation of 1900m. The snow conditions depend heavily on a good snowfall early in the season, to ensure a good base, and the local ban on snowmaking doesn't help the situation. Luckily, Les Diablerets lies at the edge of the Swiss Alps, so is often the first place to get dumped on. Following fresh snowfall, the best conditions are to be found on the glacier, where the north and east facing slopes have the added advantage of sheltering the snow. The best time for the powder hounds is usually between the end of January and February. Pure freestylers will find summer and autumn is the best time to ride. The glacier opens until 2pm each day in the summer, and until 4pm in the autumn. Snow reports are available from the ticket office -

Ticket Office
Tel: +41 (0) 492 33 58 or at
www.diablerets.ch.

Lifts & Piste_ The resort of Les Diablerets is divided into three sections - Glacier 3000, Isneau and Meilleret. The first two areas are accessible via the gondola, while the third area, which also connects to the neighbouring village of Villars, is accessible via a chairlift. The valley lift station in Diablerets is very busy, so expect to queue, although hopefully not for too long. One drawback here is that once you go to Meilleret, you have to stay there, as there's no connection between the two areas. Isneau has the advantage that you can ride down to the village and then take the gondola to the glacier.

Freeriding_ The high altitude and glacial terrain make for some good freeride terrain. Running from the glacier down towards Oldenalp is the Combe d'Audon, a wide gully

© Piat Vermeulen / Rider Fred Joggi

with steep walls and lots of cornices. Another good glacial route involves a short hike to the summit of Oldenhorn. From there, you'll find a slope that takes you down to Cabane. The run is quite steep in places, so check on the snow conditions with the ski patrol or the mountain office before you go. Floriettaz is a great run in Isneau, with a few good cornices. To get a bit more mileage out of this run, hike further up the ridge at the summit of the tow lift. Floriettaz brings you out onto the other side of the mountain towards

Reusch. Hiring a guide is an excellent idea, as this run is one of the better ones in the area, and you don't want to get it wrong. Meilleret has some nice tree runs.

Freestyling_ On the glacier, the freestyle scene heats up in summer and autumn. The snowpark provides two lines: one for experts and one for beginners. There are seven mid-sized jumps, a larger jump, quarters, and a pipe. A lot of top riders find their way here over the year, including the likes of Romain de Marchi, Jonas Emery,

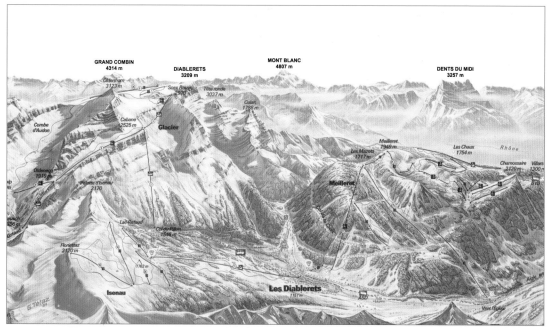

"ON THE GLACIER, THE FREESTYLE SCENE HEATS UP IN SUMMER AND AUTUMN."

and Wille Yli Luoma. During the winter the snowpark is located in Isneau, along with a boardercross course. The size of the jumps varies depending on the snow. Floriettaz has some inviting ridge lines and drops, ideal for busting out some stoopid dope fresh moves… and on the journey home, the trashers amongst you will find plenty of assorted jibs and rails to session.

Carving_ The pistes at Isneau and Jorasse in Meilleret are suitable for carving.

Beginners_ Isneau is the best area to learn in, but be careful you don't end up in Floriettaz, where it could get quite hairy! Despite the fact that the glacial terrain is quite flat and not too bad for learning, it is quite a walk to get there.

Lessons can be taken at the local ski school - Ecole Suisse de Ski - Tel: +41 (0) 244 922 002 or at the New Devils School - Tel: +41 (0) 244 923 431, who also do specialised freestyle lessons.

Mountain Restaurants_ Diablerets has four

restaurants and two snack bars. All four restaurants are good, and offer the usual resort fare of spaghetti and chips as well as specialities such as a fondue. The cheaper meals cost between Sfr 10 and Sfr 15 (€6.80 - €10.20) The glacier restaurant, designed by the well known Swiss architect Botta is a little more expensive, but worth a visit.

IN THE TOWN »
Accommodation_ The hotel prices begin at around Sfr 40 to Sfr 50 (€27 to €34) depending on the

season. Just so you know, Les Diablerets would not be what it is today without the legendary Mon Abri and its B-Bar. This place is the nerve centre of the summer camp scene, a meeting place for riders, and the starting point for many a wild party. Mon Abri - James B Organisation - Tel: +41 (0) 244 923 481 info@monabri.ch

During the summer camps, they offer a special package deal that includes lift tickets.
The one star Hotel Les Diablotins is in about the same price range as Mon Abri and is located just above »

vonzipper
Stef Lochon @ Spartacus

G.S.M. EUROPE: ph: 33 (0) 5 58 70 70 70 - fx: 33 (0) 5 58 43 40 89

"A LOCAL LEGEND TELLS OF ONCE LUSH GREEN FIELDS TRANSFORMED INTO A DESERT OF STONE, WHEN A HEARTLESS SHEPHERD WOULDN'T HELP SOME HIKERS WHO WERE IN DESPERATE NEED OF HELP."

LES DIABLERETS
SWITZERLAND

© Diablerets Tourisme

» the village. Tel: +41 (0) 244 923 633 diablotins@freesurf.ch www.diablotins.ch Further info regarding prices and availability: Diablerets Tourisme Tel: +41 (0) 244 923 358 info@diablerets.ch www.diablerets.ch

Food_There are three supermarkets. Cheaper restaurants include the Mexicaner El Clandestino, opposite the train station, and the Pizzeria Locanda Livia, above the MTB Bar. For something a little more special, and to try the traditional specialities (Papet vaudois), head to Vioz - Tel: +41 (0) 244 923 245.

Nightlife_The MTB and the Ormonan are typical Aprés Ski

bars, the latter being more popular with the locals. Later on hit the Bar Le Passage and the hotel bar at Mon Abri. Later still, go to MTB for value or the B-Bar for good music. There is also a disco - La Pote.

Other Activities_A skate park at the Congress Hall is open summer and autumn. As well as the endless touring possibilities, there's a 30km sled run - Tel: +41 (0) 491 25 03

LOCAL TIP »
If you're up for the hike, check out Pierre Pointe, it's a must! The area is not patrolled, so take a qualified guide. The hike up from the Pillon Pass requires snowshoes. This run is a dream, with cornices, windlips, natural quarters and beautiful tree runs.

"THE SNOWPARK PROVIDES TWO LINES: ONE FOR EXPERTS AND ONE FOR BEGINNERS. THERE ARE SEVEN MID-SIZED JUMPS, A LARGER JUMP, QUARTERS, AND A PIPE. A LOT OF TOP RIDERS FIND THEIR WAY HERE OVER THE YEAR, INCLUDING THE LIKES OF ROMAIN DE MARCHI, JONAS EMERY, AND WILLE YLI LUOMA."

PROS & CONS »
+ Giant area.
+ Good freeriding.
+ Great snowparks - Thyon and Les Crosets.

− Busy during holidays
− Low altitude, gets slushy.

"CONDITIONS AT THE BEGINNING OF THE SEASON ARE GENERALLY BETTER THAN ANYWHERE ELSE IN THE REGION."

LES PORTES DU SOLEIL
SWITZERLAND

LES PORTE DU SOLEIL »
www.lesportedusoleil.com
tourist office tel: +41 (0)24 4792020
location: Champéry
population: 1130
altitude: 1050m

ON THE MOUNTAIN »
season: December - May
Lifts
vertical drop: 930-2280m
amount of lifts in total: 211
gondolas: 14
chair lifts: 81
drag lifts: 116
Slopes
amount of prepared slopes: 650 km
runs w. snowmaking machines: yes
easy runs: 170 km
intermediate runs: 380 km
advanced runs: 100 km
Facilities
night riding: yes
amount of halfpipes: 3
amount of funparks: 9
heliboarding:
Lift-ticket prices in Euro
1/2 day: 26
day: 34
week: 184
season:

SNOWBOARD TUITION »
Freeride Company Ski and Snowboard School
Tel: +41 (0)244791000
www.freeridecompany.com
Swiss Ski and Snowboard School
Tel: +41 (0)244791615
www.esschampery.ch

SNOWBOARD SHOPS »
Berra Sports
1874 Champéry
Tel: +41 (0)244791390

GETTING THERE »
Car
Geneva - Champéry: 91 km
Geneva - Vésenaz - (Swiss/Fr) - Thonon les
Bains (Fr/Swiss) - Champéry
Zürich - Champéry: 235 km
Zürich - Bern - Fribourg - Montreux - towards
Martigny - exit Aigle - Monthey - Champéry
Milan - Champéry: 290 km
Milan - Cavaglia - Quincinetto - Aosta -
(It/Swiss) Tunnel du Saint Bernard - Martigny
- towards Lausanne - exit Bex - Monthey-
Champéry
Train/Bus
Departing from Lausanne with the train to
Aigle, then with the private AOMC line
towards Monthey
Champéry - train from Aigle towards Monthey.
Les Crosets and Champoussin - train Aigle-
Monthey, get off at Val d'iiliez and travel on
with the bus.
Morgins - train Aigle-Monthey, travel on with
the bus to Troistorrents where you'll need to
change again.
Torgon - train Aigle-Monthey, bus to Vionnaz
and change
Air
Geneva Airport to Morgins: 83 km
Geneva Airport to Champéry: 123 km

© Philipp Bericlaz **Rider** Joel Strecker

LES PORTES DU SOLEIL »
Intro_ Portes du Soleil is situated right on the Swiss French border; a small part of the combined Europe, in the only country that doesn't have an open border. The freeriders will find their off piste runs, the freestylers a good snowpark, and a nightlife which doesn't end too early! Combined with the French side, this resort belongs to one of the largest in Europe. Here, we'll only look at the Swiss side of things, including Champéry, Les Crosets, Morgins, Champoussin, and Torgon. The French section can be found in the 'France' chapter.

ON THE MOUNTAIN »
Snow reliability_ Portes du Soleil gets its first snowfall when the Atlantic low pressure systems begin to move in. This is the reason why conditions at the beginning of the season are generally better than anywhere else in the region. On the main runs you'll find artificial snow making facilities, but they rely on the natural stuff for the rest. The powder hunters will find the best times being between the beginning of January and February. The freestylers will have

their best sessions at the end of the season, especially around the end of March.

Snow and weather conditions at the respective lift stations:
Porte du Soleil Switzerland
+41 (0) 244 772 361
www.portesdusoleil.com
Champéry
+41 (0) 244 792 020
www.telechampery.com
Champoussin
+41 (0) 244 768 300
www.telecrosets.com
Les Crosets
+41 (0) 244 772 077
Torgon
+41 (0) 244 813 131

Lifts & Piste_ The best way into the resort is via Les Crosets. Six lifts from the valley lift station heading up in different directions. Just take the one with the smallest queue. Most of the people at Champéry are transported with the large gondola. Morgins, while Champoussin and Torgon are generally less popular and will get you to the resort a lot quicker. Take note of the timetables for the return times when riding into France. Most lifts

operate until 4.15 pm or 4.30 pm. Every Monday and Wednesday night, the Planachaux in Les Crosets and Piste La Follieuse in Morgins open.

Freeriding_ The off piste terrain in Portes du Soleil varies greatly. Sometimes you'll need to take a short hike, but there is also a lot to do close to the piste. The best tree runs can be found in the pine forests at Savolaire, running down to the village of Morgins. There are steeper and easier sections in the forests and it is the best place to go when the visibility or snow is bad. Tour de Don and Roc de Morclan, in Torgon are great runs, but look out for the rock faces. Located between Les Crosets and Morgins is the Vallée de la Grande Jeur, which is worth a detour, a valley without lifts going down to Morgins. Pointe de l'Au is also worth a look, with its small hills, wind lips and snow bridges. The slope at Pas de Chavanette called Mur Suisse is one of the steepest and best runs in the world, you'll need strong legs for this one!

Freestyling_ The Pointe de l'Au is

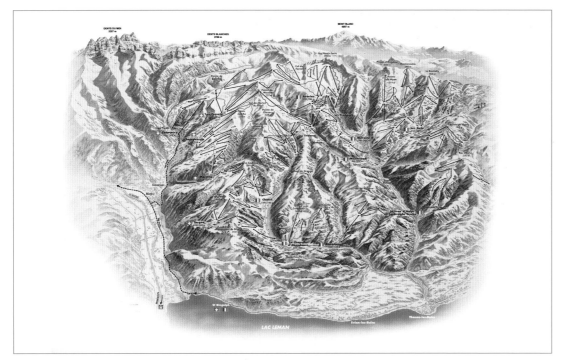

© Phillipo Berclaz

"THE SLOPE
AT PAS DE
CHAVANETTE
CALLED MUR
SUISSE IS
ONE OF THE
STEEPEST AND
BEST RUNS
IN THE WORLD,
YOU'LL NEED
STRONG LEGS
FOR THIS ONE!"

a natural snowpark. Another one is located between Avoriaz and Les Crosets by the small Cuboré chairlift, which also services the Pointe des Mossettes. Mother Nature has made everything so perfect here that shapers aren't needed. The snowpark at Les Crosets has three lines. The easy and intermediate lines have their own area with 2 hips and 4 jumps, and the more challenging line has its own section which includes 2 hips and a large table. Maybe you'll meet up with pro riders such as Darius Heristchian, Thomas Brunner, Thierry Schalcer or Cox, who ride here at times. A big jam session is organised at the start and at the end of every season. Further info at www.superpark.ch. For those who have their snowskate with them, check out the snowskate park at Morgins.

Carving_ The pistes at Les Crosets are normally used for ski training, but when they're not, they are great for carvers.

Alpine riders and beginners should avoid the Pas de Chavannette, the moguls can really ruin your day.

Beginners_ Beginners should keep to the lower sections of Les Crosets, Morgins or Champéry. Lessons are available from Ecole Suisse de Ski.

Ecole Suisse de Ski
www.esschampery.ch
Tel: +41 (0) 244 791 615

Beginner courses in freestyle or freeriding are available at the:
Freeride Compagny
Tel: +41 (0) 244 792 029
www.freeridecompagny.com

In Morgins, lessons are available from Snowline, www.snowline.ch - Tel: +41 (0) 244 772 906

Mountain Restaurants_ The La Lapisa restaurant - on the Grand Paradis piste at Les Crosets - has excellent food and tasty cakes. The panorama, the food and the Walliser wines definitely make Chez Coquoz worth a visit, the oldest restaurant in Portes du Soleil. Chez Gaby is for those looking for a cosy place to eat in Champoussin. The goat's cheese raclette is one of life's more sublime pleasures.

IN THE TOWN »
Accommodation_ Champoussin: the best tip is the Chez Gaby, next to the piste, overnight with breakfast - Sfr 52.- (€35.40) **Morgins:** Beau Site, a classic which has been newly renovated - Sfr 57.- (€38.75). **Champéry:** the best deal at Auberge du Grand Paradis - Tel: +41 (0) 244 791 167 www.grandparadis.ch
Les Crosets: is a village with a lot of regular guests, a better option is to move to the village of Val d'Illiez located opposite.

Further accommodation, reservation and tourism info:
Champéry
+41 (0) 244 792 020
www.champery.ch
Champoussin
+41 (0) 244 768 300
www.valdiliez.ch
Les Crosets
+41 (0) 244 772 077
www.valdiliez.ch
Torgon
+41 (0) 244 813 131
www.torgon.ch
Morgins
+41 (0) 244 772 361
www.morgins.ch

Food_ Supermarkets and small shops are located in every village. The Pub pizzeria or Pervenches Asian food in Champéry are both cheap and good. Vieux Valais in Morgins is good too. Cantine des Rives and Mitchell's are recommended in Champéry, and, for a really traditional evening, the Hôtel du Nord. The Assiette Valaisanne is a great combo of dried out meat and raclettes.

Nightlife_ The best places for a cool beer in Champéry are, Mitchell's, Café du centre and Bar des guides. In Champussin, we recommend Poussin and in Morgins, the T'bar

and Reines des Alpes are the places where the snowboarders hang out. The locals in Champéry generally head to Café du Levant later in the evening, and then onto Disco La Crevasse. The early hours of the morning can be spent at Le Farinet. Morgins locals head to the T'bar, Yucatan or SAF. The other villages are rather quiet, so if you're after action, go to Champéry or Morgins.

Other Activities_ When the weather is playing havoc, or you just need a days rest, then the Centre sportif de Champéry provides the alternative day plan with a swimming pool, curling, fitness studio and badminton. In Champéry you can also try snow kiting or paragliding. Morgins offers archery in the forest, or ice skating. For planning a tour in the scenic Massive der Dents du Midi, contact Montagne Expérience - Tel: +41 (0) 244 791 430

LOCAL TIP »
For those looking for the purist freeriding vibe, travel to the Massiv des Dents du Midi. A high level of expertise is required to navigate your way through the steep chutes here.

PROS & CONS »
+ Glacier open all year round.
+ Snowpark on the glacier.
+ High standard of living.

– Lift ticket prices are high.
– Slopes face north – tends to become icy.
– Parking is expensive.

"RIDERS FLOCK TO THE GLACIER DURING AUTUMN AND SUMMER, MAINLY TO RIDE THE PIPE AND BOARDERCROSS COURSE."

SAAS FEE
SWITZERLAND

SAAS-FEE »
www.saas-fee.ch
tourist office tel: +41 (0)279581858
location: Saas-Fee
population: 1600
altitude: 1800m
linked resorts: Saas-Grund, Saas-Balen, Saas-Almagell

ON THE MOUNTAIN »
season: late October to early May
Lifts
vertical drop: 1800–3600m
amount of lifts in total: 22
gondolas: 8
chair lifts: 1
drag lifts: 13
Slopes
amount of prepared slopes: 100 km
runs w. snowmaking machines: 5
amount of easy runs: 25
amount of intermediate runs: 50
amount of advanced runs: 25
Facilities
night riding: yes
amount of halfpipes: 1
amount of funparks: 1
heliboarding: -
Lift-ticket prices in Euro
day: 32.50
week: 223
season: 634.50

SNOWBOARD TUITION »
Schweizerische Ski- und Snowboardschule
Tel: +41 (0)279572348
www.home.sunrise.ch/skischool
Bananas Swiss Snowboard School
Tel: +41 (0)279574904
www.bananas.net

SNOWBOARD SHOPS »
Wild One Snowboard Shop
Tel: +41 (0)279574112
Popcorn the Snowboardpoint Shop
Tel: +41 (0)279571914

GETTING THERE »
Car
Geneva - Saas Fee 226km
Geneva - Lausanne A1 - Martigny - Sion/Sierre A9 - exit Susten - Visp - Saas Fee
Zürich - Saas Fee 345km
Zürich - A1 Bern - A12 Fribourg - A9 Montreaux - A9 Martigny - A9 Sierre - exit Susten - Visp - Saas Fee
Milan - Saas Fee 224km
Milan - A8 Gallarate - A26 Borgomanero - Ornavasso (It/Swiss) - Gondo - Visp - Saas Fee
Bus/Train
Train from Lausanne to Viège, then walk to the local bus stop, and catch the bus to Saas Fee.
Train from Bern to Brig, changing to the local Saas Fee bus
Air
Geneva Airport 225km
Zürich Airport 101km
Milan-Malpensa Airport 182km

SAAS FEE »
Intro_Saas Fee is a pretty little village set in chocolate box surroundings. Nestled at the end of a deep valley, it is surrounded by gigantic summits and distant, seemingly unreachable glaciers. Guests leave their cars parked on the edge of the village, as the only form of transport allowed here are the little electric carts that trundle through Saas Fee's narrow streets.

ON THE MOUNTAIN »
Snow reliability_The resort of Saas Fee lies in the highlands of the Swiss Alps, its highest point the glacier at 3600m. Snow conditions are generally good, even late into spring. However, expect icy runs from the lower section of the glacier down into the village. The constant deep base of the glacier ensures perfect conditions following a snowfall. The entire resort is equipped with snow making – particularly useful on the run down to the village, which lies at 1800m.

Further Information
http://home.sunrise.ch/luseil/index.html
Tourism Info - www.saas-fee.ch
Tel: +41 (0) 279 581 858

Lifts & Piste_Twenty-two lifts service around 100km of piste.

"DUE TO ITS ALTITUDE AND GEOGRAPHY, SAAS FEE GETS CONSISTENTLY GOOD SNOWFALL, AS GOOD AS ANYWHERE IN THE ALPS. THE BEST AREA TO GO FREERIDING IS BELOW THE GLACIER AT MASTE AND LÄNGFLUH. WINDLIPS, CORNICES AND ROLLERS ADD VARIATION TO THE RUNS, WHICH CONTINUE DOWN INTO SOME NICE TREE RUNS."

Saas Fee is home to Métro Alpin, the highest subway in the world. Most of the other lifts are tows. There are two main areas to ride here, Plattjen and Felskinn, the latter being the larger and more popular one. If there are long queues at the Alpin Express, the Spielboden-Längfluh gondola is often a better option. Plattjen is less popular with the tourists, and therefore more popular with you. Skiers and snowboarders are banned at the third section Hanning, as it is reserved for hikers and sledders.

When riding the glacier, be prepared for a pair of burning thigh muscles – the drag lifts here are fairly steep.

"SAAS FEE IS A PRETTY LITTLE VILLAGE SET IN CHOCOLATE BOX SURROUNDINGS. NESTLED AT THE END OF A DEEP VALLEY, IT IS SURROUNDED BY GIGANTIC SUMMITS AND DISTANT, SEEMINGLY UNREACHABLE GLACIERS."

© Philipp Berclaz **Rider** Fredy Kalbermatten

Freeriding_ Due to its altitude and geography, Saas Fee gets consistently good snowfall, as good as anywhere in the Alps. The best area to go freeriding is below the glacier at Maste and Längfluh. Windlips, cornices and rollers add variation to the runs, which continue down into some nice tree runs. Don't, however, attempt to ride off piste on the glacier without a guide – there are hidden crevasses. The piste Nationale in Plattjen will lead you to some good tree runs. Although Hanning is not accessible from the gondola, you can hike it in about an hour, and once you are cruising down, you'll know the effort was worth it!

Freestyling_ Riders flock to the glacier during autumn and summer, mainly to ride the pipe and boardercross course. Every year three different pipes are cut, each suited to a different level of rider. The closer it gets to winter, the higher the walls become, until eventually they reach almost superpipe proportions. There is a big influx of Japanese kids, as well as local heroes such as Frederik Kalbermatten, Nicolas Müller and Daniel Bumann. During the winter there's also a pipe and snowpark, but it is pretty ordinary in comparison to the summer offering. Natural kickers can be found at Maste and Längfluh.

Carving_ Saas Fee's runs are groomed with a precision characteristic of the Swiss. Without a doubt, the best ride is from Mittelallalin down to Längfluh. The Längfluhwand is perhaps too steep for carving, but a blast for speed freaks!

Beginners_ The pistes at Saas Fee are relatively steep, so you'll need to have spent a bit of time on a board before heading up. A nice beginner area is situated in the village and is serviced by three easy lifts. Lessons are available from the Swiss Ski and Snowboard School - Tel: +41 (0) 279 572 348 and the Bananas Snowboard School www.bananas.net Tel: +41 (0) 279 574 904

Mountain Restaurants_ Ten restaurants service the mountain. Amongst them is the 'highest rotating restaurant in the world'. The prices at the rotating Métro

Alpin Mittelallalin are pretty high too. Our recommendation is Gletschergrotte, where the portions are good, and the prices fair.

IN THE TOWN »
Accommodation_ Bed and breakfast: Sypcher, all rooms have a shower and toilet, and cost around Sfr 65 (€44). All rooms are non-smoking. www.myspycher.com Rooms: Dorfblick, www.dorfblick.ch, perfect for families and groups, one week in the high season costs around Sfr 230 (€156) per person. Both places are next to the Alpin Express valley lift station. The best option for accommodation in Saas Fee is in an apartment, especially in the autumn, when the prices are extremely low. You'll have no problem finding a hotel in Saas Fee. Further Info from the tourism office www.saas-fee.ch

Food_ Saas Fee has a decent supermarket in the middle of town. The Tea Room Imseng is a good place for a sandwich. Good restaurants include Pizzeria Boccalino, Feeloch and the Spaghetteria Da Rossa, none of which are too spendy. La Gorge and at Mistral are popular, as is Waldrestaurant Bodmen.

Nightlife_ The village bars and

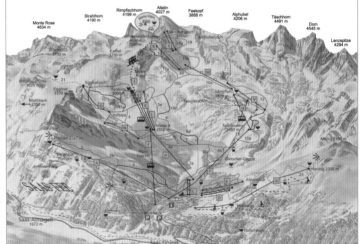

terraces are the Aprés Ski meeting places of choice, especially Nesti's Skibar or Ruud 66. Popcorn is one of the most popular Bar-Clubs, with good DJ's and occasional live concerts. Other nightspots include the Go Inn, Why Not and the Happy Bar, who all have Happy Hours and good music.

Other Activities_ If it is not buried beneath snow, check out the skatepark at the far end of town. There's a mini ramp, a cool little rolling 'wave', and a funbox. If it's

covered in snow, take your snowboard... Saas Fee also has a cinema and an indoor swimming pool with sauna, gym, etc. There is also an ice-climbing wall on the side of the Saas Fee car park.

LOCAL TIP »
The run from the glacier into the village is one of the longest in Switzerland. It will take you around 30 - 45 minutes and can be the perfect end to a perfect day. Top it all off with a beer, and enjoy the view of the amazing mountains.

ST. MORITZ
SWITZERLAND

PROS & CONS »
+ Highest summit lift station is at 3303m above sea level.
+ Freeriding at its best.
+ Perfect piste and modern facilities.
+ Season begins in mid November and ends around the beginning of May.

- Expensive.
- Overcrowded during the high season.
- The Engadine Valley is slightly off the beaten track.

ST MORITZ »
www.skiengadin.ch
tourist office tel: +41 (0)818300000
location: St. Moritz
population: 18889
altitude: 1750 m
linked resorts: Aela (Maloja), Furtschellas (Sils Maria), Corvatsch (Silvaplana), Corviglia, Marguns (St. Moritz-Celerina), Diavolezza/Lagalb (Pontresina), Muottas Muragel, Survih (Samedan), Müsella (La Punt-Chmues-ch), Albas (Zuoz)

ON THE MOUNTAIN »
deason: late November to early May
Lifts
vertical drop: 1750–3303m
amount of lifts in total: 56
gondolas: 1
chair lifts: 18
drag lifts: 27
Slopes
amount of prepared slopes: 350 km
runs w. snowmaking machines: 70
amount of easy runs: 31
amount of intermediate runs: 22
amount of advanced runs: 35
Facilities
night riding: yes
amount of halfpipes: 1
amount of funparks: 1
heliboarding: -
Lift-ticket prices in CHF
day: 61
week: 348
season: 914
Events
Swiss Snowboard Series Halfpipe (January 03)
Swiss Snowboard Series Giant Slalom, Parallel Giant Slalom (March 03)
Hangloose Cup (April 03)

SNOWBOARD TUITION »
Schweizer Skischule St. Moritz
Tel: +41 (0)818300101
www.skischool.ch
Suvretta Snowsports School
Tel: +41 (0)818363600
www.suvrettasnowsports.ch

SNOWBOARD SHOPS »
Blue Motion Snow Sports
Tel: +41 (0)818330832
www.bluemotion.ch
Playground in Paradise
Tel: +41 (0)818322363
www.playground.ch

GETTING THERE »
Car
Geneva - St.Moritz 488km
Geneva - Lausanne - Bern - Zurich - Chur - Tiefencastel - Silvaplana - St.Moritz
Munich - St.Moritz 290km
Munich - Lindau (Ger/Au) - Bregenz (Au/Sw) - Chur - Tiefencastel - Silvaplana - St.Moritz
Milan - St.Moritz 164km
Milan - towards Lecco - Còlicio - Castasegna (It/Sw) - Maloja Pass - Silvaplana - St.Moritz
Train
Zurich - St.Moritz approx. 3.5 hours
Swiss Railways: www.sbb.ch
Air
Zurich Airport 204km

ST.MORITZ »
Intro_ St. Moritz is located in the beautiful region of Engadine in south east Switzerland. The surroundings are characterised by powerful mountains, frozen lakes and pretty villages. The people here are multi-lingual and while Swiss German is the main language, you will also hear Italian, and the much older, much rarer Rhaeto-romanic. The prices in St. Moritz are not exactly an encouragement to visit the place, but the amazing variety of terrain in the 'Engadine Boarders Valley' make it simply irresistible.

ON THE MOUNTAIN »
Snow reliability_ The Engadine is a highland valley (1800m) and is surrounded by the highest mountains in the Eastern Alps. The resorts are located at above 3000m, thus guaranteeing good snow. One real plus about the Engadine is the mix of both north and south facing slopes. The season begins in the middle of November and extends right through to the beginning of May. The best time for riding is regardedto be between mid-February and mid-April, though everything depends on the snow fall, of course. The resort has modern snow making facilities so perfect pistes are guaranteed right down into the valley.

Lifts & Piste_ Overview of the Engadine Boarders Valley

Silvaplana/Corvatsch
Most people travel over the Julier Pass into Engadine. As you're driving round that last hairpin bend you'll catch a glimpse of the Piz Corvatsch. Towering up to 3303m, it looks down onto the village of Silvaplana. A gondola will connect you to this area, a dream for every freerider.

Sils/Furtschellas
St.Moritz is located to the left of Silvaplana, to the right is Lake Silvaplana and in the further distance there's the village of Sils. A gondola leaves from Sils and heads up to the Furtschellas. This area has a lot of cliffs and cornices, and is also connected to the Corvatsch area. Even further to the south east is the town of Maloja, which has a ski lift that's worth checking out in bad weather.

St.Moritz/Corviglia
St.Moritz is approximately 7km

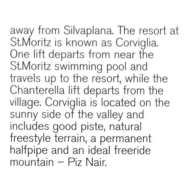

away from Silvaplana. The resort at St.Moritz is known as Corviglia. One lift departs from near the St.Moritz swimming pool and travels up to the resort, while the Chanterella lift departs from the village. Corviglia is located on the sunny side of the valley and includes good piste, natural freestyle terrain, a permanent halfpipe and an ideal freeride mountain – Piz Nair.

Celerina/Marguns
Corviglia is connected to the resort of Marguns, which is above Celerina. The two areas, both with south-facing slopes, spread out to form the largest region in the Boarders Valley. Travel another 15km down the valley, and you'll come to Zuoz, where you'll find more lifts and slopes.

Pontresina/Diavolezza
Pontresina is located in a side valley approximately 6km away from St.Moritz. The resort of Diavolezza is a 10 minute drive from Pontresina over the Bernina Pass towards the Italian border. In Diavolezza there's is a natural halfpipe, long powder runs and wide pistes.

Useful information about the

Engadine Boarders Valley and regional pro riders (Michi Albin, Dani Sappa, Reto Lamm, Therry Brunner, Franco Furger etc) can be obtained from www.boarders-valley.com

Corviglia/Marguns, which is above St.Moritz, is without doubt one of the most modern resorts in the world. There area only two tow lifts in the entire resort, the rest being comfortable chairlifts fitted with wind-protecting bubbles. You'll have a choice of four lifts to help you access the resort by taking you on a fast and efficient ride to the top. And once in the resort, you won't find yourself having to queue too long - even in the high season - thanks to the fast and modern chairlifts. All this Swiss efficiency does. however, mean that there are always lots of people on the pistes!
At Corvatsch in Silvaplana you'll find the giant gondola. You may have to queue for a bit longer than usual here, but once you're in the resort you'll find that the lift facilities keep the public well distributed. Sils/Furtschellas is connected to Corvatsch, and is generally a quieter area. Over the past few years, Furtschellas has become popular with snowboarders.

"IN ALL THE RESORTS YOU'LL FIND COUNTLESS COULOIRS, CLIFFS OF EVERY HEIGHT AND STEEP SLOPES. MOST LINES CAN BE SPOTTED BY EXPERIENCED RIDERS AS THEY LOOK OUT FROM THE GONDOLAS AND LIFTS."

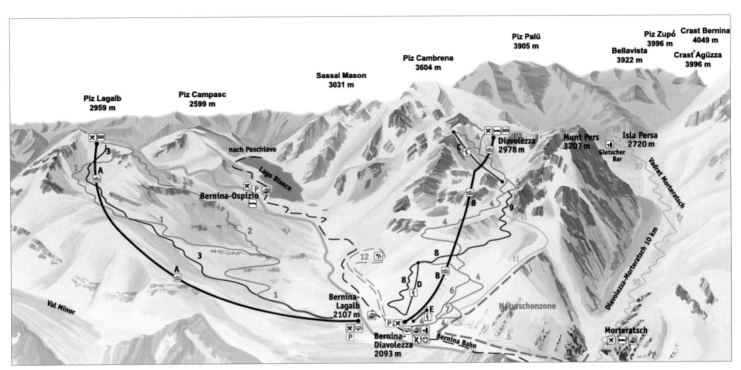

A larger gondola also enables you to reach the resort of Diavolezza at 2978m. When you get to the top, you'll be rewarded with an amazing panoramic view of the famous Engadine mountains including, Piz Palü (3905m) and Piz Bernina (4048m). Another gondola can then transport you up to Piz Lagalb - one mountain with one gondola, a good alternative when the other areas get too crowded.
TIP: Zuoz and Maloja are the quietest areas.

Freeriding_ Engadine is one of the best freeriding regions in Europe. Michi Albin, who has filmed in all corners of the world, still likes his local Engadine valley best. In all the resorts you'll find countless couloirs, cliffs of every height and steep slopes. Most lines can be spotted by experienced riders as they look out from the gondolas and lifts, and most are accessible without having to walk for hours. Spring is the time to ride the north faces of Corvatsch and Diavolezza, while the southern faces of the Corviglia provide ideal mid-winter riding. The upper regions of Engadine are fantastic for backcountry touring. The routes here are often very dangerous, though, and can extend into glacial »

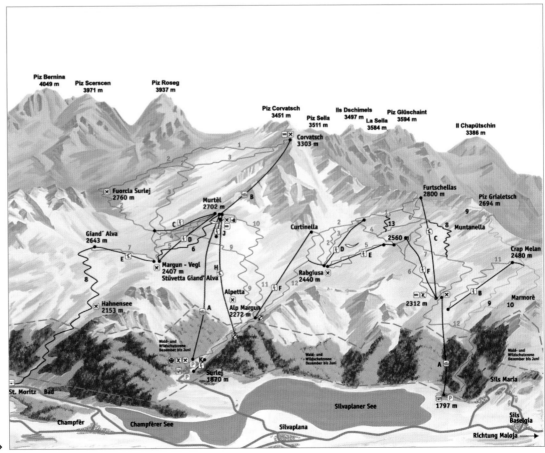

© Jeff Webb

"THERE'S ALWAYS A JUMP TO BE HAD AT CORVIGLIA/ MARGUNS. ROLLING TERRAIN AND SMALL GULLIES PROVIDE THE IDEAL SETTING FOR BUILDING KICKERS OR JUST CRUISING."

ST. MORITZ
SWITZERLAND

© Peter Mathis **Rider** Dani "Kiwi" Meier

» areas, so don't go exploring on your own - always seek help from a qualified guide or an experienced local.

Freestyling_ There's always a jump to be had at Corviglia/ Marguns. Rolling terrain and small gullies provide the ideal setting for building kickers or just cruising. At Corviglia you'll find a halfpipe, the San Murezzan lift, and a small funpark. Marguns has a few jumps but these are more suitable for beginners.
  A natural halfpipe can be found under the lift at Diavolezza. Nearby there's a little bit of off piste freestyle heaven called La Collina, where, after making a short hike, you'll enjoy a kicker paradise where you won't even need a shovel.
  The terrain near the quad chairlift at Furtschellas will keep any freestyler happy and includes lots of cliffs for that freeride, freestyle crossover.
  Another freestyle spot is the resort of Zuoz - endless rollers and cornices.

Carving_ The St.Moritz lift company at Corviglia specialises in wide pistes that offer a wide range of challenges. St.Moritz is the venue of the ski World Championships in February 2003 and has vast experience when it comes to preparing the piste. The whole mountain has the added advantage of being equipped with snow making facilities. The night piste at Corvatsch is also a lot of fun - open until 2 am on Friday nights - and always kept in excellent condition; or try the full moon run at Diavolezza for a really special experience.

Beginners_ There are plenty of slopes suitable for beginners here. The easiest runs are around the village lift at Pontresina or close to the valley lift stations at Marguns, Corvatsch and Diavolezza. The beginner lift at Corviglia is known as the Sass Runzöl. The villages of Samedan and La Punt also have ideal beginner lifts.

Mountain Restaurants_ The usual resort meals of things such as Bratwust and chips, spaghetti, etc can all be found in the many restaurants on Corviglia/Marguns. Prices are high everywhere on the mountain. The summit restaurant at Corviglia has a restaurant for those

© Peter Mathis Rider Tommy Brunner

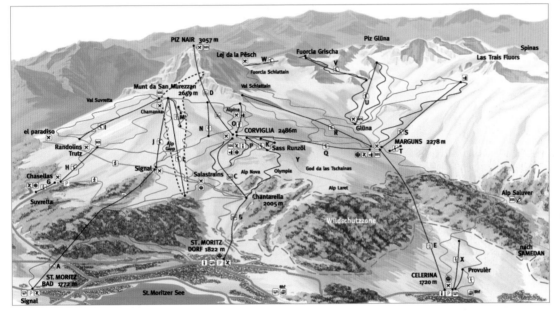

> "ST. MORITZ IS THE VENUE OF THE SKI WORLD CHAMPS IN FEBRUARY 2003 AND HAS VAST EXPERIENCE WHEN IT COMES TO PREPARING THE PISTE."

with a taste for fine food, but you won't find much here for under 80 SF (€54). One of the cheapest options is Snack Away at the bottom of the pipe chair lift, San Murezzan - where you'll get a great burger. Tasty food can be had in the Alpina Hütte at Corviglia. The snow bar has the best view of the whole valley. The Chamanna, close to the halfpipe, is also reasonable. The Hossa Bar at Corvatsch serves good snacks and there's even a DJ to add to the entertainment.

Tip: The summit restaurant at Sils/Furtschellas has a monthly menu for around 5 or 6 Swiss Francs (€3,50/4).

IN THE TOWN »
Accommodation_It doesn't matter whether you're looking for a hotel or a holiday apartment, it's expensive to stay in St. Moritz. The hotels in St. Moritz Bad are slightly less expensive or you might go for a double room at an informal youth

hostel - Jugendherberge. The bottom line is that the further away you are from the middle of St.Moritz, the less you pay. The Alte Brauerei is a popular place with visitors in Celerina - approximately 5 minutes' walk from the valley lift station Celerina/Marguns. The Hotel Inn-Lodge is another cheaper option in Celerina. Pontresina has a youth hostel and the Hotel Allegra is a cool place to stay and close to the village lift.

Food_There are lots of good restaurants in St.Moritz, and Italian cuisine is a speciality throughout the region. Good pizzas at a cheaper price are on the menu at the Pizzeria Boccalino in St.Moritz Bad. Across from the pizzeria is the Veltlinerkeller, where you can eat the best Pizzoccheri - a pasta dish with vegetables and lots of garlic. The Restaurant Laudinella in St.Moritz Bad has excellent pizzas and fast service. If you want to cook

for yourself, shop at the Co-op Centre which is between the village and the swimming pool.

Nightlife_Wall-to-wall Après-Ski parties 'til the sun goes down! Salastrains in Corviglia and the Hosser Bar in Corvatsch both offer this experience. In St.Moritz village, there's usually a good crowd at the Roo Bar in the centre of town. Your first visit of the evening should be the Cava or the Stübli - both in the centre of town. Your next stop might be the Scala Bar at the top end of the village, close to the cinema, where the sounds are good A short stagger further and you'll come to the Prince where you can dance the night away. If you're still out and about at 4 am and still have enough energy, then head to the Hemingway, where you can party 'till the sun comes up.

A good alternative to the nightlife in St. Moritz is the Pitschna Szena in Pontresina – close to the new Congress Centre in the middle of the village which has a regular program of live music.

Other Activities_St.Moritz is known as the home of winter tourism. The needs and whims of every winter tourist are catered for - every kind of winter sport can be experienced here from cross country skiing over a frozen lake, curling and snow-shoe tours to one of the bob-sled runs St.Moritz is famous for. In St.Moritz and Pontresina you'll find a cinema and swimming pool. St.Moritz also has a casino and an indoor tennis complex.

Tip: Try a sled run at Muottas Muragl. There's an amazing view at the top across the Engadine landscape, and the run down is crazy.

LOCAL TIP »
Daniel Sappa, born in St.Moritz. Northwave, Rad Air and Level Pro Rider._ "If you don't know where to go in Corviglia, then check out Lachtal - basically travel left from the halfpipe. This is the place where the locals learned all their tricks. Even when the weather craps out, you can still pull off a few easy tricks in Lachtal. When going out, head to the Scala Bar. This is where all the local riders and local chicks hang out. Don't forget our internet address - www.boarders-valley.com"

PROS & CONS »
+ Excellent freeride terrain.
+ Lively nightlife.

− Strong danger of avalanches.
− Lots of high level snowboarders and skiers -
− rapidly tracked out.

"VERBIER'S REPUTATION FOR EXTREME TERRAIN HAS GONE DOWN IN THE HISTORY OF SNOWBOARDING AND FREERIDING, AND IS ONE OF THE TOP SPOTS IN SWITZERLAND."

VERBIER
SWITZERLAND

VERBIER »
www.verbier.ch
tourist office tel: +41 (0)277753888
location: Verbier
population: 2500
altitude: 1500m
linked resorts: La Tzoumaz, Veysonnaz, Nendaz, Thyon, Bruson

ON THE MOUNTAIN »
season: end of November to end of April
Lifts
vertical drop: 1500-3300m
amount of lifts in total 38
gondolas: 8
chairlifts: 18
drag lifts: 10
cable cars: 2
Slopes
amount of prepared slopes: 150km
runs w. snowmaking machines: 15km
amount of easy runs: 21
amount of intermediate runs: 31
amount of advanced runs: 5
Facilities
night riding: yes
amount of halfpipes: -
amount of funparks: 2
heliboarding: yes
Events
22. March 2003 Xtreme Snowboard Contest
Lift-ticket prices in CHF
day: 43
week: 266
season: 1066

SNOWBOARD TUITION »
La Fantastique
Tel:+41 (0)277714141
www.lafantastique.com
Adrenaline
Tel: +41 (0)277717459
www.adrenaline-verbier.ch

SNOWBOARD SHOPS »
No Bounds
Tel: +41 (0)277715556
www.nobounds.ch
Hardcore
Tel: +41 (0)41277717820
www.hardcore-snowboard.ch

GETTING THERE »
Car
Lyon - Verbier 312km
Lyon - Geneva - Lausanne - Martigny - towards Grand St.Bernard - Verbier
Zurich - Verbier 280km
Zurich - Bern - Neuchatel - Vevey - Martigny - towards Grand St.Bernard - Verbier
Milan - Verbier 270km
Milan - towards Turin - Aosta - Grand St. Bernard Tunnel (It/Sw) - via Sembrancher - Verbier
Train
Take the train from Lausanne or Sion to Martigny. Change to the Grand St. Bernard Express to Châble. From there, either take the gondola or the bus.
Air
Geneva Airport 163km

VERBIER »
Intro_Verbier is part of the massive ski area known as Les Quatre Vallées (La Prinzte - Thyon - Veysonnat - Nendaz). It's in the Swiss canton of Wallis, and is home to the famous Verbier Extreme contest. Alongwith Mt.Fort, Verbier's reputation for extreme terrain has gone down in the history of snowboarding and freeriding, and is one of the Top Spots in Switzerland.

ON THE MOUNTAIN »
Snow reliability_Snow conditions are almost always good, thanks to a great number of the north/north-east facing pistes. The end of March is considered the best time for freeriding because the snow has had a chance to settle by then and the snow layers have had more time to bind. One small plus for Verbier - Nendaz is the fact that the sun is often smiling down on you, which means the snow is a little softer and the days are a little longer. In the lower lying areas of the resort, the direct sunlight can wreak havoc with the snow base, especially towards the end of the season. Southern frontal systems are held up by the Mt. Fort Massif, which then forces good snowfalls, allowing Mt.Fort to be one of the early winter openers. Snow making facilities are hand in the centralareas of the resort.

Further information
Tourism Office:
+41 (0) 277 753 888

Lifts & Piste_Verbier is divided into two sections, Ruinettes/ Mt. Fort and Savoleyres/La Tzouma (Mayens de Riddes). Both sections are connected by tow lifts located close to the village. The Verbier lift ticket also allows you to ride at Brusons, on the opposite side of the valley. You can also buy a lift ticket for the entire 4 Vallées region. Verbier is almost solely equipped with chairlifts or gondolas. The chairlift from Medran is a quicker option for accessing the pistes at Ruinettes for those who want to avoid the long queues at the gondolas — the only problem is that it'sa long ride and hell in bad weather. Savoleyres doesn't get so overcrowded so you'll not have to wait as long. A similar ride to the top is taken from Tzouma/Mayens de Riddes. The crowds generally head to the Funispace d'Attelas - a bigger 30-seater gondola serving the Ruinettes area. But if you don't want to have to fight your waythrough the crowds, head to the older Attelas gondola. The La Chaux and Lac des Vaux chairlifts (return trip down to Verbier or Tortin) should be avoided in late afternoon because they're always full.

Freeriding_The slopes in the high alpine regions of Mont Fort, Mont Gelé and Olympique offer an ideal playground for experienced freeriders, with couloirs, ridges and cliffs and excellent snow conditions. This area is not recommended for everyone though. It requires a high level of riding ability and detailed knowledge of the mountains and the dangers they hold. You absolutely must check outthe avalanche situation , especially when heading off on tour. For those whose goal is to ride on the famous Bec des Rosses (site of the Extreme contests), you'll need to be physically strong and fit. When riding in the Massiv des Mont Fort you're very likely to come across freeriders such as Alex Coudray or Cyril Néri. Vallon d'Arbi is also a great freeriding spot, located behind the Lac des Vaux. The run begins in a long, wide gully before heading into some tighter tree runs and ending up on the Mayens de Riddes. Boarders searching for good terrain not so high up can head to the tree runs in the direction of Verbierat Ruinettes. These are not as dangerous but are still a lot of fun. Untracked powder fields can often be found at Savoleyres, although they're not very steep.

Freestyling_Lac des Vaux and Vallon d'Arbi are not only great freeriding areas, but also offer quite a lot of terrain for freestyling, including natural quarters and spines. The snowpark is at Chaux, where the park shapers have built stuff all over the place. The runs have been designed for intermediate to experienced riders, although there is one jump that's suitable for beginners. The park sound system reverberates around 5 tables, 1 spine and 5 rails. A section of the park is reserved for snowskating with rails, boxes and a hut. Snowskates can be hired for 10 SF a day (€6.80).

Carving_The need for speed can be satisfied on the piste from Attelaz to Ruinettes. The piste is steep and fast. The best time to ride is early in the morning if you want to avoid collisions with uncoordinated skiers.

Beginners_The beginners slope is at Esserts. The level of difficulty in this area is generally intermediate, with one black run on Mt.Fort. The best Après-Ski bar is

"THE NEED FOR SPEED CAN BE SATISFIED ON THE PISTE FROM ATTELAZ TO RUINETTES. THE PISTE IS STEEP AND FAST. THE BEST TIME TO RIDE IS EARLY IN THE MORNING IF YOU WANT TO AVOID COLLISIONS WITH UNCOORDINATED SKIERS."

the Carrefour. On a sunny day, it's a great place to chill.

Mountain Restaurants_There are 15 restaurants on the mountain (10 at Ruinettes and 5 at Savoleyres) They're all close to the respective lift stations and are self-service cafeterias serving relatively cheap meals such as spaghetti or bratwurst. If you happen to catch the last gondola back up to Savoleyres after a day's riding, rent a sled from the Evasions Sport shop and travel down to the Restaurant des Marmottes (halfway between Col des Gentianes and La Chaux) for a great cheese fondue. After a good sledding race, the fondue tastes twice as good.

IN THE TOWN »
Accommodation_The best deal for snowboarders in Verbier is the Bunker - Tel: +41 (0) 277 161 01 - the old bomb shelter at the

sports centre. Overnight accommodation and breakfast costs25 SF(€17), and you'll need a sleeping bag.
Overnight accommodation is available at Les Touristes for around60 SF (€41). Guesthouses with rooms to rent are also available - check them out with Madame Luisier, Real Estate Agent
Clair de Lune:
+41 (0) 277 723 256
Chantal Crettenand:
+41 (0) 277 714 147
Fabienne Michellod:
+41 (0) 277 712 329
And regular holiday apartments are available too, of course.

Further information
Verbier Tourist Office
Tel: +41 (0) 277 753 888
www.verbier.ch

Food_There are supermarkets in the village, so self-catering is a cheap option. You can get snacks

at the Pub Mt. Fort, the Off-shore Bar, and during the season at Snack Michellod,next to the lift station which has great takeaway sandwiches. Hearld Burger is your fast food stop in Verbier for cheap food and Internet access. Pizza is on the menu just about everywhere including; Chez Martin, Borsalino, Al Capone and Fer à Chreview. One of the best restaurants in Verbier is the Rosalp, but you'll need a thick wallet or dish washing skills.

Nightlife_Après-Ski begins at Pub Mt.Fort where the drinks are half priceup to 5pm. Farinet has live music every day and Vaux (next to No Bounds) has free pizza. Pub Mt.Fort is also a favourite meeting place in Verbier for later on in the evening. Tuesdays, Thursdays and Sundays are Special Shots nights, when shots cost €0.70 between 10.30 and 11.30pm. Other well-patronized pubs include: the Big Ben, Nelson, and Murphy's Bar.

Crok No Name provides daily live music or a DJ. Jack's Bar and Bar Jo are also okay. The evening generally continues on to a disco in the village -the Taratata, Marshall, Scotch or the Farm perhaps.But be warned! Drink prices rise sharply once you hit the clubs.

Other Activities_Verbier has two cinemas, where they usually show films in English. Visitors to Verbier should definitely try the snow carts, basically regular carts on snow. Paragliding in Verbier is just as popular in winter as it is in summer, and the climate provides an ideal location for gliding.

LOCAL TIP »
The craziest thing to do is to spend New Year's Eve in Verbier, where the crowds hang out in the town centre at midnight to hear the bells ring. And Faschings Tuesday (Shrove Tuesday) in Verbier is like carnival time in Rio.

ZERMATT
SWITZERLAND

ZERMATT »
www.zermatt.ch
tourist office tel: +41 (0)279668100
location: Zermatt
population: 5600
altitude: 1620m
linked resorts: Cervinia

ON THE MOUNTAIN »
season
winter: Nov – May
Summe-Glacier: May - Nov
Lifts
vertical drop: 1620-3820m
amount of lifts in total: 41
cable cars: 2
gondolas: 16
chair lifts: 5
drag lifts: 18
Slopes
amount of prepared slopes: 150km
snowmaking machines: 230
easy runs: 43,5km
intermediate runs: 62,5km
advanced runs: 44km
Facilities
amount of halfpipes: yes
amoun t of funparks: yes
heliboarding: yes
Lift-ticket prices in Euro
1/2 day: 34
day: 43,80
week: 247,50
season: 1414,-

SNOWBOARD TUITION »
Schweizer Ski- und Snowboardschule
Tel: +41 (0)279662466
www.zermatt.ch/skischule
Stoked Swiss Snowboardschool
Tel: +41 (0)279674340
www.stoked.ch
Alpin Center Zermatt
Tel: +41 (0)279662460
www2.zermatt.ch/alpincenter

SNOWBOARD SHOPS »
Julen Sport
Stoked Snowboard Shop
Tel: +41 (0)279674340
www.julensport.ch

GETTING THERE »
Car
Zurich - Zermatt 231km
Zurich - A1 Bern - A6 Thun - Kandersteg - Lötschberg (train connection - €17.20 per car incl. passengers) - Steg - Viége/Visp - Täsch (car park) - connecting train into Zermatt
www.bls.ch Auto transport Lötschberg
Zurich - Zermatt 347km
Zurich - A1 Bern - A12 Fribourg - A9 Montreux - A9 Martigny - A9 Sierre - Susten exit - Visp - Täsch (Car park) - connecting train into Zermatt
Geneva - Zermatt 238km
Geneva A1 - Lausanne A1 - Sion/Sierre A9 - Viége - Täsch (car park) - connecting train into Zermatt
Milan - Zermatt 228km
Milan - A8 Gallarate - A26 Borgomanero - Ornavasso (It/Swiss) - Gondo - Visp - Täsch (car park) - connecting train into Zermatt.
Train
Zürich to Bern, change at Brig, transfer to the regional BVZ line's Zermatt service.
Geneva to Brig, transfer to the regional BVZ line at Viége or Brig then on to Zermatt
For Swiss Railways info: www.sbb.ch
Air
Zürich Airport 244km
Geneva Airport 236km
Milan-Linate Airport 247km
Milan-Malpensa Airport 186km

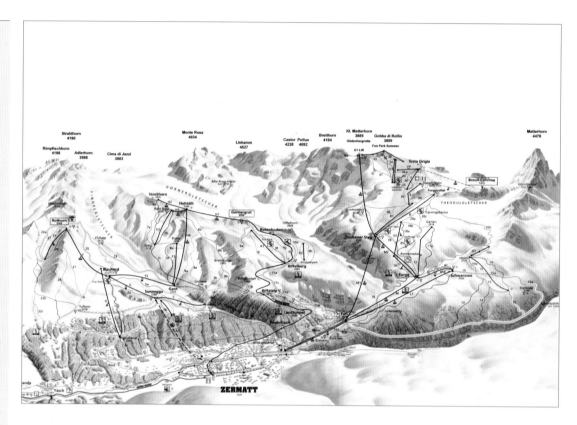

ZERMATT »
Intro_Zermatt is a blue-blooded, expensive resort with breathtaking views of Switzerland's best known mountain, the Matterhorn which is 4478m above sea level. Money plays a big role in Zermatt – the prices in the town and on the mountain have escalated beyond control. On the plus side, the resort is a car-free village, has heli-boarding, an excellent park and pipe and perfect freeriding terrain, all in the shadow of one of the most spectacular mountains in the world.

ON THE MOUNTAIN »
Snow reliability_Zermatt is 1620m above sea level and is at the end of a long valley which is sheltered from the wind and thus has its own microclimate. This, combined with the fact that it faces north/north-east makes for great snow conditions all year round. There is also a glacier which is open from July through to May. The best time for riding is in March. The early winter months are generally cold, so wrap up warm. For further info go to www.zermatt.ch
Gornergrat lift
Tel: +41 (0) 2792 147 11
Matterhorn lift

Tel: +41 (0) 2796 761 62
Rothorn lift
Tel: +41 (0) 2796 627 40

Lifts & Piste_Taken together with Cervinia over the border in Italy, the resorts between them have 250km of piste and 71 lifts, and are divided into four sections: Blauherd, Gornergratt, Klein Matterhorn and Cervinia. The best-known area (so the one that gets the most overcrowded) is the Klein Matterhorn, and from here you can ride into Italy. During the busiest periods, it's not unusual to find the 6-seater gondola crammed with tourists hoping to catch a glimpse of the Klein Matterhorn which towers up to 3885m above sea level. But if you want to avoid the crowds your best option is to exit at the Trockener Steg station, and from there either access the pipe and park or take one of the numerous other lifts. If you are planning to cross into Italy, you'll need to keep a close eye on the lift operating times and remember your passport! You'll also have to decide whether you want to ride on the Klein Matterhorn or on the Gornergrat/Blauherd because the transfer

takes far too long to ride both in one day. Your basic lift ticket, which is more expensive here than anywhere else in the world, is valid for these three sections, but if you want to go riding in Cervinia, you'll have to shell out even more.

Freeriding_Due to the high altitude and north-facing slopes, the powder here remains mostly soft and dry. Freeriding on the Theodul glacier is relatively dangerous and riders regularly need to be rescued from the crevasses. Your best option is to travel with a guide and go riding early in the morning. The zone below the glacier is ideal for a day's riding off piste. A few good lines, including some great cornices to drop, are accessible from the Garten am Fugg station. The runs from Schwarzsee or Hörnli down towards Stafelalp are first class and you can go through the forest for big powder fields with lots of natural jumps. Due to the size of the resort, good powder can be found just about everywhere. From Gornergrat, take the gondola to Hohtälli and/or Stockhorn at 3405m. Around the

"THE RESORT IS A CAR- FREE VILLAGE, HAS HELI-BOARDING, AN EXCELLENT PARK AND PIPE AND PERFECT FREERIDING TERRAIN, ALL IN THE SHADOW OF ONE OF THE MOST SPECTACULAR MOUNTAINS IN THE WORLD."

© Philipp Berclaz **Rider** Franco Furger

"DUE TO THE HIGH ALTITUDE, THE POWDER IS SOFT AND DRY."

summit area, the entries are quite steep and tight (chutes), but they then open up further down. It pays to check the depth of the snow base since the terrain here is made up of rock and scree. If you can afford it, consider taking a helicopter up to the summit.

Freestyling_ Summer and autumn are the best times for riding in the

Klein Matterhorn glacier park, where there's a large freestyle scene awaiting you. The park has a superpipe, two large and two small jumps, and two rails. Reto Kestenholz is the man who keeps the park in great shape. Santa Cruz team riders and Italian riders from Cervinia session this park for most of the season. And there's another funpark a bit lower down at

Trockenen Steg. The jumps aren't all that wonderful, but they do have some good rails – five in all, including a rainbow, kink and flat. When snow conditions permit, another pipe is prepared at Sandiger Goden as well. The pipe at Gornergratt is also worth a visit - good height, good length and a rope tow running alongside it.

Carving_ Zermatt has its own carving terrain on the Klein Matterhorn. The piste travels from the Furggsattel and the descent is perfect: - long, wide and varied in pitch. Rotenboden - Gornergrat is also a good spot for carving - not too steep, but wide enough for some nice 'Vitelli' turns.

Beginners_ Blauherd is the best bet for beginners, as it has been sectioned off specially and isn't too steep. The beginner zone at Klein Matterhorn is next to the funpark at Trockenen Steg, just above the rails.

Mountain Restaurants_ For those who go riding at Klein Matterhorn and have the right ticket, the best places to eat are on the Italian side. Whether you use Swiss Francs or Euros, you'll pay half the price you'd pay on the Swiss side. We recommend Polenta all Valdostana or Pasta ai Funghi, just two of the many culinary delights that await you. If you don't have the Italian lift pass, your best bet is the restaurant at Testa Grigia, right on the Italian border. Après Ski bars on the piste include the Hennu Stall, the Olympia and the Blauherd. Don't stay there too long though, the sun goes down very quickly in Zermatt.

IN THE TOWN »

Accommodation_ Zermatt has a big pedestrianised area and private transport has to left at the Täsch car park, 5km away from the village. So if you were thinking about camping in your van, forget it! Zermatt is expensive, but if you know where to look, you can still find cheaper accommodation. The Matterhorn Hostel is probably one of the cheapest options in town, with a shared room without breakfast costing between 29 and 39 SF (€20 to €27). Breakfast costs around 7 SF (€4.80) - Tel: +41 (0) 279 681 919 or log onto www.matterhornhostel.com
The Naturfreunde Hotel does great

deals for groups, and in the low season a double room with half board costs 70 SF (€48) per person Tel: +41 (0) 279 672 788 or check out naturfreunde.zermatt@spectraweb.ch The youth hostel costs 48 SF (€33) per person in a shared room Tel:+41 (0) 279 672 320 www.youthhostel.ch/zermatt. For further information and last minute deals check out www.zermatt.ch or call +41 (0) 279 668 100

Food_A few years ago, there wasn't a single supermarket in Zermatt, and even now there's only one. The Walliserkanne serves up good traditional food, including regional specialities such as Rösti, Raclette and tomato fondue. The Arvenstübli does an excellent Chinese fondue. Chez Max et Gretti, a 30 minute walk away in neighbouring Zumsee, is a small restaurant with good local cuisine.

Nightlife_ Paperla Pub, Pöstli and Grampi's all come within the category of Après Ski bars. Pöstli and Grampi's also do snacks, including great pizza, and the Pöstli is also an evening bar featuring live music. Grampi's is a disco well worth visiting, especially if you're on the pull! It's hard not to drink yourself into oblivion with the excellent choice of cocktails on offer at Z'Alt Hischi. A good old reggae sound and a nice vibe can be found at The Pipe, which also serves food.

Other Activities_ Zermatt has two cinemas if you fancy a sit. But if your energy levels are still up to it, it has an artificial and a natural ice rink where you can practice your curling, and while there's no public swimming pool, seven of the town's hotels have pools so it shouldn't be too hard to sneak into one.

LOCAL TIP »

You should definitely include a helicopter ride in your budget for Zermatt. The Mountain Guides Association offers four setting-down places (Monte Rosa, Alphubel, Test Grigia and Rothorn) and excellent snow conditions can generally be found at all of them. Info at www.zermatt.ch/alpinecentre/
Your alternative is the Air Zermatt service where a flight will set you back between 100 SF and 500 SF (€70 to €345)
Info at www.airzermatt.ch or Tel: +41 (0) 279 668 686

ENGLAND
SCOTLAND

IRELAND
WALES

NETHERLANDS
GERMANY

BELGIUM
FINLAND

ARTIFICIAL SLOPES
EUROPE

»

© Russ Shea **Rider** Thorne/Norwich

"IN RECENT YEARS DRYSLOPE DESIGN HAS EVOLVED RAPIDLY, AND MANY SLOPES NOW OFFER WHOLE 'PARKS'. THE OTHER MAJOR INNOVATION IN RECENT YEARS HAS BEEN THE INDOOR 'REAL' SNOW SLOPE, AGAIN FEATURING JUMPS, JIBS, AND BOARDER-ONLY SESSIONS."

ARTIFICIAL SLOPES »

UK_Although Scotland has mountain resorts, for the majority of English snowboarders, they are no easier to get to than the Alps. But this doesn't stop us from having a thriving snowboard scene. Across the UK, there are well over sixty plastic 'dryslopes', most of them having a selection of jumps and jibs, plus regular boarder-only nights. In recent years dryslope design has evolved rapidly, and many slopes now offer whole 'parks', while Sheffield Ski Village even has its own halfpipe! The other major innovation in recent years has been the indoor 'real' snow slope, again featuring jumps, jibs, and boarder-only sessions.

'REAL' SNOW SLOPES »

If pretending plastic is snow isn't your thing, there are 2 slopes in England that offer the real thing... sort of.

TAMWORTH
The Snowdome_130m indoor snow slope. Assorted jumps and rails, and a VW Beetle! Snowboard sessions every Tuesday and Saturday night.
Tel: +44 (0)990 000011
www.snowdome.co.uk

MILTON KEYNES
Xscape_Britain's biggest real snow slope. Two 170m slopes plus nursery slope. Assorted jumps and jibs. Bigger, with better snow than Tamworth, but more expensive with it. Snowboard sessions every Friday night.
Tel: +44 (0)1908 230260
www.xscape.co.uk

DRYSLOPES »

What the UK's tight, thriving snowboard scene lacks in snow, it certainly makes up for in dendix and, more recently, Snowflex. Snowflex is a new surface that features foam padding which makes for softer and safer slams. Look out for Snowflex parks at Sheffield, Halifax, Kendal, Gloucester and Hillend slopes.

ENGLAND »

ALDERSHOT
Alpine Ski Centre_Gallwey Road, Aldershot Hants GU11 2DD
Tel: +44 (0)1252 325889
www.alpineski.co.uk

BIRMINGHAM
Ackers Outdoor Activity Centre_Waverly Canal Basin. A fairly small slope of 100 metres. Session: 6 – 9 Thursdays.
Tel: +44 (0)121 7725111
www.ackers-adventure.co.uk

BALLATER
Ballater Ski Slope_Craigendarroch Hotel Braemar Road, Ballater
Aberdeenshire AB35 5XA
Tel: +44 (0)13397 55858

BRACKNELL
Bracknell Ski & Snowboard Centre_Amen Corner Bracknell Berkshire RG12 8TN
3 slopes with a 150 metre main slope. Session: 7 – 10 Mondays.
Tel: +44 (0)1344 789000
www.nikegroup.co.uk/jnl/bracknell.htm

BRENTWOOD
Warley Ski Centre_Holdens Wood Warley Gap, Brentwood CM13 3DP
Tel: +44 (0)1277 211994

BRISTOL
Avon Ski Centre_Lyncombe Lodge Churchill Bristol Avon BS25 5PQ
170 metre slope curving almost 180 degrees over a bridge and onto a wide run off. Session: 7 – 10 Sunday and Wednesday.
Tel: +44 (0)1934 852335
www.highaction.co.uk

CARLISLE
Carlisle Ski Centre_The Edenside Cricket Ground, Carlisle Cumbria CA3 9EW
Tel: +44 (0)1228 514569

CHATHAM
Chatham Ski Centre_Alpine Park Capstone Road ME7 3JH
200 metre slope with Britains longest toboggan run. Session: 8 –10 Mondays.
Tel: +44 (0)1634 827979
www.nikegroup.co.uk/jnl/chatham.htm

CHRISTCHURCH
Christchurch Ski Centre_Matchams Lane Hurn, Christchurch, Dorset BH23 6AW
3 slopes with a 120 metre main slope. Session: 6 onwards Thursdays and Sundays.
Tel: +44 (0)1202 499155
www.christchurch-skicentre.com

CLITHEROE
Pendle Ski Club_Clitheroe Road Sabden, Clitheroe, Lancs BB7 9HN
Tel: +44 (0)1200 425222

DURHAM
Spectrum Leisure Centre_Hunwick Lane Willington, Co. Durham DL15 OJA
Tel: +44 (0)1388 747000

DORCHESTER
Warmwell Ski Centre_Warmwell Leisure Resort Warmwell, Dorchester, Dorset DT2 8JE
Tel: +44 (0)1305 852911

ESHER
Sandown Ski School_Sandown Park More Lane, Esher, Surrey KT10 8AN
Tel: +44 (0) 1372 467132
www.sandownsports.co.uk/

EXETER
Exeter & District Ski Centre_Belmont Road, Exeter EX2 2DJ.
Tel: +44 (0)1392 211422

FALKIRK
Polmont Hill Ski Slope_Polmont Farm Polmont, Falkirk, Stirlingshire FK2 0YE
Tel: +44 (0)1324 503835

FOLKESTONE
Folkestone Ski Centre_Radnor Park Avenue. Folkestone, Kent CT19 5HX
Tel: +44 (0)1303 850333

GATESHEAD
Whickham Thorns Outdoor Centre_Market Lane Dunston Gateshead NE11 9NX
Tel: +44 (0)191 460 1193

GILLINGHAM
Chatham Ski & Snowboard Centre_Alpine Park, Capstone Road Gillingham, Kent ME7 3JH
Tel: +44 (0)1634 827979
www.jnll.co.uk

GLOUCESTER
Gloucester Ski and Snowboard Centre_Robinswood Hill Gloucester GL4 9EA
240 metre main slope and a friendly bunch of boarders. There is also a Playgrass funpark with a variety of hits and quarters. Session: 6 – 10 Fridays and Sundays.
Tel: +44 (0)1452 414300

GOSLING
Gosling Ski Centre_Stanborough Road Welwyn Garden City, AL8 6XE
Super fast 160 metre slope with speaker system. Session: 7 – 10 Tuesdays.
Tel: +44 (0)1707 384384/331056
www.goslingsports.co.uk

GUILDFORD
Bishop Reindorp Ski School_Larch Avenue, Guildford, Surrey
Tel: +44 (0)1483 504988
www.brski.co.uk

HALIFAX
Halifax Ski Centre_Bradford Old Road Swales Moor, Halifax HX3 6UG
135 metre slope. Recently upgraded with Snowflex board park. Cost: £6ph
Tel: +44 (0)1422 340760
www.dryski.tv

HEMEL HEMPSTEAD
Hemel Ski Centre_St. Albans Hill Hemel Hempstead HP3 9NH
4 slopes, the longest being 180 metres. Two slopes are for training sessions and one is a 100 metre wavy mogul run. Session: 7 – 10 Sundays. Cost: £9.50
Tel: +44 (0)1442 241321

HERTS
Bassingbourn Ski Centre_1, Rose Villas
Jacksons Lane, Reed, Royston, Herts SG8 8AB
Tel: 01763 848114
http.community.net.uk/~bassingbourn/

IPSWICH
Suffolk Ski Centre_Bourne Terrace
Wherstead, Ipswich IP2 8NG
Tel: +44 (0)1473 602347
www.suffolkskicentre.co.uk

KENDAL
Kendal Ski Club_Kirkby Kendal School
Thorny Fields, Kendal, LA8 5HT
Despite being quite short, the black snowflex
slope of Kendal is well worth a visit, with a
variety of hits and quarters. Session: 5.30 –
7.00 Thursdays and 6 – 9 Sundays. Cost:
£6ph (non- members), £3ph (members)
Tel: +44 (0)1539 732948/01539 733031
www.kendalski.co.uk

KENT
Bromley Ski Centre_Sandy Lane
St. Paul's Cray, Orpington, Kent BR5 3HY
Fairly steep 120 metre slope and nursery
slope. Session: 7 – 10 Tuesdays.
Tel: +44 (0)1689 876812
www.c-v-s.co.uk/bromleyski

LONDON
Beckton Alps_Beckton Alpine Centre
Alpine Way, London E6 4LA
Newly refurbished with board park,
summer 2002
Tel: 020 7511 0351
www.learntoski.co.uk

NORWICH
Norfolk Ski Club_Whitlingham Lane
Trowse, NR14 8TW
4 slopes with a 180 metre main slope. Fairly
new club in great condition. Session: 6 – 10
Mondays and 8.30 – 10.30 Thursdays.
Cost: 1 day membership costs £11 inc. 1st
hour of boarding. Members £3ph
Tel: +44 (0)1603 662781
www.norfolkskiclub.co.uk

PLYMOUTH
Alpine Park_Marsh Mills
Plymouth, PL9 8QL
3 slopes and the UK's longest Toboggan run.
Tel: +44 (0)1752 600220
www.nikegroup.co.uk/jnl/plymouth.htm

RAWTENSTALL
Ski Rossendale_Haslingden Old Road
Rawtenstall, BB4 8RR
3 slopes with a 200 metre main slope.
Session: 5 – 7 Sunday. Cost: £8.10
Tel: +44 (0)1706 222426/226457
www.ski-rossendale.co.uk/

RUNCORN
**Runcorn Ski and Snowboard
Centre**_Town Park, Palace Fields
Runcorn, WA7 2PS
2 slopes situated amongst 800 acres of
landscaped parkland. Session: Thursdays.
Cost: £6.50 for an hour and a half.
Tel: +44 (0)1928 701965
www.runcornskicentre.co.uk

SHEFFIELD
Sheffield Ski Village_Vale Road
Parkwood Springs, S3 9SJ
The biggest, most technical slope in the
country with 8 runs to choose from including
rails, jumps and a halfpipe. Cost: £10.20ph or
£23.60 for a whole day.
Tel: +44 (0)114 2769459
www.sfa-sheffield.co.uk

SOUTHAMPTON
**Southampton Ski and Snowboard
Centre**_The sports Centre, Bassett,
Southampton, SO16 7AY
3 slopes all interconnecting with various
little chicken runs and 'tree runs'.
Session: 7 - 9 Wednesdays. Cost: £8
Tel: +44 (0) 2380 780676
www.southampton.gov.uk/leisure

STOKE
Stoke Ski Centre_Festival Park
Stoke-on-Trent, ST1 5PU
120 metre main slope with plenty to offer
snowboarders. Session: 8 - 10 Tuesdays.
Cost: £15
Tel: +44 (0)1782 204159
www.stokeskicentre.co.uk

SURREY
Sandown Ski Centre_Sandown Park,
More Lane, Esher, Surrey KT10 8AN
100 metre long, 35 metre wide slope
overlooking a racecourse.
Session: 9 – 11 Mondays. Cost: £7ph
Tel: +44 (0)1372 467133
www.sandownsports.co.uk

SWADLINCOTE
Swadlincote Ski Centre_Hill Street
Swadlincote, Derbyshire, DE11 8LP
160 metre main slope with a nursery
slope and 650-metre toboggan run.
Session: 8 – 10 Wednesdays. Cost: £8
Tel: +44 (0)1283 217200
www.nikegroup.co.uk/jnl/swadlincote.htm

TELFORD
Telford Ski Centre_Court Street
Madeley, Telford TF7 5DZ
Fairly short 85 metre slope. Big, well-built
kickers. Session: 6 – 9 Sundays. Cost: £10
Tel: +44 (0)1952 586862
www.telfordleisure.co.uk

WYCOMBE
Wycombe Summit_Abbey Barn Lane
High Wycombe, Bucks HP10 9QQ
Europe's longest dry slope, clubhouse at the
top. Sessions: 6 – 10 Wednesdays, Fridays
and Sundays. Cost: £10ph
Tel: +44 (0)1494 474711
www.wycombesummit.com

YEOVIL
Yeovil Ski & Activity Centre_Addlewell
Lane, Nine Springs, Yeovil, BA20 1QW
110 metre main slope. Ideal for beginners.
Session: 6 – 10 Wednesdays. Cost: £5ph.
Tel: +44 (0)1935 421702
www.yeovilski.com

SCOTLAND »

AVIEMORE
Glenmore Lodge_Aviemore
Inverness-shire PH22 1QU
Tel: +44 (0)1479 861256

DUNDEE
Ancrum Centre for the Environment_10
Ancrum Road, Dundee Tayside DD2 2HZ
Tel: +44 (0)1382 435911

EDINBURGH
Midlothian Ski Centre_Hillend Park,
Biggar Road EH10 7DU
5 Slopes with a 200 metre main slope,
including a Snowflex funpark. Session: 6 – 9
Fridays. Cost: £6.30 1st hour, £2.thereafter.
Tel: +44 (0)131 4454433

GLASGOW
Bearsden Ski Club_Stockiemuir Road
Bearsden, Glasgow G61 3RS
4 slopes with a 100 metre main slope.
Session: Tuesdays and Fridays.
Tel: +44 (0)141 9431500
www.skibearsden.co.uk

Glasgow Ski Centre_Bellahouston Park
16 Drumbreck Road, Glasgow G41 5BW
Tel: +44 (0)1414274991/3
www.ski-glasgow.co.uk

IRELAND »

BELFAST
Mount Ober Ski Centre_Ballymaconaghy
Road, Belfast, Northern Ireland BT8 4SB
Tel: +44 (0)1232 401811

WALES »

CARDIFF
Cardiff Ski Centre_Fairwater Road, Cardiff
Glamorgan CF5 3JR
Tel: +44 (0)1222 561793
www.skicardiff.com

DYFED
Pembrey Country Park_Pembrey Nr
Llanelli, Dyfed, South Wales SA16 0EJ
Tel: +44 (0)1554 834443

GWENT
Pontypool Ski Centre_Pontypool Park
Pontypool, Gwent Wales NP4 8AT
Tel: +44 (0)1495 756955
www.amc-comm.demon.co.uk/pontypoo.htm

GWYNEDD
Plas-y-Brenin National Centre_Capel
Curig, Gwynedd LL24 0ET
Tel: +44 (0)1690 720214

ARTIFICIAL SLOPES »

NETHERLANDS »

WESTERHOVEN
Montana Snowcenter_Track Length: 140m
Kempervennendreef 4
5563 VB Westerhoven
Tel: +31(0)40-2071888
http://www.montana-snowcenter.nl/

RUCPHEN
Skidôme_Track length: 160m
Baanvelden 13
4715RH Rucphen
Tel: +31(0)165-343134
http://www.skidome.nl/

LANDGRAAF
Snowworld Zoetermeer_Track length:
520m. New 3rd indoor skislope under
construction. Parallelstraat 21, 6372 XD.
Tel: +31(0)79 3202 211
http://www.snowworld.nl/

DEN HAAG
Snowdome De Uithof_Track length: 210m
Jaap Edenweg 10
2544 NL Den Haag
Tel: +31(0)70-3599000
www.deuithof.nl/snowdome/

VELSEN-ZUID
SnowPlanet_Track length: 230m
Heuvelweg 6-8, 1981 LV Velsen-Zuid
Tel: +31(0)255-545848
www.snowplanet.nl/

BIDDINGHUIZEN
Snow Village_Spijkweg 15
8256 RJ Biddinghuizen
Tel: +31(0)321-330441
http://www.snowvillage.nl/

LANDGRAAF
Snowworld_Track length: 520m
Parallelstraat 21, 6372 XD Landgraaf
Tel: +31(0)45-5470700
http://www.snowworld.nl/

GERMANY »

BOTTROP
Alpincenter Tetraeder_Europe's larges
indoor snow slope. Track Length: 640m
Prosperstraße 299 – 301, 46238 Bottrop
Tel: +49(0)2041/7095-500
www.alpincenter.com

NEUSS
Allrounder Winter World_Track Length:
300m
An der Skihalle 1, 41472 Neuss
Tel. +49 (0)2131/1244-0
www.allrounder.de

BELGIUM »

PEER
Skicentrum Snow Valley_Track Length:
235m
Deusterstraat 74. 3990 Peer
www.snowvalley.be

KOMEN
Ice Mountain_Track Length: 210m
Kapellestraat 16. 7780 Komen
Tel: 056 55 45 40
www.ice-mountain.com

FINLAND »

VUOKATTI
DNA Ski Tunnel_Vuokatinhovintie 2
88610 Vuokatti
Tel: (08) 6178 600
www.skitunnelvuokatti.fi

GERMANY
FRANCE

ITALY
NORWAY

AUSTRIA
SWITZERLAND

»

SUMMER CAMPS 2003
EUROPE

»

© Danny Burrows **Rider** Ashley Call/Folgefona

GERMANY »

GAP1328_A big and fun summer camp with many international visitors, a large snow park, the only superpipe in Germany and a nice chill area on the glacier with barbecue, music and a jacuzzi. GAP is also pretty notorious for its wild parties!

Location Garmisch-Partenkirchen
Date May – June
Park Superpipe, Halfpipe, Kickers, Big Air, Corner, Rails
Price* not including accommodation, lift ticket, or glacier transfer
2 Days: €56
1 weeks: €120
5 weeks: €225
7 Days accommodation, lift tickets, glacier transfer: €424

Car
Munich – Garmisch-Partenkirchen: 88km
Munich – A95 GAP – Oberau – Garmisch-Partenkirchen
Innsbruck – Garmisch-Partenkirchen: 60km
Innsbruck – Zirl – Seefeld – Mittenwald – Garmisch-Partenkirchen
Air
Munich Airport: 126km
Innsbruck Airport: 61km

Tel +49 (0)8821 90 95 26
Email sommercamp-info@gap1328.de
Homepage www.gap1328.de

FRANCE »

FACCIOSNAO SNOWBOARD CAMP_A small camp, organised by Italians, and mainly visited by Italians. Other guests are however more than welcome. An opportunity to practice your languages alongside your tricks!

Location Les Deux Alpes
Date July – August – September
Park 2 Pipes, Quarter, Rails, Big Air, BoarderX
Price* 2 People: €270 to €320
3/4 People: €340 - €514

KOMMUNITY CAMP_A legendary camp run by Neil McNab, who also runs a camp during the winter in Chamonix. The majority of campers, pros and coaches are British, and the range of activities on offer here are unsurpassed.

Location Les deux Alpes
Date July
Park 2 Pipes, Quarter, Rails, Big Air, BoarderX
Price* £495 per person/ per week including 6 day lift pass, 7 nights accommodation with half board and coaching.

Tel + 44 1546 830 243
Email shelagh@mcnab.co.uk
Homepage www.mcnab.co.uk/sbd/

Car
Lyon – Les Deux Alpes: 179km
Lyon - Grenoble – exit Gap, Briançon – Vizille - Barrage du Chambon - Les Deux Alpes
Geneva – Les Deux Alpes: 218km
Geneva – (Swiss/F) - Saint-Julien-en-Genevois – Chambéry – Montmélian – Grenoble - Barrage du Chambon - Les Deux Alpes
Milan – Les Deux Alpes: 309km
Milan – Torino – Rivoli – Oulx (I/F) – Briançon - Barrage du Chambon – Les Deux Alpes
Air
Lyon Airport: 166km
Grenoble Airport: 117km

Tel +33 (0)347 15 99 507
Email info@facciosnao.com
Homepage www.facciosnao.com

NAZCA CAMP_An Italian summer camp in the French Alps. The park at Tignes is the biggest snowpark in France during the summer.

Location Tignes
Dates Summer Camps: June – July – August
Autumn Camp: October
Park 2 Pipes, Kickers, Corner, Rails
Price* -

Car
Torino – Tignes: 152km
Torino – A32 Rivoli – exit Susa – (I/F) Col du Mont-Cenis – Lanslevillard
Geneva – Tignes: 175km
Geneva (Swiss/Fr) – Annecy – Albertville – Moûtiers - Bourg-Saint-Maurice - Tignes
Lyon – Tignes: 233km
Lyon – A43 Bron - La Tour-du-Pin – Chambéry – Montmélian – Aiton – Aigueblanche – Moûtiers - Bourg-Saint-Maurice - Tignes
Air
Chambery Airport: 139km
Geneva Airport: 175km
Lyon Saint Exupéry Airport: 214km

Tel +39 0165 87680
Email nazca@nazcacamp.com
Homepage www.nazcacamp.com

ITALY »

BIG A CAMP_The biggest camp in Italy. The great facilities for snowboarders and the short travelling distance to the glacier make this camp a popular one.

Location Val Senales (Schnalstal) – Maso Corto
Dates Summer Camps: July – August
Autumn Camp: October
Park 2 Halfpipes, Kickers, Gaps, Quarters, 15 Rails, Snowskate Park, Skatepark und Miniramp.
Price* Apartment for two: €498 to €559
Half board for two: €567 to €750
Half board for one: €653 €750
This includes coaching, accommodation, 7 day lift ticket and video analysis.

Auto
Milan – Maso Corto: 333km
Milan – Brescia – Affi – Bolzano – Naturno - Maso Corto
Zurich – Maso Corto: 282km
Zurich – Sargans – Susch – Zernez (Swiss/It) – Glorenza – Spondigna – Naturno - Maso Corto
Innsbruck – Maso Corto: 183km
Innsbruck – Brennerpass (AUT/I) – Bolzano – Naturno – Maso Corto
Air
Innsbruck Airport: 184km
Milan-Linate Airport: 336km

Tel +39 333 460 8698
Fax +39 012 575 1882
Email big_a@iol.it
Homepage www.big-a.it
MDY PINK SOMMER CAMP_
Location Macugnaga or Cervinia
Park Kickers, Funboxen, Spines, Railpark

Tel +39 0331 773224
Homepage www.mdysnowparks.com

© Christian Stadler/Gap1328

© Jul/Zugspitze

POSITIVITY CAMP_A relatively new camp put together by Italy's oldest snowboarding organisation. The accommodation is located next to the piste, in a mountain hut on the glacier.

Location Valle Formazza, Siedel Gletscher
Dates June – July
Park Funboxen, straight Jumps, Rails, Snowskate Park, Miniramp.
Price* €125 per weekend
(incl. lift ticket & full board)
€365 1 week (incl. lift ticket & full board)

Car
Milan – Formazza: 163km
Milan – Lainate – Ornavasso – Crevoladossola – Formazza
Turin – Formazza: 211km
Turin – Biandrate – Ornavasso – Crevoladossola - Formazza
Zurich – Formazza: 281km
Zurich – Steinhausen – Brunnen - Tunnel del Gottardo – Bellinzona – Locarno (Swiss/It) – Domodossola – Crevoladossola – Formazza
Air
Milan-Malpensa Airport: 122km

Tel +39 0347 280148
Email maurino@snowbox.it
Homepage www.positivity.it

NORWAY »

FOLGEFONNA SNOWBOARD CAMP_A classic summer camp. Not exactly cheap by Central European prices, but definitely an unforgettable experience. A whole camp site gets taken over each summer, complete with its own lake, skate ramps, trampolines and pub. Best of all, everyone speaks good English!

Location Folgefonna
Dates July
Park Halfpipe, Boxen, Jumps, Rails & BoarderX
Price* €400 per week
(sleeping in your own tent)
€450 per week (renting a hut)
Price includes transport to the glacier and one week lift pass

Car
Oslo – Jondal: 397km
Oslo – Tanum – Geilo – Kinsarvik – Utne - Jondal
Bergen – Jondal: 75km
Bergen - Indre Arna – Norheimsund – Tørvikbygd – Jondal
Air
Oslo Airport: 390km
Bergen Airport: 80km

Tel +47 53 66 88 18
Email post@folgefonna.no
Homepage www.folgefonna.no

STRYN SOMMER CAMP_This camp is now going into its sixteenth successful year. Stryn is the most popular glacier in Norway and is known for more than its snowpark.

Location Stryn
Dates End of June – July
Park Halfpipe, Kickers, Quarter, Rails, Snowskate Park
Price* 2,900 NOK (ca. €395) per week (including 7 day lift ticket, glacier transfer, 5 day freestyle course). Accommodation/food not incl. The cheapest accommodation option is to bring your own tent. Camping fees - €7 per person/per night. To sleep under a fixed roof, budget for €17 to €24 per person/per night. The camp recommends you stay in Hotel Hjelle- www.hjelle.com.

Car
Bergen – Stryn: 266km
Bergen – connection to Lavik – Førde – Skei – Byrkjelo – Stryn
Air
Bergen Airport: 280km
Oslo Airport: 442km

Tel +47 22 69 30 30
Email halengen@online.no
Homepage
www.snowboard.no/camp/campenglish.htm

AUSTRIA »

BASE YOUTH SÖLDEN_The Sölden snowpark has seen considerable investment in the past two years. A good skate park and a great bowl can also be found in the glacier's car park.

Location Sölden
Date June – July - August
Park Big Air, Spine, Roller, Straight Jump, Railpark
Price* €460 per week including 6 nights half board accommodation, 6 day lift ticket, 2 x Pro Coaching and 2 x Video Coaching

Car
Munich – Sölden: 190km
Munich - Inntal motorway (A 12) Kufstein-Innsbruck – towards Bregenz – exit Ötztal - Sölden
From Italy: via Brennerautobahn (A13) to Innsbruck - towards Bregenz – exit Ötztal - Sölden.
Air
Innsbruck Airport: 85km
Munich Airport: 230km

Tel +43 (0)5254 508
Email base@soelden.com
Homepage www.base.soelden.com/

SPCC55 CAMP_The best known summer camp in Europe. Last year saw the move from Hintertux to Stubai glacier. SPC is famous for its 'mega roller' jump and party scene, where pros, campers, and strippers party happily together.

Location Neustift - Stubaier Gletscher
Dates (May) - June – July – August
Park Kingsize Park – Superpipe, Halfpipe, Kickers, Corner, Rails, Snowskate Park
Price* 1 week from €390 to €690
(camp ground – 5* Hotel)
Includes: 6 nights accommodation and evening meals, 6 day lift ticket, park entry.

Car
Innsbruck – Neustift: 24km
Innsbruck – Motorway towards Brenner – exit Schönberg (Toll station) - Telfes – Fulpmes – Neustift.
Verona – Neustift: 270km
Verona – Brenner (Toll station) – Additional Stubaital (Toll station) – Telfes – Fulpmes – Neustift.
Air
Innsbruck Airport: 25km
Munich Airport: 228km

Tel +43 (0)522 630 524
Email info@spc55camps.com
Homepage www.spc55camps.com

SWITZERLAND »

ICERIPPER SNOWBOARD CAMP_The Titlis glacier is the location of the biggest Summer Camp in Switzerland, with international pro riders and coaches.

Location Engelberg
Dates Summer Camp: July
Autumn Camp: October
Park Halfpipe, Kickers, Rails, Corner & Snowskate Park
Price* Sfr 850 (€590) for accommodation in a 3* Hotel, with breakfast and evening meals, 5 day lift ticket, coaching and video analysis.

Car
Zurich – Engelberg: 88km
Zurich – A4 toward Gotthard Luzern 20km – A 14 towards Gotthard Luzern 14km – A2 towards Engelberg
Milan – Engelberg: 247km
Milan – A8 towards Lugano – Como (I/Swiss) – A2 towards San Bernardino – Gotthard Pass – via Stans – Engelberg
Munich – Engelberg: 398km
Munich – towards Lindau (Ger/Aut) – towards St. Gallen (Aut/Swiss) – Zurich Ost – towards Luzern – A2 exit Emmen – via Stans - Engelberg
Air
Zurich Airport: 99km
Bern Airport: 148km

Tel +41 79 332 89 80
Email office@iceripper.com
Homepage www.iceripper.com

JAMES B FRUITASTIC CAMP_The park at Les Diablerets is getting bigger and better, and is becoming a popular destination for Europe's freestylers, especially during the autumn.

Location Les Diablerets
Dates Summer Camps: June – July
Autumn Camps: October – November
Park Halfpipe, Kickers, Rails, Slopecross
Price* Sfr 798 (€545) without coaching
Sfr 898 (€612) with coaching
Price includes: room and breakfast, 6 day lift ticket, video analysis

Car
Zurich – Les Diablerets: 240km
Zurich – Bern – Fribourg – Vevey – towards Grand St Bernard/Martigny - exit Villeneuve – Aigle – Le Rosex – Les Diablerets
Geneva – Les Diablerets: 123km
Geneva – Lausanne – towards Grand St Bernard/Martigny – Exit Villeneuve – Aigle – Le Rosex – Les Diablerets
Milan – Les Diablerets: 196km
Milan – Santhià – Ivrea - exit Aosta - Colle del Gran San Bernardo (I/Swiss) – Martigny – towards Lausanne – exit Bex, Saint-Maurice - Aigle – Le Rosex – Les Diablerets
Air
Geneva Airport: 123km

Tel +41 24 492 3481
Email info@monabri.ch
Homepage www.monabri.ch

*Prices correct at time of print - summer 2002

FRANCE
AUSTRIA

ITALY
SWITZERLAND

»

252
BACKCOUNTRY &
FREERIDE CAMPS
EUROPE

© Pascal Boulgakow Rider Jean Nerva

BACKCOUNTRY & FREERIDE CAMPS »
EUROPE

© Christian Stadler Rider Alex Schmalz and Jan

FRANCE »

KOMMUNITY FREERIDE CAMPS & BACKCOUNTRY COURSE_
Location Chamonix
Packages available Different courses are run in the Chamonix area, for inexeperienced through to more experienced freeriders. Run by British freeride legend Neil Mcnab.
Dates February – March - April
Price Kommunity Freeride Camp: £475 (€755) including 6 day lift tickets, coaching and half board accomodation.
Backcountry Riding Course: £785 (€1250) including 6 day lift ticket, 5 days with a mountain guide, backcountry equipment, half board accommodation.
High Mountain Freeride Course: £970 (ca. €1500) including 6 day lift ticket, 5 days with a mountain guide, backcountry equipment, half board accomodation.

Tel + 44 (0)1546 830 243
Email shelagh@mcnab.co.uk
Homepage www.mcnab.co.uk/sbd/freeride

SNOWLEGEND FREERIDE CAMP_
Location La Grave-La Meije
Package available Freeriding in one of Europe's best spots, in groups of 2 - 6 people. Snow kiting is also available.
Dates December – May
Price Prices do not include accommodation and lift ticket.
1 Day €70
5 Days €310
Every additional day €50
Accommodation in two star Hotel Edelweiss Inn - 2002, €4750 per day for 2 people with breakfast and dinner. Tel: +33 (0)476 799 093

Tel +33 (0)476 799 622
Email snowlegend@waw.com
Homepage www.snowlegend.com

© Scalp Rider Phil Lallement

AUSTRIA »

SAAC LAWINEN & FREERIDE CAMPS_
The Snowboard Avalanche Awareness Camps are free and run by experts in avalanche safety. Two day courses are also held in Germany, Switzerland and Italy. Details can be found on the SAAC Website.

Location Austria, Germany, Switzerland and Italy
Dates Free Avalanche Camps 2003
Day 1 - Theory - indoors
Day 2 - Practical - outdoors
Things to bring: Snowboarding equipment, avalanche transciever, shovel and avalanche probe. Rental equipment is available. Lift tickets are free!
Kaunertaler Glacier Tirol (AUT)   29 – 30 Nov
Axamer Lizum Tirol (AUT)   07 – 08 Dec
Illwerke – Golm Vorarlberg (AUT)   14 – 15 Dec
Hochzillertal Tirol Tirol (AUT)   21 – 22 Dec
Seegrube Innsbruck Tirol (AUT)   03 – 04 Jan
Westendorf Tirol (AUT)   10 – 11 Jan
Silvretta Nova Vorarlberg (AUT)   18 – 19 Jan
Mayrhofen (AUT)   08 – 09 Feb
Seegrube Tirol (AUT)   14 – 15 Feb
Diedamskopf Vorarlberg (AUT)   21 – 22 Feb
Hochzillertal Tirol (AUT)   22 – 23 Feb
Further dates available from the SAAC Website.

Email anmeldung@saac.at
Homepage www.saac.at

BACKYARD CAMP_
Rather than hardcore freeriders, this camp is more suited to freestylers who don't mind a short hike in the morning and a good backcountry kicker session in the afternoon. Accommodation is at 1700m, next to a small funpark with rails and its own piste grooming machine. Gigi Rüf, whose uncle owns the Neuhornbach Lodge, along with Backyard Team members Basti Balser and Lars Oesterle are often to be found here.

Location Neuhornbach Lodge, Vorarlberg
Package available Hikes, powder runs, backcountry kickers, park sessions
Dates April
Price €290, 1 week, full board, touring, park session

Tel +49 (0)7551 970306
Email camp@backyard.de
Homepage www.backyard.de

KAUNERTAL FREERIDE CAMPS_
Top Snowboarding Kaunertal organises a 3 or 5 day course, where you are taught how to use an an avalanche transciever and about the dangers of alpine terrain, as well as taking part in some great tours.

Location Kaunertal
Packages available Rookie Camp, Advanced Camp, Expert Camp, Touring in Arlberg, Silvretta, La Grave and Alagna
Dates Touring and Expert Camps - see Website
Rookie Camps 02/03
21 Nov – 24 Nov
28 Nov – 01 Dec
12 Dec – 15 Dec
02 Jan – 05 Jan
30 Jan – 02 Feb
06 March – 09 March
Advanced Camps 2003
Feb – 07 Feb
04 May – 09 May
Price including half board, lift tickets, safety equipment
Rookie Camps €330
Advanced Camps €520

Tel +43 5475 297
Email top-snowboarding-kaunertal@aon.at
Homepage www.top-snowboarding-kaunertal.at

ITALY »

FREERIDESPIRIT CAMP_
Unfortunately, at the time of going to print, the leader of the Freeride Spirit Camp was busy making his way to the summit of Coh Oyu at 8202m, in Tibet, and so was unable to provide any information about his camp. However, by the time you read this he'll hopefully have returned home and will be able to give you the information personally!

Tel +33 5 6243916
Email emilio@freeridespirit.com
Homepage www.freeridespirit.com

SWITZERLAND »

MOUNTAIN SURF CLUB_
The Mountain Surf Club offers a variety of courses, ranging from a simple refresher course pre-winter, through to a full five day camp.

Location Various Swiss resorts
Package available Mountain guide, theory and learning material, overnight accommodation
Dates November - April
Price between Sfr89 and Sfr1079 (€60 to €730)

Tel +41 (0)33 823 27 24
Email info@mountainsurfclub.ch
Homepage www.mountainsurfclub.ch

HELIBOARDING
EUROPE

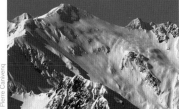

HELIBOARDING IN EUROPE »

Heliboarding. Who doesn't think of Alaska, and steep, endless runs through deep powder? However, although heliboarding is traditionally a reserve for pro riders armed with somebody else's credit card, there are plenty of opportunities for us mere mortals to experience the rush of a heli drop into virginal powder runs. And, by cutting down on travel costs and staying in Europe, it needn't cost the earth either.

FRANCE »

In France, for environmental reasons, use of helicopters for winter sports is prohibited. However, it is possible to charter a flight from Italy into France and Val d'Isere, Montgenèvre, La Plagne and Courchevel.

ITALY »

The Aosta valley is home to some of the steepest and most technical mountains that can be accessed by helicopters in the whole of Europe.

SCUOLA DI ALPINISMO MONTE ROSA_c/o Hôtel Dufour, Fraz. Edelboden, 34
11020 Gressoney La Trinité
Tel: +39 0125 366 139
http://www.guidemonterosa.com

Destination and price in euros per person
Monte Rosa 4.632m -   150,-
(incl. mountain guide).
Extra per person per 1000m   50,-

MONTEROSA EXPRESS_Katarina
Bangata 79, S-116 42 Stockholm
Tel: +46 70 5771305
www.monterosa.com

Destination and price in euros per person
Monte Rosa 4.632m – Beginner
(groups of 7 People)   184,-
(incl. mountain guide)
Monte Rosa 4.632m – Expert
(groups of 3 People)   235,-
(incl. mountain guide)

AUSTRIA »

Heli flights in the Tirol region are prohibited. However, heliboarding is available on the Swiss Vorarlberg side of Arlberg.

WUCHER HELICOPTER_Hans-Wucher-Platz 1, A-6713 Ludesch
Tel: +43 (0)5550 2261 111
www.wucher.at/

Destination and price in euros - for four people
Flexenpaß – Orgelscharte ca. 2.300m   330,-
Flexenpaß – Mehlsack 2.652m   310,-
Kriegerhorn – Orgelscharte ca. 2.300m   280,-
Kriegerhorn – Mehlsack 2.652m   280,-
Flights only from Monday - Friday
Mountain guides are obligatory and not included in the price

SPAIN »

The Pyrenees are the cheapest destination for heliboarding in Europe.

HELIPUERTO BAQUEIRA BERET_25598 salardu Leirida
Tel: + 34 (9) 73645797

Destination and price in euros - for four people
40 destinations are on offer in Val d'Aran, for eg. Colomers (2932m), Saboredo (2829m), Montardo (2832m) or Mulleres (3010m).
Per 1000 vertical meters - €140

SWITZERLAND »

Switzerland, while being the most expensive, also has the widest choice of heliboarding in Europe.

HELICOPTERE SERVICE SA_Rte des Ronquoz 146, CH-1950 Sion
www.heliservice.ch
Tel:+41 (0) 27 327 30 60

Destinations and Prices in euros - per person
Arolla - Pigne d'Arolla 3.796m   90.-
Arolla - Petit Combin 3.672m   160.-
Arolla – Rosa Blanche 3.340m   120.-
Croix de Coeur - Petit Combin 3.672m   120.-
Croix de Coeur - Pigne d'Arolla 3.796m   145.-
Croix de Coeur – Rosa Blanche 3.340m   100.-
Croix de Coeur - Glacier du Trient 3.170m 125.-
Le Chable - Petit Combin 3.672m   120.-
Le Chable – Pigne d'Arolla 3.796m   175.-
Le Chable – Rosa Blanche 3.340m   120.-
Le Chable - Glacier du Trient   125.-
Orsière - Petit Combin 3.672m   110.-
Orsière – Trient 3.170m   110.-
Finhaut - Petit Combin 3.672m   200.-
Finhaut – Trient   120.-
Bec de Nendaz - Petit Combin 3.672m   130.-
Bec de Nendaz - Pigne d'Arolla 3.796m 140.-
Bec de Nendaz – Rosa Blanche 3.340m   100.-
Ayent – Wildhorn 3.250m   100.-
A mountain guide is required, and not included in the price.

AIR ZERMATT AG_Sion Airport:
CH-1950 Sion
www.airzermatt.ch
Tel: +41 27 966 86 86

Destination and price in euros - per person
Zermatt - Aeschihorn 3.562m   80,-
Zermatt - Pigne d'Arolla 3.796m   175,-
Zermatt - Rosa Blanche 3.340m   215,-
Zermatt - Trient 3.170 m   340,-
Zermatt – Ebneflue 3.962m   300,-
Testa - Monte Rosa 4.634m   150,-
Testa - Alphubel 4.206m   170,-
Mörel - Ebnefluh 3.962 m   546,-
Mörel - Petersgrat 3.200m   480,-
Mörel - Ebneflue & Petersgrat   720,-
Mörel - Jungfraujoch 3.580m   785,-
A mountain guide is required, and not included in the price.

AIR GLACIERS_Heliport Postfach 22
CH-3822 Lauterbrunnen.
Tel: +41 (0)33 8 560 560
www.airglaciers.ch

Destination and price in euros - per person
Lauterbrunen – Jungfraujoch 3.580m   95,-
Lauterbrunen – Petersgrat 3.200m   105,-
Lauterbrunen – Ebnefluh 3.962m   110,-
Lauterbrunen – Rosenegg 3.470m   115,-
Gstaad/Saanen – Wallegg 2.050m   65,-
Gstaad/Saanen – Gumm 2.060m   75,-
Gstaad/Saanen – Gstellihorn 2.770m   100,-
Gstaad/Saanen – Wildhorn 3.250m   110,-
Gstaad/Saanen – Zanfleuron 2.870m   110,-
Air Glaciers has a further 38 destinations in the Swiss Alps.

HELIBERNINA_7503 Samedan
Tel: + 41 (0)81 850 00 50
www.bernina.ch

Destination and price in euros
Oberengadin - Fuorcla Chamuotsch (2923m)
Three or more people €80 per person. A mountain guide is required, and is not included in the price.

HELISWISS_Bern-Airport
CH-3123 Belp
Tel. 031 818 88 88
www.heliswiss.ch
Flight Destination: Flights from Gstaad and Meiringen
Wildhorn (3250m), Zanfleuron (2870m), Staldenhorn (1930m), Wallegg (2050m), Gstellihorn (2800m), Gumm (2060m).
Price on enquiry.

HELI CHABLAIS_Heliport Leysin
CH-18954 Leysin
Tel: +41 (0)24 494 34 34
www.helichablais.com
Destination and price in euros - for 5 people
Zanfleuron 2.870m   410,-
Gumm 2.060m   375,-
Wildhorn 3.250m   545,-
Trient 3.170m   650,-
Rosablanche 3.336m   615,-
A mountain guide is required, and is not included in the price.

Tracer Goggles

Jet Iron-cross Helmet

Jet wing Helmet

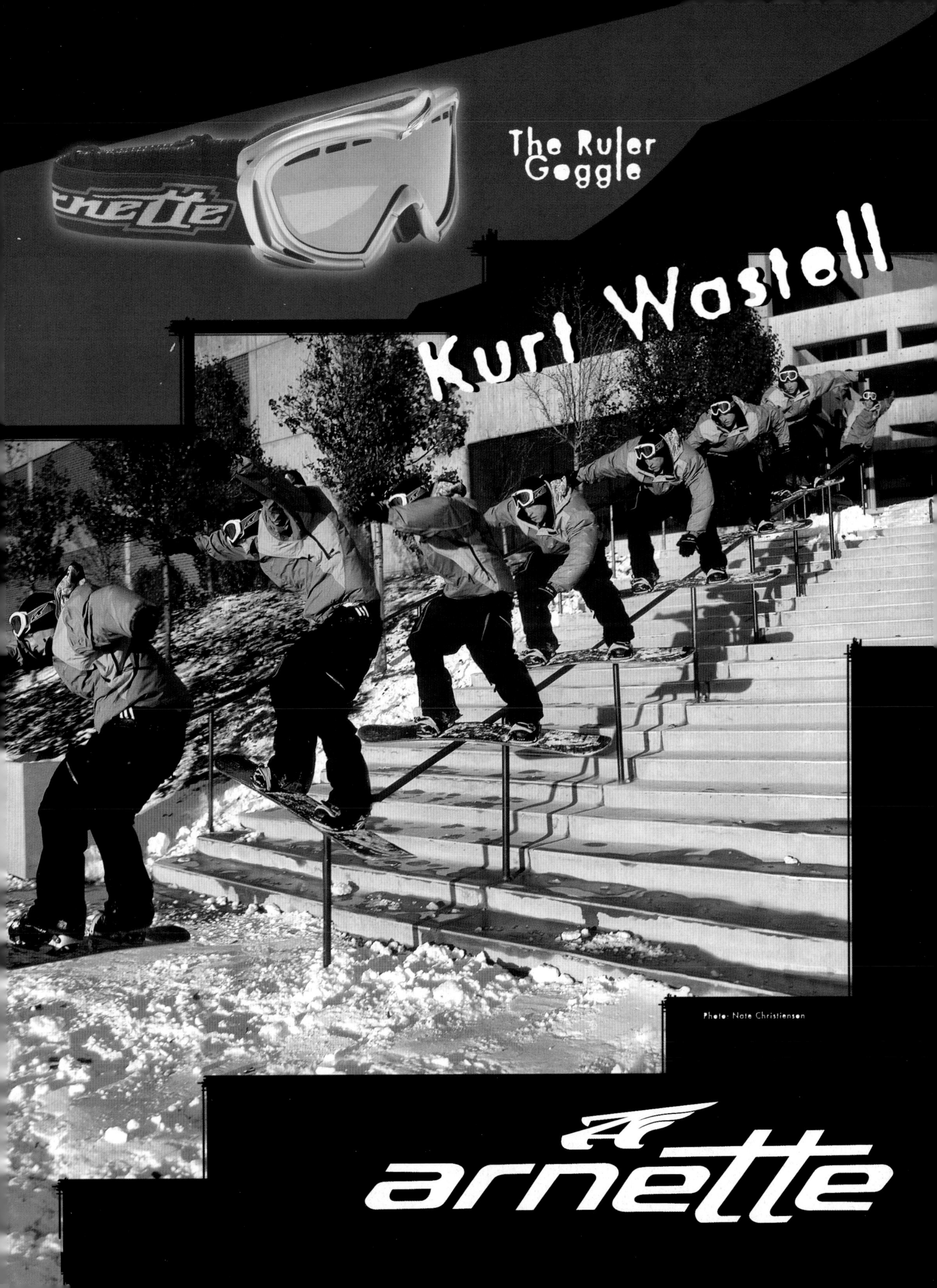
The Ruler Goggle
Kurt Wastell
Photo: Nate Christienson
arnette

Riders Fredy Kalbermatten/Nicolas Müller

INDEX

52 O2
O'NEILL
50
YEARS
DAY ONE

find your spot on earth and ride it

O'NEILL

gian simmen

www.**oneilleurope**.com

Martín
Černík